EXTENDING

SCIENCE CONCEPTS

IN THE LABORATORY

Unit Authors

A. S. Atal
N. L. Drugge
M. R. Duncan
J. A. Petrak
W. H. Rasmussen
L. E. Wade

Edited by

Manfred C. Schmid, B.A., B.Ed., M.Ed.

Science Department Head
King George Secondary School
Vancouver, British Columbia

p
h
PRENTICE-HALL OF CANADA LTD.

Illustrations by Loates Visual Arts.

PRENTICE-HALL, INC., ENGLEWOOD CLIFFS, NEW JERSEY
PRENTICE-HALL INTERNATIONAL, INC., LONDON
PRENTICE-HALL OF AUSTRALIA, PTY., LTD., SYDNEY
PRENTICE-HALL OF INDIA, PVT., LTD., NEW DELHI
PRENTICE-HALL OF JAPAN, INC., TOKYO

Library of Congress Catalog Card No. 75-129559

0-13-298034-7

PRINTED IN CANADA   1 2 3 4 5 74 73 72 71 70

CONTENTS

PREFACE   xi

ACKNOWLEDGEMENTS   xiii

UNIT I   CELLS, REPRODUCTION AND HEREDITY   1

Introduction 1

Section I   The Compound Microscope 2

I-1 The Parts of a Microscope 2 • I-2 Operation and Care of the Micro-scope 5 • I-3 Characteristics of The Image 8 • I-4 Depth of Field 9 • I-5 Magnification With The Microscope 11 • I-6 The Stereoscopic Microscope 13

Section II   The Cell 17

I-7 The Purpose of Stains 18 • I-8 Living and Non-Living Plant Cells 19 • I-9 Observing the Various Kinds of Cells In a Leaf 22 • I-10 A Leaf Impression 25 • I-11 Human Skin Cells 27 • I-12 Blood Cells 28 • I-13 Microscopic Organisms 30

Section III   Reproduction of Organisms 33

Asexual Reproduction 34 • I-14 Budding 34 • I-15 Cell Binary Fis-sion 35 • I-16 Vegetative Reproduction 37 • I-17 Regeneration 39 • I-18 Spore Production 40 • Sexual Reproduction 43 • I-19 Flower Structure 43 • I-20 A Life Cycle – Alternation of Generations 47

Section IV   Genetics – The Study of Inheritance 51

I-21 Variations in Living Things 52 • I-22 Variations in Your Family Tree 53 • I-23 The Laws of Inheritance 55 • Review of Mendel's Investigation 58 • I-24 Segregation 59 • I-25 Gene Segregation and Recombination 62 • I-26 Drosophila Technique 64 • I-27 Mutant Characteristics of Fruit Flies 69 • I-28 Inheritance of a Single Trait 71 • I-29 Cells From an Actively Growing Region of a Plant 74 • I-30 Mitosis in Plant and Animal Cells 75 • I-31 Meiosis – Reduction-Division 79 • I-32 Effect of The Environment on Plant Development 84

UNIT II   ELECTRICITY AND MAGNETISM   87

Introduction 87

*II-1 Static Electrical Charges 88 • II-2 Transfer of Electric Charge 91 •
A Model of the Atom 92 • II-3 A Steady Flow of Electrons 101 • A
Model to Help You Visualize What Has Taken Place 104 • Using the
Model to Explain the Results of Procedure 2 107 • Using the Model to
Explain the Results of Procedure 3, 4 and 5 107 • II-4 Measuring Cur-
rent in Electrical Circuits 110 • Notes on the Use of a Multi-Range
Milliameter 111 • II-5 Relationship Between Current and Voltage for
a Carbon Resistor 115 • Using the Code 116 • II-6 Series and Parallel
Circuits 120 • II-7 Household Circuits (Demonstration) 127 • II-8
Properties of Magnets 134 • II-9 Properties of Magnets: Comparison
with Electrostatic Charges 137 • II-10 Properties of Magnets: Direction
of Magnetic Fields (May be Demonstrated) 142 • II-11 Magnetic Effects
of An Electric Current (Demonstration and Student Activity) 146 • II-12
Magnetic Effects of A Current-Carrying Solenoid (Demonstration and
Student Activity) 153 • II-13 Application of Principles: The Galvanometer – Interaction Between a Current-Carrying Coil and a Permanent
Magnet 159 • II-14 Interaction of a Moving Magnetic Field and a Solenoid 166*

UNIT III   ATOMS, MOLECULES AND IONS   171

Introduction 171

*Section I   A Comparative Study of the Electrical Conductivity of Ele-
ments, Compounds and Solutions 175*

*III-1 Electrical Conductivity of The Chemical Elements 175 • III-2
The Electrical Conductivity of Compounds 178 • III-3 Investigating
Chemical Change During Electrolytic Conduction 185 • III-4 Observing
the Electrical Properties of Zinc Chloride – Solid, Dissolved and Molten
(Demonstration) 193 • A Model of Electrolytic Conduction 198*

Section II   Properties of Ionic and Covalent Compounds 200

III-5 Comparing Ionic and Covalent Compounds 200

Section III   Electrolysis 204

*III-6 "Magic" Writing by Means of Electrolysis 204 • III-7 Electro-
plating 208*

Section IV   Electron Transfer During Chemical Changes 212

III-8 The Formation of Ions – Electron Transfer 212 • III-9 The Nature of the 'Gremlin' In a Dry Cell (Demonstration) 214 • A Further Application of the People Model 220 • III-10 The Electrochemical Cell – A Study of Minimum Requirements 220 • III-11 Corrosion – Unwanted Electron Transfer 223 • III-12 The Daniell Cell – Electron Transfer and Ion Migration (Demonstration) 225 • III-13 A Chemical Analysis of Electron Transfer In An Electrochemical Cell 227 • III-14 The Lead-Acid Storage Cell – Further Application of Electron Transfer (May be demonstrated) 231

Section V   Reactions Involving Ions 234

III-15 Reactions Between Ions in Solution 234 • III-16 A Quantitative Study of the Ionic Reaction Between Barium Chloride and Potassium Chromate 236

Section VI   Classification of Electrolytes 239

III-17 Classification of Electrolytes 239 • Reactions Between Electrolytes (Acids and Bases) 244 • Summary and Additional Notes 246

UNIT IV   SOUND AND WAVE MOTION   **249**

Introduction 249

IV-1 Requirements for Sound 250 • IV-2 Mediums Which Transmit Sounds 253 • IV-3 Sound Waves (Part Demonstration) 256 • IV-4 Representation of a Sound Wave (Demonstration) 263 • IV-5 Natural Frequency 267 • IV-6 Transverse (S) Waves (Demonstration) 272 • IV-7 Music and Noise (Demonstration) 276 • IV-8 Waves In Two Dimensions 280 • IV-9 The Negative Effects of Noise 286

UNIT V   THE PLANET EARTH   **291**

Introduction 291

V-1 The Lithosphere 293 • V-2 The Atmosphere 296 • V-3 The Hydrosphere 305 • V-4 Diastrophism and Volcanism 308 • V-5 Detecting An Earthquake – The Seismograph (May be Demonstrated) 312 •

*V-6 Locating the Epicenter of An Earthquake 319 • V-7 How Earth-
quakes Tell Us About the Earth's Interior 323 • V-8 Earthquake Damage 329 • V-9 Geological Time Scale (may be done as a class project)
372 • V-10 Identifying Common Minerals 335 • V-11 Rocks 347 •
V-12 Sedimentary Rocks 359 • V-13 Metamorphic Rocks 364*

UNIT VI RADIOACTIVITY   **369**

Introduction 369

*VI-1 Observing Radioactivity (Demonstration) 370 • VI-2 Detecting
Radioactivity With a Geiger Counter 371 • VI-3 Radioactivity and
Time 375*

BIBLIOGRAPHY   **379**

PREFACE

Extending Science Concepts in the Laboratory is a resource laboratory manual from which teachers can select the investigations which seem to them most worthwhile. IT IS IMPOSSIBLE TO DO ALL OF THE LABORATORY EXERCISES THAT ARE INCLUDED IN THIS BOOK in the time normally allotted for science in a one year school program. Teachers are therefore cautioned that they must carefully plan the year's work well in advance in order to give the major concepts of each unit sufficient attention. The exercises in each of the six areas of investigation are written to enable students to proceed with as little oral instruction about procedure as possible. This design enables students to proceed at different rates; it also allows the course to be tailored to suit the interests and abilities of individual students. The order in which the units are studied is a matter of choice, with two exceptions: the first four exercises of Unit II should be done before Unit III; the properties of waves in Unit IV should be studied before earthquakes in Unit V.

For most experiments, it is expected that students will work in pairs. Some demonstrations are included, but they are written in such a way that students can imagine themselves doing the experiments.

A number of features are employed to prevent students from floundering. Each experiment is preceded by a short introduction which outlines the nature of the investigation, *reviews pertinent ideas that have already been developed* and, when necessary, supplies background information. The introduction is followed by a list of the apparatus and the materials required for each experiment. The instructions for procedures in the laboratory are written in point form for easy reading. They are interspersed with questions that lead the student to make significant observations and/or draw conclusions from what he is doing. Following each experiment is a series of questions organized and labelled according to difficulty. The questions consolidate what the student has learned and apply the principles developed to interesting situations. References and suggestions for further investigation follow most exercises. Each exercise is therefore a *learning package*, tightly structured, yet flexible enough to accomodate individual differences.

While the student is becoming familiar with the *method* of this course, he will not acquire knowledge as quickly as he might in a traditional science course. He must *first* develop skill in doing the procedures and confidence that he can work and investigate by himself. The teacher must accept this and bridge any *temporary* gap by summarizing the main principles at the end of each section.

Many students are discouraged by the lack of specific direction from the teacher and frequently require attention and direction; this can be given by a teacher moving from station to station during laboratory periods. Frequent quizzes on sections of work emphasize to the student the importance of learning the main principles of each exercise. Students should be encouraged to carry out regular library research to expand the knowledge they have gained in the laboratory. *An extensive bibliography, listing many useful books, is included at the end.*

An unvaried year-long routine of discovering scientific principles may eventually cause interest to lag. Teachers may therefore wish to vary the routine periodically by carrying out some of the exercises as demonstrations and discussing them with their classes.

Independent laboratory work by the student, however, *is not* a substitute for teaching. The laboratory exercises are designed to give the teachers and students common experience to serve as a basis for teaching.

EXPLANATION OF SYMBOLS USED:

* indicates that the question is a basic one and should be answered by all students.

† indicates that the question or experimental procedure is for enrichment.

†† indicates that the question is designed for students with a deep interest in the topic.

In addition to the student aids that have been mentioned, a pronunciation guide for words with which the student may not be familiar is included. The key to this guide is as follows:

GUIDE TO PRONUNCIATION

a, ah	like a in father
ai,	like ai in fair
ay,	like a in cake
aw,	like aw in saw
e, eh,	like e in bed
ea,	like ea in fear
double e,	like double e in feed
ew,	like ew in mew
i, ih,	like i in fin
y, ye, eye,	like i in find
o,	like o in hot
double o,	like double o in food
oh,	like o in home
oi,	like oi in boil
ow,	like ow in fowl
u, uh,	like u in fun
er,	like er in finer
ur,	like ure in future
g,	like g in gas
j,	like j in jump
z,	like s in his
zh,	like z in azure

ACKNOWLEDGEMENTS

This book is the product of practicing classroom teachers and was initiated by the British Columbia Science Teachers' Association of the B.C. Teachers' Federation. The scope and sequence of the material was developed by the Junior Secondary Science Revision Committee of the British Columbia Department of Education.

We would especially like to recognize the great contribution to this book made by the following:

Mr. A. G. Creelman
Dr. W. R. Danner
Mr. J. G. Loudon
Miss M. Murphy
Mr. J. T. Young

Other contributors we would like to thank are:

Mr. K. Armstrong
Dr. J. W. Bichard
Dr. R. M. Ellis
Professor J. C. Lawrence
Mr. S. Louie
Dr. M. McClaren
Dr. J. G. Souther
Dr. J. O. Wheeler
Professor R. D. Wild

CELLS, REPRODUCTION AND HEREDITY

INTRODUCTION

Perhaps the most important feature that distinguishes living things from non-living things is the former's ability to reproduce and so continue their form of life. We can usually recognize the relation between parents and offspring because of the many features they have in common. In a farmyard the parents of chicks are never confused with those of goslings and calves. However, offspring are not exact duplicates of their parents and individual differences in both structure and personality can be recognized. In reproduction a provision must therefore exist for the passage of both similarities and differences to the offspring. The study of this transmission or inheritance of characteristics is called *genetics*.

The experiments in 1865 of an Austrian monk named Gregor Mendel (MEN-dal) were the first major scientific investigations of inheritance. Most of the important discoveries, however, have been made in this century and genetics has become one of the most rapidly advancing biological sciences.

Since all living things must reproduce their kind, all are theoretically suitable for inheritance studies. We find, however, that some organisms are easier to rear and care for in the laboratory than others. The fruit fly (Drosophila melanogaster) is especially suitable for genetic studies because it is easy to rear in large numbers and because it has a short life span. Thus, many generations can be examined in a short time. The fruit fly will be used in this unit in order to determine some of the principal controls of inheritance; however, you should be alert to inherited features in all life forms.

Corn, sweet peas, mice, guinea pigs and even man himself are well suited for genetic studies. In fact, in one of the following exercises, some of the features you and your classmates have inherited will be examined.

It seems in science that every answer to a problem suggests two or more further problems. The science of genetics is no exception. As you proceed through the activities in this unit, many questions will be raised. It is hoped that this unit will not only make you aware of the work that has been done in genetics but also make you curious about many questions that have yet to be answered. More understanding in genetics is the key to the solution of many extremely important human problems.

Section I
THE COMPOUND MICROSCOPE

Man's curiosity has led him to investigate his environment. His instruments have enabled him to probe the vast distances of space, the depths of the ocean and the interior of the earth. He discovered long ago that a piece of glass with a curved surface would magnify the size of objects. Anton Von Leeuwenhoek (LAY-wen-hook), a Flemish cloth merchant and amateur lens grinder of the seventeenth century, devised a single glass bead in a metal holder to look at small objects. With this single lens or simple microscope he observed minute living organisms whose existence had been previously unknown. He found them in pond water, cheese and even in the material he scraped from between his teeth. The simple microscope was improved by the addition of a second lens which magnified the image produced by the first lens. Such a microscope is called *compound*. By the nineteenth century, compound microscopes of excellent quality had made it possible to examine in detail the cellular structure of living things.

The following exercises will show you the correct way to use the compound microscope.

I–1   THE PARTS OF A MICROSCOPE

Remove the microscope from its storage area using both hands: one grasping the arm and the other supporting the base. Hold it in an upright position keeping the stage horizontal, and place it on the table directly in front of you with the light source or mirror away from you. Examine the microscope and Fig. I-1-1 carefully. Locate and examine the following parts:

base and pillar which support the parts of the microscope.

inclination joint which allows the microscope to be tilted.

arm, or curved support, by which the microscope should be carried (with one hand while supporting the base with the other).

stage which supports the slide to be examined.

stage clips to prevent movement on the slide while it is being viewed. A slight movement of the slide may move the object which you are viewing out of sight.

body tube which holds a set of lenses at each end.

ocular lens, or eye piece, containing a magnifying lens which is fitted into the top of the body tube. It may be lifted out easily and replaced by another of different magnification.

revolving nose piece, a disc-shaped piece at the lower end of the body tube, which holds a number of objective lenses. Turn it gently by

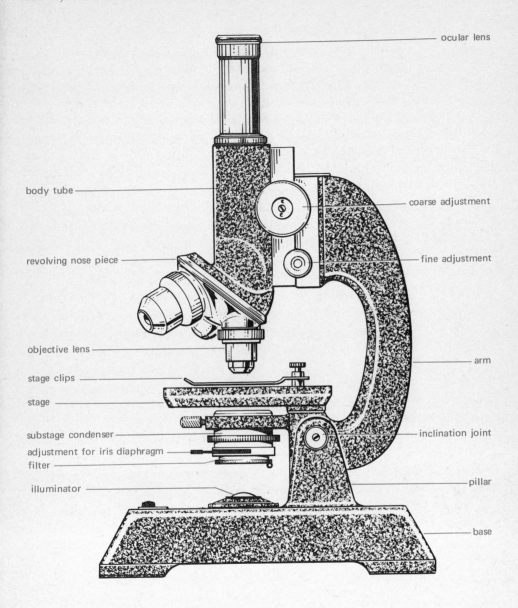

Fig. I–1–1   The compound microscope

grasping the objectives. When a lens moves into the proper position below the body tube you will hear a faint click.

objective lenses, three lens assemblies attached to the revolving nosepiece. Note that they are of different lengths; the longer objectives
have a higher magnification.

coarse adjustment, operated by the larger milled wheel near the top
of the arm. It is used only when the low- or the medium-power
objective lens is in place. Never use the coarse adjustment with the

high-power objective lens. Do not turn the coarse adjustment down (that is, away from you) when looking through the eye-piece. The gap between the slide and the high-power objective lens is usually too small to permit much downward movement of the body tube without damage to the slide.

fine adjustment, operated by a smaller milled wheel attached below the coarse adjustment. It is used for adjusting the sharpness of the image viewed under medium or high power.

substage lamp, a lamp in a housing which usually shines through a blue filter to light the specimen being examined. Some microscopes are equipped with a mirror to reflect light from other sources.

condenser lens, a converging lens system that focuses light from the substage lamp onto the object to be viewed. It may be a fixed lens set into the stage opening or part of a movable unit below the stage. The height of this movable unit is controlled by the *substage condenser adjustment*.

iris diaphragm, a device used to reduce the amount of light entering the microscope. It consists of a series of overlapping metal plates regulated by a lever to vary the size of the opening. On some microscopes it is replaced by a *light control disk* which has several openings of different sizes. It may be rotated to vary the amount of light.

Questions:
*1. How does a compound microscope differ from a simple microscope?
*2. What is the proper method for carrying a microscope?
*3. When the microscope is put away, the low-power objective should be directly beneath the body tube. Why?
*4. Name the parts of the microscope through which light passes from the lamp to the observer's eye.
*5. What parts of the microscope are involved in changing the focus to obtain a clear image?
*6. What effect has the condenser lens on light rays passing through it?
*7. What is the purpose of the iris diaphragm or light control disk?
†9. What advantage would an adjustable condenser lens have over a fixed condenser lens?
†10. Make a report on the work of an early microscopist such as Zacharias Jansen, Anton Von Leeuwenhoek or Robert Hooke.

References and Suggestions for Further Investigation:
1. You may wish to make a duplicate of one of Leeuwenhoek's simple lenses. To construct a spherical lens, heat the centre of a six or seven inch length of solid glass rod in a burner flame. Rotate the rod as it heats. When the glass is soft pull the ends apart to form two filaments. Heat the end of each filament in the flame to form a glass bead

approximately two millimeters in diameter. Place a prepared slide against a light source (a window will do). Using the rod as a handle, hold the bead lens close to the prepared slide and examine it.

I–2   OPERATION AND CARE OF THE MICROSCOPE

Microscope lenses are accurately ground from soft glass. They are easily scratched and permanently damaged by improper handling. Any film of dust, grease or moisture on the lens will produce a fuzzy indistinct image. The following precautions are necessary in caring for lenses.

(a) Before using the microscope, clean only the lens surfaces that are exposed. Do not remove the ocular or objective lenses from the microscope.

(b) Use only lens paper provided by your instructor for wiping lenses. Clean all lenses before each use, then discard the lens paper. Do not substitute facial tissue or paper towel.

(c) If there is an oil or grease film on the lens, it can be removed with lens tissue dampened with xylol (xylene). Do *not* use alcohol for this purpose.

(d) Never touch a lens surface with your fingers.

APPARATUS AND MATERIALS REQUIRED (per station)
> *Compound microscope*
> *lens paper*
> *colored magazine (not newspaper) photograph*
> *slides and cover slips*
> *medicine droppers (pipettes) and forceps*
> *xylol (xylene)*

Procedure:

PART A   PREPARING A SLIDE

1. Clean a slide and a cover slip with paper towelling moistened with water. To clean the fragile cover slip, fold the paper around the slip; then use a finger and thumb to wipe both sides at the same time.
2. Cut a piece approximately 1 cm square from a colored magazine photograph. Examine it carefully to see how the picture was printed on the paper.
3. Place the square of paper on the slide, then add a drop of water to the paper with a pipette (medicine dropper).
4. Using forceps or holding the cover slip by the edges only, lower the slip over the paper square and water.

Did you trap any air bubbles under the cover slip? How could you lower it to avoid this happening?

PART B   EXAMINING THE SLIDE WITH LOW POWER

Before placing the prepared slide on the microscope stage, carry out the following procedures.

5. Check to ensure that the lowest power objective lens (the shortest one) is in place directly under the body tube.

6. Using the coarse adjustment, raise the body tube to approximately 2.5 cm above the stage.

7. Look through the ocular lens and adjust the light until the field of view is bright and evenly illuminated.

8. Place the slide on the stage so that the square of paper is centered over the opening in the stage. Use the stage clips to hold the slide in position. If there is a surplus of water on the slide or on the top of the cover slip, remove this by gently blotting it with a paper towel.

9. Sight along the stage (your eye should be level with the stage) and use the coarse adjustment to lower the body tube until the objective lens is about .5 cm above the cover slip. Some microscopes are provided with a stop which prevents lowering the low-power objective too far.

10. Keep both eyes open while looking through the ocular lens with one eye. Slowly raise the body tube with the coarse adjustment until the dots on the paper are in clear focus. (Both eyes are kept open to reduce fatigue from squinting, but you may find that blocking out the vision of your other eye with your hand will help at first.)

11. Slowly rotate the *fine* adjustment clockwise and then counter-clockwise.
    What effect does this rotation have on the image? Would you normally use the fine adjustment with the low-power objective lens?

12. Adjust the iris diaphragm or light control disk.
    What effect has this control on the image?

13. Draw three circles of 5 cm diameter in your record book. These will represent your fields of view (the complete area you see) as you look through the ocular lens.

14. When you have adjusted all the controls to obtain a clear image of the dots at low power draw *one* of the dots in the first circle. Draw the dot to show its area relative to the area of the field.

PART C   EXAMINING THE SLIDE WITH MEDIUM
OR HIGH POWER

NOTE: *Always rotate the nosepiece carefully and slowly while at the same time sighting along the level of the slide to make sure that the objective lens does not touch the cover slip or slide. If it appears that it will touch the slide, request assistance from your teacher.*

the nosepiece so that the medium-power objective (middle length objective lens), is under the body tube. It will click into place.

16. With the medium-power objective in place, look through the ocular lens.
How does the light intensity (brightness) now compare with the intensity when you were examining the dots under low power?
Adjust the iris diaphragm or disk to compensate for this difference.

17. If the object is not in focus, use the fine adjustment first and later, if necessary, a slight movement of the coarse adjustment. If your micro-scope is *parfocal,* all three objective lenses will be in focus at the same position of the body tube. You should be able to switch from low power to medium power, and even to high power, with very little focusing.
How many dots can you see in the field of view now? Can you see how the various shades of color were obtained on the paper?

18. In the second circle of your record page draw the same colored dot that you previously observed and drew at low power as it appears now under medium power.

19. To examine the dot under high power, repeat Procedures 15 to 18 with one important exception. When using the microscope with the high power you should use *only the fine adjustment*, never the coarse adjustment. In the third circle draw the same dot as seen under high power. Beside each circle label the name of the objective lens that was used.

*20. If you have time, continue to practice using the microscope, examin-ing the dot with the three objective lenses in turn. Practice focusing throughout these initial technique exercises. Although the operation of the microscope may require much thought at this stage, it will become easier with practice.

21. When you have finished your examination of the dots under high power, remove and clean the slide and cover slip. (Recall Procedure I.) Clean all the lenses of the microscope with lens paper and leave the low power objective in position below the body tube. Cover the microscope with its plastic dust cover and carry it by the arm and base to its storage place.

Questions:

*1. What does parfocal mean? Why is it advantageous to have a micro-scope that is parfocal?

*2. Why is it desirable that the coarse adjustment knob be a little stiff or difficult to turn?

*3. Why would it be difficult to use an objective lens of higher power than the 40 power objective lens on your microscope? (Hint: What changes occur when objectives lenses of higher magnification are used?)

*4. Why are fewer dots seen at a time with the high power objective lens?

References and Suggestions for Further Investigation:
1. For further practice in the operation of the microscope you will find it interesting to examine such things as a razor blade edge, an insect's leg, a butterfly wing, a fish scale and a phonograph needle.

I–3 CHARACTERISTICS OF THE IMAGE

There are differences between the image of the object as seen through the microscope and the object as seen directly. The most important difference, of course, is that the image is larger. In this exercise we will examine another difference, one which sometimes causes difficulty when the microscope is first used.

APPARATUS AND MATERIALS REQUIRED (per station)
> *Microscope*
> *slide*
> *cover slip*
> *pipette*
> *printed magazine or newspaper page*

Procedure:
1. Cut a 1 cm square piece of newspaper or magazine containing the printed letter c, h or p.
2. Prepare a slide of this paper as in Exercise I–2.
3. Examine the letter under low power.
   Estimate how many times larger the size of the image is than the size of the actual letter as seen by your unaided eye. What differences do you observe in the appearance of the letter?
4. Move the glass slide slowly to the right. Observe the direction in which the image moves. In turn, move the slide to the left, away from you, toward you and then rotate it clockwise and counter-clockwise. Describe the direction of movement of the image in each of these cases.
5. Repeat Procedure 4 under medium power.
   Do you obtain the same result as under low power?

Questions:
*1. Compare the size, appearance and brightness of the object as seen with the unaided eye and the image as seen with the microscope.

*2. Why was the letter x or w not selected for this exercise?
*3. How could you arrange a slide in order to see the letter "c" so that its image is not inverted?

I-4   DEPTH OF FIELD

The eye has an automatic way of quickly changing focus, enabling it to examine objects close at hand and then objects that are far away. From your previous studies of the eye you will perhaps remember how its lens is able to focus light rays from objects at different distances. In this exercise you will observe how a microscope can be focused on different levels of an object from its top to its bottom surface.

APPARATUS AND MATERIALS REQUIRED (per station)
> 2 dissecting needles
> forceps
> 1 cm square pieces of several types of cloth (cotton, silk, wool, nylon), preferably each a different color
> slide
> cover slip
> pipette
> microscope

Procedure:
1. Simultaneously use one dissecting needle to hold and another to tease a single thread from each of the three fabrics mentioned as materials required. Place a 1 cm length of each of the threads on a slide so that they will all cross at the center of the slide. (See Fig. I-4-1.) Use a pipette to put a drop of water on the threads.

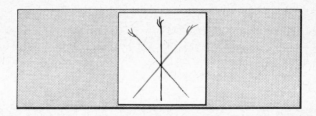

Fig. I-4-1   Crossed threads used to show depth of field

2. Try to separate the fibres of the threads using the dissecting needles.
3. Add a cover slip using the technique of Exercise I-2.
4. Note which thread is on the top and which is on the bottom at the cross-over point. Then examine the threads under low power. Move the slide to see where the three threads cross. Experiment to obtain the best position for the iris diaphragm (or the light control disk) and the substage condenser lens, if it is adjustable. Change the depth at which the microscope is in focus by rotating the coarse adjustment knob clockwise and counter-clockwise.
Which thread appears to be in the top position? How many threads are in clear focus under low power? Can all three threads be simultaneously in focus?
5. Rotate the nosepiece to the medium-power lens and repeat Procedure 4.
6. Rotate the nosepiece to the high-power objective and repeat Procedure 4. This time slowly rotate only the *fine* adjustment back and forth.
Which of the three objectives gives the greatest depth of field (that is, the depth of the specimen that is simultaneously in focus for any one position of the nosepiece)? Under high-power, does the rotation of the fine adjustment knob produce any increase in the depth of field?
7. Under high power, scan the field of view (i.e. let your eye travel over it from one side to the other).
Are the center and the edges of the field of view equally sharp or do you have to adjust the focus to see the entire field clearly? Can you identify the type of cloth used in each sample?

Questions:
*1. You have seen that under high-power the microscope must be almost continually adjusted with the fine adjustment knob to see "in depth." How does your eye adjust to enable you to see both near and distant objects clearly? Try to read this page and see a distant object at the same time.
*2. State two reasons why material being examined under a microscope must be very thin. (Hint: How is the amount of light which passes through the specimen affected by this thickness?)

References and Suggestions for Further Investigation:
1. You may wish to try photographing objects through a microscope. To do this the camera lens must be held very steady against the ocular lens. If the camera has an adjustable diaphragm, set the camera lens focus at infinity using its largest opening, (that is, with the f stop to its lowest number). You will have to experiment to deter-

mine the best shutter speed. Do you think it would be possible to photograph the threads used in Exercise I-4 under high-power so all three will be clear in the picture? In what ways is a drawing superior to a photograph?

2. Hair can be identified by its surface markings. Examine the surface markings on the hairs of several different animals and record their characteristics.

I-5 MAGNIFICATION WITH THE MICROSCOPE

The magnifying power of the microscope has been referred to as low-, medium- or high-power. You will now try to determine how great each of these magnifications is and how much material can be examined in each field of view.

MATERIALS REQUIRED (per station)
Microscope
small plastic ruler with millimeter scale

Procedure:
1. Examine the millimeter scale on the edge of a plastic ruler under low power.   Place the millimeter scale on the stage across the diameter of the field of view.   Move the ruler sideways so that one of the millimeter division marks is on the extreme left side of the field of view. Determine the diameter of the observed field in millimeters as seen through the ocular lens.

NOTE: *The unit used for the measurement of distances under a microscope is the micron (usually abbreviated as the Greek letter mu (mew) which is written µ). A micron is 1/1,000 of a millimeter or approximately 1/25,000 inch.*

What is the diameter of the low-power field in millimeters? in microns (MY-krons)?

2. Repeat Procedure 1 using the medium-power objective and answer the same question. Do *not* use high-power. Examine the ocular lens to find its magnifying power (a number followed by an X).

3. Examine the markings on the objective lenses.   (Do not remove the lenses.) There are usually several sets of numbers. The larger numbers usually refer to magnification. Record the magnification produced by each objective lens.

NOTE: *The total magnification of the object which the microscope produces is found by multiplying the magnification number found on the ocular lens by the magnification number that is on the objective lens in use.*

4. Copy and complete the following table as instructed.

	(i)	(ii)	(iii)	(iv)	(v)	
	DRAWING OF OBJECTIVE LENS	MAGNIFICATION OF OBJECTIVE LENS	MAGNIFICATION OF OCULAR LENS	TOTAL MAGNIFI-CATION	DIAMETER OF FIELD IN MM AND MICRONS	
					mm	*μ*
LOW POWER						
MEDIUM POWER						
HIGH POWER						

(i) In the first column draw the low-, medium- and high-power objective lenses to show their relative lengths.

(ii) In the second column record the markings on the barrels of the objectives that show their magnifying power.

(iii) In the third column record the marking on the ocular lens that shows its magnifying power. (If the ocular lens is not changed, this figure is the same for all three cases.)

(iv) In the fourth column show the total magnifying power. (This is the product of the ocular and the objective magnifications since the first magnification by the objectives is further magnified by the eye-piece.)

(v) In the fifth column record the diameters of the fields in millimeters and microns. These were previously found for low and medium powers. Calculate the product of the total magnification and diameter of field for low power and for medium power. Use these products and the total magnification at high-power to calculate the diameter of the high-power field.

5. The photograph in Fig. I-5-1 represents a micro-organism viewed at the magnification shown.

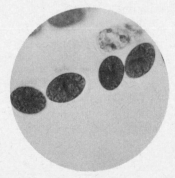

Fig. I–5–1   Micro-organism magnified 100x

Use your previous calculations to determine the diameter of the field in millimeters and microns.

- **What is the approximate length in millimeters and microns of the micro-organism?**
6. Draw two circles of equal diameter in your notebook. Sketch the micro-organism as it would appear at low and high power.

Questions:
*1. A student draws a fish and labels it ¼X. What does this label mean?
*2. A student observes a rectangular-shaped cell under a magnification of 40x. He calculates its length to be approximately 50 μ (microns). He makes a drawing of the cell, 1 cm in length.
  (a) What is the magnification of this drawing?
  (b) He then decides to make another drawing of the cell at a magnification of 1000x. What length should this cell be drawn?
*3. If an object stretches across 2/3 of the low-power field, what is its actual length? If you draw it 15 cm long, what is the magnification of your drawing?
*4. An object stretches across 1/5 of the high-power field. What is its length? You are told to draw it with a magnification of 900x. What length will the object be in your drawing?
*5. An organism swims across the low-power field in 30 seconds. How fast is it swimming in microns per minute?
†6. State the relationship between microns and millimeters; microns and centimeters; microns and meters; millimeters and meters; centimeters and meters.

References and Suggestions for Further Investigation:
1. How thick is a human hair? Prepare a slide of a short length of your hair and examine it under high-power. What is the diameter of the hair in millimeters and microns?

I-6 THE STEREOSCOPIC MICROSCOPE

The compound monocular (one eye-piece) microscope has both upper and lower limitations in its ability to magnify (e.g. 40x to 400x). Other types of microscopes are used in the ranges above and below the limits of the compound monocular microscope. Very high magnifications are made possible with the electron microscope. With this microscope the image is produced by electrons instead of light rays. Compare the extra detail shown in the electron microscope photograph of the head of a plant louse (Fig. I-6-3) with that taken through a compound microscope (Fig. I-6-2).

Fig. I–6–1   Aphid (plant louse) viewed with a stereo binocular microscope. Note the mouth parts projecting from the lower side of the mouth.

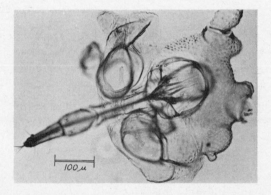

Fig. I–6–2   Head of aphid viewed with a compound monocular microscope. Note the small hairline projections at the tip of the mouth parts.

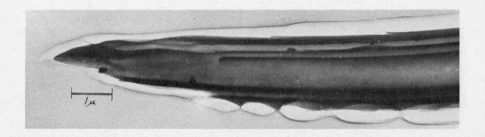

Fig. I–6–3   One hair-like projection viewed with an electron microscope

For magnifications below the range of the compound monocular microscope, the stereoscopic microscope is used. In this exercise you will note the similarities and differences between these latter two microscopes.

APPARATUS AND MATERIALS REQUIRED (per station)
> *Stereoscopic microscope and lamp*
> *dissecting needle*
> *petri dishes*
> *slides*
> *four classes of objects for examination:*
> > *opaque objects (e.g. coin, leaf, razor blade, pencil)*
> > *translucent objects (e.g. lens tissue, newspaper, cloth)*
> > *transparent objects (e.g. microscope slide, cover slip, cellophane)*
> > *live and moving objects (e.g. earthworm, mealworm, beetle)*

Fig. I–6–4   Compound monocular
microscope

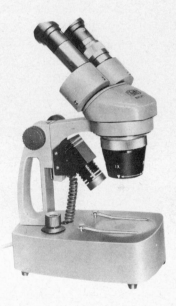

Fig. I–6–5   Stereoscopic binocular
microscope

Procedure:
1. Examine your stereoscopic microscope for the following features.
   (a) *Illumination.* An object on the stage can be illuminated from above, from below or from the side. Approximately what area of the stage can be illuminated from below?
   (b) *Focusing.* How many knobs are used to raise and lower the body tube?

(c) *Ocular lenses.* How many ocular lenses and body tubes are there? How can you adjust the distance between the ocular lenses to match the distance between your eyes? Notice that one of the ocular lenses is fixed while the other can be rotated. What magnification by the ocular lenses is indicated?

(d) *Objective lenses.* Locate the objective lenses by looking upward from the stage. How many objective lenses are there? Are they all of different lengths or are some of the same length? What are the objective magnifications indicated? How do you change from one magnification to another?

2. From your observation of the number of ocular lenses, body tubes and objective lenses, what conclusions can you reach regarding the number of pathways taken by light from the object to your eyes?

3. Place an opaque object such as a coin on the center of the glass stage plate.   Adjust the nosepiece for low-power magnification and lower the body tube as far as it will go.

4. Look through the ocular lenses.   If you see two overlapping circles of light, adjust the distance between the ocular lenses so that the circles coincide.

5. Use the adjustment knob to obtain an initial focus on the coin.   Because the vision in each of your eyes is different, it is necessary to focus each ocular lens separately.   First, focus for the eye looking into the *fixed* ocular lens while keeping the other eye closed.   Then use only the other eye and focus for it by rotating the ridged ring just below the ocular lens on the body tube.

6. Observe the different effects produced by shining light on the coin from various positions.   Close one eye, then the other and compare the two images of the coin.
Is a three dimensional (stereoscopic) effect produced when you view the two images simultaneously?

7. Stack three or more coins in a staggered pile.   How many coins can you see in clear focus at one time?   Repeat at the higher magnification. Compare the depth of field at the two magnifications.

8. Place one of the living specimens in a petri dish and examine it through the microscope.   Move the dish to keep the specimen in view.   Compare the specimen's direction of movement with that of its image. A dissecting needle may be used gently to move the specimen within the field of view.

9. Examine other objects provided, varying the magnification and the illumination to obtain best results.

Questions:

*1. Compare the "working" spaces between the objective lenses and the stage in two types of microscopes shown in Figs. I-6-4 and I-6-5.

Which microscope provides the greatest amount of space for manipulating specimens?

*2. Compare the ranges of magnification possible when using the two microscopes.

*3. What is the meaning of the term "stereoscopic"?

*4. How does a stereoscopic microscope help us to judge depth when viewing an object?

*5. Which microscope would you use to examine the dial of a wrist watch? Give several reasons for your choice.

*6. Which microscope would you use to examine the surface detail of a pollen grain? Give a reason for your choice.

Section II
THE CELL

The cell is considered to be the basic unit of life and thus it is the basic unit involved in reproduction. With remarkably few differences, both plant and animal cells are much the same in their composition and structure. By examination of both your own and manufactured slides you will see *some* of the parts of cells. If the extremely powerful electron microscope were available to you, much more could be seen of the fine structure of cells. (See Figs. I-7-1 and I-7-2.) You should consult reference texts to find other photographs showing recently discovered details of the structure of cells.

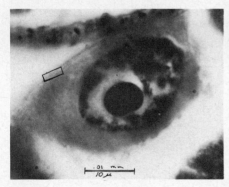

Fig. I–7–1   A cell from the digestive tract of an aphid viewed with a compound monocular microscope

Fig. I–7–2   The membrane from the cell above viewed with an electron microscope

Several techniques that make cell parts easier to see are outlined in the following exercise. Which of these techniques is used depends on the type of material to be examined. Some structures can be clearly seen with very little preparation. From the several slides you will make, you can obtain a composite or generalized picture of the structure of plant and animal cells.

I–7 THE PURPOSE OF STAINS

When specimens are too transparent or too uniform in color and texture to allow their structures to be seen clearly, stains may be used to highlight the parts.

APPARATUS AND MATERIALS REQUIRED (per station)
Monocular microscope
slides
cover slips and pipettes
iodine stain
white blackboard chalk
starch

Procedure:
1. Put a small amount of starch (about the size of a pin head) on one end of a slide and spread it out into a thin layer using the edge of a second slide.
2. Put a small amount of finely powdered chalk dust on the other end of the slide and spread it out in the same way.
3. Observe both kinds of particles under low-, medium- and high-power. **What do the grains of each powder look like? How do they compare in size? in color? in the shape of their granules? Can you tell them apart easily?**
4. Use the edge of the second glass slide to scrape the powders to the center of the prepared slide and mix them together. Add a drop of water to the mixture and cover it with a cover slip. Observe the mixture through your microscope. **Can you now distinguish the starch from the chalk particles more easily?**
5. Put a drop of iodine stain at the edge of the cover slip as shown in Fig. I-7-3. **What happens to the drop of stain? Does it spread under the cover slip?**
6. Touch the opposite edge of the cover slip with a small piece of paper towel as shown in Fig. I-7-4. **What happens to the stain?**

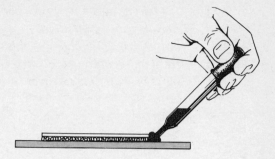

Fig. I–7–3   Adding stain to a slide

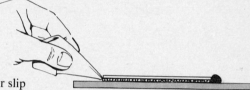

Fig. I–7–4   Drawing stain under the cover slip

7. Observe the starch-chalk mixture again, first under low and then under medium power.
Can you distinguish the starch grains now? What has happened to each of the powders?

Questions:
*1. Can soluble materials be examined by the methods used in Procedures 4 to 7? Explain.
*2. What effect should a stain have on the material being examined?
*3. Suggest which common household materials might usefully serve as stains.
*4. Under what conditions would it not be necessary to stain the material being viewed?

I–8   LIVING AND NON-LIVING PLANT CELLS

The word "cell" as a descriptive term for the unit of structure of living things was first used by an English microscopist, Robert Hooke (1635-1703). He examined thin slices of cork and found that they were composed of tiny empty structures arranged in rows. He named them "cells" because they resembled bare rooms or cells in a monastery. In this exercise you will compare cells in cork, pith and balsa wood with cells of living plants. You may judge for yourself how appropriate the name "cell" is for such structures.

APPARATUS AND MATERIALS REQUIRED (per station)

> *Materials for examination:*
>> *bottle cork, pith ball and balsa wood*
>> *fresh onion bulb*
>> *moss or water plant leaves*
> *razor blade*
> *microscope*
> *slides*
> *cover slips*
> *forceps*
> *pipettes*
> *iodine stain*
> *methylene blue stain (or blue ink)*
> *eosin stain (or red ink)*
> (If the inks are used, dilute them half and half with water.)

Procedure:

1. Prepare the cork, pith and balsa wood in the following way. Use a sharp razor blade to cut a *thin*, wedge-shaped section from the sample supplied. At the narrow edge of the wedge there should be an especially thin layer in which you can see the cells clearly. Cut several sections until you are satisfied you have a thin enough wedge.

2. Mount this wedge in a drop of water on a slide and add a cover slip. Examine only under low and medium powers. On low power you should scan the entire slice to locate the thinnest area. Then turn to medium power for a detailed examination of the cells in that area.

3. Using the method learned in Experiment I-6, add a drop of one of the stains and observe the effect it has on the material.

4. Draw four or five representative cells from each of your samples to indicate their general shape and arrangement. Draw each cell at least 2 cm long. Estimate and record the sizes of the cells in microns. What is the magnification of your drawing?

   If you had been in Hooke's position as one of the first people to see these materials under a microscope, what might you have used for a name instead of "cells"?

   Each of the materials used comes from a different region of a tree trunk; cork from the bark, balsa from the stem and pith from the soft center of the stem.

   Do you see any indication of their source when looking at these cells through a microscope? These materials float in water. From your observations, can you suggest an explanation for their buoyancy? Compare the thicknesses of the walls of the various kinds of cells. Can you relate these thicknesses to the textures of the three kinds of wood? Which was hardest? Which was softest?

5. Peel off and discard the brown papery covering of an onion bulb. Take one crisp, fleshy layer from the bulb and bend it backwards against its natural curl so that it breaks near its middle. Although the inner tissues of this specialized "leaf" break cleanly, the outer skin usually will not. This makes it possible to readily peel off a thin layer of skin with a forceps.

6. Spread out a small piece of the onion skin (epidermis) evenly on a slide and add a drop of water and a cover slip. Observe the epidermis under low power. Scan the field of view under low power to select a suitably thin area and then observe this area under medium and high power. Add iodine stain.

    Has the addition of stain enabled you to see more detail of the structure of the cell? What structures do you now see that you did not see before?

    Draw a few cells showing the structures observed. Indicate the cell sizes in microns.

7. Repeat Procedure 6 but this time have your partner prepare a slide using eosin (EE-oh-sin) stain while you prepare a similar slide using methylene blue stain.

    Compare the effects of the various stains on the cell structures. Are some parts more deeply stained? What are the clear spaces in the cell?

8. Place a small leaf from a moss or water plant on a slide, add water and a cover slip and examine it under low and medium powers.

    What region of the leaf is thinnest? How many cells thick is it at the thinnest part? You will have to rotate the coarse adjustment knob to raise and lower the position of focus and count the layers as they come into focus.

9. Look for chloroplasts. These are small, oval, green-colored bodies inside the cells. Estimate their number.

    Describe any movement detected within the cell. Can you locate any other internal cell structures such as the denser nuclei?

Questions:

*1. Compare the structure and contents of non-living cells (cork, pith, balsa wood) with living cells (moss, onions, water plant).

*2. Do stains have the same effect on all cell contents? Explain.

*3. When iodine is added to a group of cells, parts of some cells turn purple. What does this indicate? (Hint: Refer to Experiment I-6.)

Consult a reference book to answer questions 4-7.

*4. What is the function of a chloroplast? a cell wall? a nucleus?

*5. Where in a cell are the cell membrane, nuclear membrane, cytoplasm (SY-toh-plaz-um), nucleolus (noo-KLEE-o-lus) located?

*6. What is a vacuole (VA-kew-ohl)? Where is it found?
*7. Find out about the early work done on cells by Matthias Schleiden
     and Theodor Schwann.

I–9 OBSERVING THE VARIOUS KINDS OF CELLS IN A LEAF

Living organisms are usually made up of many different kinds of cells. In this
activity you will observe some of the specialized cells of a green leaf. The
principal function of a green leaf is to manufacture food for the plant by the
process of photosynthesis. The chemical change during photosynthesis can be
summarized by the following reaction statement:

$$\text{carbon dioxide} + \text{water} + \text{light energy} \longrightarrow \text{simple sugar} + \text{oxygen}$$

To perform its function the leaf must
(a) permit light to enter,
(b) obtain carbon dioxide and water,
(c) transport manufactured sugar to other parts of the plant,
(d) remove surplus oxygen.

APPARATUS AND MATERIALS REQUIRED (per station)
        A "soft" leaf such as geranium, begonia, grass, pea or bean
        a "hard" leaf such as laurel, poplar or holly
        monocular microscope
        slides
        cover slips
        pipettes
        forceps
        razor blade

Procedure:
1. Examine both surfaces of one or more kinds of soft and hard leaves.
    Note how the surfaces differ. Describe the vein pattern. Veins serve
    the leaf in two ways. As a form of skeleton, they support the leaf.
    As "highways" they allow the transport of water and dissolved sugar.
    **How is the vein pattern related to these functions? If possible, suggest
    a more efficient pattern.**
2. Break a "soft" leaf sharply in half across its midrib or flex it several
    times before tearing it into two parts. Do this in such a way that the
    center part of the leaf becomes partially separated from the epidermal
    surface layer. At the upper and lower surface of the broken edges
    look for projecting, thin, almost transparent layers of skin. These
    are the epidermal cells.

3. Remove a projecting piece of the delicate epidermal layer from the top surface of the leaf while your partner removes a similar layer from the bottom. Mount each layer on a slide, add water and cover slip. In turn, scan each slide on low power to select a suitably thin area. Then examine the types of cells present on medium and high power. Compare your leaf surface with that shown in Fig. I-9-1.

Fig. I–9–1   Leaf epidermis

How many different types of cells can you find?
Draw one cell of each type.
Can you think of a reason for the shape of the most abundant type of cell? Plant leaves breathe through openings called stomata. Can you see any of these openings? How many can you count in the high-power field? Are they as concentrated on the upper epidermal layer as on the lower one? Two curved cells called guard cells are on either side of each stoma. What effect would straightening the guard cells have on the size of the opening? Do any of the cells in the epidermal layer contain chloroplasts?

4. Select an area of a "hard" leaf that has no thick veins and cut out a section slightly narrower than the width of the slide. Sandwich the leaf section between two slides. The top slide should be offset from the bottom slide by about 1 cm with the leaf blade projecting from under it as shown in Fig. I-9-2.

5. Arrange with your partner so that one of you cuts a thin section of

Fig. I–9–2   Cutting a leaf cross section

leaf with the top side of the leaf uppermost and the other with the bottom side uppermost. To cut a section hold the slides firmly together on the desk with one hand. With the edge of the upper slide as a guide, use a razor blade to make a vertical cut across the leaf (Fig. I-9-2). Without moving the slides or leaf, prepare a very fine wedge of leaf material by using the slide edge as a guide and by cutting with the razor blade at an angle (Fig. I-9-3). Remove the thin cross-section formed between the two cuts using forceps. Repeat the procedure making several of these sections. With a little practice you will be able to make thin, even sections. You will probably find that suitably thin sections will tend to curl up slightly.

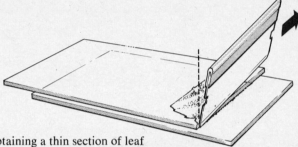

Fig. I–9–3   Method of obtaining a thin section of leaf

6. Mount *several* sections on a slide in a drop of water and add a cover slip. Observe these under low, medium and high powers.

   Are all parts of your section equally thin? Why was your partner asked to cut his leaf with the opposite side up? Scan the slide to find an area where the number of different layers of cells from top to bottom can be counted. How many layers of cells are there? Is each cell layer made up of one, or more than one cell type? Can you locate any guard cells?

   Draw a typical cell from each layer. (Fig. I-9-4 is a photograph of a cross-section of a leaf and Fig. I-9-5 names the various parts.) Compare your drawings of the epidermal cells as seen from the side with your previous ones (Procedure 3) of the same cells as seen from the top. Based on these two views of the same cells, describe their overall shape.

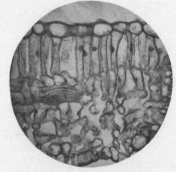

Fig. I–9–4   Cross section of a leaf

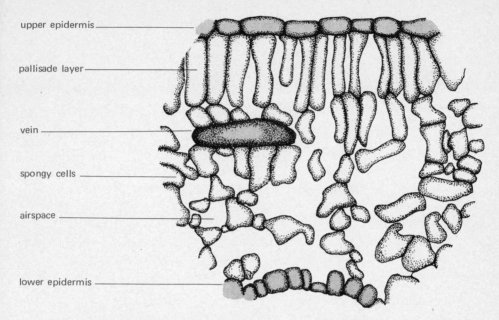

upper epidermis

pallisade layer

vein

spongy cells

airspace

lower epidermis

Fig. I–9–5   Parts of a leaf

Which cell types or layers have chloroplasts? Which layer has the most chloroplasts? How are the cells in this layer arranged? Are the chloroplasts in any particular part of the cell?

Questions:
Consult a reference book to find the answers to the following questions.
*1. A tissue is a group of similar cells which usually perform a single function. What tissues are found in a leaf vein? What are their functions?
*2. Where is the cuticle or layer of cutin (CEW-tin) located? How does it protect the leaf? How does it differ in structure from the other layers of the leaf?
*3. Name the cell layers in a leaf. Each layer forms a tissue.
*4. What materials pass through the stomata?
*5. Which layer of the leaf permits the freest movement of materials between cells?
†6. How does an organ differ from a tissue? What are the organs of a green plant?

I–10   A LEAF IMPRESSION

In this exercise you will use the surface of a leaf as a mold on which to make a cast in a transparent plastic film. In this way you will obtain a very different view of the surface cells of a leaf.

APPARATUS AND MATERIALS REQUIRED (per station)
> *Acetone*
> *cellulose acetate plastic strip (about 1 in x 3 in heavy gauge as used in electrostatic experiments in Unit 2)*
> *glass petri dishes*
> *monocular microscope*
> *slides and cover slips*
> *pipettes*
> *forceps*
> *scissors*
> *leaves*

Procedure:

1. Cut two small pieces from a leaf, one square and the other triangular. Place them in a glass petri dish about 1 cm apart with the upper surface of the square section to the glass and the lower leaf surface of the triangular section to the glass. The shape can be used to identify the surface to be studied.

CAUTION: Acetone is extremely flammable. Ensure that the room is well ventilated and that no open flames are present.

2. Cut off a piece of cellulose acetate plastic strip sufficiently large to cover both leaf sections. Soften one side of it by adding a drop of acetone (ASS-eh-tohn).
3. Place a drop of acetone on each leaf portion.
4. Place the softened side of the plastic over the leaf portions, then press down firmly with your thumb.
5. After about one minute, when the acetone has evaporated, life the film from the glass.
6. Remove the leaf portion from the acetate film with forceps or by gently scraping with your fingernail.
7. Examine each of the impressions on the strip under low and medium power. Light from the side (side-light) is best for observation in this case. Reduce the intensity of light from below or omit it entirely. **How many types of cells can you distinguish in the field? Can you locate the small openings called stomata? How many of them are there in the field at medium power?** Compare the relative numbers of stomata on the upper and lower surfaces of the leaf.

Questions:

*1. In what ways does viewing an impression of the leaf surface differ from viewing the surface itself?

*2. What are the functions of the openings (stomata) in the leaf surface?

*3. Why are there usually more openings in the lower surface than in the upper one?

References and Suggestions for Further Investigation:

1. Examine impressions of surfaces of leaves that have been collected from different habitats – some moist, some dry. Be sure to include a grass and a water plant in your samples.

2. Try to estimate the number of stomata on both surfaces of a leaf.

   (a) Count the number of stomata in the field for both surfaces.

   (b) You have previously measured the diameter of the field in mm. Now calculate its area (Area = 3.14 × radius²).

   (c) Determine the total area of the leaf in mm².

   (d) Therefore, the total number of stomata per surface = number of stomata in a field $\times \dfrac{\text{area of leaf in mm}^2}{\text{area of field in mm}^2}$.

3. Two books which contain electron photomicrographs of cells and cell parts are: *Cell Ultrastructure* by W. Jensen and R. Park (Belmont, California: Wadsworth Publishing Co., 1961) and *The Microstructure of Cells* by S. Hurry (Boston: Houghton Mifflin Co., 1968).

NOTE: *This is the recommended time to prepare cultures of micro-organisms for Experiment I-12.*

I–11   HUMAN SKIN CELLS

In the previous exercises you examined epidermal cells covering surfaces in plants. When you examine corresponding animal cells, use tissue obtained from the skin on the inside of your cheek. The layers of your skin exposed to air are not suitable because they are composed of dead tissue that lack the detail of living cells. Cheek cells are protected from drying out by the mucus in saliva.

APPARATUS AND MATERIALS REQUIRED (per station)

   Monocular microscope
   slides
   cover slips
   pipettes
   toothpicks
   methylene blue and eosin stains

Procedure:

1. To prepare a slide, *gently* rub or scrape the inner lining of your cheek in one direction with a toothpick. Smear the material obtained over the center of a clean slide. Discard the toothpick. Each partner should prepare a slide.

2. Stain the material on the slide. One partner should use a drop of methylene blue and the other a drop of eosin. Add a cover slip.

3. Examine the cells under low, medium and high power. Draw two or three typical cells.

   Does each cell have a cell wall? Are there clear spaces in the cytoplasm? Does each cell have a nucleus and a nucleolus? What structures are accentuated (stained more deeply) with the blue stain? with the red stain?

   Draw several cells to show the structures you have observed.

Questions:

*1. Compare the structures of typical plant and animal cells. How are they similar? How do they differ?

*2. The skin of plant leaves is composed of epidermal cells while the skin of animals is said to be made of epithelial cells. Compare these cells. Consult a dictionary or other reference book to find the difference in meaning between these terms.

†3. Man's skin is a much more complex tissue than the covering of a leaf. In a reference book try to find information about the structure of human skin.

I–12   BLOOD CELLS

Animal blood consists of cells suspended in a fluid. By using a smear technique, we can examine several different kinds of cells in this fluid. Convenient sources of fresh blood are frogs, fish or your own body. However, if you have any objection to using your own blood you will not be required to do so.

APPARATUS AND MATERIALS REQUIRED (per station)

Monocular microscope
new slides
cover slips and pipettes
sterile lancets
Wright's stain
methyl alcohol
sterile absorbent cotton

Procedure:

1. Clean a slide thoroughly with alcohol and wipe it dry with a clean paper towel. The slide must be free of grease so handle it only by its edges. If new slides are available use them.

2. If you are to be the donor of a drop of blood, first wash your hands well with soap and water. Then disinfect the tip of a finger using a swab of cotton that has been immersed in methyl alcohol.

NOTE: Only sterile lancets should be used in this experiment.

3. Unwrap a sterile lancet. Avoid touching its pointed end. Puncture the disinfected tip of your finger and put a drop of blood on one end of the cleaned side as shown in Fig. I-12-1.

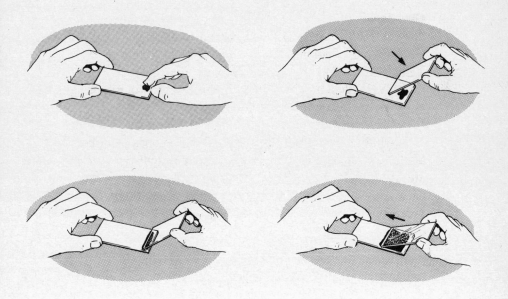

Fig. I–12–1   Making a blood smear

4. To spread the blood drop, bring the edge of a second slide along the surface of the first until it touches the drop. (See Fig. I-12-1.)
What happens when the drop is touched?

5. With a smooth motion *push* the second slide along the surface of the first away from the drop. Do not break contact with the lower slide. The drop should now be spread out as a thin film. Let the slide dry in the air for a few minutes.

6. To stain the specimen, first place the slide on a paper towel, then place several drops of Wright's stain on the smear, counting the number of drops used. Wait one to three minutes. Add the same number of drops of tap water. A green scum will form. Again wait two or three minutes.

7. Rinse the smear *gently* with tap water and wipe the bottom of the slide dry. Dry the top by shaking off the water and blowing on it.

8. When the blood smear is dry, examine it with a microscope. A cover slip is not required. Examine the slide to find areas where the film is thin.

   How many different types of cells can you locate using high power?

9. Draw a sample of each type of cell observed. Determine the size of each in microns.

   What is the magnification of your drawing? Do all of the observed cells have nuclei? What type of cell is most abundant? How could you best estimate the number of cells in the field of view under high power? Make an estimate of the number of each type in the field.

Questions:

*1. Are there any cells which are stained more than one color? What does this observation tell you about Wright's stain?

*2. The cells examined in the leaf cross-sections generally had flattened sides. Were the animal cells used in this exercise round- or flat-sided? How do you account for the differences?

†3. In references to the blood we often hear the terms "red blood cells" and "white blood cells." Are these colors the ones you observed?

†4. Use a reference book to find how many different types of cells there are in normal blood. Give a brief description of each type and the percentage of the blood that is composed of each type.

†5. Use a reference book to find out where blood cells are made in the body.

References and Suggestions for Further Investigation:

1. Ask the school nurse or public health nurse if blood typing serums are available. If so, try to determine your blood type. Place one drop of blood at each end of a slide. Put one drop of the first typing serum on one drop of blood and a drop of the second typing serum on the second drop of blood. Stir each with a separate toothpick. Blood is classified into groups: O, A, B and AB according to the reactions caused by the serums.

2. The red blood cells of some animals such as the frog have nuclei. If possible, examine blood from several other animals to see if their cells have other differences from yours.

I–13 MICROSCOPIC ORGANISMS

Several days in advance of this exercise your teacher may instruct you to prepare cultures of micro-organisms (very small plants or animals) by various techniques. Some examples of materials which may be used to grow these cultures are

(a) water from a pond or ditch mixed with a small amount of bottom mud or soil,
(b) chopped, dried grass in water and a pinch of soil. (Chlorinated tap water may be used if it is allowed to sit in an open container for at least 24 hours before being used.)
(c) aquarium water with scrapings from the side of the aquarium or material from the filter,
(d) pond water and a pinch of powdered milk, dried yeast or a few grains of boiled wheat or peas,
(e) pond or ditch water to which has been added the scrapings from submerged plant leaves or twigs,
(f) rainwater collected from a puddle.

The jars containing these cultures should be labelled according to the date, the location from which the culture was collected and food materials that were added. These cultures may be shared by the class for the exercise. Evaporation of water from the jars may be retarded by placing a loose cap or cover over the jar.

APPARATUS AND MATERIALS REQUIRED (per station)
Micro-organism culture
monocular microscope
slides
cover slips and pipettes
iodine stain

Procedure:
1. Some organisms may congregate near the surface of the water, others at the sides or bottom. You should select samples from several parts of the jar using a pipette. Compress the pipette bulb before placing the pipette in the water, then release it to gather the sample. (If the bulb is compressed under water, the air expelled will force organisms away from the pipette opening.)
2. With a pipette add a drop of water from a culture to a slide and cover it with a cover slip. Examine the slide under low power first to obtain an idea of the variety and types of organisms present. Repeat the procedure using other cultures. Not all cultures will contain an abundance of micro-organisms and different types of organisms will be found in different cultures.
3. Use medium and high power to examine these organisms for detail. Under this magnification they may appear to move very quickly. Remember that you are magnifying their speed as well as their size.

If you are having difficulty, look for organisms that are trapped by debris on the slide or slowed down near their food supply. Alternatively, you can kill them by using iodine stain but do so only after you have made an attempt to observe the living cells.

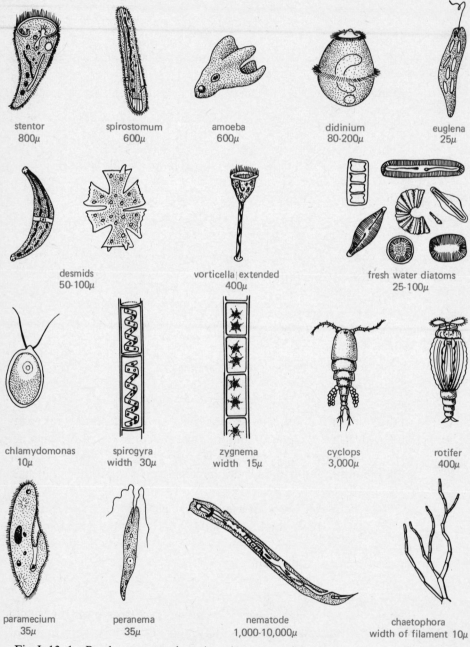

Fig. I–13–1   Pond water organisms (not drawn to scale)

4. A sampling technique that you might try is to place one cover slip on the bottom of the culture container and to float another slip on the surface of the water. Leave these overnight to allow organisms to attach themselves to the surfaces. To examine these samples, dry one side of each slip with towelling and place the other on a drop of water on a slide.

5. A few of the micro-organisms commonly found in fresh water are drawn in Fig. I-13-1. Compare your specimens with them. There are many thousands of kinds of small aquatic organisms so it is advisable to obtain additional reference books from the library to assist you in your identification. In the cells you should look for
   (a) the presence or absence of chlorophyll,
   (b) the shape of chloroplasts if any are present,
   (c) the thickness of the cell wall if one is present,
   (d) the general shape of the organism, (Has it a fixed shape or can its shape be changed?)
   (e) any special structures that help the organism to move.
   What types of micro-organisms did you find? Which are one-celled and which are many-celled?
   Draw one organism of each type you observe.

   Questions: (Consult a reference book.)
*1. Compare the cell covering of spirogyra (spy-roh-JY-ra) with that of amoeba (a-MEE-ba).
*2. What structures do plant cells and animal cells have in common? In what respects are they different?
*3. What are cilia (SIL-ee-a), flagella (fla-JEL-a), pseudopodia (SEW-do-POH-dee-a)? Give examples of organisms possessing each.
*4. In what respects does euglena (you-GLEE-na) resemble an animal cell? a plant cell?

Section III
REPRODUCTION OF ORGANISMS

In Section II you examined various kinds of cells, noting their similarities and differences. The walls of some plant cells were thick, others thin, but all plant cells possessed walls of some sort. The nuclei of some cells were large and spherical, others were small and oval, but nearly all cells possessed nuclei. The green color of chlorophyll was observed in some cells while in others it was absent.

In Section III you will investigate reproduction, an important life process of all cells and of all organisms. A basic difference between living organisms and non-living materials is that living organisms die. The life span of organisms may vary from a few minutes to several centuries. All living things must, therefore, reproduce their kind before they die or it will disappear from the earth. Name some plants and animals which have become *extinct*.

Asexual Reproduction:

Some living things are able to reproduce their kind by the division of a single individual into two parts. Others reproduce by the repeated separation of the parent organism into numerous immature individuals. When only one organism is involved as a parent, the type of reproduction is called *asexual* ("a" – without; "sex" – involving two parents). Some forms of asexual reproduction occur naturally while others can be made to occur by removing a part of the organism and encouraging it to grow separately. In each of the following exercises you will see an animal or plant which demonstrates a form of asexual reproduction.

I–14   BUDDING

Yeasts are one-celled plants commonly found on the surfaces of leaves or fruits as a grayish film or "bloom." They may be stored in a dried condition in pellet or cake form. They will reproduce rapidly when moisture and a food supply such as a sugar solution are supplied at the right temperature.

APPARATUS AND MATERIALS REQUIRED (per station)
> *Dried pellets of baking yeast*
> *sugar (sucrose or glucose)*
> *small glass container (e.g. baby food jar)*
> *monocular microscope*
> *slides and cover slips*
> *stain (e.g. methylene blue, neutral red)*
> *pipette*

Procedure:
1. Add 4 or 5 pellets of dried yeast to 25 ml of tap water. Mix in approximately one tablespoonful of sugar by shaking. Then allow the mixture to settle.
2. Use a pipette to obtain some clear solution from the container. Apply a drop to a slide, add a cover slip and examine under low- and high-power. Do you find any evidence of yeast cells?
3. Set the mixture of yeast and sugar solution aside in a warm place. In

successive class periods examine a drop of the solution, using a stain to improve visibility.

Is there evidence that the yeast cells are multiplying? If so, is the increase in numbers small or large?

Under what magnification can you see the yeast best?

What is the approximate size of a yeast cell in microns? (How many yeast cells would fit in a line across the diameter of the field?)

Are all of the yeast cells the same size and shape?

Try to locate yeast cells which have small projections or buds. How abundant are these cells compared to those with no projections or buds?

Can you find any small free floating cells which are the same size as the attached buds?

Questions:
*1. What was the energy source for the growth of the yeast cells?
*2. Could the growth of yeast cells in your sugar solution continue indefinitely? Was there any indication of an eventual decrease in the rate of reproduction of yeast cells in your culture?
*3. What factors could affect the rate of growth of an organism?
*4. Consult a reference book to find what other organisms reproduce by budding.
†5. What is the role of yeast in bread-making?
†6. Fermentation is the process of converting natural sugars in fruit or grain into alcohol. How are yeasts involved in this process?

I–15 CELL BINARY FISSION

The term *binary fission* (BY-na-ree) means a splitting into two approximately equal parts. If this fission occurs "from head to tail" it is called longitudinal fission. If it occurs from side to side it is called transverse fission.

APPARATUS AND MATERIALS REQUIRED (per station)
> *Slides of paramecium showing binary fission*
> *monocular microscope*
> *culture of paramecium*
> *iodine stain*
> *slides and cover slips*

Procedure:
1. Put a drop of paramecium culture on a clean slide and add a cover slip. (See Fig. I-15-1.) Examine the slide. Add a drop of iodine

Fig. I–15–1   Paramecia

stain at the edge of the cover slip to kill the paramecium. This will enable you to see their structures.

Are there any indications that some paramecia were dividing or about to divide? Such signs include an abnormal shape of the nucleus or a constriction around part of the cell which seems to pinch it in two.

2. Using the permanent mount slide of paramecium supplied, locate the large nucleus (macronucleus) which is stained darker than the remainder of the cell. Close to the large nucleus is a smaller one, the micronucleus.

What are the positions of the nuclei in the cell? How many times larger is the macronucleus than the micronucleus?

3. Examine the nuclei of cells which are dividing.

Have either of the nuclei changed their position? Have either changed their shape? Does either of the nuclei divide, like the rest of the cell, to make two nuclei?

4. After examining a number of cells in various stages of division, draw a sequence of these cells undergoing binary fission to show the successive changes a cell undergoes while dividing to form two cells.

Questions:

*1. Why do we call this method of reproduction asexual?

*2. In what ways is this method of reproduction different from budding?

*3. What is the fate of the parent cell in binary fission? Is it immortal (does it live forever)?

*4. Use a reference book to help you describe binary fission as it occurs in amoeba and spirogyra.

*5. How does a paramecium obtain its food to supply energy and materials for division and growth? Compare the method used by a paramecium with that used by spirogyra.

References and Suggestions for Further Investigation:

1. Protococcus is a simple one-celled green plant that is often found in shaded locations on fence posts or sides of buildings. It occurs in

large colonies which give the appearance of weathered green paint. Scrape some of this powdery material onto a slide and examine it at low and high magnifications. Look for groupings of cells which might indicate that binary fission has occurred.

I–16   VEGETATIVE REPRODUCTION (Can be done as a home experiment.)

Some methods of asexual reproduction result from the growth of cuttings or otherwise separated parts of a growing plant. (See Figs. I-16-1 and I-16-2.) These methods are called *vegetative* because they involve parts of plants not usually thought of as being reproductive.

Fig. I–16–2   An example of asexual reproduction

Fig. I–16–1   Bryophyllum plant. Numerous small plants are produced asexually on the leaf margins. Note the large number that have dropped and taken root in the pot.

APPARATUS AND MATERIALS REQUIRED (per station)
  Planting containers such as tin cans
  potato
  carrot
  house plant (african violet, begonia, geranium, etc.)
  soil
  sand or vermiculite
  *a woody branch which includes side and terminal buds (willow, for-
    sythia, cherry or apple tree branch)*
  one package of rooting hormone (Rootone) is desirable

Procedure:

1. Prepare planting containers with soil and sand (or vermiculite). Soak the contents well with water.
2. Plant the following in the containers:
   (a) a slab cut from the side of a potato,
   (a) a one inch section cut from the top of a carrot,
   (c) a portion of stem with attached leaves from a house plant,
       (Remove the two lowest leaves, dip the cut end in rooting hormone and insert it in the sand to at least the depth of the removed leaves.)
   (d) a woody branch. This may be inserted in the sand or in a container of water.

   In each case, periodically add water to keep the sand or vermiculite moist. The best location in which to place the containers is one that is both cool and dark. Maintain a regular, careful watch of the plant's progress and record the changes which take place. Keep your record in the form of a diary, noting the time, date and type of change you see. Be patient; some changes are slow and take several weeks. Include measurements of size in your observations.

   What changes did you first notice in your plants? What were the initial signs of active growth? Did these changes occur at specific locations on the cut portion of the original plant? With what parts did you start (e.g. root, stem, leaf or fruit)? What parts were the first to grow?

   As you continue to observe the growth, list in order the other parts of each plant as they appear. Suggest a reason for this order.

   What differences did you find in the rates of growth of the various parts of the developing plants?

Questions: (Consult a reference book to answer questions 4-6.)

*1. In each case, do you consider the method of growth to be a method of reproduction (in which a new plant is formed) or do you consider it to be a continuation of the growth of the original plant? Give some reasons to support your answer(s).

*2. What other *types* of plants do you think you could make grow in one of the above ways?

*3. What other *parts* of plants do you think you could use to demonstrate vegetative growth or reproduction?

†4. Describe a method for grafting plants. What are the purposes of grafting? Is grafting a method of reproduction? Explain.

†5. What vegetative methods of reproduction are illustrated by the tulip, crocus and iris?

†6. Gardeners may reproduce several plants from one by the technique of tip layering. Describe this method.

I–17   REGENERATION

Most animals and plants have the ability to repair or heal wounds. In some organisms, when the wound is severe enough to divide it in two, both parts may heal to form two individuals. In this experiment you will examine the ability of planaria, a form of flatworm, to regrow lost parts.

APPARATUS AND MATERIALS REQUIRED (per station)
Living planaria
glass containers with glass covers
pipette
clean sharp razor blades
hand lens or stereoscopic microscope

Procedure:
1. Partly fill a clean glass container with water from an aquarium or with tap water that has been allowed to stand for 24 hours. Do not use water directly from the tap.
2. Transfer a planarian (pla-NAIR-ee-an) to your dish with an eye dropper pipette. (Planaria should not have been fed for several days before this exercise.) Observe it with a hand lens or stereo microscope. Examine both the dorsal (upper) and ventral (lower) sides. **What features can you distinguish? Does it have an anterior (front) and a posterior (hind) end? How can you turn it over to see its lower side? Record your observations in the form of diagrams.**

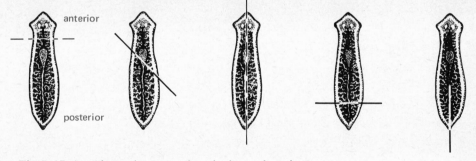

Fig. I–17–1   Alternative ways of sectioning a planarian

NOTE: Depending on the number of planaria available, your teacher will make arrangements to ensure that as many students as possible have the opportunity to section (cut) a planarian. Planaria can be cut in a variety of ways, some of which are shown in Fig. I-17-1. Your class may be divided into teams and the members of each team may be asked to try a different method.

3. Obtain a clean, sharp razor blade and, unless otherwise instructed, cut your planarian in one of the ways suggested by Fig. I-17-1. Do not show disrespect for a living creature by being careless or by needlessly maltreating the organism. Keep the razor blade edge dry and wrapped when not in use to prevent rust.
4. Store the cut planaria in dishes containing the same water used in Procedure 1. Posterior pieces may be kept in one dish, anterior pieces in a second and partially sectioned but still complete animals in a third.
5. Use a glass square to cover each dish and set them aside in a cool somewhat darkened place. Do not attempt to feed the planaria. Observe them at intervals over the next several weeks. Record your results in the form of diagrams to show the changes that take place. **Did any parts die? How is the ability of a part to survive related to its size? How is it related to the end from which the part was taken? Did the regenerated worm replace all the parts which it had lost? Did it grow to its original size?**
    Were the renewed parts always correctly oriented (e.g. Did a head always grow where a head had been removed?)?

Questions:

*1. Where are planaria normally found? Consult a reference book to learn more about their structure, method of feeding and methods of reproduction.
*2. If possible, find out how planaria can best be kept in a laboratory.
*3. Can planaria reproduce naturally by regeneration or must they first be attacked and damaged before regenerating?
*4. Describe how animals such as starfish, earthworms and crabs regenerate lost parts.
*5. Can man regenerate any of his body parts if they are removed?

I-18   SPORE PRODUCTION

A large number of plants reproduce by forming very small cells called spores. These reproductive cells are abundant in the air about us but are unnoticed because of their very small size. Spores may be formed on a simple stalk or encased in a covering called a *sporangium* (spoh-RAN-jee-um). In some spore-forming plants there are elaborate devices for the protection and release of spores. Some of the plants which use this means of asexual reproduction are illustrated on the following pages.

APPARATUS AND MATERIALS REQUIRED (per station)

Source of spores (fern, moss, horsetail, bread mould, citrus fruits, mushroom, puffball, bracket fungus)
monocular microscope
slide and cover slip
forceps
pipette
stereo microscope
hand lens

Procedure:
1. With forceps, remove a small portion of material containing spore-producing structures.
2. Mount this portion in water on a slide, add a cover slip and examine it under low-power. Note the structure of the spore container.
3. Press gently on the cover slip with the forceps to break open the spore containers and to disperse the spores in the water on your slide.
4. Note the shape, size and number of the spores. Do they appear to be all alike or is there variety in their size and shape?

   Approximately how many spores can you count in the field under high-power? Considering the size of the sample you have examined in relation to the plant from which you obtained it, can you estimate the total number of spores produced by the plant? (Multiply the number of spores on the slide by the number of black dots on the surface of the bread mould or use some other such approximation.)

   If there is time to examine several specimens, compare their methods of releasing spores. Examine them with a hand lens, stereo and monocular microscope. A number of spore-forming plants are shown in Fig. I-18-1.

Questions:
*1. In what ways are spores similar to buds? In what ways are they different?
*2. How are spores dispersed so that they can populate areas far away from the parent plant?
*3. Where do each of the spore-forming plants shown in Fig. I-18-1 normally grow? Are there any features common to their natural habitats?
*4. If spores are produced in such large numbers, why do the spore-forming plants not overpopulate the world? (A single puffball may produce over a billion spores.)

References and Suggestions for Further Investigation:
1. Using *A Sourcebook for the Biological Sciences* by Morholt, Brand-

Spore forming plants

Fig. I–18–1(a)   Underside of fern frond showing clusters of sporangia

Fig. I–18–1(b)   Several fern sporangia with enclosed spores

Fig. I–18–1(c)   Clump of moss plants with stalked sporangia

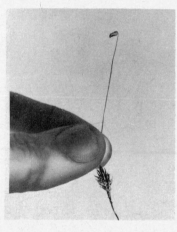

Fig. I–18–1(d)   Mature moss sporangia

Fig. I–18–1(e)   Mushroom showing gills on lower surface

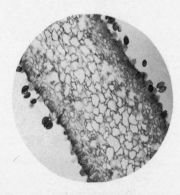

Fig. I–18–1(f)   Cross section of a single mushroom gill showing groups of spores

wein and Joseph (New York: Harcourt, Brace & World, 1966) as a guide, prepare dishes of several types of food materials suitable for cultures of spore-producing plants. You can then sow a "garden" of these plants by crushing the sporangia enclosing their spores or by merely exposing the dishes to air-borne spores.

2. Collect several different mushrooms. Remove the stalks and place the mushroom caps, lower side down, on white paper. Cover them with a beaker or plastic wrap to prevent their drying out. Next day, examine the color and pattern formed by the released spores.

Sexual Reproduction:

In asexual reproduction the characteristics of the offspring are inherited from a single parent organism.

In sexual reproduction two parents act as donors of material for the growth of a new individual. The cells donated by the parents are called *gametes* (GA-meets). The female gamete is the *egg* cell and the male gamete is the *sperm*. When these gametes unite at *fertilization*, the cell formed, the *zygote*, will grow and subdivide to become the offspring. Since two parents contribute living material to form the zygote, the offspring will have features from both of them and will therefore differ from each of them. Such differences between the offspring and its parents may give the offspring an advantage or disadvantage in survival. Differences which encourage survival include those which encourage reproduction and thereby the continuation of the race. Not all variations are advantageous; some may cause the death of organisms or impair their ability to reproduce. Differences which cause the death of an organism are said to be *lethal* (LEE-thal).

The species of plants and animals alive today represent a small fraction of the total number of species that have at one time lived on the earth. Many species which have failed to produce variations favorable for survival in their offspring have become extinct. Can you think of some? Successful species have been able to multiply and distribute themselves to nearly all parts of this planet. Included in this group are man, the dandelion, the rat and the cockroach. What other species would you include?

I–19   FLOWER STRUCTURE

In the sexual reproduction of higher plants a highly specialized structure, the flower, has developed. Flowers not only assist in the production of the gametes but they also ensure that the sperms reach and unite with the eggs to form the zygotes. The sperms and the eggs are usually produced by separate plants.

Although these gametes are microscopic, the anthers and ovaries, the structures in which they are formed, are easily visible. Examination will acquaint you with the details of their structure.

APPARATUS AND MATERIALS REQUIRED (per station)

> *Flower(s)*
> *forceps*
> *fine pointed scissors*
> *hand lens*
> *razor blade*
> *stereo and monocular microscopes*
> *slides*
> *cover slips*

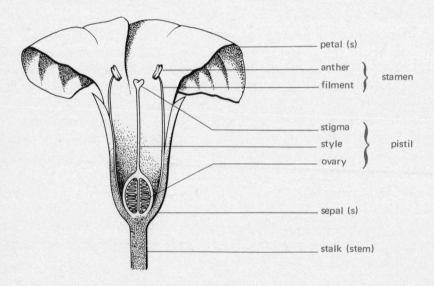

Fig. I–19–1   Flower structure

Procedure:

1. Examine the flower parts and their arrangement. Compare your flower with the one drawn in Fig. I-19-1 and the one photographed in Fig. I-19-2. Do not remove any parts at first; bend them aside to see hidden structures. Note the different types of flower parts and the arrangement and position of each. You may find it convenient to record your answers to the following questions in the form of drawings.

Fig. I–19–2   Tulip – what parts can you locate?

Is the stem swollen at the point of attachment of the floral parts? Is there more than one flower attached to any one part of the stem? Are several flower-bearing stems joined together in a cluster?

Does the flower have several small leaf-like structures around its lower outer edge? How many of these leaflets (sepals) are there? How do they compare with the ordinary leaves of the plants?

How many petals are there? Where are they attached to the stalk relative to the sepals? What are their color and shape? Can you locate nectar-secreting glands at the base of the petals?

How many stamens (STAY-mens) are there? Are they attached to the petals or are they separate? Are they longer than the petals or are they covered and hidden?

The central core which remains is called the pistil. It is the female portion of the flower. Has it the same diameter throughout its length? What does the tip, the stigma, look like? Is it split into two or more parts? Does its tip project beyond the other floral parts or is it enclosed by them?

2. Use scissors to remove the sepals and petals carefully. If the stamens are attached to the bases of the petals they will be removed as well. Sometimes like parts are fused together. For example, petals may be fused together to form a tube. In other cases dissimilar parts such as stamens and petals may be fused together.

3. Crush an anther on a slide to release some of its *pollen*. Add water and a cover slip. Examine the pollen with your microscope.
    What is the appearance of a pollen grain? Are the pollen grains from the same type of flower all alike? If possible, examine pollen from different flowers. How do they compare?

4. With a razor blade, cut across the swollen base of the pistil as shown in Fig. I-19-3. This swollen part is called the *ovary* of the pistil. Examine it with the binocular microscope.

Is the ovary divided into chambers? How many?
Squeeze the ovary.
What comes out? These are called ovules and contain the eggs.

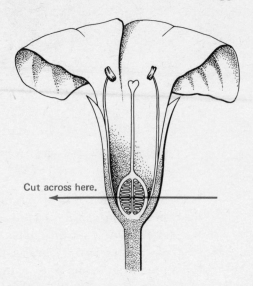

Cut across here.

Fig. I–19–3   Ovary cross section

NOTE: The egg is fertilized by the sperm from the pollen grain to form a zygote. The ovule which contains the zygote will then develop to form a seed. The seed contains the fertilized egg plus stored food.

5. If the fruit of this plant is available, examine it and compare it to the flower to see if you can tell what parts of the flower were involved in the production of the fruit. You will have to cut the fruit open. Once you have located the position of the seeds you should be able to determine the origin of the other parts of the fruit.

Questions:
*1. What is the sex of a flower? Explain.
*2. What flower parts are most prominent, or easily seen, in its bud phase? pollination phase? fruiting phase?
*3. What flower parts are essential for reproduction? Which parts assist in reproduction?
*4. Of what advantage is it to the flower to support the anthers on long stalks and to embed the ovary deep within the petals?
*5. Use reference books to find out the role played by the contents of the pollen tube during the fertilization of the eggs of a flower.
*6. The transfer of pollen between flowers (cross-pollination) is usually assisted by insects or wind. In what ways are the flower's parts specialized to assist in pollination by insects? by wind?
*7. How might a flower prevent self-pollination (pollen from its own anthers falling on its stigma)?

References and Suggestions for Further Investigation:

1. We can duplicate the germination of the pollen by the following method.

   (a) Select a flower which is shedding pollen. It is important that pollen be fresh because it loses its ability to germinate after a few weeks.

   (b) Prepare an egg albumin solution by mixing together equal parts of glycerine and egg albumin (egg white).

   (c) Place two or three drops of the solution at one end of a slide and spread it with your finger tip.

   (d) Dust pollen grains from the flower anther onto the solution.

   (e) Crush one or two stigmas on the slide near the pollen. (This will aid germination of the pollen.)

   (f) Place a circle of paper towelling in a petri dish bottom, soak it with water and then pour off any surplus water. Place the slide on the moist towelling with the fixative side facing upwards. Add the petri dish cover and store the preparation at room temperature or slightly higher (ideally 75°-85°F). This will provide a warm, moist atmosphere for the pollen.

   (g) Examine the slides for growth of pollen tubes in successive class periods. Some growth may be evident only a short while after preparing the slide.

   Normally the pollen grain will germinate (begin to grow) when it is deposited on the sticky surface of the stigma. A swelling of the pollen grain, called a pollen tube, is produced. It is in this tube that the sperm cell may travel to the egg.

I-20   A LIFE CYCLE – ALTERNATION OF GENERATIONS

In Section III you observed some of the characteristics of asexual and sexual reproductive methods. These can be summarized as follows.

Asexual:
1. Only one parent is involved.
2. Great numbers of offspring are produced.
3. Offspring are distributed over a large area quickly.
4. Offspring show little or no variation from the parent.

Sexual:
1. Two parents are involved.
2. In general, fewer offspring are produced by this method than by asexual methods.
3. Offspring show a general resemblance to the two parents but many variations in details of structure.

For the survival of a species there are advantages and disadvantages to each method of reproduction. If environmental conditions are favourable, the offspring of asexual reproduction multiply quickly and flourish; however, if environment conditions change they may all perish. There is considerable evidence that this kind of change has occurrred frequently in the Earth's history.

In sexual reproduction, although the offspring have general characteristics in common with their parents, they differ in many details. Some of these differences may enable the offspring to survive more successfully than others in the face of changing environmental conditions. Variations which increase the chances of survival lead to adaptation to the environment.

A number of organisms have successfully combined both asexual and sexual methods of reproduction in alternate phases of their life cycle, thus obtaining the advantages of each method and at the same time cancelling out some of the disadvantages. The alternation of an asexual, spore-producing cycle with a sexual, gamete-producing cycle is known as *alternation of generations*. Some plants exhibiting this type of life cycle are mosses, ferns and flowering plants. You will confine your study to the moss.

Mosses are generally found in moist shaded locations. They are thought to be transitional forms between aquatic (water) and terrestrial (land) plants. Keep this in mind as you examine the moss and consider how the structures observed are related to its mode of life.

APPARATUS AND MATERIALS REQUIRED (per station)
> *Moss plants with both gametophytes and sporophytes (preserved and fresh)*
> *compound and stereoscopic microscopes*
> *slides*
> *cover slips and pipettes*
> *fine pointed forceps and dissecting needles*
> *hand lens*
> *prepared slides of moss antheridia and archegonia*

Procedure:
1. Look at a clump of moss plants. Notice the green colored mat of leafy shoots. These make up the *gametophyte* (ga-MEE-toh-fite) or gamete-producing stage of the plant.
   What is a gamete? What is the meaning of the term "phyte"?
   Examine a leaf from this plant and observe the chloroplasts in the cells (as described in Experiment I-8, Procedure 8).
   At this stage in the life cycle, is the moss able to manufacture its own food by photosynthesis?
2. Choose a green leafy shoot of a moss plant that has a tall hair-like stalk growing out of it. (See Fig. I-18-1D.) Examine the swollen tip (the capsule) on the stalk with a hand lens or stereoscopic micro-

scope. If the capsule has a cone-shaped covering, remove it with forceps. The stalk and capsule form the *sporophyte* or spore-producing stage of the plant. (See Fig. I-20-1.)

3. Observe the color of the sporophyte. You may see sporophytes of different colors on one clump of moss plants. The small, immature sporophytes are green while the larger, mature sporophytes are brown. **What does this color change indicate about the methods by which the young and the mature sporophytes obtain food?** Draw a moss plant showing the mature sporophyte and gametophyte.

4. Place a capsule from a fresh moss plant in a drop of water on a slide. Remove the capsule cover and tease it apart thoroughly. Apply a cover slip and examine under low, medium and high powers. The single cells floating free in the water are spores. **Approximately how many are there in the field at low power? Do they all look alike?** Draw a few spores at high power.

5. Examine the gametophyte using commercially prepared slide sections as well as fresh or preserved moss gametophytes.

NOTE: *The permanent mount slides issued to you are stained, vertical sections or "slices" through the tips of the male and female gametophytes. Sex organs on the male gametophytes, called the antheridia (sing. antheridium) produce sperm; the sex organs on the female gametophytes, called the archegonia (sing. archegonium), produce eggs.*

Refer to the diagrams of antheridia and archegonia (ahr-keh-GOH-nee-ah) in Fig. I-20-1. Then scan the slides at low power to locate these structures.

How many antheridia can you locate in the field at low power?
Move the slide to place one antheridium in the center of the field, then examine it at medium and high powers. Within the cells of the antheridium are developing sperms. Approximately how many are there?

How many archegonia can you find in the field at low power?
Scan the slide to locate an archegonium "slice" which shows a large dark-stained egg cell in the chamber and a long "neck" leading from it. Examine this archegonium under medium and high powers. Compare the numbers of eggs and sperms.

6. Refer to the diagrams of male and female moss gametophytes. **How do their tips differ in appearance?** Examine preserved or fresh gametophytes with a hand lens. Try to identify the male and female plants by shape. Remove several of each type.

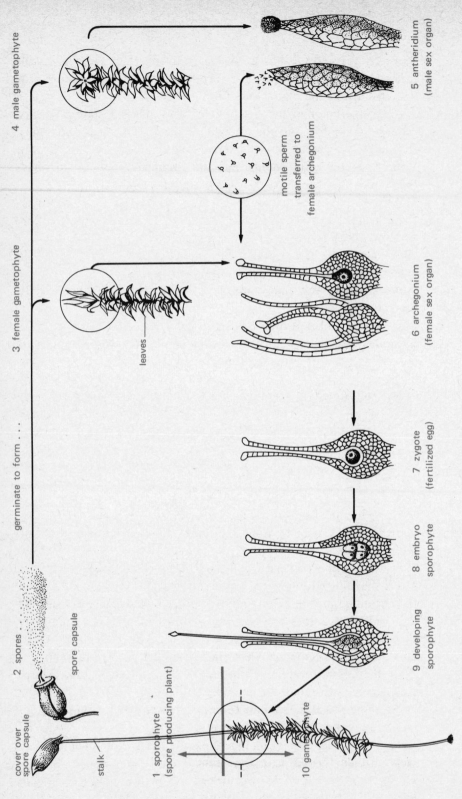

Fig. I-20-1 Moss life cycle

4 male gametophyte

5 antheridium (male sex organ)

motile sperm transferred to female archegonium

3 female gametophyte

leaves

6 archegonium (female sex organ)

7 zygote (fertilized egg)

8 embryo sporophyte

9 developing sporophyte

germinate to form . . . .

2 spores . . . .

spore capsule

cover over spore capsule

stalk

1 sporophyte (spore producing plant)

10 gametophyte

7. As you have observed, both antheridia and archegonia are found in the tips of the gametophytes. Place a drop of water on a slide. Over the drop squeeze the tip of the green plant between your fingers to release fragments into the water. Tease these fragments apart thoroughly. Apply a cover slip and examine the slide for either antheridia or archegonia. Near antheridia you may see small cells moving quickly and erratically. These are sperms which are provided with small hair-like *flagella* for swimming in water.

Questions:

*1. Which is the most prominent or conspicuous generation in the moss—the sporophyte or the gametophyte?

*2. How does each generation obtain its food supply?

*3. How does the moss sperm travel to the egg? What does this tell you about the environmental conditions necessary for survival of the moss?

*4. Compare the relative numbers of spores, sperms, eggs and zygotes produced by a moss plant. Which of these cells develops into an offspring?

*5. Which generation of the moss would produce the most offspring?

*6. How are moss sperms and spores distributed? Which would be distributed over a greater area?

*7. Which generation of moss plant is produced by the germination of a spore? of a zygote?

*8. Explain how the phrase "alternation of generations" applies to the life cycle of mosses.

*9. Describe how the moss combines the advantages of both asexual and sexual methods of reproduction?

Section IV
GENETICS – THE STUDY OF INHERITANCE

One advantage of sexual reproduction is that different combinations of characteristics occur in each offspring.

You may have previously studied some of the work of Charles Darwin on natural selection, the selection of organisms by the natural forces of the environment. Darwin showed us that some organisms had advantageous characteristics (traits) which enabled them to survive in their environment and thus form the breeding portion of their population. Consequently, their traits were passed on to future generations. Traits that tended to harm the individual were often lost as these individuals often did not survive to reproduce.

Darwin investigated the development of new types of organisms and the role of variation in evolution but he did not explain the mechanism by which these changes are produced.

In this section we will study how later scientists discovered the method by which traits are passed between successive generations and how these traits are changed to permit evolution to occur. Genetics is a young science, barely more than a century old, but within this short period of time it has become one of the most active and important areas of scientific research.

I-21   VARIATIONS IN LIVING THINGS

By looking around at your classmates you will realize that each one is a unique individual. You would be able to recognize each one easily from among all others in your class. But you also recognize that all pupils in your class are really very similar in structure and that their differences are usually only in the expression or appearance of individual traits.

In this exercise you will see how great the differences can be in any one trait.

APPARATUS AND MATERIALS REQUIRED
Ruler
radish seeds
petri dishes
paper towelling

Procedure:
1. Measure to the nearest 2 mm the length of your partner's right ear from the top to the tip of the lobe.
2. Make a list of ear lengths for the class in 2mm steps, from the smallest ear size to the largest. Every 2 mm interval between these extremes must be included whether or not someone has that measurement. Record the number of students having each ear size by placing an "x" after the measurement for each occurrence.
   What was the difference between the largest and smallest ear size in the class? What was the most common size? What was the average size? How many pupils in your class could you isolate or separate on the basis of ear length alone (i.e. How many of the students were the only ones with their ear size?)
3. If you can obtain the results from other classes, compare them with your class.
   Are there significant differences between the ranges or average values? What other features could be measured for this experiment?

†4. Germinate a large number of radish seeds on wet paper towelling in petri dishes. Show the variation that occurs in the lengths of their radicles (roots) by repeating the method of Procedure 2.
Can you suggest factor(s) other than hereditary characteristics that could effect the results? What other living things can be used so that a large sample of a population is measured?

Questions:

*1. Would you expect the offspring of asexually reproducing organisms such as parmecia and yeast to show more or less variation in structure from their parents than the offspring of sexually reproducing organisms? Why?

*2. Some species of animals and plants appear to us to show little variation in individual structure. For example, all sparrows probably look alike to you. Do we easily recognize the differences between humans because we show more variation or because we are more familiar with certain groups of humans? Explain.

*3. You have seen that although some people possess long ears and others short ears, these are just extremes for a continuous range of ear sizes. Can you think of any other features which humans possess for which this is not the case?

*4. Prepare a graph of the results of your measurements by plotting the number of cases possessing a given length of ear (y-axis) against the length of ear sizes (x-axis). Is your graph "bell-shaped"?

NOTE: *This may be a convenient time to plant seeds for Exercise I-24. See page 60.*

I-22   VARIATIONS IN YOUR FAMILY TREE

Sometimes a family trait is expressed by many members of a family. For example, the Hapsburgs, a ruling family of Austria, had a protruding lower jaw which gave them a "bulldog" appearance. In this exercise look for the occurrence of a trait which might be said to be "typical" of your family.

Procedure:

1. If it is possible, consult with your parents to see if there is a simple family trait expressed by some members of your present and past family. Characteristics you might look for are attached ear lobes, widow's peak hair line, ability to roll the tongue, eye color, ability to bend the last joint of the thumb back to a 45° angle, hair on the middle joint of the fingers, placing the left thumb over the right thumb when hands are folded naturally, etc.

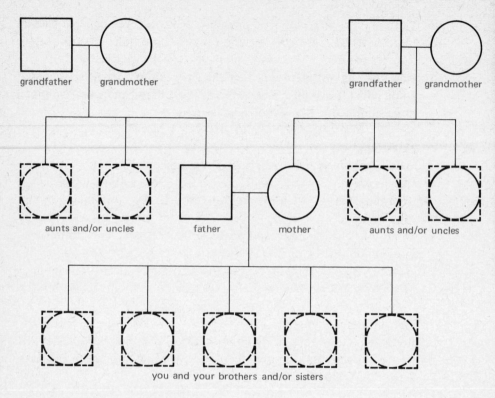

Fig. I–22–1   Your family tree

2. Make a copy of the record sheet in Fig. I-22-1. Squares are used to represent males, and circles, females. In cases where dotted squares and dotted circles are both included, you will have to outline the ones which apply, (i.e. square for your brother or circle for your sister). If there are too many spaces or not enough you may add some or leave them blank to suit the situation. Notice that three types of connecting lines are used in this type of "family tree." A horizontal marriage line is drawn between husband and wife; a second horizontal fraternal line is drawn above their children; a vertical descent line connects a marriage line to a fraternal line.
   How would you arrange the charts to show a second marriage of the parent? How would you show twins?

3. On the chart, record the way your family trait was expressed by the various members of your family.
   Was the trait shown by all members of your generation? just by the boys? just by the girls?
   Was the trait shown only on your mother's side? your father's side? both sides? Did the trait seem to skip a generation, (appear in one generation but not the next)?

Questions: (Consult reference books to answer these questions.)

*1. List several defects that humans can inherit.

†2. Make reports on the inheritance of the following characteristics: eye color, hair color, tallness, baldness and skin color.

††3. Blood types are sometimes used to establish the parentage of a child. Find out how this is accomplished.

I-23   THE LAWS OF INHERITANCE

Gregor Mendel, an Austrian priest and teacher, laid the foundation for the science of genetics in 1865 with the publication of his paper "Experiments in Plant-hybridisation." The significance of this major contribution to science was not recognized until about forty years later when other scientists arrived at the same conclusions independently and acknowledged Mendel's work. This unfortunate gap of forty years illustrates the importance of communication among scientists to avoid duplication of efforts in overlapping fields of work.

Mendel chose the common garden pea as his experimental organism. This was a fortunate choice because the garden pea is normally self-pollinated. As a result, plants produced from seeds show only the traits possessed by pollen and ovules from the same plant. (What could be the result of using a cross-pollinating plant?)

Mendel observed that pea plants and their seeds showed differences in many individual traits. Some plants were tall, others short (dwarf). Some had colored flowers, others white. Some produced yellow pea seeds, others green.

Mendel first obtained, by careful breeding, several different strains of peas, each of which could be classified as a pure strain for one particular trait. For example, he collected seeds from tall plants, planted them and then noted and recorded the type of offspring produced. He then repeated the procedure many times until he obtained seeds that would consistently produce only tall plants. He used similar procedures for other traits until he had seeds which were *purebred* for such things as dwarfness, colored flowers and smooth seed coat. Mendel wisely decided to study only one trait at a time instead of several simultaneously. Because his plants and seeds were purebred for one trait only, his work differed from that of most other plant breeders of his time.

After he had obtained seeds purebred for one trait, Mendel's next step was to "cross" purebred plants for a given characteristic. Examples of such crosses are:

Tall plant (long stem)	x*	Dwarf plant (short stem)
Smooth seed plant	x	Wrinkled seed plant
Green seed	x	Yellow seed
Yellow pod	x	Green pod

*x means crossed or bred with.

To make a "cross" such as the first one listed above, Mendel planted seeds pure-bred for producing tall plants and seeds purebred for producing dwarf plants. When the plants were fully grown, he removed pollen from the flowers of the tall plants and applied it with a small brush to the stigma of the flowers of the dwarf plants. In other words he cross-pollinated or crossed the two purebred strains. (Why did Mendel have to remove the pollen from one plant and transfer the pollen by hand to these plants?) When egg cells in the ovules of the dwarf plants had been fertilized by the sperm nuclei from the pollen of tall pea plants, the resulting zygotes developed into seeds. Mendel collected these seeds and planted them in turn.

Since the seed now planted presumably had a mixture of traits, one might expect that the plants produced from these seeds would be midway in height between the original tall and dwarf pea plants. This Mendel did not find. The plants produced were all tall and appeared to be identical in height to the original purebred tall plants. He repeated this procedure for other traits and found that the results were consistent. There was no averaging, mixing or blend-ing of the original characteristics; instead, only *one* of the original shapes or colors appeared. The following chart indicates some of the results.

PARENT		PARENT		
PUREBRED STRAIN	x	PUREBRED STRAIN	=	RESULT F_1 *
1. Tall	x	Dwarf	=	all tall
2. Yellow seeds	x	Green seeds	=	all yellow
3. Smooth seeds	x	Wrinkled seeds	=	all smooth
4. Green pods	x	Yellow pods	=	all green pods

*The term F_1 is often used to describe the first generation (first filial generation) resulting from a cross.

From experimental evidence with many such crosses between pure-bred plants, Mendel came to the conclusion that one trait (e.g. tallness) com-pletely masked the alternative trait (e.g. dwarfness), since only one factor was apparent. He described the tallness trait as *dominant* over the dwarfness trait and the dwarfness trait as *recessive* since it was hidden completely. This fact has since been stated as the *Law of Dominance*.

When Mendel used these first generation seeds to produce a second generation of plants (F_2) he found that most of the plants that resulted were tall but a few were dwarf (recessive). To explain this unexpected reappearance of the recessive trait, Mendel assumed that the plants in the F_1 generation pos-sessed factors for both tallness and dwarfness (one received from each pure-bred parent). He also assumed that in the production of sperms and eggs, the factors became separated or *segregated* from each other so that each sperm or egg had only one factor. When a sperm fused with an egg the resulting zygote brought these factors together again.

To show the combination and separation (segregation) of the factors conveniently in diagrammatic form, geneticists use the following short-hand method:

(a) Capital letters are used for dominant characteristics and *corresponding* small letters are used for recessive characteristics.

DOMINANT CHARACTERISTIC	RECESSIVE CHARACTERISTIC
T – tall	t – dwarf
Y – yellow seed	y– green seed
S – smooth seed	s – wrinkled seed
G– green pod	g– yellow pod

(b) A purebred tall plant is shown as TT. This is because it has received a factor T from the sperm and a factor T from the egg to produce the zygote (TT) from which the plant developed.

Geneticists now know that the control for a single factor such as tallness is located on a specific part of one *chromosome* in the nucleus. This specific structure is called the *gene*. We now speak of the gene for tallness rather than the factor for tallnesss. Mendel did not know of the existence of chromosomes or genes and their role in inheritance. These discoveries were made by later workers in genetics.

We can show the segregation of factors (genes) for purebred tall parents as follows.

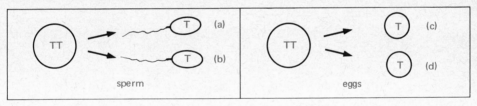

Fig. I–23–1   Segregation of factors during the production of sperm (left) and eggs (right)

If these purebred tall plants are crossed, four possibilities for fertilization exist. Sperm (a) could fertilize either egg (c) or (d); sperm (b) could fertilize either egg (c) or (d). A simple device to show these possibilities is the *Punnet* (PUN-net) square as shown in Fig. I-23-2.

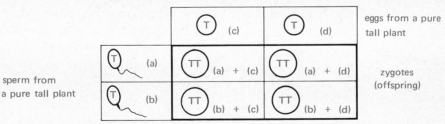

Fig. I–23–2   A Punnet square

Mendel's cross of purebred tall plants (TT) with purebred dwarf plants (tt) would be shown as:

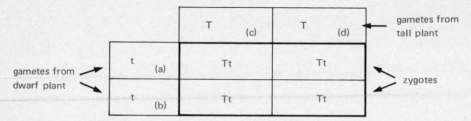

Fig. I–23–3   The four possible chance combinations during fertilization

Since the gene for tall stem is dominant, all offspring appear tall but all possess the gene for dwarfness.

Questions:
*1. Describe the method Mendel used to obtain
   (a) purebred strains of seed,
   (b) cross-bred strains of seed.
*2. What advantages has the garden pea as an organism for genetic study? What disadvantages?
*3. Describe the appearance of pea plants having the following genetic combinations: Yy, TT, Tt, tt, GG, gg, Gg, Ss, ss, SS. (Consult the table on page 57 showing dominant and recessive characteristics.)
*4. Is it possible to have a dwarf plant whose cells carry a factor (gene) for tallness? Explain.
*5. Use Punnett squares to show the results of the following plant crosses.
   (a) GG x gg.
   (b) SS x ss.
   (c) Yy x Yy.
*6. Can you see any advantage to a farmer of planting seed that will produce plants that are all alike in one trait (for example, plants which are all tall)? Explain.
*7. Look up the term "hybrid" in a reference book. Give its meaning. From your study of the garden pea give examples that show which characteristics may be combined to form a hybrid.

Review of Mendel's Investigation so far:
1. He bred pure strains: TT, tt, YY, yy, GG, gg, etc.
2. He crossed pure strains to produce an F_1 generation, all of which were *hybrid* and all of which showed only *dominant* characteristics.

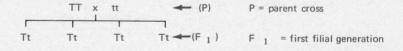

3. Next, Mendel planted seed from the F_1 or hybrid plants. The plants produced from this seed (the F_2 or second filial generation) were of two kinds: most were tall and resembled the F_1 plants but some were dwarf and resembled the dwarfs in the original parent generation.

```
        Tt    x   TT            (F 1 )
    ┌──────┬──────┴──────┬──────┐
    Tt    Tt     Tt     tt      (F 2 )
```

I–24   SEGREGATION

In the following exercise you will observe the results of planting hybrid (F_1) seeds. Remember that Mendel devoted years to his plant breeding investigations. He planted thousands of seeds and kept accurate records. You cannot expect to achieve similar accuracy in a short time, studying only a few cases.

When Mendel planted a great many seeds resulting from the cross of F_1 (hybrid) peas, the numbers of the two types of plants that resulted in the F_2 generation were found to be approximately in the ratio of 3 to 1.

He repeated this F_1 cross using several different traits. No matter which trait he worked with, the ratio remained approximately 3 to 1. For example, as shown in the Punnett square (Fig. I-24-1), there were 3 tall plants to every dwarf plant or 3 dominants to every recessive. How would his results from crossing hybrid green pod and hybrid yellow pod plants be shown? from crossing hybrid yellow seed and hybrid green seed plants?

	T		t	
T	TT	(tall)	Tt	(tall)
t	Tt	(tall)	tt	(dwarf)

Fig. I–24–1   A dihybrid cross

The term *phenotype* (FEE-noh-type) is used to describe the outward appearance of organisms with respect to certain traits. For example, pea plants which possess two dominant genes for tallness (TT) outwardly look exactly like those which possess only one such gene (Tt). Only by further crossing can you determine that these plants are not genetically identical. The term used to describe the genetic composition is *genotype* (GEEN-oh-type). In Fig. I-24-1, three genotypes are shown: TT, Tt and tt.

If the genotype is such that the organism is pure breeding then we say the organism is *homozygous* ("homo" means same). If, however, the genotype shows us that the chromosomes carry both the dominant and recessive traits, then the organism is *heterozygous* ("hetero" means different). Thus, the plants shown as TT and tt are homozygous and the plants shown as Tt are heterozygous.

APPARATUS AND MATERIALS REQUIRED (per class)
>   *Hybrid seed such as:*
>   *tobacco (green, albino)*
>   *soybean (green, light green, yellow)*
>   *corn (green, albino; or tall, dwarf) or sorghum (green, albino)*
>   *cobs of genetic corn*
>   *planting trays*
>   *soil*

Procedure:

1. Plant 10 to 20 of the seeds provided in shallow pans or boxes that have small drainage holes. Set the seeds in regularly spaced rows so that if any fail to germinate and grow an empty space will show this. After arranging the seeds, cover them with a thin layer of soil. Water them lightly every day or two (do not let them dry out). If they are stored in a warm, dark place they will probably germinate in 7 to 10 days.

2. Examine the trays of different plants and note the two or more contrasting traits which are to be counted (green, light green, albino, tall, dwarf etc.).

3. Count the number of plants showing each trait. State the ratio between these numbers. For example

PLANT	NO. OF PLANTS	RATIO
Tobacco, green	62	62:19 = 3.2:1
Tobacco, albino	19	

4. Observe the trays having albino (al-BEE-noh) and green plants over a period of at least two weeks. What happens to the albino plants? Albino is a lethal gene for green plants. Explain the meaning of "lethal gene" and suggest why the albino characteristic would be lethal to the plant.
   Are the white plants (albino) homozygous or heterozygous? Explain your answer.

5. Examine the green plants carefully at intervals over a period of more than two weeks. Are they all the same shade of green? If they are dark green and light green how can you account for this? (See a reference book for an explanation of incomplete dominance.) The green plants are a mixture of homozygous and heterozygous types.
   How could you determine which of the green plants were homozygous for the green trait?

6. Examine the cobs of "genetic" corn. These are corn ears bred for the purpose of illustrating Mendelian ratios. For example, if pollen from an F_1 (hybrid) plant which has the genotype Ss (smooth seed/ shrunken seed) is applied to the stigmas of another F_1 plant having

the genotype Ss, the resulting kernels on the corn cob form the F_2 generation. A count of smooth and shrunken kernels on this cob will provide a Mendelian ratio of one trait to the other. The cob you are examining shows the result of segregation of genes to form the F_2 generation.

What are the contrasting traits on each cob? (Some of these are: shrunken seed/smooth seed; purple color/yellow color; purple color/white color.)

7. Make a count of the numbers of kernels for each trait separately. Be careful not to remove any of the kernels. You may find it helpful to mark the first row counted and the row you are counting with straight pins so that you avoid counting any row twice.

8. Determine the ratio for each pair of traits.

   Which trait appears to be dominant? How do you account for any discrepancy between your results and the expected results?

Questions:

*1. Figure I-24-1 represents a cross of two heterozygous (tallness-dwarfness) plants in which 16,000 plants were produced.

  (a) Approximately how many would be tall?

  (b) Approximately how many would be dwarf?

  (c) What is the ratio between the numbers of tall and dwarf plants?

*2. In the F_1 generation all plants are alike but in the F_2 generation the characteristics for tall and dwarf separate again. What is another name for this separation?

*3. Draw Punnett diagrams for the crosses shown below. State the ratio produced and describe the appearance of each.

  (a) GG and gg,

  (b) Ss and Ss,

  (c) TT and Tt,

  (d) Yy and Yy.

*4.(a) When purebred short-haired guinea pigs were mated with purebred long-haired guinea pigs, the offspring are all short-haired. Which trait is dominant? What letters would you use to show the genetic makeup of the offspring?

  (b) If hybrid short-haired guinea pigs are mated with each other, what would be the expected ratio of short-haired and long-haired offspring produced?

  (c) What genotypes would be produced? Show this cross by a diagram.

†5. How many students in your class (or school) are blond? How many are red-haired? How many have dark or brunette hair? From these figures what do you infer about dominant and recessive hair colors?

Would your figures be affected by the racial makeup of the population of your school? Explain.

I-25   GENE SEGREGATION AND RECOMBINATION

In your study of Mendel's Laws of Inheritance, you have seen that a dominant trait will hide the presence of a recessive trait. Accordingly, a recessive trait will appear only when both genes for that feature are recessive. When you diagrammed the results of Mendel's experiments, you observed that when an individual that is pure strain for a dominant trait is crossed with an individual that is pure strain for a recessive trait, the offspring (the F_1 generation) all appear to have the dominant trait. However, if these F_1 individuals are then crossed, the recessive trait would appear in ¼ of their offspring (the F_2 generation). The recessive trait must therefore be present in the F_1 individuals even though they do not show it; when they produce gametes the traits must segregate so that half the gametes contain the recessive gene.

You will examine a model to illustrate how chance is involved in the selection of gametes for recombination in the offspring. Beginning with a model for pure strain parents you will produce an "F_1 generation." The members of this generation will then be crossed to produce an "F_2 generation."

APPARATUS AND MATERIALS REQUIRED
> *Two jars or boxes*
> *dried white beans and dried colored beans, e.g. red (approximately 50 of each)*

Procedure:
1. Add approximately equal numbers of white and colored beans to two separate containers. The beans will represent the gametes of the parent stock and their color will represent the gene for color possessed by each gamete.
   How many different genetic types of gametes can each parent (container) produce? Could each of the parents be considered pure strain?
2. Select one gamete from each of the parent containers. Place the pair side by side (to represent union at fertilization). Repeat this procedure until all the gametes in one container have been used up.
   Are all the resulting pairs identical? Why would the model be incorrect if you used two beans from the same container? Describe the phenotype of the "offspring." (See the note on page   59 .) Assume the gene for color is dominant. What is the genotype of these crosses?
3. Assume that the first half of the pairs were male and put them in one container. Put the other half of the paired beans in the other con-

tainer. (About 25 pairs of beans will go into each container). These beans now represent the gametes of the F_1 generation.

How do they differ from those of the parent generation? Is the F_1 generation pure strain?

4. Again select one bean at random from each container and set the two beans side by side. Repeat this procedure until all of the beans have been used.

Are the offspring all alike this time? How many types of pairs are there? What generation does this represent? Describe the phenotype of each distinct combination. Describe the genotype of each distinct combination.

5. Fill in the table which follows with the data for your random assortment (selection). Record your results on the board as well so that class totals may be determined. When these are known, fill in the second half of the table.

Assume the colored gene (R) to be dominant over the white gene (r).

DATA TABLE FOR THE MODEL OF GENE COMBINATION

	PHENOTYPE (RED OR WHITE)	GENOTYPE (RR, Rr or rr)
YOUR RESULTS	No. of red pairs .... No. of white pairs	No. of RR .... No. of Rr .... No. of rr ....
	Ratio of red:white = ... :	Ratio of RR : Rr : rr = ...:........:........
CLASS RESULTS	No. of red pairs .... No. of white pairs	No. of RR .... No. of Rr .... No. of rr ....
	Ratio of red:white = ... :	Ratio of RR : Rr : rr = ...:........:........

Questions:

*1. What are the expected ratios for the F_2 generation from this model? Which ratios matched them more closely, your ratios or the class ratios? Explain why the class results would normally be closer to the expected ratios.

*2. In the model, what determined the type of gamete chosen? Do you think that this same factor controls the selection of gametes in living things?

References and Suggestions for Further Investigation:
1. (Home assignment) Use two coins which are alike (e.g. two pennies). Toss the two coins and tally the result in a table like that shown below. Repeat the toss at least fifty times. Bring your tally to class where totals may be made and ratios calculated for the whole class.

TWO HEADS	ONE HEAD ONE TAIL	TWO TAILS
ЖІ ІІ 7	ЖІ ЖІ І 11	ІІІІ 4

2. In a short paragraph relate the tossing of the coins to Mendel's work with garden peas. What does each side of the coin represent? What does the grouping into three categories represent? How do the results compare with Mendel's? What determines the grouping?

1–26   DROSOPHILA TECHNIQUE

The most widely used animal in genetic studies has been the fruit fly (drosophila melanogaster). It can be found on rotting fruits on which it lays its eggs. Some of the advantages of using drosophila are:
1. it is easily raised under laboratory conditions,
2. it has a relatively short life cycle,
3. large numbers of offspring are produced,
4. it can be anaesthetized easily for sorting and counting,
5. it is hardy,
6. it possesses a small number of chromosomes (4 pairs),
7. it possesses giant chromosomes in the cells of its salivary glands which can be studied using simple procedures.

At room temperature the life cycle of Drosophila is usually completed in about 14 to 16 days with the egg-larval period requiring about 8 days and the pupal stage about 7 days. The purpose of this exercise is to acquaint you with the techniques to be used in handling and culturing Drosophila for use in genetic experiments.

One half of the class will culture stocks of "wild" flies and the other half stocks of a "mutant" variety. For the purposes of this exercise you need not be concerned with the differences between the flies. The reproductive cycle is the same for both. It will be useful, however, to have in quantity *pure* stocks of two or more types of flies for the genetics experiments to follow.

APPARATUS AND MATERIALS REQUIRED (per station)
> *Etherizer*
> *re-etherizer*
> *ether and pipette*
> *camel hair brush*
> *culture medium*
> *culture container (shell vial or test tube)*
> *cotton or foam plug*
> *stereomicroscope*
> *examination plate (white tile)*
> (per class)
> *stock cultures of flies (wild and mutant)*
> *stock of dead (over-etherized) wild strain flies*
> *culture vials containing only virgin female flies (wild and mutants)*
> *morgue for dead flies (bottle of oil)*

NOTE: *Female flies that have not mated can be obtained from a flourishing culture by removing all adult flies at the beginning of the school day. Since females usually do not mate for 12 hours after emerging from the pupa, all females collected through the day are probably virgins. Once their sex becomes distinguishable (after about 4 hours) the male flies can be disposed of. The virgin females can be kept separate or together in clean vials that contain a small amount of culture medium until they are required.*

Procedure:
PART A   EXAMINING DROSOPHILA

1. From a stock of dead flies pour about six or seven flies onto an examination plate. With a hand lens or a stereomicroscope, examine the flies to observe details of their structure. Note particularly that
   (a) in dead flies the wings are vertical over the back,
   (b) males have rounded abdomens with a solid black tip while those of females are pointed and larger with separated bands of pigment (See Fig. I-26-1.),
   (c) males are smaller than females,
   (d) males have a "sex" comb of black bristles on the fourth segment of the front leg. (See Fig. I-26-2.)
2. Separate the flies with a brush so that males are on one side of the plate and females are on the other. Check your work by exchanging plates with another team.
3. Make a tally of the number of male and female flies for the class (or for several classes). Can you make any inferences about the ratio between male and female flies from this random sampling?

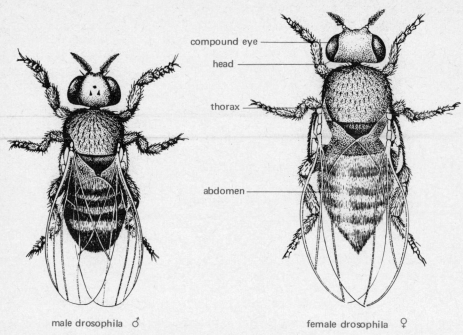

Fig. I–26–1   Comparing male and female drosophila

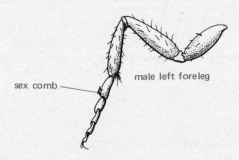

Fig. I–26–2   Left foreleg of the male drosophila

PART B   MATING FLIES OF DIFFERENT STRAINS

4. Prepare a vial for breeding flies by adding the culture medium to a depth of about 1 cm. (If dry Instant Drosophila medium is used, read the instructions on the container label. Remember to add yeast if it is required.)

5. Your teacher will demonstrate how to etherize the flies and transfer them from one container to another. (See Figs. I-26-3, 4 and 6.) Follow his instructions and etherize the wild or mutant flies from the stock bottles that you have been given. Half the class will use wild flies, half will use mutant flies.

CAUTION: *Ether vapors are highly flammable! Do not bring ether near an open flame. Make sure that the bottle of ether is securely stoppered at all times when not in use. Do not use it in a confined area.*

Fig. I–26–3   Culture bottle with foam plug

Fig. I–26–4   Etherizing equipment   Fig. I–26–5   Re-etherizing awakening flies

NOTE: *One method of etherizing and handling the flies is as follows. Put a few drops of ether on the cotton of an etherizer made by wrapping cotton string around the stem of a funnel (See Fig. I-26-6(a).). Rest the funnel on the mouth of the glass bottle. Make sure that the ether is confined to the cotton so that it will not touch the flies and thereby kill them. Tap the stock container against the palm of your hand in order to drive the flies down to the bottom of the rearing container.*

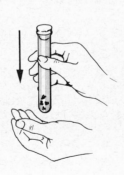

Fig. I–26–6(b)   Driving flies to bottom of stock bottle before removing plug

Fig. I–26–6(a)
Preparing etherizer

Fig. I–26–6(c)   Driving flies into etherizer

(See Fig. I-26-6(b).) Quickly remove the cotton plug from the stock container and invert the vial into the funnel of the etherizer. (See Fig. I-26-6(c).) Tap the bottom of the bottle gently to force the flies down into the etherizer bottle.

When the last fly ceases to move about (after about 1 minute), remove the etherizer funnel and dump the flies onto a white plate or the stage plate of the dissecting microscope. If you over-etherize, the flies will die. Flies should be re-etherized for a few seconds if they show signs of overcoming the effect of the ether while being examined. (They may be expected to move their legs while etherized.) To do this apply a few drops of ether on the cotton of a re-etherizer (cotton gauze in a petri dish) and place it over the flies until motion ceases. (See Fig. I-26-5.)

6. Place etherized flies on the examination plate and separate the males from the females. Only the males from this separation will be used in following procedures.

7. Add four of your male flies to the culture vial which you prepared in Procedure 4 and seal the vial with a plug. Remember, half the class is using wild (+) males and half the class is using mutant (M) males. Keep the vial in a horizontal position until the etherized flies recover sufficiently to avoid becoming stuck in the culture. Return all unused flies to the stock culture bottle from which they were originally taken.

8. Transfer two virgin female flies to your culture vial for breeding purposes as follows. Students with "mutant" strain male flies should transfer two "wild" strain virgin females to their culture vials. Students with "wild" strain male flies should use mutant strain females.

9. Label your culture bottle with the date, your names and a description of the flies. Use the following symbols:

   ♂ - male;   ♀ - female;   + - wild;   M - mutant.

A sample label is shown in Fig. I-26-7. Store your culture at normal room temperature. (Avoid windowsills.)

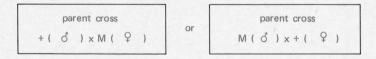

Fig. I–26–7   Label for fly culture

NOTE: *If you are to carry out Exercise I-28, you must remove the parent flies from your culture after about 7 days. (See Procedure 1, page 71.)   Keep these culture vials for use in Experiment I-28.*

Questions:

*1. Observe your culture bottle for a short time each succeeding class period to answer the following questions.

 (a) Look for eggs on the culture medium surface with a hand lens. What are their size and color? (You may have observed eggs more closely while examining etherized female flies that have just laid an egg.)

 (b) After how many days do you first observe the larvae? (Larvae make tunnels in the culture medium as they feed.)

 (c) For how many days does the larval stage last?

 (d) The larvae moult twice as they feed on the culture medium. After two moults, they climb onto a dry surface to enter the pupal stage during which they do not move about. After how many days do you first see pupae on the sides of the container?

 (e) How does the pupa differ from the larva? How long does the pupa stage last? When do flies emerge from the pupa cases?

 (g) How does the appearance of a newly hatched fly differ from the appearance of one hatched some time before?

 (h) What does the term "metamorphosis" mean? Does it apply to the development of Drosophila?

†2. Using a reference book, find out what the larvae are feeding on in the culture medium.

†3. What could be done to hasten the changes in the life cycle of Drosophila?

†4. What other animals undergo the same type of changes as Drosophila in their development?

I–27 MUTANT CHARACTERISTICS OF FRUIT FLIES

We tend to describe varieties of living things by the characteristics which occur in most individuals and are therefore considered normal for that group. For example, the common fruit fly, referred to as the "wild" type, possesses a certain eye color (red), wing length and shape, body color and bristle (body hair) pattern.

Occasionally, an individual that has no abnormal characteristic is found. Such a find was made in 1910 by Thomas Hunt Morgan when he observed a white-eyed Drosophila in a jar of supposedly red-eyed (normal) flies. These abnormal forms or mutations (mew-TAY-shuns) can be produced by exposing the parent stock to certain chemicals, excessive heat or radiation such as x-rays. This exercise is designed to introduce the student to a study of certain eye and wing mutations.

APPARATUS AND MATERIALS REQUIRED (per station)
> *Dead male and female flies of the following varieties:*
>> *wild type*
>> *eye mutation (type A) e.g., sepia eye*
>> *wing mutation (type B) e.g., vestigial wing*
> *camel hair brush*
> *dissecting microscope*
> *drosophila reference books (two are listed at the end of this experiment)*

Procedure:

PART A   EYE MUTATION

1. Obtain one each of a male and a female wild type fly and a male and a female type A mutant fly. Place the flies on the dissecting microscope plate. Arrange the flies so that their dorsal or top surface is up. Use a camel hair brush to move the flies into position so that the two wild flies are side by side and the two type A mutant flies are immediately below them and side by side. Examine the flies and answer the following questions.
   (a) What is the eye color of the male wild type fly? the female wild type fly? Are they the same?
   (b) What is the eye color of the male type A mutant fly? the female type A mutant fly? Are they the same?
   (c) Are the eye colors of the males of the two types (wild and type A) the same? of the females?
   (d) Do the eyes of the wild type and type A flies differ in any respects other than color? If so describe the difference(s).
2. With the aid of suitable reference material, answer the following questions.
   (a) What other eye colors may occur in mutant flies?
   (b) What other eye characteristics may occur in mutant flies?

PART B   WING MUTATIONS

3. Obtain a male and a female wild type fly and a male and a female type B mutant fly. Arrange them on the dissecting microscope plate in the same manner as indicated in Procedure 1. With the aid of the microscope, answer the following questions.
   (a) Make a simple sketch of the wings of the male wild type fly. Label your diagram.
   (b) Are the wings of the male and female wild type similar?
   (c) Make a simple sketch of the wings of the male type B mutant fly. Beside the diagram write the type of mutant.
   (d) Are the wings of the male and female type B mutant fly similar?

Questions:

*1. Are mutant forms capable of reproducing their own kind? Explain.
*2. What might have caused mutant characteristics to appear in fruit flies?
*3. Do you expect most mutations to be detrimental or beneficial to the organisms?

References and Suggestions for Further Investigation:

1. Two reference books for information on Drosophila are *Drosophila Guide*, 7th edition, by M. Demerec and B. P. Kaufmann (Washington, D.C.: Carnegie Institute of Washington, 1964), and *Experiments in Genetics with Drosophila,* by M. W. Strickberger (New York: John Wiley and Sons, Inc., 1962).

I–28   INHERITANCE OF A SINGLE TRAIT

In this exercise you will determine what will happen if two flies showing different traits for a single structural feature are crossed. Will the offspring show a merging of the parental appearances or show one or the other separately? Contrasting features of a trait are known as *alleles* (a-LEELZ); e.g. vestigial (ves-TIJ-ee-al) wing is an allele of normal wing and white eye is an allele of red eye.

APPARATUS AND MATERIALS REQUIRED
   Basic equipment as in Exercise I-26
   cultures prepared in Exercise I-26

NOTE: In Exercise I-26, half the class started culture bottles containing four male wild type flies (+) and two virgin female mutant flies (M) and the other half of the class started culture bottles containing four male mutant flies (M) and two virgin female wild type flies (+). (Why did you not use only one male fly and one female fly in the culture bottle?)

Procedure:

1. When the cultures are 7 or 8 days old, etherize and remove the adult (parent) flies from the bottle. Discard these flies in the morgue. This procedure allows time for mating and egg laying. If parent flies remain in the culture after this time they may be counted with the offspring.
2. In successsive class periods remove the new adult flies as they appear. Keep several males and females for cross breeding in Procedure 4 to

follow. The others may be put in the morgue after you have counted how many of each show the wild trait and how many of each show the mutant trait.

3. Continue separating males and females for 7 or 8 days. Then answer these questions.
   (a) What is the total number of flies?
   (b) How many are male? female?
   (c) How many show a wild strain trait (e.g. normal wings)?
   (d) How many show the mutant strain trait (e.g. vestigial wings)?
   (e) Which trait is dominant?
   (f) What name is given to the generation of flies you have produced?
   (g) Which of Mendel's laws is illustrated by your results?
   (h) Show the cross you have performed diagramatically in a Punnett square.

4. To a fresh culture vial transfer four males and three females obtained in Procedure 2. These are offspring (F_1 generation) of a parent cross. If there is insufficient time in class, your teacher may suggest that you complete your observations of this hybrid cross as a home assignment. After seven days, remove the parent flies. When a sufficiently large number of new adults has developed, etherize and examine them to answer the following questions.
   (a) How many of the F_2 flies showed the wild trait?
   (b) How many of the F_2 flies showed the mutant trait?
   (c) What is the ratio between the numbers of wild and mutant flies?
   (d) Show the genotypes expected from this cross in a diagram.
   (e) Which of Mendel's Laws is illustrated by this cross?

Questions: (Consult a reference book to answer the following questions.)

*1. Give several reasons for choosing drosophila as an organism for genetic studies.

*2. Define the term "mutation." Describe the various ways in which mutations are produced.

*3. Are mutations "good" or "bad"? Explain.

*4. In drosophila, normal wings are dominant over stubby wings. If you mated equal numbers of purebred normal winged flies with stubby winged flies what would be the appearance (phenotype) of the offspring?

*5. If the offspring of the cross in the previous question were mated (selfed) and 240 offspring (F_2) were produced, approximately how many flies would have normal wings? stubby wings? medium length wings?

†6. List several mutations that have been discovered in drosophila.

*7. How did Hermann J. Muller increase the rate of mutations in drosophila? Would this apply also to humans?

*8. How did Thomas Hunt Morgan's work with drosophila contribute to our knowledge of genetics?

Mendelian Principles:

We can summarize the results of Mendel's work as follows.

1. Each characteristic is inherited as a single independent factor *(The Law of Unit Characters)*.

2. For any given characteristic or trait, there are two factors *(genes)*. Each gene pair may be alike or different in any one organism. If different, one may be dominant and the other recessive *(The Law of Dominance)*.

3. When gametes are formed, the factors (genes) are separated or segregated so that each gamete carries only one factor (gene) from each pair. At fertilization, gametes unite to form a zygote which again contains paired genes. The traits are completely independent of each other *(The Law of Segregation)*.

More recent research has shown us that Mendel's clear-cut ideas are somewhat oversimplified. For example, complete dominance and recessiveness do not always occur; in fact, complete dominance is far rarer than is partial dominance or partial recessiveness. The idea that one gene operates independently of all other genes is not always true. For these reasons, you may find difficulty in accounting for the occurrence of some traits, such as eye color or skin color in man.

Section V
REPRODUCTION OF CELLS

From his study of the inheritance of a number of traits in garden peas, Mendel proposed several basic principles which form the basis of modern genetics. Later discoveries of cell structure and the behavior of cells during division now make it possible to account for these principles.

There are two basic patterns in cell division. The first, *mitosis* (my-TOH-sis), is the process by which the zygote and succeeding cells divide to form the bulk of the organism's body. The second, *meiosis* (my-OH-sis), is the process by which the gametes are produced in the reproductive organs.

A cell produced by *mitosis* (i.e. a body cell) divides again to form further similar cells. A cell produced by *meiosis* (i.e. a sex cell or gamete) unites with another gamete to form a zygote. It is important to remember this difference when we are considering the two processes.

I–29 CELLS FROM AN ACTIVELY GROWING REGION OF A PLANT

In a previous science course you may have measured the rate of growth of a seedling root tip by marking it with a series of lines. The resulting relatively large spread of the lines near the tip showed this region to be one of active growth. The tip of the root is therefore a convenient source of cells dividing by mitosis.

Cells can be separated for easier examination by the application of an acid which will break down the substances that bind the cells together. After staining, the cells which remain can be separated by squashing them between the slide and cover slip.

APPARATUS AND MATERIALS REQUIRED (per station)
> *Monocular microscope*
> *well slides*
> *slides*
> *cover slip*
> *pipettes*
> *germinated seeds*
> *growing root tips (bean, pea or onion)*
> *aceto-carmine stain (or aceto-orcein stain)*
> *razor blades*
> *1M HC1*
> *burners*
> *preservative solution (18 parts ethyl alcohol, 1 part formalin and 1 part glacial acetic acid by volume)*

Procedure:
1. Grow root tips by either germinating a bean or pea seed or allowing an onion bulb to sit in the mouth of a water-filled jar so the base of the bulb in touching the water. (See Fig. I-29-1.)
2. Cut off about 1 cm of several root tips. These may be used immediately or stored in a preservative.
3. Place the root tips in the depression of a well slide and cover them with 1 M HCl. Carefully warm the slide for several minutes above a bunsen burner flame but do not boil the acid. Then soak up the acid with a paper towel and cover the tips with aceto-carmine stain. Again warm the slide as before for several minutes.
4. Soak up the stain with a paper towel and transfer the stained tips to a flat, clean slide with forceps.

Fig. I–29–1   Growing onion roots

5. Cover the specimens with a cover slip and place a small square (about 4 cm) of paper towel over the slip.
6. With the slide on the table, apply pressure to the cover slip with your thumb to squash or macerate the root tips. Press directly downward on the paper over the slip so that the slip does not move sideways.
7. Examine the root tips under your microscope. Scan the slide under low power and then observe the individual cells at higher powers.
   Can you determine the shape of the cells? Therefore, what was the effect of the acid? What parts of the cells seemed to have absorbed most of the stain? Are all of the cells the same age? How might you account for any differences in size? Are the nuclei distinct and round in all root tip cells or are they replaced by fine strands in a few? If you can locate a cell with fine, deeply stained nuclear strands, draw a much enlarged view of this cell to show the number, arrangement and position of the strands.

Questions:
*1. Look up the word "chromosome" in a reference book. What are the roots of this word?
*2. How many chromosomes should there be in each cell of the material you are examining? How many can you count?
*3. Very briefly, what is the role of the chromosome in the cell?

I–30   MITOSIS IN PLANT AND ANIMAL CELLS

In multicellular organisms individual cells must reproduce themselves to replace cells that die and to provide for growth. In human blood the life span of a white corpuscle is one to two days while that of a red blood corpuscle is 125 days.

For survival, these cells must be duplicated or replaced continually. Growth is also the result of repeated cell divisions. By this means, after countless divisions, the zygote of the human finally becomes the adult human. The process by which cells divide and duplicate themselves is similar in all organisms and is called mitosis. In this exercise you will examine the stages of cell division by mitosis in a plant and in an animal.

APPARATUS AND MATERIALS REQUIRED

Monocular microscope
prepared slides of onion root tip (longitudinal sections)
prepared slides of whitefish eggs

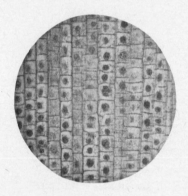

Fig. I–30–1   Dividing cells in an onion root tip

Procedure:

PART A   PLANT CELL DIVISION

1. Scan a prepared slide of an entire root tip under a microscope.
   Into how many distinct areas could you divide the root based on the type and arrangement of cells?
2. Examine the cells behind the root cap at the tip. These are in the region of rapid cell division.
   In what ways do they differ from the cells farther back from the tip (in the region of cell elongation)?

NOTE: In mitotic cell division three major phases occur. (See Fig. I-30-2.) The first is the replication of the chromosome. *In this phase chromosomes replicate (or duplicate) themselves. The duplicate strands of the chromosome are known as* chromatids.

3. Using medium power, find a cell that contains stained chromosomes that have contracted in length as much as they can, so that they appear as distinct thread-like bodies.

How many chromosomes are there in the nucleus? You may have to count them in several cells. Do the chromatids appear to be coiled? Why do you suppose the chromosomes appear to become shorter and thicker during the division of cells?

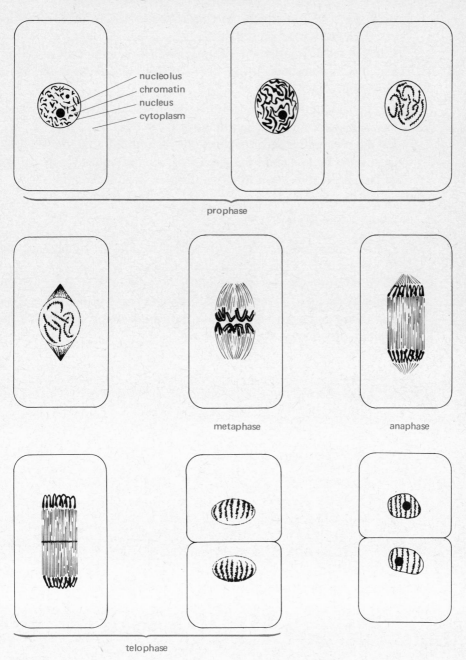

Fig. I–30–2   Phases of mitosis

NOTE: *The second phase during cell division is the* separation of the chroma-tids. *The chromosomes do not separate completely into chromatids but remain joined in an area called the* centromere. *At this stage they line up in the center of the cell.*

4. Look for a cell in which the chromosomes are arranged in a line across the center of the cell.
Can you see any pattern or a connection between the ends of the cell and the chromosomes at the center? This connection is known as the spindle.

5. Locate a cell in which the chromatids appear to have separated and moved away from the center of the cell.
Do the chromatids seem to resist this separation? Can you see what parts separate first and what parts resist separation the most? Do any of the chromatids seem to lag in position behind the others?

NOTE: *The re-formation of the nuclei initiates the third phase, the* separation of the cytoplasm.

6. Locate a cell in which the chromatids have fully separated and seem to be gathering in the form of nuclei again.
What resulting changes do you notice in the chromatid structure and depth of staining? What resulting changes can you see in the cyto-plasm and cell walls? Is there any indication that a new wall is de-veloping to separate the cell into two?

Questions:
*1.(a) From the diagrams in this manual and from your own observa-tions, what general remarks can you make about the relative numbers of chromosomes in a parent cell and a daughter cell?
   (b) What does your answer imply about the numbers of chromosomes in all body cells?

*2. Chromosomes are the structures that control hereditary character-istics.
   (a) Do new cells produced by mitosis contain identical or different hereditary traits (genes)?
   (b) Therefore, does any change in hereditary characteristics result from mitosis?

*3. The second phase of cell division is sometimes further subdivided into prophase, metaphase, anaphase and telophase. These stages overlap and are continuous. (See Fig. I-30-2.) Using reference books, describe what is happening in each of the phases.

*4. Formerly, the period before the replication of the chromosome was called an interphase or resting stage. Are these terms appropriate? Suggest why that description of this stage was changed.

PART B   ANIMAL CELL DIVISION

Cell division in animals can be observed in the embryo of the white-fish, immediately after the zygote has started to develop.

Procedure:
7. Follow the instructions given in Part A as they apply and answer the questions asked, substituting "whitefish embryo" for each reference to "onion root tip."
8. Compare the activity of the chromosomes and the methods of final division of the whitefish and onion cells.
How does the direction in which the chromosomes line up in the second phase affect the shape of the cell? Does the spindle seem to originate from specialized structures near the ends of the cell? Eventually the onion and whitefish cells will form organisms very different in appearance. Since these cells have so many similar features, what do you think is responsible for this difference?

I–31   MEIOSIS–REDUCTION-DIVISION

In sexual reproduction two parents contribute hereditary material in their chromosomes to a new cell, the zygote. It follows that the zygote will contain more chromosomal material than either of the cells contributed by the parents (the gametes). For example, in the human, the sperm and egg contain 23 chromosomes and the zygote has 46 chromosomes.

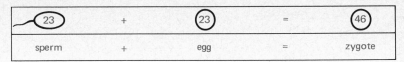

In your study of mitosis you have seen that when the zygote divides to form new cells by mitosis there is a replication of chromosomes followed by a separation of the chromatids to form *identical* daughter cells. The daughter cells are identical to the parent cell in both number and kind of chromosomes.

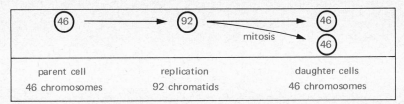

If sperm and eggs were produced by *mitosis* from sex organ cells in the human, they too would possess 46 chromosomes. The zygote then resulting from the union of sperm and egg would contain 92 chromosomes. How many chromosomes would zygotes and body cells of the next generation have? and the next? Clearly this would lead to generations having hundreds of thousands of chromosomes. We know that this does not happen; counts of chromosomes in body cells and gametes show a constant number, with no increase from one generation to the next.

There is also a constant number of chromosomes in the sperm and eggs; however, the number in both types of gametes is exactly half the number in the zygotes and body cells. The number of chromosomes in gametes is described as being *monoploid* (n) and that in zygotes or body cells as being *diploid* (2n) (DIP-loid). The chart shows the number of chromosomes in various organisms.

EXAMPLE	MONOPLOID (n) (GAMETES)	DIPLOID (2n) (BODY CELLS)
Human	23	46
Fruit fly (Melanogaster)	4	8
Corn	10	20
Onion	8	16
Horse	33	66
Moss (Bryum)	10	20
Garden Pea	7	14
Rhesus Monkey	24	48
Potato	24	48
Shrimp	127	254
Spirogyra	12	24
Fern	32	64
Chicken	39	78

The process by which specialized diploid (2n) cells divide and reduce the number of chromosomes to half or monoploid (n) is called meiosis or *reduction-division*. During their life cycle, plants and animals which reproduce sexually must perform meiosis to reduce the number of chromosomes in their sperms and eggs to half that of the body cells. In some organisms meiosis occurs in the sex organs when sperms and eggs are manufactured. This is the case in human ovaries and testes. In other organisms meiosis occurs at another stage of the life cycle. For example, during the alternation of generations of the moss (refer to the diagram on page 50), meiosis occurs in the capsule when spores are produced. The monoploid spores germinate to form gametophytes in which *all* cells, including sperm and eggs, are monoploid.

The exercise which follows shows in simplified chart form the basic differences between meiosis and mitosis and the recombination of chromosomes during fertilization.

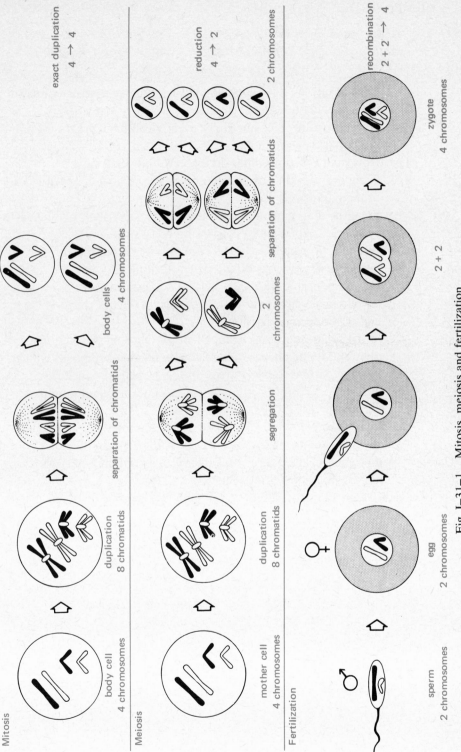

Fig. I-31-1　Mitosis, meiosis and fertilization

Procedure:

NOTE: *Refer to the chart in Fig. I-31-1. The cells illustrated are diagram-*
         matic and are not drawn to scale. Only chromosome detail is shown.

1. Describe briefly what is happening in each stage of mitosis by answering the following questions.
   (a) How many chromosomes does a body cell have before division?
       Note that they are in pairs.
   (b) How many chromosomes do the new body cells have?
   (c) Compare the kind of chromosomes in the new cells with those
       of the parent cell.
2. Examine the diagrams representing meiosis. Describe briefly what is
   happening at each stage by answering these questions.
   (a) What parts of meiotic process are different from the correspond-
       ing parts of mitosis? What parts are similar?
   (b) How many times does cell division occur in meiosis? How many
       chromosomes are in the cells at the end of the first division? at the
       end of the second division?
   (c) In the separation (segregation) of chromosomes in the first cell
       division, do the chromosome pairs segregate or remain together?
       Are the chromosomes paired in the new cells produced?
   (d) Do the cells produced by meiosis contain equal numbers of
       chromosomes? Explain.
   (e) If the parent cell in meiosis had a tall characteristic on one chro-
       mosome and its allele (the corresponding gene on the other chro-
       mosome of the pair) was dwarf, would both characteristics
       appear in any resulting gamete?
   (f) How many cells are produced from one mother (parent) cell in
       mitosis? in meiosis?
3. Examine the diagram representing fertilization and answer these
   questions.
   (a) How many chromosomes are there in the sperm, the egg and the
       zygote?
   (b) Compare the numbers and arrangements of chromosomes in the
       zygote, the mother cell of meiosis and the original body cell of
       mitosis.

Questions:
*1. Using a blank outline similar to Fig. I-31-2, complete the chart us-
    ing the letters Aa for the straight chromosome pair and the letters
    Bb for the bent chromosome pair.
*2. Complete a second outline chart using three pairs of chromosomes

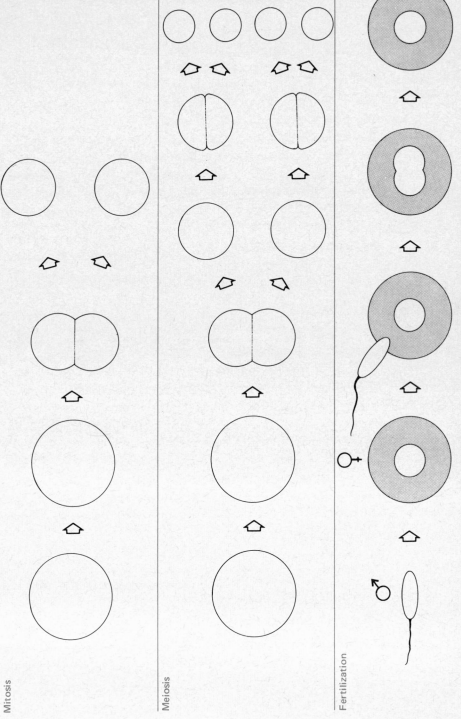

Mitosis

Meiosis

Fertilization

Fig. I-31-2   Blank outline of mitosis, meiosis and fertilization

instead of two. It is suggested that colors be used to represent the chromosomes,

e.g.   pair 1:   light red, dark red
        pair 2:   light green, dark green
        pair 3:   light blue, dark blue

*3. Refer to the diagram of the moss life cycle on page *50*.

(a) Where does meiosis occur in the moss?

(b) What parts of the diagram are monoploid (n)?

(c) Where does fertilization occur?

(d) What parts of the diagram are diploid (2n)?

(e) The zygote of the moss has 20 chromosomes. How many chromosomes has a leaf cell? a spore? a cell from the spore capsule wall? a sperm?

†(f) Does meiosis produce identical cells (identical from the standpoint of traits or genes carried on the chromosomes)?

†(g) Would the spores released from the moss capsule carry identical hereditary traits or genes, or would they show variation?

Section VI
HEREDITY AND THE ENVIRONMENT

From your study of genetics, you may feel that your total physical development is determined before birth by the genes in your chromosomes. Is there no opportunity for change once the zygote is formed? Does the environment play any role in influencing our growth? To answer such questions, animals and plants of a single genetic type are usually exposed to different environmental conditions. The resulting growths are then measured and interpreted to establish the cause of any differences.

To study environmental effects on man's development, a difficulty arises in trying to get genetically similar types. The best subjects are identical twins who have identical genetic patterns. This is because both develop from the division of one fertilized egg. The resulting two cells then grow into two separate individuals. There have been cases of identical twins who were reared in different areas subsequently showing noticeable differences in physical and mental growth.

I–32   EFFECT OF THE ENVIRONMENT
       ON PLANT DEVELOPMENT

You will first examine the effects of a single environmental influence in a controlled situation in the laboratory. Then, outside the laboratory, you will examine the combined effect of all environmental influences on a genetically similar population.

APPARATUS AND MATERIALS REQUIRED (per station)
Bean seedlings grown in the light
bean seedlings grown in the dark
a ruler

Procedure:
1. Examine and compare the seedling plants provided. What differences do you see in the
   (a) color of leaves?
   (b) size of leaf area?
   (c) length of stem from cotyledons to first leaves?
   (d) length of stems from first to second whorl of leaves?
   (e) rigidity of the stem?
   If hormones usually promote growth, which plant do you think shows the greatest hormone influence?
   Light influences the production of hormones. Can you tell from the results whether it increases or decreases their production?
2. This part of the exercise must be done individually at home. Select one type of plant for your examination. A good example is the dandelion commonly found as a weed on lawns and in flower beds. (Other species of single pasture plants or forest plants could be used as well.) Compare the growth of dandelions in the center of your lawn, at the margins, in a walked-on area, in an open area, in a shaded area and in flower beds. You might best record your observations in the form of a chart relating the location of the plants to each of the following characteristics:
   (a) the color and general form of the leaves,
   (b) the quantity and quality of the flowers and seeds produced,
   (c) the length of the flower stalks,
   (d) the length of the tap roots. (Dig carefully so that you don't break the root),
   (e) the diameter of the leaves. (Leaves arranged in a circle in this way are called a rosette.)
   Speculate as to what environmental factors are causing the differences observed.

Questions:
*1. What environmental factors could influence the height and weight of a person?
*2. Are all features shown by a baby at birth the result of inheritance?

Fig. I–32–1(a)

Fig. I–32–1(b)

Compare trees growing in different locations

*3. What features of a person are most likely to be the result of inherited characteristics only and not environment?

*4. Compare the extent of growth of the trees in Fig. I-32-1a and 1b. What environmental factors might account for any differences?

UNIT ▊▊   M. C. Schmid & J. A. Petrak

ELECTRICITY AND MAGNETISM

INTRODUCTION

If you are like most people, you take electrical energy very much for granted.
Yet only two hundred years ago there were no electric lights, telephones, radios,
refrigerators, electric motors, electrochemical cells, electronic computers or
thousands of other electrical devices that help to make us comfortable and en-
rich and expand our lives.

When you use electricity you seldom need to do more than push a
button or flick a switch because electrical energy is easily controlled and most
electrical appliances are simple to operate. There will be times in your life,
however, when it will be important that you make intelligent decisions regarding
electricity; some of these decisions may affect your safety. You should also be
able to make minor electrical repairs. You should, therefore, acquire sufficient
knowledge about the nature of electricity and what it is capable of doing.

II-1   STATIC ELECTRICAL CHARGES

You have no doubt discovered that a blouse or a shirt made of synthetic material clings to you when you try to take it off and that a cat's fur crackles when stroked on days when the humidity is low. These and many similar observations are clues to the electrical nature of matter. In the following experiment you will systematically examine the effects of electrical charges to determine some of the rules which describe the electrical behavior of matter.

NOTE: *To ensure that this experiment is successful on humid days, warm the plastic strips and cloths to decrease their moisture content by placing them above a heat register or under a heat lamp. Better results can also be obtained if the strips or rods to be charged are washed in warm soapy water or wiped with a cloth that has been dampened in methyl alcohol.*

APPARATUS AND MATERIALS REQUIRED (per station)
>   *A 35 cm length of stiff wire*
>   *burette clamp*
>   *support stand*
>   *single strand nylon thread*
>   *2 vinyl plastic strips or ebonite rods*
>   *wool square or cat's fur*
>   *2 acetate plastic strips*
>   *cotton square or paper towel*
>   *6 cm diameter watchglass*
>   *meter stick*
>   *metal rod (approx. 25 cm long and 5 mm in diameter)*

Procedure:

NOTE: *You need not spend much time on this experiment. When you have observed the effect in each procedure, go on to the next.*

1. Bend a 35 cm length of stiff wire to form a cradle in which a vinyl plastic strip (or ebonite rod) can be supported. (See Fig. II-1-1.) Suspend the cradle below the base of a support stand by means of a single strand of nylon thread so that the cradle can rotate freely. Note the way the string should be tied. If necessary, allow the thread to unwind until the cradle remains stationary.

2. Hold a strip of vinyl plastic (or an ebonite rod) at its center, vigorously rub both ends with a piece of dry wool or cat's fur and place it in the wire cradle.

3. In the same way, rub one end of a second identical strip with the

same material. Then bring this rubbed end close to, but not into contact with, each end of the suspended strip in turn. (If the reaction is
indefinite, repeat Procedures 2 and 3.)

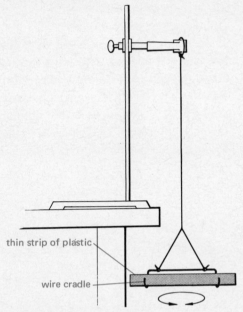

thin strip of plastic

wire cradle

Fig. II–1–1   Apparatus for testing electrical charges

**How do the ends of the suspended strip respond when the second
strip is brought near? How is the force between the strips changed
when the distance between the strips is increased? Since the two strips
used were made of the same material and since they were each given
the same treatment, how must the electric charges that they obtain
compare?**

4. Vigorously rub an acetate plastic strip with a piece of cotton or paper
   towelling. Bring its rubbed end close to, but *not* into contact with,
   each end of the suspended vinyl strip in turn. (If the reaction is indefinite, repeat Procedures 2 and 4.)
   **Is the suspended strip attracted at both ends or is it repelled at one
   end and attracted at the other? Is the electric charge on the acetate
   strip the same as that on the vinyl strip? Explain.**

5. Remove any electric charge that might be present on another vinyl
   plastic strip and on the acetate strip by bringing all parts of their surfaces into contact with your hand. Then determine the effect of each
   strip on the suspended, charged vinyl strip.
   Rub the vinyl and acetate plastic strips together. Test for any
   electric charges by bringing each strip, in turn, near to the ends of the
   suspended, charged vinyl strip. Compare the effects with those previously observed.

Did rubbing the strips together cause them to become charged? Did both materials develop the same charge? Explain.

6. Repeat Procedures 2 and 3 but use acetate plastic strips and cotton cloths (or paper towelling) in place of the vinyl strips and wool (or fur).

    Is the result the same as when vinyl plastic was used? Therefore, does the charged acetate strip have the same charge as a charged vinyl strip? (Recall your results for Procedure 4.)

†7. Balance a meter stick on a watchglass as shown in Fig. II-1-2. Bring a charged vinyl strip close to, but not into contact with, each end of the meter stick in turn. Describe the results. Repeat this procedure using a charged acetate plastic strip and again describe the results.

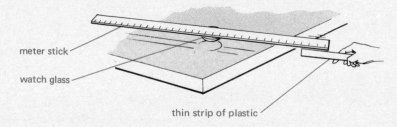

meter stick
watch glass
thin strip of plastic

Fig. II–1–2   Bringing a charged rod near a rotatable meter stick

When the charged vinyl was brought near the neutral (uncharged) meter stick, was the meter stick attracted or repelled? When the charged acetate was brought near the meter stick, was the meter stick attracted or repelled?

†8. Rub a metal rod with wool or cotton and test its effect on the balanced meter stick.

    What charge does the metal rod appear to have?

†9. Test the apparent charge of a thin stream of water from a tap by bringing, in turn, a charged vinyl and a charged acetate strip near to it.

    What is (are) the apparent charge(s) on the water?

NOTE: *The charges developed on the strips during the experiment are referred to as static electrical or* electrostatic *charges.*

Questions:

*1. In Procedures 2 and 4, when the vinyl and acetate strips were rubbed, was there any *apparent* change in
    (a) their physical properties such as color, odor, hardness and so on?
    (b) their sizes or volumes?
    (c) their electrical charges?

*2. It is known that some matter is transferred from one object to another when objects are being charged. Would you expect the amount

of transferred matter to be a very large or a very small part of the original object? (Consider the amount of charge in the appearance of the object.)

*3. Describe the difference between the charge produced on the vinyl strip and that produced on the acetate strip in terms of their effects on a charged vinyl strip.

NOTE: *The electrostatic charge that a vinyl strip (or ebonite rod) develops when it is rubbed with wool is called a* negative *charge; that produced on an acetate strip when it is rubbed with cotton is called a* positive *charge.*

*4.(a) Is the resulting force one of attraction or of repulsion when

(i) a negatively charged object is brought near a positively charged object?

(ii) a positively charged object is brought near a negatively charged object?

(iii) a positively charged object is brought near a positively charged object?

(iv) a negatively charged object is brought near a negatively charged object?

(v) a charged object is brought near a neutral object?

(b) Make a general statement about the effect of bringing

(i) similarly charged objects near each other.

(ii) dissimilarly charged objects near each other.

†5. Try to explain in terms of the transfer of some matter, the fact that when a vinyl and acetate plastic strip were rubbed together (Procedure 5) they gained opposite charges.

References and Suggestions for Further Investigation:

1. Rub an inflated balloon against your clothing, then place the balloon against a wall or a ceiling. Explain why the balloon does not fall.

2. Pages 403-406 of *Physical Science, A Basic Course* by J. C. Hogg, J. B. Cross and K. E. Vordenberg (Toronto: D. Van Nostrand Co. Inc., 1959), discuss several facts about static electricity.

II–2 TRANSFER OF ELECTRIC CHARGE

(May be demonstrated by projecting a shadow of the electroscope on the wall.)

You have observed that
(a) two kinds of electrostatic charge may be produced by rubbing objects,
(b) vinyl plastic (or ebonite) becomes negatively charged when rubbed with

wool whereas acetate plastic becomes positively charged when rubbed with cotton or paper towel,

(c) objects with like electrical charges repel each other while objects with unlike electrical charges attract each other,

(d) electrical forces become greater as the distance between the charged objects decreases,

(e) when objects become charged there is no visible change in their appearance.

Although these facts were discovered over 400 years ago, it was not until almost the turn of this century that the cause of these effects began to be understood. The following information will enable you to explain them.

You have already learned that all substances are made up of atoms. At first it was thought that atoms were indivisible but the discovery of the *electron* in 1897 and the *proton* in 1919 disproved this idea. In 1911, Ernest Rutherford proposed a model of the atom that showed how electrons were arranged in atoms. Even though much more has been learned since, you will find that, for the purposes of this course, this model of the atom is adequate to describe the electrical behavior of matter. A third very important atomic particle, the *neutron,* was discovered in 1932 and has been included along with the proton in the following description of the Rutherford atom.

A Model of the Atom: (See Fig. II-2-1.)

Every atom contains a very small nucleus made up of a number of protons and neutrons. Because neutrons have no electrical charge while protons have a positive charge, every nucleus has a positive charge. The particles in the nucleus are bound together by very strong nuclear forces, which overcome the repulsive forces between the positive charges on the protons.

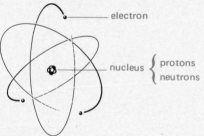

Fig. II–2–1   1911 Rutherford model of the atom

Travelling separately in orbits around the nucleus are electrons. Each electron possesses a negative charge equal and opposite to that of a proton. Because the charges are opposite, there are attractive forces between the electrons and the nucleus. These attractive forces cause the electrons to orbit the the nucleus.

The atoms of each element can be identified by the number of protons contained in their nucleii. An individual atom of an element tends to hold as many electrons as there are protons. Therefore, even though atoms contain two kinds of charged particles, they have no net charge and may be considered neutral.

The mass of an electron is negligible in comparison with the mass of either a proton or a neutron – about 1/1840 of the mass of either one. Therefore, almost all of the mass of an atom exists in the nucleus of that atom.

The outermost electrons, being farther away from the positive nucleus, are less strongly attracted than the inner ones; they are repelled by those closer in. As a result, the outermost electrons are more easily removed from an atom. When materials such as wool and vinyl plastic are rubbed together, the frictional effects cause the *outer electrons* of some atoms to be transferred from one material to the other. Since protons are inside atoms and strongly bound to neutrons and other protons, *only electrons are removed from atoms* when electrostatic charges are produced. This means that a material like rubbed vinyl, which possesses a net negative charge, carries an excess of electrons that have been gained from atoms on the wool. On the other hand, a material like rubbed acetate, which possesses a net positive charge, has a deficiency of electrons because it has lost some to the cotton on which it was rubbed.

In the following experiment you will be required to use Rutherford's model to explain the observed behavior of a device called an electroscope.

APPARATUS REQUIRED (per station)
> *Electroscope (leaf type)*
> *2 metal cans supported vertically on 2 plastic rods*

MATERIALS REQUIRED (per station)
> *Vinyl plastic strip (or ebonite rod)*
> *wool square or cat's fur*
> *acetate plastic strip*
> *cotton square or paper towel*
> *samples of copper, nickel and silver (coins will serve), wood, glass rod, rubber tubing, tygon tubing, iron, sealing wax, large copper sulphate crystal, string, carbon rod and so on*

Procedure:

PART A   USING AN ELECTROSCOPE TO DETECT ELECTROSTATIC CHARGES

1. Study the leaf type electroscope provided. It has three major components as shown in Fig. II-2-2:
   (a) an outer case of metal and glass

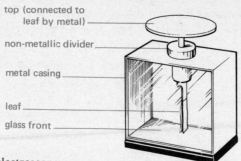

top (connected to
    leaf by metal) ——

non-metallic divider ——

metal casing ——

leaf ——
glass front ——

Fig. II–2–2   A leaf type electroscope

(b) a non-metallic divider made of sulphur, wax or plastic that separates the outer case from the central working part,

(c) a central metallic unit which includes one or two very delicate metal leaves attached at only one end. *This is the working part of an electroscope.*

2. Touch the top of the central unit of the electroscope with your finger and note the position of the leaf (or leaves) when the electroscope is neutral. In this procedure, and those following, record your observation in the form of a simple sketch like that in Fig. II-2-3 and include a brief note that describes what you did.

Fig. II–2–3   Sketch of neutral electroscope

3. Bring a negatively charged strip such as rubbed vinyl close to, *but not into contact with*, the sides and then the top of the electroscope. Observe the effect on the leaf. Take care not to tear the delicate leaf. **In which position did the charged vinyl produce the greatest effect on the leaf? the least effect?**

4. Again bring the negatively charged strip close to, *but not into contact with*, the top of the neutral electroscope. Sketch the electroscope with the leaf as it is when the negatively charged strip is nearby. Include the charged strip in your sketch.
What happens to the electroscope leaf when a negatively charged rod is brought near the top of the electroscope? Is there a force acting on the leaf? If so, is it one of repulsion or of attraction? What happens when the strip is removed?

5. Now *touch* the top of the electroscope with the negatively charged strip and slide its charged end across the top of the electroscope. Then remove the strip. Sketch the electroscope (and the charged strip, when appropriate) both during and after contact.
   What happens to the electroscope leaf when the top of the electroscope is touched with a charged strip? When the charged strip is removed? Does the leaf become charged? Give a reason for your answer.

6. Recharge the vinyl strip and slide its charged end across the top of the charged electroscope.
   What happens to the electroscope leaf? Have you increased or decreased the charge on the electroscope?

7. Touch the top of the charged electroscope with your finger. Sketch the electroscope after it has been touched.
   Does the electroscope maintain its charge when you touch it with your finger?

8. Repeat Procedures 4 to 7 using a positively charged acetate strip. Sketch the electroscope each time as before. Whenever the strip is present, include it in your sketch.

9. Charge the electroscope using a negatively charged strip as in Procedure 5. Remove this strip and then bring a positively charged strip close to, but not into contact with, the electroscope.
   What happens to the leaves as the positively charged strip approaches?

10. Touch the top of the electroscope with the positively charged strip.
    How does the leaf of the electroscope behave?

†11. Repeat Procedures 9 and 10 using a positively charged electroscope and a negatively charged strip.

†12. Charge a plastic comb or plastic ruler by rubbing it on wool or through your hair. Use a charged electroscope to determine the charge on the comb.

PART B   TESTING MATERIALS FOR THEIR ABILITY TO CONDUCT CHARGE

13. Charge a leaf type electroscope negatively. Touch the top with your finger.
    What evidence is there that negative charges (electrons) can move through your body? Why do electrons leave the negatively charged electroscope?

NOTE: *When you provide a path from the charged electroscope to the ground, you are said to be* grounding *the electroscope.*

14. Charge the electroscope negatively. In turn, hold one end of each of the sample materials mentioned under Materials Required and touch the other end to the top of the electroscope as shown in Fig. II-2-4.

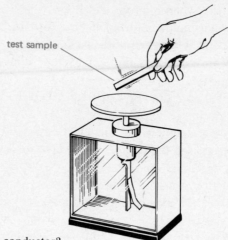

Fig. II–2–4   Is the material a conductor?

NOTE: *If a material allows the electroscope to discharge, that material is a conductor. If necessary, you must recharge the electroscope before testing the next sample. Those materials which allow the electroscope to discharge slowly or not at all are poor conductors or insulators.*

List the materials under two headings:

GOOD CONDUCTORS	POOR CONDUCTORS

NOTE: *In Procedure 14 it was observed that metals allow electrons to move freely through them. Therefore, when a charged strip is brought near to an electroscope, electrons in the metallic part of the electroscope move either closer to or farther away from the charged strip, depending on whether the strip is positively or negatively charged. When the charged strip touches the electroscope, electrons move from the electroscope to a positively charged strip or to the electroscope from a negatively charged strip. In each case the electroscope becomes charged with the same charge as the strip.*

15. Use the previous information about electron movement and the model of the atom described in the introduction to this experiment to interpret your observations in Procedures 4, 5, 7 and 9. Use the symbols + and — to represent protons and electrons respectively. Equal numbers of the two symbols then indicate a neutral charge and an excess of + or — symbols indicates a positive or negative charge respectively. For example, your sketches for Procedures 2

and 4 should be labelled as shown in Fig. II-2-5 and Fig. II-2-6 respectively.

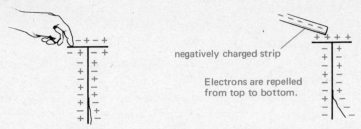

Fig. II–2–5   A neutral electroscope   Fig. II–2–6   Causing a separation of charges

PART C   OBSERVING THE SEPARATION OF CHARGES

16. Mount on 2 plastic rods 2 metal cans from which the labels have been removed. Support them in a vertical position *so that they are in contact* with each other. (See Fig. II-2-7.) Remove any charge on the cans by touching them with your hands.

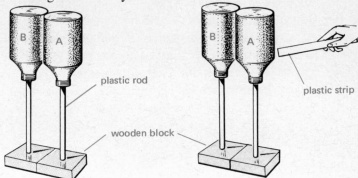

Fig. II–2–7   Neutral cans   Fig. II–2–8   Bringing a negatively charged strip close to can A

17. Give an electroscope a slight negative charge. (This charge will be used to test the nature of the charge on the cans in Procedure 19.)

18. Bring a negatively charged strip close to, *but not into contact with* can A. (See Fig. II-2-8.) Note that the charged strip is farther away from can B than it is from can A. While the strip is in this position separate the two cans. Do not allow your hands to touch the tins while you are separating them.

19. Use the electroscope to test first can A and then can B to determine the nature of any charge on them. Observe the electroscope closely since the effect may be slight.

Do both cans have the same charge? Account for any difference in terms of the movement of electrons. In what way is this effect similar to the effect observed when a charged strip was brought near the top

of an uncharged electroscope in Procedure 4? Why were the cans separated while the strip was still nearby? Why were the cans mounted on plastic rods?

Questions:

*1. Explain how you would charge a leaf type electroscope positively. negatively.

*2. Explain how you would use an electroscope to determine whether an object was positively charged or negatively charged.

*3. In terms of electron movement, describe what happens when a vinyl strip is rubbed with wool.

*4. In terms of electron movement, describe how an acetate strip becomes positively charged when rubbed with cotton.

*5. Is it possible to charge an object negatively by rubbing it without charging some other object positively? Explain. (Is your answer supported by your results in Procedure 5 of Experiment II-1?)

*6. The incomplete diagrams below represent two sequences of procedures which you carried out in the laboratory. The first diagram in each sequence represents a neutral electroscope (indicated by equal numbers of + and — symbols). Copy the diagrams in each sequence into your notebook and complete each one by

   (a) drawing the leaf as it would appear in each situation represented,

   (b) showing all of the resulting net charges,

   (c) using an arrow to indicate the direction in which electrons moved to produce or reduce net charges.

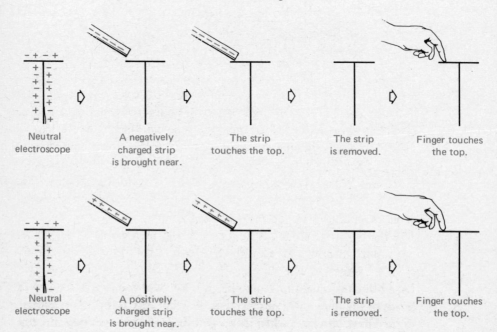

Neutral electroscope   A negatively charged strip is brought near.   The strip touches the top.   The strip is removed.   Finger touches the top.

Neutral electroscope   A positively charged strip is brought near.   The strip touches the top.   The strip is removed.   Finger touches the top.

*7. Explain in terms of electron movement why small pieces of paper are first attracted to and then repelled from a charged comb.

*8. What name is given to materials through which electrons are able to move easily? to materials through which electrons cannot move easily?

*9. In Experiment II-1 you observed that an electrically charged rod attracted neutral objects such as a meter stick. Use your knowledge of electron movement to explain why attraction occurred.

*10. When aircraft are refuelled, the metal nozzle of the hose is always connected to the metal of the plane by means of a conductor. Gasoline trucks drag a chain on the ground behind them. Explain the reasons for these safety precautions. (Hint: Do rubber tires conduct electrons?)

*11. If you walk on a rug on a dry cool day it is possible for a static charge to build up on your body. On touching a metal door knob under these circumstances you will probably feel a shock. How could you tell the sign of the charge you are carrying? Why would you not see a spark or feel a shock if you touched the wooden part of the door?

*12. What general name would you give to the material which separates the functioning part of an electroscope from its case? (See Fig. II-2-2.)

†13. Suggest the purpose of the outer metal case which surrounds the delicate leaf of an electroscope.

†14. Gold is much denser than other metals such as magnesium, aluminum, copper and iron. Why then are the leaves of a very sensitive electroscope usually made of gold?

References and Suggestions for Further Investigation:

1. A short description of the operation of a leaf type electroscope is given on pages 407-409 of *Physical Science, A Basic Course* by J. C. Hogg, J. B. Cross and K. E. Vordenberg (Toronto: D. Van Nostrand Co. Inc., 1959).

2. Use a reference book to find the cause of lightning. List a number of ways of protecting yourself from lightning when you are (a) indoors (b) outdoors. Why does thunder accompany lightning?

3. (a) Charge a leaf type electroscope negatively. Bring your finger to within 1 cm of the top of the electroscope. Does the electroscope discharge? Explain the observed behavior.

   (b) Place a lighted match close to but not touching a positively charged electroscope. Repeat, using a negatively charged electroscope. Does the result depend on whether the electroscope is positively or negatively charged?

   Hold a lighted match far enough away from a charged electroscope so that the latter will not discharge. Then fan the heated air gently toward the top of the electroscope. Do your experiments suggest that the electroscope discharges because the top is heated or because heating causes the air to become a conductor? Explain.

4. If a van de Graaf generator is available, carry out the following procedures.

(a) Ground the dome by touching it with a grounded conductor. Then bring a neutral pith ball into contact with the dome, holding it by means of an insulating thread. Then charge the dome and repeat the procedure.

(b) Charge the pith ball negatively by bringing it into contact with a charged vinylite rod. Then bring the pith ball near the charged dome. What is the nature of the charge on the dome?

(c) Set up a meter stick as shown in the diagram. Observe what happens when the generator is running. Replace the meter stick with a long metal rod from a support stand. Leave a larger gap at each end of the rod. Again turn on the generator. Observe the results.

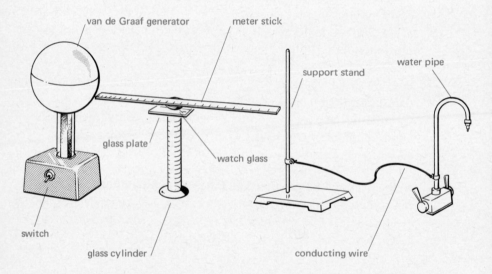

(d) Connect conducting wire to both terminals of a receptacle containing a neon glow lamp. Ground one of the wire ends and bring the other wire end near to the dome while the generator motor is running. Does the dome discharge to ground through the conducting wire?

(e) Ground the dome and place a thumb tack with its pointed end facing upward on top of it. Charge the dome. Use the neon glow lamp assembly to determine whether the dome becomes as charged as before. Investigate the use of pointed devices in lightning rods and electric precipitators. (The latter are often used in air conditioning systems to remove dust particles.)

5. Refer to a text book to find out how an electroscope can be charged by *induction*. Charging by induction eliminates the need for contact between the charged and uncharged objects. The technique is described in most physics reference books that discuss electrostatics. Pages 272-275 of *Basic Physics for Secondary Schools* by H. L. Eubank, J. M. Ramsay and L. A. Rickard (Toronto: MacMillan Co. of Canada Ltd., 1957) illustrate this technique in detail.

6. The electrophorus is an interesting device which you can make at home. It provides an almost continuous supply of electrostatic charge. Almost every reference book that discusses electrostatics describes this device.

II–3   A STEADY FLOW OF ELECTRONS

Electrons flow readily through electrical conductors such as metals but are almost unable to pass through electrical insulators such as plastic or porcelain. In other words, materials vary in their ability to conduct electrons.

You have observed that the charge on an electroscope is quickly lost when the electroscope is touched by a wire conductor held in your hand. Since both ends of the conductor quickly reached the same charge condition, the time during which electrons flowed through the conductor was very brief. If a steady flow of electrons is to be maintained through a wire conductor, a *difference in charge* must be maintained between the two ends of the conductor. Free electrons must be added continuously to one end of the conductor while electrons are being removed at the other end.

A dry cell is a device that will fulfill these requirements under normal operating conditions by having two terminals to which a conductor can be connected, one being a *source* of electrons and the other a *receiver* of electrons. The dry cell therefore *maintains* a small difference in charge between these two terminals.

In this experiment you will observe that a steady electron flow can be used to produce heat and light energy. You will also learn how dry cells should be connected.

After preliminary observations of the effects of steady electron flow, you will be presented with a model which will help you to visualize what takes place in a simple electrical circuit.

APPARATUS REQUIRED (per station)
Insulated copper wire
2 1.5 volt dry cells
electrical switch
3 volt flashlight bulb and receptacle

Procedure:

1. Examine a dry cell (or flashlight cell) and note the positions of the two terminals. These are usually marked + and –. (See Fig. II-3-1.)

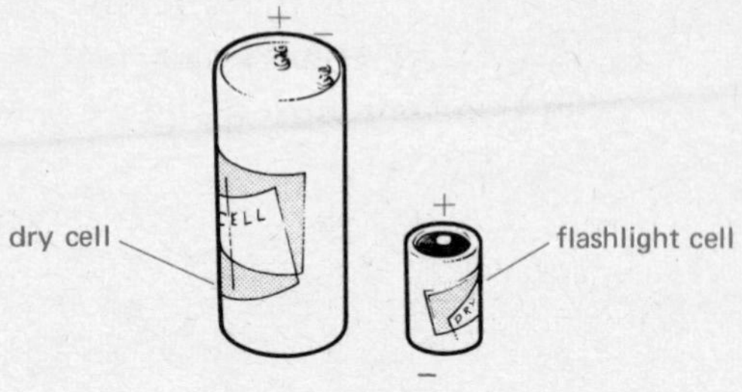

Fig. II–3–1 Dry cells

NOTE: The center terminal of a dry cell is called the positive terminal *and the outside terminal is called the* negative terminal. *However, to be accurate, all that can be truly said is that the center terminal is* more positive *or* less *negative than the outside terminal. Although the difference in charge between the terminals is generally constant, the actual charge on a terminal depends upon the circumstances.*

The symbol used for a dry cell in an electrical circuit is —|▌— *The long, thin line represents the positive terminal and the short, thick line represents the negative terminal.*

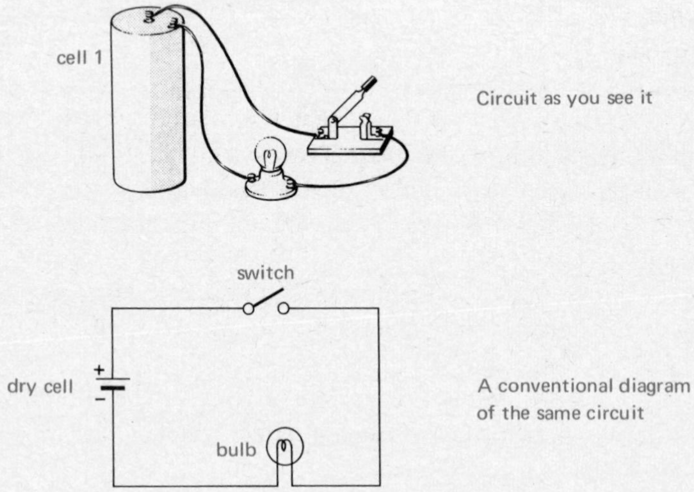

Fig. II–3–2 A circuit – an electrical path

2. Use the copper wire, electrical switch and flashlight bulb assembly to provide a conducting electrical path from the negative terminal of a dry cell to its positive terminal as shown in Fig. II-3-2.

NOTE: *A light bulb consists mainly of a short length of thin tungsten wire*
          surrounded by a chemically inactive gas encased in glass. (See Fig.
          II-3-3.)

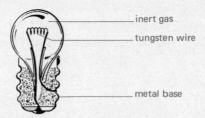

inert gas

tungsten wire

metal base

Fig. II–3–3   A light bulb

Close the switch to make the bulb glow and then open the switch.
Sketch the circuit in your notebook and record the result.
What kind of material covers the copper wire? What is its function?
What problem will result if some of the covering on the copper wire
is not removed from the ends and hence forms a part of the electrical
path?

3. With the switch open, disconnect the wire to the negative terminal
   of the cell used in Procedure 2 and connect this end to the negative
   terminal of a second cell (cell 2 in Fig. II-3-4). Before you close
   the switch, make a prediction. Will the electrons *flow* (from the
   source to the receiver)? Test your prediction by closing the switch.

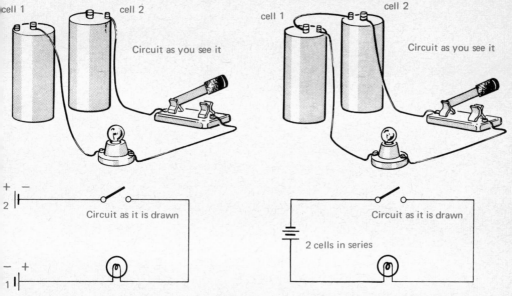

Fig. II–3–4   An open circuit   Fig. II–3–5   A circuit containing two cells in series

NOTE: *To prevent "burning out" bulbs which are intended for use with one*
          cell only, always be ready to open the switch in any circuit that
          causes a bulb to glow too brightly.

Will free electrons arrive at the positive terminal of a cell if its negative terminal is not simultaneously providing them? Will electrons move in the wire if the charges at its two ends are the same?

4. Open the switch again and connect negative terminal of cell 1 to the positive terminal of cell 2 as shown in Fig. II-3-5. Again close the switch briefly. Sketch the circuit and record the result.

NOTE: *When two or more cells are connected so that they function as a unit, the combination is called a* battery. *In Procedure 4 you formed a battery by connecting two cells in series. That is, the positive terminal of each cell was connected to the negative terminal of the other.*

5. Form a battery by connecting two cells *in parallel*. That is, join the positive terminals of both cells with one wire conductor and the negative terminals of both cells with another wire conductor. Then join the two wire conductors using the switch and lamp assembly as shown in Fig. II-3-6. Close the switch briefly.

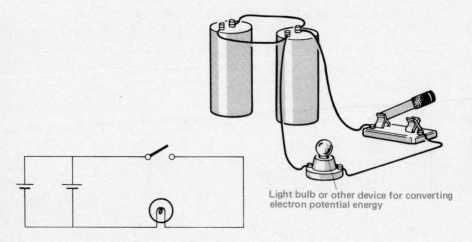

Light bulb or other device for converting electron potential energy

Fig. II–3–6   A circuit containing cells in parallel

Which battery produces the most heat and light in a bulb, two cells in series or two cells in parallel?

A Model To Help You Visualize What Has Taken Place:
When a conducting path, including a bulb, was provided from the negative terminal to the positive terminal of a dry cell, the light bulb glowed steadily. This glowing indicated two things:
(a) that there was a steady flow of electrons through the bulb, and
(b) that these electrons were releasing energy in the bulb in the forms of heat and light.

Where did this energy come from? How was the difference maintained between the electrical charges on the two terminals? Why must electrons be simultaneously received at the positive terminal if they are to flow from the negative terminal?

To account for these results consider the following model. When necessary, reference will be made to this model in later sections.

Suppose that inside each dry cell there lives a conscientious gremlin. This gremlin has the job of moving any "extra" electrons that arrive at the positive terminal to the negative terminal. (See Fig. II-3-7.) Because the electron is attracted to the positive terminal and repelled by the negative terminal, the gremlin must exert a force and do work to transfer each electron. By being so moved, each electron gains *potential energy*.

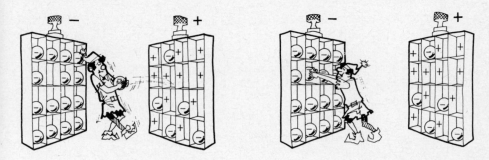

Fig. II–3–7   The gremlin takes electrons off the positive terminal and puts them onto the negative terminal.

When necessary, and provided he is healthy,(that is, the dry cell is new), the gremlin can work very quickly. However, by removing electrons from the positive terminal, he makes that terminal more positive and increases its force of attraction for electrons. At the same time, as he adds more electrons to the negative terminal, he makes that terminal more negative and hence increases its force of repulsion against electrons. Like you, the gremlin is limited in the size of the force he can exert. Unless charges are lost from the negative terminal and added to the positive terminal outside the cell, a point is reached when he is no longer able to transfer electrons and must stop doing work. Once the cell terminals have achieved their maximum difference in charge, the gremlin's job can be carried out only if
(1) electrons are removed from the negative terminal, and
(2) electrons are added to the positive terminal.

Although Fig. II-3-7 provides a more accurate description, it is more difficult to visualize than that given in Fig. II-3-8. In future diagrams we will show the gremlin working in the latter way since you are more familiar with gravitational potential energy. Imagine the gremlin doing a fixed amount of work on each electron by lifting it through a fixed distance. For the gremlin to give each electron potential energy, two requirements must be satisfied. A free electron must be available at the lower (positive) tube and a space available at the upper (negative) tube so that the gremlin can lift an electron and push it into the upper tube.

Fig. II–3–8   The supplier of potential energy in a cell

Consider the wire conductor. As you know, a solid conductor consists of fixed atoms whose outer boundaries are made up of electrons. Very few of the total number of electrons in a conductor are able to escape from their atoms. Only those that can escape can move through the conductor. Furthermore, in order to move in a given direction, each of these "free" electrons must
(1) be pushed (repelled) and/or pulled (attracted) in that direction, and
(2) have a space to move into.

As cars that are bumper to bumper on a highway, each electron moves only when the one in front of it has moved to provide space. Therefore, picture a wire conductor as a tube with "free" electrons inside it. Such a conductor is represented in Fig. II-3-9. (You already realize, however, that the diagram is an oversimplification of a conducting wire, since the "free" electrons which move make up only a very small portion of the wire.) Because air and the insulation on the wire are non-conductors, electrons cannot escape from the wire. Therefore, the conductor is shown to be surrounded by a region that they cannot enter. Usually very little of the potential energy possessed by electrons is lost in a good conductor such as the copper wire used in your experiments. Therefore, a good conductor is shown as a *horizontal* tube, as you will notice. A horizontal tube, then, indicates that there is no difference in the potential energy of the electrons between the two ends of the conductor.

Fig. II–3–9   A wire conductor surrounded by insulation (including air)

In contrast with the copper wire, the light bulb is a poor conductor. The bulb converts most of the potential energy possessed by each electron into energy in the forms of heat and light. The light bulb is therefore represented in the model as a vertical mechanical arrangement such as is shown in Fig. II-3-10.

Fig. II–3–10   The gremlin at work

Using The Model To Explain The Results Of Procedure 2:

A space is made available at the positive terminal each time the gremlin picks up an electron there, and each electron along the conductor is then pushed in turn, by repulsion, one space closer to the positive terminal. Thus, as each electron shifts one space toward the positive terminal, the gremlin is able to place the electron that he picked up onto the negative terminal. The electrons, pushing on the paddles of the vertical belt, cause the belt to move as they fall and so lose their potential energy to the belt. The gremlin works as fast as electrons and spaces are available; consequently, the entire process occurs at a steady rate.

The model which has been presented to you has a number of obvious flaws, not the least of which is the suggestion of a gremlin! However, it serves as a starting point. As you gain understanding, the model will be modified. Even the chemical nature of the gremlin will be revealed to some extent in Unit III. However, while applying the model, keep in mind that

1. electrons with potential energy have potential *electrical* energy rather than the potential mechanical energy suggested here. Therefore, when you are using the dry cell, it does not matter whether the cell is used sideways or up-side down. The energy stored by each electron is more like the energy stored in a compressed spring than that stored in an elevated mass.
2. the kinetic energy that results in the bulb is not kinetic mechanical energy as the model suggests but rather heat and light energy.
3. millions of electrons are simultaneously involved in the flow of electricity.

Using The Model To Explain The Results Of Procedures 3, 4 and 5:

In Procedure 3, the cells are connected as shown in Fig. II-3-11. No electrons are able to flow because neither of the gremlins in the two cells can complete his job – but for a different reason. One finds no free electrons at the positive terminal while the other finds no space at the negative terminal. The charge at the negative terminal of cell 2 and that at the positive terminal of cell 1 very quickly equalize when connected by a conductor (even a poor one).

In this case, the light bulb is unable to convert the potential energy of the electrons to heat and light.

Fig. II–3–11   An incomplete circuit

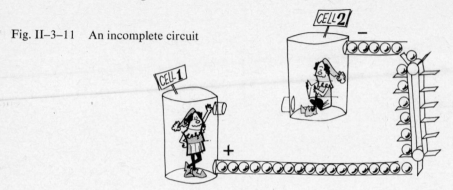

In Procedure 4, the cells are connected as shown in Fig. II-3-12. A good conductor joins the negative terminal of cell 1 to the positive terminal of cell 2. Therefore, these two terminals will very quickly reach the same energy level (and the same net charge). As a result, the gremlin in cell 2 lifts the electron to a still higher potential energy level. As spaces become available to allow movement, each electron on the paddles of the vertical belt will yield twice the energy that it would if only one cell were used.

Fig. II–3–12   A closed circuit with the cells in series

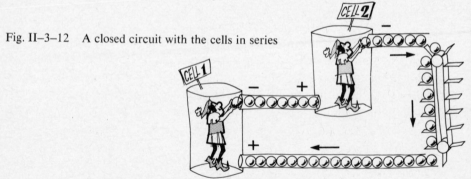

In Procedure 5, the cells were connected as shown in Fig. II-3-13. Each electron which moves onto the paddles of the vertical belt has the same energy as if one cell were used. However, there is an advantage to the gremlins, because using two cells in parallel requires that each gremlin work only *half as rapidly* as when his cell alone is used.

NOTE: *You should have noticed that the dry cells which you used are referred to as 1.5 volt dry cells. A volt is a unit which describes the amount of potential energy which a unit charge possesses. Thus, the 1.5 volt rating describes the amount of potential energy given to each of the charges by the gremlin in the cell. A battery consisting of two cells in series as in Fig. II-3-12 is a 3 volt battery; one consisting of two cells in parallel as in Fig. II-3-13 is a 1.5 volt battery.*

The term unit charge *may confuse you. It may refer to a charge equal to the charge on an electron. However, just as it is more convenient to measure eggs in dozens, it is often more convenient to group a large number of these smaller charges into a much larger unit of charge which is called a* coulomb. *One coulomb is 6.2 x 10[18] electron charges.*

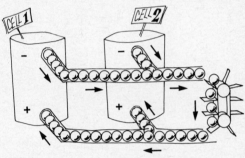

Fig. II–3–13   Two cells connected in parallel

Questions:

*1.(a) Draw the following arrangements of cells, wires, switch and bulb, using the conventional symbols shown in previous diagrams.

(b) Would four cells cause the light bulb to glow noticeably brighter than a single cell in case 1? in case 2?

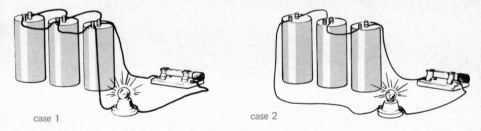

case 1   case 2

(c) Are the cells connected in series or in parallel in case 1? in case 2?

(d) What voltage does the battery provide in case 1? in case 2? (Use the model to help you to find the answer.)

*2. If you counted the number of charges passing a point along the wire before the light and at a point past the light *for the same length of time,* how would the numbers of charges compare?

†3.(a) In which case of Question 1 (a) will the rate of electron flow be greatest? Why?

(b) In which case will the potential energy lost by each electron be greatest? Why?

(c) Therefore, does increasing the voltage across a light bulb increase the amount of energy released in the light bulb?

†4. If you were provided with a very sensitive instrument to detect the rate of electron flow, how could you test to see if two cells produced the same voltage?

†5. Under what condition would two new cells in parallel produce a brighter light than a single new cell? (Hint: What limitation does a gremlin have?)

NOTE: *The history of current electricity is relatively recent. (A current is a flow of electrical charges.) It began somewhat by accident when Luigi Galvani (1737-1798) discovered that a dissected frog's leg twitched when probed by two unlike metals. By 1800 Alessandro Volta had determined the essential ingredients of a chemical cell and they were soon in common use.*

Surprisingly, the rules that govern the flow of electricity were known before the discovery of the electron in 1897. Because early workers could not actually observe the direction of the electric charges that flowed to produce a current, they had to make an assumption about it. Electric current was described as a flow of charges from the positive to the negative terminal of a cell. *(This is the direction in which the empty space moves in our model.)*

In liquids and gases it is common for positive particles to be moving in the direction of the current. When it was later discovered that the charged particle that moved in a solid conductor was the electron, a distinction had to be made between electrical current *and* electron flow.

The direction of electric current is from positive to negative.

The direction of electron flow is from negative to positive.

II-4   MEASURING CURRENT IN ELECTRICAL CIRCUITS

One of the advantages of any model is that it allows predictions to be made which can later be tested experimentally.

The model of a dry cell and electrical circuit introduced in the previous experiment suggests several things about the rate of flow of electric current in various parts of the circuits you examined. In this experiment you will be asked first to make predictions based on the model and then to determine experimentally whether the predictions are, in fact, correct.

You will require a meter which measures the current (opposite to the direction of electron flow). A meter is not a battery. It simply detects how much current there is while taking very little energy from the electrons. Meters are called *ammeters* (A) if they record in a unit called the *ampere,* and *milliammeters* (mA) if they record in thousandths of an ampere. The meter you will probably use allows a range of sensitivities so that both large and small currents can be measured accurately. Such a meter is called a multi-range meter. Because these meters can be easily damaged through care-less use, the following safety rules must be obeyed.

Notes on the Use of a Multi-Range Milliammeter:

1. Always begin by moving the dial to the largest setting, (1000 mA range on the meter in Fig. II-4-1). This is the least sensitive range and thus the range least likely to allow damage to the meter.

Fig. II–4–1   Multirange current meter

2. Never attempt to force the dial clockwise from the maximum setting or counter-clockwise from the minimum setting.
3. Always use the *brush technique* before making the final connection which closes the circuits. It should become a habit to brush the wire quickly over the terminal to which you intend to make the connection while observing what happens to the meter. This will tell you if:
   (a) there is too large a current, causing the needle to go beyond the scale, or
   (b) the meter connections are backwards, so that the needle is deflected in the wrong direction.
4. If after momentarily closing the circuit, the meter reads zero, check all connections and ensure that any bulbs in the circuit are screwed in. Then repeat the brush technique. If the meter shows more than a full scale deflection when it is on the largest setting, report it to your teacher. Such behavior indicates a damaged meter.
5. Always check the meter terminals before making connections. They will either be marked + or — or be color-coded. *Red means positive and black means negative.* If you start at the positive terminal of a cell and trace the electrical path you should arrive at the red terminal of the meter.
6. If the circuit is closed and it is found that a more sensitive scale is desirable, the dial should be turned one setting at a time until the most sensitive scale capable of accommodating the current is reached. Fig. II-4-1 shows a multi-range milliammeter with the dial set on the

100 mA (milliampere) range. With this setting, a needle deflection to the extreme right of the scale occurs when the current through the meter is 100 milliamperes.

When the dial is set at 5 mA, a needle deflection to the center of the dial indicates that there is a current of 2.5 mA through it.

APPARATUS REQUIRED (per station)
Two dry cells
3 volt bulb and receptacle
milliammeter
wire leads for circuit connections

Procedure:
1. Re-examine the model suggested for a dry cell, conductor and flash-light bulb as illustrated in Fig. II-3-10 on page 107. Predict how the current into the bulb will compare with the current out of the bulb.
2. Set up the circuit as shown in Fig. II-4-2. Test your prediction by placing the milliammeter in first one and then the other of the two positions shown. Record the current reading in each case.

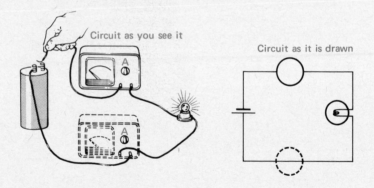

Fig. II–4–2   Is the current into the bulb equal to the current out of the bulb?

3. Re-examine the model for a circuit composed of two dry cells in series, wire conductors and a bulb as illustrated in Fig. II-3-12 on page 108 . Predict how the currents into the bulb, out of the bulb and between the two dry cells compare.
4. To test your prediction set up this circuit and place the milliammeter, in turn, in each of the three positions shown in Fig. II-4-3. Record the current readings.
   Does the addition of another dry cell in series increase the current through the bulb?

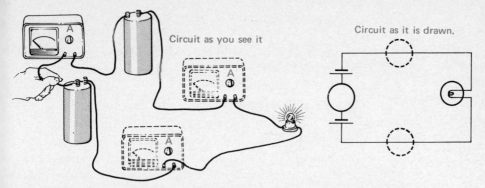

Fig. II–4–3   Is the current the same at all three positions of the meter?

†5. Re-examine the model for a circuit consisting of two dry cells in parallel, wire conductors and a bulb as illustrated in Fig. II-3-13 on page 109 . Predict how the currents will compare at the four positions of the milliammeter shown in Fig. II-4-4.

†6. Set up the circuit shown in Fig. II-4-4 to test your predictions. Record the current readings.

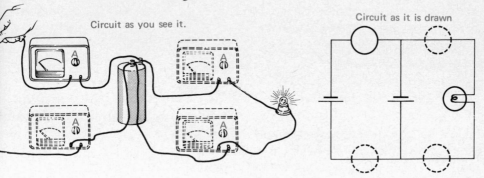

Fig. II–4–4   Is the current the same at all three positions of the meter?

Does the addition of another cell in parallel increase the current through the bulbs?

NOTE: *The meter offers a slight resistance to electric current; consequently, your results may not be exactly as you have predicted.*

Questions:
*1. When there is an electric current flowing in a circuit
 (a) what unit measures the current or rate of flow of charge?
 (b) what unit measures the available potential energy per electron charge?
*2. To describe various aspects of the flow of water through pipes, the following units might be used: gallons, gallons/minute, feet/minute, foot-pounds, foot-pounds/minute or foot-pounds/gallon.

(a) Which of the above units could be used to measure the current (rate of water flow), and is therefore comparable to the ampere?

(b) Which of the above units could be used to measure the potential energy per unit amount of water, and is therefore comparable to the volt?

*3. Milliammeters are placed in various parts of the electrical circuits shown below. The current measured at position 1 is 900 milliamperes and that measured at position 7 is 300 milliamperes. Assuming that all cells have equal voltage and that the meters offer no resistance to the current, what current will the other meters in the circuits measure?

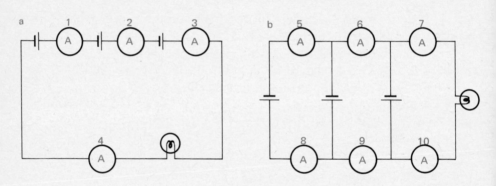

*4. Use a solid arrow (———→) to indicate the direction of the electric current in Questions 3(a) and 3(b). Use a broken arrow (←----) to indicate the direction of electron flow.

*5. Use the gremlin model to explain why the current in one part of the circuit shown in Question 3(a) cannot be greater than that in another part.

*6. In the circuit shown in Question 3(b), does any of the charge flowing from cell X enter cells Y or Z? (All cells have equal voltage.) Explain why or why not.

*7. Would the lamps in the circuits shown in Question 3 continue to emit light if the conductor were cut

(a) near position 1?

(b) near position 4?

(c) near position 5?

(d) near position 8?

†8.(a) If equally stretched springs together have a total of 240 foot-pounds of potential energy,

  (i) calculate the potential energy per spring.

  (ii) calculate the potential energy per dozen springs.

(b) Do both of these calculated values provide basically the same information?

(c) How is this fact related to the description of voltage given on
     page 108 ?

II-5   RELATIONSHIP BETWEEN CURRENT AND VOLTAGE FOR A CARBON RESISTOR

So far in your experiments with electricity you have learned
1. that the voltage applied "across" a bulb can be varied merely by increasing
   or decreasing the number of dry cells connected *in series.*
2. that the direction of the current in a circuit can be reversed by reversing the
   dry cell connections.
3. that when dry cells are connected in series the current into and out of each
   cell is the same and equal to that which the battery provides to the rest of
   the circuit.
4. that when dry cells are connected in parallel the current supplied by *each*
   cell may not be the same and is not equal to the current provided by the
   battery to the rest of the circuit.
      The voltage between two points, A and B, in an electrical circuit
is a measure of the potential energy of each unit charge that is converted to
some other form of energy while the charges move from A to B. (See Fig.
II-5-1.) If C is a point between A and B, then the voltage (potential energy
per unit charge) between C and B is less than that between A and B. In the
model shown in Fig. II-5-1, the difference in the potential energy of electrons
between point C and point B would be about half that between point A and
point B.

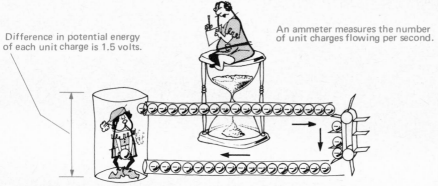

Difference in potential energy
of each unit charge is 1.5 volts.

An ammeter measures the number
of unit charges flowing per second.

Fig. II–5–1   A drop in potential energy across one resistor

      The part of an electrical circuit in which most of the potential
energy of unit charges is lost, such as a light bulb, toaster or radio tube,

is called a *resistor*. Such a device offers resistance to the electric current and in so doing limits the current. Electrical resistance is measured in units called *ohms*. In this experiment you will determine how current (amperes), potential energy per unit charge (volts) and electrical resistance (ohms) are related.

APPARATUS REQUIRED (per station)

Milliammeter
a selection of at least 4 carbon resistors in the 100 to 2,000 ohm range
4 dry cells
insulated wire leads
voltmeter (if available)

NOTE: *Radio manufacturers' colors codes for resistors:*

Color: Black Brown Red Orange Yellow Green Blue Violet Grey White
Number
Value: 0   1   2   3   4   5   6   7   8   9

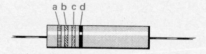

a b c d

Fig. II–5–2   A carbon resistor

Using the Code:

The first and second rings (a and b in Fig. II-5-2) represent the first and second digits respectively of the resistance value. The third ring (c in Fig. II-5-2) represents the number of zeros which follow the first two digits. The fourth ring (d in Fig. II-5-2) gives the tolerance of the resistance value given.

No marking means	± 20%
Silver means	± 10%
Gold means	± 5%

Suppose a, b, c and d on the diagram are red, brown, yellow and silver. Then the resistance of the resistor would be within 10% of 210,000 ohms. That is, the manufacturer has stated that the resistance of the resistor is greater than 189,000 ohms and less than 231,000 ohms.

Procedure:

NOTE: *If a voltmeter is not available for each station, it will be necessary to use dry cells of very nearly identical voltages. You can check to see if cells indeed produce the same voltage by connecting them "back to back" with a milliammeter as shown in Fig. II-5-3. If there is any significant current, the cell voltages are too unequal and another cell should be tried.*

CAUTION: *Remember that milliammeters are very sensitive. Always use the*
           brush technique to ensure that the meters deflect in the right direction
           and that they do not deflect too far.

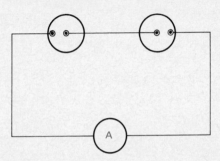

Fig. II–5–3   Finding whether cells are of equal voltage

1. Select the highest range on the milliammeter and use the brush technique as you connect a milliammeter, dry cell and 1,000 ohm resistor
   (or another resistor between 100 and 2,000 ohms), in the electrical
   circuit shown in Fig. II-5-4. Note that the symbol for an electrical
   resistance is a zig-zag line. If a voltmeter is available, connect it
   "across" the carbon resistor as indicated. (Use the brush technique.)
   (The maximum voltage obtainable from one dry cell is 1.5 volts.)
   Record your results in a table with these headings: RESISTANCE USED
   (OHMS); NUMBER OF CELLS OR VOLTAGE (VOLTS); CURRENT (MILLI-
   AMPERES).

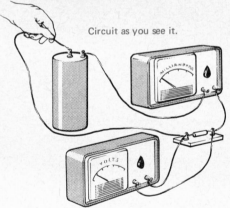

Circuit as you see it.

Circuit as it is drawn

1,000 ohms

Fig. II–5–4   A circuit with a single resistor

2. Repeat Procedure 1 using batteries of 2, 3 and then 4 dry cells connected in series. The last circuit is shown in Fig. II-5-5. If a voltmeter is not available for each station, use dry cells whose voltages
   are nearly equal to that used in Procedure 1. (See the note at the
   beginning of the Procedure.) If identical cells are used, assume the

voltage of each to be 1.5 volts. Therefore, when 2, 3 and 4 such cells are connected in series, their total voltage output will be 3, 4.5 and 6 volts respectively.

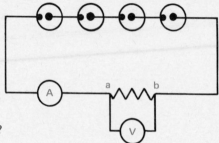

Fig. II–5–5   What is the effect of
               increasing the voltage?

3. For the rest of the time available, repeat Procedures 1 and 2 using other resistors with considerably different resistances but still in the range between 100 and 2,000 ohms.

4. For each resistor used, plot a graph of the current in milliamperes (x-axis) against voltage in volts (y-axis). Use only one set of axes, and join all points that were obtained from the same resistance. Label each of the lines on your graph according to the resistance it describes. Another point for each graph line can be obtained by answering the question, "What is the current when the voltage is zero?"

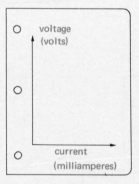

Fig. II–5–6   Arrangement of axes

In general, what do your graphs tell you about the relationship between current and voltage for a given resistance? about the relationship between current and resistance for a given voltage?

†5. (For students of mathematics.) Use your graph to determine what current there would be through each resistor if the difference in potential across the resistor were 5 volts. You have learned in your mathematics courses that the slope of a graph line is found by dividing the vertical charge between two points on the graph line by the horizontal change between the same two points. For example, in

Fig. II-5-7, the vertical change between the two points O and A is 6 volts and the horizontal change between O and A is 10 mA. Therefore, by definition, the slope is 6 volts ÷ 10 milliamperes = 0.6 volts/milliampere or 6 volts ÷ 0.010 ampere = 600 volts/ampere. (1 milliampere = 0.001 ampere.) Find the slope of each of the graph lines obtained in Procedure 5 in volts/ampere.

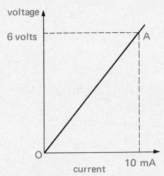

Fig. II–5–7   Determining the slope of a graph

How does the slope of your graph in volts/ampere compare with the stated (color code) resistance of the resistor used in each case? Does your answer suggest that voltage ÷ current (in amperes) = resistance in ohms? For a given resistance, what happens to the current when the voltage is doubled?

Questions:

For Questions 1 to 4, recall the model of the gremlin in the cell.

*1. For a given battery, would you expect an increase in the value of the resistance to change the voltage of the battery? Does it? If so, in what way?

*2. For a given battery, does an increase in the resistance change the current through the resistor? If so, in what way?

*3. For a given battery, does an increase in the resistance change the rate at which electrical energy is converted to other forms of energy in the circuit? If so, in what way?

*4. Does the resistance of an electrical resistor depend on the voltage applied to it or the current through it? Try to give a reason for your answer.

†5. The voltage across a resistor is often called the voltage drop or potential drop, since electrons lose potential energy as they flow through a resistor. Since the voltage drop "across" a resistor measures the loss of potential energy by each unit charge as it passes through the resistor, and amperage measures the number of unit charges flowing through a given resistor per second, what would the product or voltage and amperage be a measure of?

NOTE: *Ohm's Law states that:*

$$Current\ in\ amperes\ =\ \frac{voltage\ in\ volts}{resistance\ in\ ohms}$$

or, if conventional symbols are used: $I = \dfrac{V}{R}$

As you know from your mathematics, such equations can be written in three ways, e.g., $V = IR.$

†6. Rearrange the symbols to express Ohm's Law in a third way.

†7. Use Ohm's Law to answer the following questions.

   (a) What current is there in a circuit when a voltage drop of 2 volts is maintained across a 6 ohm resistor?

   (b) What voltage is required to send a current of 3 amperes through a 4 ohm resistor?

   (c) What is the resistance of a lamp filament which draws a current of 0.5 amperes at a potential difference of 120 volts?

   (d) When the current is 0.060 amperes through a radio resistor, the voltage drop across the resistor is found to be 12 volts. What is its resistance?

   (e) A 12 volt storage battery supplies a current of 48,000 milliamperes when the starting motor in a car is turned on. What is the resistance of the starting motor?

††8. Two dry cells, A and B, are connected in series in a circuit with a resistor and an ammeter. The ammeter reads 2 amperes. When the terminals of B are reversed so that the cells are "back to back," the ammeter reads 0.40 amperes. If the voltage of cell B is 1.0 volt, find the voltage of cell A. Draw a circuit diagram to represent each of the two situations described.

References and Suggestions for Further Investigation:

1. Almost every basic physics textbook devotes a few pages to the discussion of Ohm's Law. Examples are pages 287-288 of *Basic Physics for Secondary Schools* by H. L. Eubank, J. M. Ramsay and L. A. Rickard (Toronto: MacMillan Co. of Canada Ltd., 1957), and pages 503-505 of *Physics, a Basic Science* by F. L. Verwiebe, G. E. Van Hooft and R. R. Suchy (Toronto, Van Nostrand Co. Inc., 1962).

II-6   SERIES AND PARALLEL CIRCUITS

The previous experiment showed that a definite relationship exists between the current and the voltage for a circuit containing a single resistor whose resistance is independent of the direction of the current. This relationship is known as Ohm's Law. Although Ohm's Law describes this relationship for a single resistance, it cannot always be used directly to determine the total effect of several resistances in a single circuit.

Several resistors are often used simultaneously in electrical circuits. In such cases, resistors can be connected in either of two circuit patterns. In one pattern, where the resistors are said to be connected *in series* with each other, the circuit is formed by connecting two or more resistors across a voltage source so as to form *only one path* for the current. In the other pattern, where the resistors are said to be *in parallel* with each other, the current is formed by connecting at least two resistors across a voltage source so that the current has as many paths as there are resistors.

Connection of resistors to form series and parallel circuits will be illustrated in this experiment. It will be your job to determine what effect the arrangement of the resistors has on the current-voltage relationship you observed in the previous experiment.

APPARATUS REQUIRED (per station)
Milliammeter
voltmeter (if available)
2 dry cells
wire lead
2 1,000 ohm resistors
2 2,000 ohm resistors or their equivalent

NOTE: *It will be easier to perform this experiment if wire leads equipped with alligator clips are available.*

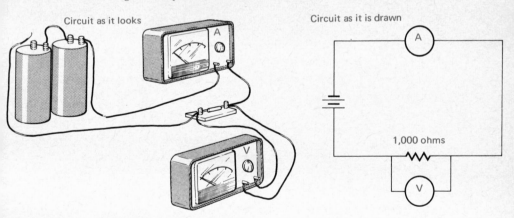

Fig. II–6–1   Measuring current and voltage in a circuit containing one resistor

Procedure:
1. Using the brush technique, complete a circuit containing a 1,000 ohm resistor, a milliammeter and two dry cells in series as indicated in Fig. II-6-1. Connect the voltmeter as shown in the figure. (If a volt-

meter is not available you will have to assume that each dry cell pro-
duces a voltage of 1.5 volts.) Record the current and voltage readings.
**How do the currents into and out of the resistor compare? (Recall
Experiment II-4.)**

2. Repeat Procedure 1 using a 2,000 ohm resistor.
**What is the effect on the current and on the voltage of doubling the
resistance?**

3. Repeat Procedure 1 using two 1,000 ohm resistors connected in
series as illustrated in Fig. II-6-2. Record the current value and the
voltage drop (V_1) across the first resistor (R_1). Next move the voltmeter so that it reads first the voltage drop (V_2) across the second
resistor (R_2) and then the voltage drop (V_3) across both resistors.
**How do the voltage drops V_1 and V_2 compare when resistances of
equal value are used (that is, when $R_1 = R_2$)? How do the voltage
drops across R_1 and R_2 compare with the total voltage drop across
$R_1 + R_2$?** Now move the milliammeter to the other position shown in
Fig. II-6-2.

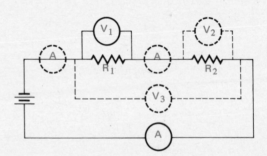

Fig. II–6–2   Two resistors in series

**How do the current values in the different parts of the circuit com-
pare with each other? How do they compare with the values obtained
when a single 1,000 ohm and a single 2,000 ohm resistor were used
in Procedures 1 and 2 respectively?**

4. Repeat Procedure 3 with the two 1,000 ohm resistors connected in
parallel as shown in Fig. II-6-3. Determine the voltage drop (V_1)
across the first resistor and then move the voltmeter to measure the
voltage drop (V_2) across the second resistor. Then move the milliammeter in turn to each of the three other positions shown in the
diagram. Record the current for each position.
**How does the voltage drop V_1 compare with the voltage drop V_2?
How do the voltage drops V_1 and V_2 compare with the voltage of the**

battery? How do the currents compare in the two paths provided by the two resistors? How does the current through each resistor compare with that through the 1,000 ohm resistor in Procedure 1? Does the sum of the currents through the two resistances equal the current at position 3? position 6?

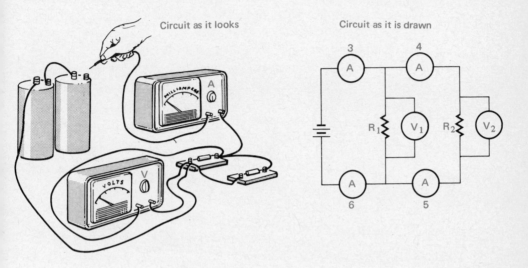

Fig. II–6–3   Two resistors in parallel

†5. If there is time, repeat Procedures 3 and 4 using two 2,000 ohm resistors and answer the same questions. In addition, make comparisons of the currents with the current through the single 2,000 ohm resistor of Procedure 2.

NOTE: The effective *resistance of a series or of a parallel arrangement of resistors is given by the ratio of the voltage of the battery and the current through the battery, $(R = V/I)$.*

In general, when several resistors are connected (a) in series, (b) in parallel, is the resulting effective resistance greater than or less than the resistance of only one of these resistors?

†6. Repeat Procedures 3 and 4 using a 1,000 ohm resistor and a 2,000 ohm resistor connected first in series and then in parallel with each other.

How do the voltage drops V_1 and V_2 compare when resistances of unequal value are connected in series? in parallel? In each case is the current through each resistance the same as it was when the single resistance was used, as in Procedures 1 and 2?

††7. Repeat Procedure 4 using 3 equal resistances in parallel.

NOTE: It is possible to use the model which was introduced in Experiment
         II-3 to illustrate the behavior of resistors connected in series and
         in parallel with each other. Fig. II-6-4 shows two unequal resistors
         in series. Remember that neither current nor voltage affects the value
         of a resistance. The diagram shows that the smaller resistance R_1
         converts less of each electron's potential energy than does the larger
         resistance R_2. Together the two resistors convert almost all of the
         electron's potential energy in the same way as the single light bulb
         did in Experiment II-3. If a third resistor (R_3) were added in series
         with the first two resistors, the potential energy lost by each electron
         in R_1 and R_2 would immediately become less. Together, then, several
         resistors in series behave like a single resistor whose resistance is
         equal in value to the sum of the individual resistances.

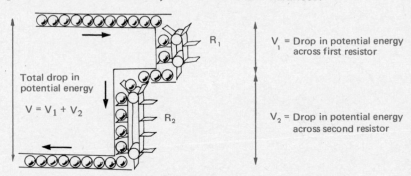

Fig. II–6–4   A potential drop across the two resistors is the sum of the individual
               potential drops.

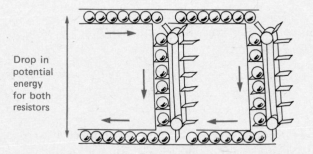

Fig. II–6–5   The drop in potential is the same across both resistors.

The two resistors in parallel shown in Fig. II-6-5 need not
be of equal resistance. If they are not, the one with the lower resistance allows a larger current through it than the other. Resistors in
parallel behave just as they would if they were by themselves — provided the gremlin is able to keep up with the extra work that is involved. As additional resistors are connected in parallel to produce
more electrical paths, the current from the battery increases.

Questions:

*1. How many conducting paths are there in a circuit consisting of
   (a) three resistors connected in series with each other?
   (b) three resistors connected in parallel with each other?

*2. There is a limit to the voltage provided by a dry cell. The energy gained by an electron (the voltage) in the cell is lost in the resistors of the circuit. How is this voltage drop distributed across two resistors when
   (a) they are of equal resistance and are connected in series with each other?
   (b) they are of equal resistance and are connected in parallel with each other?

*3. For the same voltage drop, what change in current occurs when a single resistance is replaced by two equal resistors that are connected (a) in series, (b) in parallel with each other?

*4.(a) What electrical quantity remains the same in all parts of a series circuit?
   (b) What electrical quantity remains the same across all resistors in a parallel circuit?

*5. Cheaper types of Christmas tree lights are connected so that when one bulb burns out the entire string goes out. Are these bulbs connected in series or in parallel with each other?

*6. Are the appliances in your home connected in series or in parallel with each other? Give evidence to support your answer.

*7. If too many appliances (resistors) are used simultaneously in one circuit in your home, what is the result?

*8. How is the effective resistance of a circuit with a series arrangement of resistors calculated?

*9. In a parallel circuit, which quantity remains constant for all resistors? Which quantity varies according to the branch of the circuit you are testing?

†10. Draw a series circuit which contains a dry cell, a switch, a 1 ohm resistor, a 2 ohm resistor, a 3 ohm resistor and an ammeter. Use Ohm's Law and the facts you have just learned to calculate the following:
   (a) the effective resistance in the circuit,
   (b) the total current through the circuit,
   (c) the current through each resistance in the circuit,
   (d) the voltage drop across each resistance in the circuit.

†11. Draw an electrical circuit which contains a 1 ohm resistor, a 2 ohm resistor and a 3 ohm resistor connected in parallel with each other. Include a dry cell, switch and ammeter in your circuit. Use Ohm's

Law and the facts you have just learned to calculate the following:

(a) the voltage drop across each resistance in the circuit,

(b) the current through each resistance in the circuit,

(c) the total current through the circuit,

(d) the effective resistance of the circuit.

†12. Eight small electric lamps of equal resistance are connected in series to form a string of Christmas tree lights. The voltage across all of them together is 120 volts and the current is 1 ampere. Draw a diagram of this circuit and then find:

(a) the effective resistance of all the lamps taken together,

(b) the resistance of each lamp,

(c) the voltage drop across each lamp.

†13. Four appliances of resistance 50 ohms, 60 ohms, 100 ohms and 300 ohms respectively, are connected in parallel. Draw a diagram of this circuit. If the voltage across the parallel network is 120 volts, find:

(a) the voltage drop across each appliance,

(b) the current through each appliance,

(c) the total current through the circuit,

(d) the effective resistance of the circuit, that is, the current through the voltage source.

After the 100 ohm appliance has been disconnected, determine whether any of the answers you calculated above have changed. If they have, calculate their new values.

References and Suggestions for Further Investigation:

1. Pages 419-422 of *Physical Science, A Basic Course* by J. C. Hogg, J. B. Cross and K. E. Vordenberg (Toronto: D. Van Nostrand Co. Inc., 1959), as well as pages 288-291 of *Basic Physics for Secondary Schools*, by H. L. Eubank, J. M. Ramsay and L. A. Rickard (Toronto: Macmillan Co. of Canada Ltd., 1957), examine both the theory and applications of series and parallel circuits.

2. Ammeters and voltmeters both employ galvanometers. The moving coil of the galvanometer is connected in parallel with a very low resistance "shunt" in an ammeter and in series with a high resistance in a voltmeter. Use a reference book to determine how these meters are wired internally. Draw a schematic diagram of the internal structure of a galvanometer, an ammeter and a voltmeter to show how and where any internal resistance is connected.

3. Compare the behavior of a selenium rectifier with that of a carbon resistor by measuring the current through the rectifier first in one direction and then in the other. Use the method of Procedure 1 of Experiment II-6.

II – 7   HOUSEHOLD CIRCUITS (Demonstration)

Many people do not realize the danger which accompanies the 120 volts of electrical energy per unit charge that is used in their home.

If a person's body becomes the only resistance in a circuit in which there is a 120 volt drop in potential energy, there is little chance of his survival. This voltage is sufficient to produce a current large enough to be fatal. In fact, the recovery of heart action from an electric shock at this voltage is less rapid than at much higher voltages.

For this reason, you should never operate an electrical appliance near a bath tub or metallic plumbing. Contact with such plumbing (directly or via a conducting liquid such as tap water) while touching even one of the wires from a wall plug is frequently fatal. For this reason, changes made in household wiring are inspected by city officials to ensure that the wiring and the locations of outlets are safe.

Pairs of wire bringing electrical energy into your home have a potential *difference* of 120 volts. This fact by itself does not indicate the size of the charge on either wire. For example, the wires could have the dangerous charge potentials, relative to the Earth, of 2,000 volts and 2,120 volts respectively, providing the difference of 120 volts. In order to prevent the dangerous accumulation of such charges on the wires, one of the wires is connected to "ground" and so always has the same electrical potential (0 volts) as ground. This grounding means that it has the same net charge as the deep moist section below the surface of the Earth. Consequently, if you touch both this wire and some plumbing there is no effect. Since the voltage provided by hydro electric generators continuously reverses itself, the second wire alternately reaches a maximum of +120 volts and a minimum of −120 volts. Thus, a maximum difference of 120 volts is maintained between this second wire and the grounded wire. The second wire is comonly called the "hot" wire and as we have mentioned, contact with this wire and ground can be fatal. The cycle of voltage alternation is repeated exactly 60 times per second. Unless the frequency of the change is carefully controlled, electric clocks will not keep the correct time.

Up to now we have described only two of the wires that bring electrical energy into your home. In fact there are three wires. One of them has the charge of "ground" while the other two are "hot." At the extremes of voltage in the cycle, one of the "hot" wires will be a +120 volts and the other will be at −120 volts relative to ground.

Thus, by connecting the two "hot" wires to an electric range, a maximum voltage of 240 volts can be obtained. For normal household circuits, however, the grounded wire and one of the "hot" wires are used.

Various kinds of protective devices are required in electrical circuits. Household circuits generally contain plug fuses, cartridge fuses, circuit breakers or a combination of these devices to prevent an "overload" that may result in fire. In this experiment you will examine some of these safety devices.

APPARATUS REQUIRED (per class)

> *A test lamp made from a weatherproof standard socket and a 6 watt lamp*
>
> *insulated 120 volt circuit wire*
>
> *10 3 "volt"* bulbs mounted in miniature receptacles*
>
> *bare copper wire to connect the receptacles together in parallel*
>
> *3 new dry cells*
>
> *6 wire leads with alligator clips*
>
> *5 ampere range ammeter*
>
> *voltmeter*
>
> *4 1 ampere 125 volt cartridge fuses (must be straight wire such as Buss AGC 1)*
>
> *circuit breaker (if available)*
>
> *plug fuse*
>
> *(Optional: 10 6 "volt" bulbs)*

*Small bulbs are often described in terms of the most suitable voltage at which they can be used.

Procedure:

PART A   FINDING THE "HOT" WIRE

CAUTION: The bare ends of the wire leads to the test lamp should be exposed for less than about 3 mm so that it is impossible for the hands to contact bare wire when the lamp is being inserted into a wall plug. Do not use a bulb with a rating higher than 6 watts.

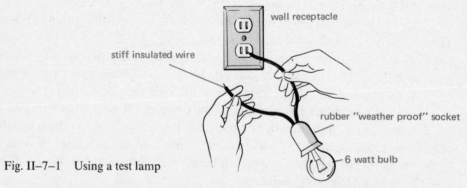

Fig. II–7–1   Using a test lamp

1. To determine the brightness of a 6 watt lamp in a 120 volt circuit, hold the insulated socket of a test lamp in one hand, and the insulated portions of the wires to the lamp in the other, and insert the wire ends into the two openings of a standard electrical outlet. DO NOT TOUCH THE BARE WIRE ENDS. (See Fig. II-7-1.)

2. To locate which of the terminals inside the electrical outlet is connected to the "hot" wire, repeat Procedure 1, but this time, insert
only one test lamp wire end into each opening, in turn, of the electrical outlet. Each time, bring the other test lamp wire into contact
with the bare end of an insulated wire which is connected to a water
or gas pipe. (See Fig. II-7-2.)

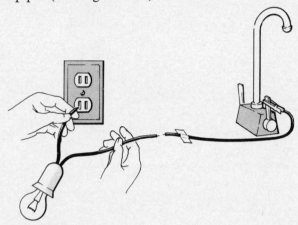

Fig. II–7–2   Which is the "hot" terminal?

**When the test lamp formed a part of the circuit from the "hot" wire
to ground, did the lamp burn as brightly as it did in Procedure 1?
What would happen if you accidentally touched only the hot wire
in a household circuit? Does your answer depend on whether or not
another part of your body is in contact with a conductor to ground?**

NOTE: *When making any minor repairs to electrical fixtures in your home,
it is essential that you stop all electrical energy flowing to the fixture.
This can be done by opening either the main switch controlling the
energy to all circuits or a circuit breaker switch in the circuit for that
particular fixture.*

PART B   SAFETY DEVICES

3. Connect ten lamp receptacles in parallel by wrapping one turn of a
length of bare copper wire around each terminal screw, in turn, and
then tightening the screw. (See Fig. II-7-3.) Then insert a 3 "volt"
light bulb loosely into each receptacle so it *does not make contact*
with the base terminal. Connect a 5 ampere range ammeter, a 1 ampere cartridge fuse, a voltmeter and the 10 lamps to a battery of 2
new dry cells in series as shown in Fig. II-7-3. You now have a
circuit that can be used to examine electrical overloads.
4. Screw in each bulb in turn and record the current and voltage readings as each bulb forms a path in the circuit.

How many bulbs were connected before the fuse opened the circuit? What is the maximum current which the fuse was able to accommodate? What finally happened to the fuse wire? Is the voltage measured by the voltmeter constant? If not, try to explain why in terms of the gremlin model.

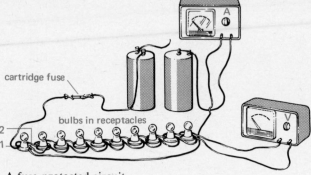

cartridge fuse

bulbs in receptacles

2

1

Fig. II–7–3   A fuse-protected circuit

NOTE: *Previously, you learned that the voltage across a resistor is a measure of the energy released* by each unit of charge *as it passes through the resistor, and that the amperage is a measure of* the number of unit charges *flowing through the resistor per second. Thus the product of voltage and amperage is a measure of the* rate *at which energy is used in a resistor.*

When there is a current of 1 ampere and a potential difference of 1 volt, the rate *at which electrical energy is used is called* 1 watt. *Therefore:*

1 volt $\times$ 1 ampere = 1 watt

In order to determine the total amount of energy used, the time of use as well as the rate of use must be considered. Hence:

volts $\times$ amperes $\times$ time in hours = watt-hours

(1 kilowatt-hour = 1,000 watt-hours)

5. Calculate the wattage delivered to the circuit (Procedure 4) just before the fuse wire melted.

6. Unscrew all of the bulbs except one and replace the fuse. Use a length of conducting wire with bare ends to connect the two terminals of one of the receptacles from which the bulb has been removed. For example, positions 1 and 2 on Fig. II-7-3 can be connected with the wire.
    What happens to the fuse when a short circuit occurs?

NOTE: *When a resistance in an electrical circuit is by-passed by means of a good conductor, the result is called a* short circuit.

7. Replace the fuse and repeat Procedure 4, this time using a battery of 3 new dry cells connected in series.

This time, how many bulbs were connected before the fuse wire melted? What was the maximum current the fuse was able to accommodate? Calculate the wattage delivered to this circuit just before the fuse wire melted.

†8. Repeat Procedure 4 using 6 "volt" bulbs in place of the 3 "volt" bulbs. **How did the voltage readings across these bulbs compare with those across the 3 "volt" bulbs? How do the maximum current and wattage values compare in these two cases? At the same voltage, does a 6 "volt" bulb release energy at a greater rate than a 3 "volt" bulb?**

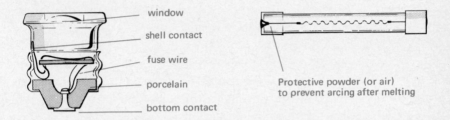

window

shell contact

fuse wire

porcelain

bottom contact

Protective powder (or air)
to prevent arcing after melting

Fig. II–7–4   A commercial 15 ampere fuse   Fig. II–7–5   A cartridge fuse

9. Various electrical protective devices are sold commercially. Some examples are plug fuses (Fig. II-7-4), cartridge fuses (Fig. II-7-5) and circuit breakers (Fig. II-7-6). Examine samples of these devices if they are available. The type of circuit breaker shown in Fig. II-7-6 operates when the bimetallic strip is overheated by too much current through it. The advantage of this device is that it can be reset merely by pressing a button or flicking a switch. Another type of circuit breaker, one which operates with the aid of an electromagnet, is not shown.

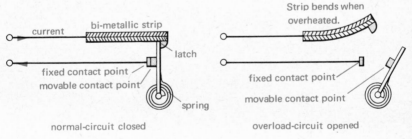

Strip bends when overheated.

bi-metallic strip

current

latch

fixed contact point

movable contact point

spring

normal-circuit closed

fixed contact point

movable contact point

overload-circuit opened

Fig. II–7–6   Operation of a circuit breaker

NOTE: *A homeowner purchases electrical energy. In order to measure the energy he uses, a meter is installed and read every two months. The unit used to measure the electrical energy consumed is the kilowatt-hour.*

Questions:

*1. Using a faulty electrical power tool, a workman drills holes in a wooden floor. While he is drilling, he steps on a drain pipe and receives an electrical shock. Why did he not receive an electrical shock before stepping on the drain pipe?

*2. Explain why, for a given electrical resistance in your body, it is current and not voltage that causes death.

*3. List two conditions that can cause an electrical circuit to become "overloaded."

*4. What is meant by the phrase "short circuit"? Give an example of a situation that may result in a short circuit. Is the effective resistance of a short circuit large or small?

†5. Some electrical plugs such as those attached to electric washing machines, refrigerators and drills have two flat prongs and one round prong. The latter is connected to the metal surrounding the appliance. Assign appropriate voltages to each of the three prongs. What is the purpose of the round prong?

†6. The diagram below shows that the wiring in a toaster is connected to a 3-prong plug. What is the purpose of the prong labelled 3?

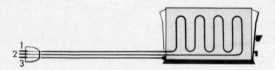

†7. What does the word fuse mean? (Use your dictionary if necessary.) Why then are some protective electrical devices called fuses? You have probably heard the expression, "the fuse has blown." Does an explosion accompany this event? Explain.

Additional Questions Pertaining to Electricity Used in Homes:

*1. Most standard household circuits contain a 15 ampere fuse.
 (a) What is the voltage in an ordinary household circuit?
 (b) Therefore, how many watts of electrical power can be delivered by such circuits before a 15 ampere fuse will melt?

*2.(a) Are household circuits connected in series or in parallel with each other? Give a reason for your answer.
 (b) Do you expect a 1,500 watt electric kettle and a 1,000 watt toaster to operate simultaneously when they are connected into a circuit that contains a 15 ampere fuse? Explain.

*3. An electric heater draws 5 amperes of current from a standard 120 volt electrical outlet.

ELECTRICITY AND MAGNETISM

(a) How much electrical power is required to operate this heater?

(b) How much electrical energy must be provided to operate the heater for five hours? Express your answer in watt-hours and in kilowatt-hours.

*4. Assuming that each of the following devices is connected to a standard household circuit, complete the following table.

APPLIANCE	CURRENT (AMPERES)	VOLTAGE (VOLTS)	POWER (WATTS)	TIME/DAY (HOURS)	ENERGY/DAY (WATT-HOURS)
light bulb	1			10.0	
hot water heater	15.00			5.0	
stereo hi-fi	2.50			3⅓	
toaster	10.00			.5	

Total Energy = ——— w.h. per day.

(a) How many kilowatt-hours of electrical energy must be supplied to operate all of the above devices *each day* for the times specified?

(b) Calculate the total cost of operating these devices for a day assuming that electrical energy costs 2¢ per kilowatt-hour.

*5. Complete the following table and then answer the questions which follow:

APPLIANCE	POWER CONSUMPTION OF APPLIANCE (WATTS)	TIME USED PER DAY (HOURS)	ENERGY USED PER DAY (WATT-HOURS)
electric clock	4	24	96 (100 approx.)
6 light bulbs	100 × 6 = 600	5	
electric iron	1,100	1	
electric range	4,000 (estimated avg.)	2	
automatic washer	600 " "	1	
automatic dryer	5,600	1	
television	200	5	
vacuum cleaner	800	1	
dishwasher	1,800	1	

Total energy/day = ——— w.h.

(a) Express the total energy which must be delivered to these appliances per day in kilowatt-hours.

(b) The cost of electricity varies according to the amount used. Meters are usually read every two months. Use the following sliding scale to determine the cost of operating the above devices for 60 days.

1st 600 K.w.h. cost 3¢ per K.w.h.
the rest cost 1.1¢ per K.w.h.

†6. One type of overhead projector bulb is rated at 600 watts. It has an estimated lifetime of 25 hours. How much electrical energy must be delivered to this bulb? Each bulb costs $14.25 and electrical energy costs 3¢ per kilowatt hour. What is the total cost per hour of operating the electrical system of an overhead projector? (Neglect the small amount of energy delivered to the cooling fan but include the cost of the bulbs.)

†7.(a) Because an electric stove draws a large amount of electrical energy, it is connected in a separate circuit. This circuit is doubly protected by two 40 ampere circuit breakers in parallel with each other. These breakers will "trip" when the power consumption of the stove exceeds 9.6 kilowatts. What is the operating voltage for an electric stove?

   (b) If you have an electric stove, locate and examine the wires that supply electricity to it. Describe what precaution has been taken to protect and isolate these higher voltage wires.

References and Suggestions for Further Investigation:

1. Read the meter which measures the amount of electrical energy you use in your house. After two days, read the meter again. Phone the electrical power authority in your area to ask the price of electrical energy in your locality. Then calculate your consumption of electricity for the two-day period and, from this, the cost of the energy used.

2. Examine the supply wires to each of the major electrical appliances in your house. Which appliances obtain energy through a cable that has a metallic flexi-shield around it? Such cables are essential when the wires carry 240 volts instead of the normal 120 volts. Which appliances in your home operate at a voltage of 240 volts? Suggest two reasons for the use of a metallic flexi-shield around higher voltage wires or wires that carry large currents in homes.

3. Household wiring, protective electrical devices and electrical power are topics discussed briefly on pages 317-322 of *Physical Science for Progress* by M. O. Pella and A. G. Wood (Englewood Cliffs, N.J.: Prentice-Hall Inc., 1964).

II-8   PROPERTIES OF MAGNETS

You are no doubt already aware of many of the properties of magnets. Did you know, however, that magnets are required to operate most of the electrical equipment found in your home? Telephones, electric motors and generators, television sets, radios, stereo phonographs and cars all require magnets in order to function.

Since the turn of the century, little has been added to our knowledge of the basic principles which govern magnetism. In fact, it was not until very recently that amazing discoveries were made in this branch of physics. For example, small crystals have been produced with fantastic magnetic strengths.

You must be able to understand the principles that govern the behavior of magnets before proceeding to more interesting problems and applications. In this experiment you will study the behavior of a bar of metal which, after being magnetized, has retained its magnetism.

APPARATUS AND MATERIALS REQUIRED (per station)
>*Two permanent bar magnets*
>*stiff copper wire*
>*single strand nylon thread*
>*support stand*
>*burette clamp*
>*magnetic compass*
>*masking tape*
>*samples of glass, plastics, soft iron, aluminum, wood, copper, chalk, nickel*

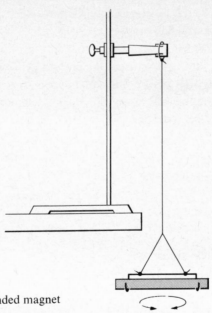

Fig. II–8–1   Horizontally suspended magnet

Procedure:
1. Using a length of thread and a cradle made from stiff copper wire, suspend a permanent bar magnet horizontally as shown in Fig. II-8-1.

The cradle should be below the level of the table. Gently rotate the magnet and note the position it takes when it comes to rest. (To save time, slow the swing with your finger.)

Can you suggest a useful application of the property which you have observed?

2. A small permanent magnet mounted on a low friction pivot inside a non-magnetic case is called a magnetic compass. Place a magnetic compass on a table away from magnetic materials and note the position its needle takes.

How does its position compare with that of the suspended magnet in Procedure 1?

3. If the suspended magnet is not already so labelled, tape its ends and mark the *north-seeking* end N and the *south-seeking* end S. If the magnet is already labelled, ensure that it is labelled correctly. Then remove the bar magnet from the cradle and replace it with another similar one. If necessary mark its ends N and S according to the geographical directions in which the ends point.

4. Hold the first magnet with its north-seeking end directed towards the suspended magnet and, in turn, approach the latter from various directions.

How does the suspended magnet respond? Which direction of approach produces the greatest effect and which the least effect on the suspended magnet?

5. Repeat Procedure 4 but with the magnet reversed in your hand so that the south-seeking end points toward the suspended magnet.

Which of the ends of the magnet in your hand seems to have the greater effect on the suspended magnet? What differences do you observe between the actions of the two ends?

†6. Test to see whether the suspended magnet is attracted to various materials such as glass, plastic, soft iron, aluminum, wood, copper, chalk, nickel (coin) and silver (coin).

†7. Test to see whether the effect of two magnets on each other is altered when one of the materials used in Procedure 6 is placed between them.

Questions:

*1. How many magnetic regions does a permanent bar magnet have? Each of these regions is called a pole. What would be suitable names for these poles?

*2. Write down a set of rules that describes the influence of the poles of one magnet on the poles of another.

*3. In a given location a suspended magnet tends to point always in the same direction. What does this fact tell us about the nature of our Earth?

*4. In the diagram below, the large circle represents the Earth. The north and south *geographic* poles are shown. The smaller circles represent magnetic compasses whose north and south-seeking poles are labelled N and S respectively. Copy this diagram into your notebook. Imagine a huge bar magnet stretching along the Earth's axis from the North Magnetic pole to the South Magnetic pole. Draw this imaginary object on your Earth model. Use your knowledge of magnetism to label the poles of this magnet correctly. Do you notice an apparent discrepancy that results? How can you resolve this problem? What decided which pole of your suspended magnet was labelled N when you named the pole?

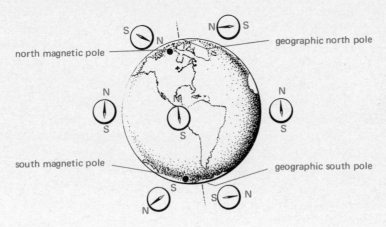

*5. When talking about magnets, some people use the phrase north pole, others, the phrase north-seeking pole. Which phrase do you think is more accurate? Why?

†6. You are given two pieces of iron which look alike in every respect. However, one piece is a strong magnet and the other is an unmagnetized piece of soft iron. Explain how you would determine which piece is the magnet.

II-9 PROPERTIES OF MAGNETS: COMPARISON WITH ELECTROSTATIC CHARGES

Recall Experiment II-1 in which you produced electrostatic charges by rubbing. You found that you could not charge conducting materials by this method; however, it would have been possible if they had been insulated. This statement is confirmed by the fact that cars and aircraft which are separated from the ground by insulating materials frequently develop electrostatic charges. *All* materials can be given electrostatic charge because they are composed of atoms that contain electrically charged particles.

In Experiment II-1 you also observed that charged objects attracted several different kinds of materials such as wood and tap water. In fact, all materials are attracted by charged objects.

In this experiment you will further investigate the magnetic properties of various materials so that you will be able to distinguish clearly between magnetism and electrostatic charges. You will answer these questions:
1. Can all materials be magnetized?
2. How do materials become magnets?
3. How can magnets become demagnetized?
4. Can a N-pole exist without a S-pole?
5. What is the source of magnetic properties?

APPARATUS REQUIRED (per station)
> *2 bar magnets*
> *watch glass*
> *meter stick*
> *a straightened paper clip*
> *magnetic compass*
> *bunsen burner and gas lighter*
> *soft iron bar*
> *handful of ½ in. finishing nails*
> *screwdriver blade*
> (per class)
> *hammer*
> *cutting pliers*
> *magnetizer (if available)*
> *support stand base*

NOTE: *A relatively inexpensive commercial magnetizer with an automatic circuit breaker will enable students to remagnetize weak magnets when necessary.*

Procedure:
1. Balance a meter stick on a watch glass as in Procedure 6 of Experiment II-1 and bring a magnet near each end of the meter stick in turn. **Is the meter stick attracted by the magnet? Was it attracted by electrically charged plastic strips?**
2. Replace the meter stick with an iron bar and repeat the procedure. **Describe the effect of the magnet on each end of the iron bar.**
3. Bring a straightened, unmagnetized paper clip near both ends of a magnetic compass. **Are both ends of the compass attracted? repelled?**
4. Rub the straightened paper clip across a permanent bar magnet sev-

eral times, but always in the same direction, as shown in Fig. II-9-1. Use the magnetic compass to determine whether the wire has become permanently magnetized.

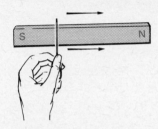

Fig. II–9–1   Stroking a paperclip

How will a permanently magnetized wire differ from an unmagnetized one?

5. Repeat Procedure 4, but this time stroke the paper clip towards the other pole of your permanent magnet.
   Does the direction of rubbing make any difference?

6. Sketch the paper clip and label its polarity. Attach a piece of masking tape marked N to the north-seeking pole of the paper clip and one marked S to the south-seeking pole. Then, using a pair of cutting pliers, cut the wire in half. Retest the polarity of the two halves and again make a labelled sketch of your observations after cutting.

7. If necessary, remagnetize one of the halves by stroking it as in Procedure 4 and then use crucible tongs to hold it in a bunsen burner flame. As soon as the paper clip has become red hot, remove it from the bunsen flame. Continue to hold it in the crucible tongs until it is cool. Then retest the wire to see if it is still magnetized.
   Does heating affect a magnet's strength?

8. Magnetize the blade of a screwdriver using the technique of Procedure 4. Place this magnetized end in a small pile of ½ in finishing nails and count the nails you can pick up. Now place the screwdriver blade flat on a hard surface (for example, a support stand base) and strike it several times with a hammer. Retest the magnetic strength of the blade by counting how many nails it will pick up.
   What happens to the magnetic strength of the steel blade when it is struck?

9. Test the strength of each of two bar magnets by counting how many small nails each can lift. Now hold the magnets together so that like poles are adjacent. Test this combination of magnets to find how many nails it will lift. Next reverse one magnet so that N and S poles are adjacent. Test the strength of this combination.
   Which arrangement produces the greatest magnetic strength? the least?

10. Dip a soft iron bar into a large pile of ½ in finishing nails. How many can you pick up? Now hold the soft iron near the pile of nails and bring a permanent magnet *near* the free end of the bar as shown in Fig. II-9-2.

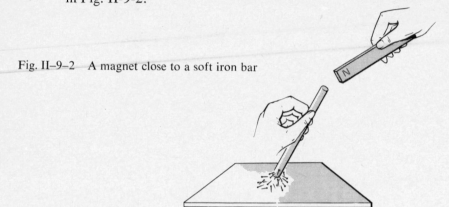

Fig. II–9–2   A magnet close to a soft iron bar

What difference do you observe?

11. Now hold the magnet against the free end of the bar.
    Is there any change in the ability of the bar to pick up nails?

12 With the magnet touching the bar, use the bar to pick up as many nails as possible. Hold the bar over the table and then remove the permanent magnet.
    Does the soft iron bar retain all of its magnetism? some of its magnetism?

Questions:

*1. Distinguish between electrostatic charge and magnetism by answering the following questions.
    (a) Can all materials be magnetized?
    (b) Can all materials be given an electrostatic charge?
    (c) List one way in which materials can be magnetized.
    (d) List one way in which materials can be electrostatically charged.
    (e) List two ways by which magnets can be demagnetized.
    (f) List one way by which a charged metal rod can be discharged.
    (g) Is it possible to separate the N and S poles of a magnet so that you have an object with only one pole?
    (h) Is it possible to separate a positive charge from a negative charge?

*2. Try to suggest a reason why dropping or heating a magnet causes the magnet to lose its magnetism. (Hint: What effect does the absorption of heat energy have on the molecules in an object?)

*3.(a) Suggest a reason why dropping a permanent magnet causes it to lose some of its magnetism. In what way is this effect similar to the effect caused by heating an object?

(b) Therefore, what do you suspect must be involved in magnetizing or demagnetizing a steel bar?

*4.(a) Try to give a reason why cutting a magnet into four pieces produces four complete magnets.

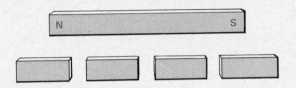

(b) The magnet shown in the diagram is broken into pieces. Label the poles of these small magnets.

*5.(a) Can you remove an electrostatic charge from an iron bar by touching it? Why or why not?

(b) Can you remove the magnetism of an object by touching it? Why or why not?

*6.(a) List as many magnetic materials as possible. Refer to a book to increase your list.

(b) Are all of the materials in your list elements?

†7. Suppose you had a very large number of identical magnets. What would the total effect of these magnets probably be if you laid them haphazardly in a pile without regard to the directions of the poles? What would be the effect if you carefully arranged them so that their north poles all pointed in the same direction?

†8. Suppose that elements with magnetic properties have atoms that are themselves small magnets. If so, how does a magnetized bar differ from an unmagnetized one? Use a sketch to show the difference.

†9. Use the idea suggested in Questions 7 and 8 to give an explanation of why steel tends to retain its magnetism more permanently than softer, almost pure iron. (Steel is iron containing a small percentage of carbon and other metals.)

†10. Sketch the diagram above and label the magnetic poles induced in each nail shown.

†11. In Canada, iron pipes usually become magnetized when they are driven into the ground. What magnetic pole would the upper end of the pipe become? the lower end? Explain. (Hint: The Earth's North Magnetic Pole is located about 1,800 miles below the crust of the Earth at the Boothia Peninsula in the Northwest Territories.)

References and Suggestions for Further Investigation:
1. Pages 295-299 of *Physical Science for Progress* by M. O. Pella and A. G. Wood (Englewood Cliffs, N.J.: Prentice-Hall Inc., 1964), present a simplified explanation of why some materials display magnetic properties and some do not. An atomic description is used to explain many of the activities in Experiment II-9.

II–10   PROPERTIES OF MAGNETS: DIRECTION OF MAGNETIC FIELDS
(May be demonstrated)

In Experiment II-8 you noticed that the effect of a magnet on another magnetic material is greatest at the poles and that it decreases as the magnetic material is moved farther away from the magnet. When an object is affected by a magnet we say the object is in the *magnetic field* of that magnet. Using this term we can rephrase the opening sentence as follows: the strength of the magnetic field around a magnet is greatest at the poles and it diminishes as we move away from the poles.

One further point must be made. The magnetic field that is created by a magnet causes other magnets, such as compasses, to point in a particular direction. When placed at a point in a magnetic field, the compass can be made to line up in *only one direction*. This direction is different at different points in the magnetic field.

In this experiment you will examine the direction of a magnetic field in different locations by observing the alignment of tiny iron filings which become magnetized in the magnetic field of a bar magnet, or alternatively, by observing the direction of a compass needle in the magnetic field.

APPARATUS REQUIRED (per station)
2 bar magnets
a U-shaped magnet
an unmagnetized block of iron about 2 cm × 2 cm × 0.5 cm
iron filings or magnetic compass
sheet of transparent plastic
(per class)
overhead projector

large non-magnetic pneumatic trough
a large darning needle
a cork.

NOTE: These exercises can be effectively demonstrated on an overhead pro-
       jector.

Procedure:
1. Place a sheet of paper or plastic over a bar magnet. Sprinkle iron
   filings onto the sheet and then tap it gently. Sketch the directions in
   which the tiny filings line up.
   **Why do the filings tend to form lines? (Hint: What happens when
   iron is placed in a magnetic field?) Does the direction of each line
   tell you the direction of the magnetic field in that region? Explain.**

NOTE: *The results of this experiment can also be obtained using a magnetic
       compass instead of the iron filings. Place the magnetic compass in
       turn at various locations about the magnet. Use a small arrow to
       denote the direction of the compass needle (let the arrow head
       represent the N pole). Then sketch the direction of the magnetic field
       in various locations about the magnet using the arrows that you have
       drawn as direction guides.*

2. Sketch the magnetic field lines for several different arrangements of
   magnets. Use arrows to show the general direction taken by the filings. Five suggestions are illustrated in Fig. II-10-1.

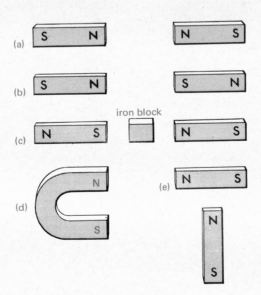

Fig. II–10–1   Possible magnet arrangements

3. (Demonstration) Place a bar magnet on the bottom of a non-magnetic container, and cover it with about three inches of water. Induce an N pole on the blunt end of a large darning needle by rubbing it on a permanent magnet as you did in Experiment II-9. Push the needle through a piece of cork so that the *north-seeking magnetic pole points downwards*. Place the cork (N pole in the water), on the surface of the water as shown in Fig. II-10-2. Release it and observe its path of travel. Repeat the procedure by releasing the cork from various positions above the magnet.

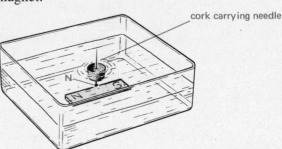

cork carrying needle

Fig. II–10–2   A free moving
                "N pole"

Does the needle move in a straight line directly toward the S pole in all cases? What path does it follow when it is released at different locations around the N pole of the bar magnet? How do these paths compare with the lines formed by the iron filings in Procedure 1?

NOTE: *It is convenient to imagine that lines of force exist around a magnet. A magnetic line of force is a line which marks the path along which a "free N pole" will travel as it leaves the N pole and moves toward the S pole. The end of the needle submerged in the water behaves like an imaginary free N pole. Of course, you have already discovered in Experiment II-9 that an N pole is always accompanied by an S pole.*

4. Use arrows to mark the path of travel of the free N pole along the "lines of force" on the diagrams you drew in Procedures 1 and 2 of this experiment.

Questions:
*1. Define a magnetic line of force.
*2. Examine the sketches which you made. Did the lines in your diagrams ever cross? (They shouldn't.)
*3.(a) When you sprinkled iron filings over the U-magnet, did they tend to concentrate in the region between the poles?
   (b) Did the filings tend to concentrate where the magnetic field is strongest?
   (c) Why does a horseshoe magnet have more lifting power than a bar magnet of the same size?

*4. Define a magnetic field.

*5. Sketch the magnetic field of the Earth on a diagram similar to that shown in Question 4 of Experiment II-8. Use lines to represent the Earth's magnetic lines of force.

†6. The N pole of a weak magnet is found to repel the N pole of a compass needle but the N pole of a strong magnet is found to attract it. Try to account for this apparently unusual behavior.

References and Suggestions for Further Investigation:

1. How does the pull exerted by a bar magnet vary along its length? If you have a meter stick, masking tape, half-inch finishing nails and an empty tin you will be able to answer this question after a short experiment. Tape the bar magnet to a meter stick as indicated in the diagram. Then hang half-inch finishing nails from the magnet until the nail chain cannot be made any longer.

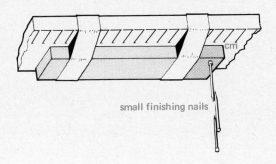

small finishing nails

Record the number of nails suspended from each position and the distance of that position from the end of the magnet. Repeat this procedure for about fifteen positions, two of which should be the very ends of the magnet. (Hint: To obtain good results, choose about five positions within 2.5 cm of each end of the magnet. Also, shake the nails in a metal container before using them in a different position on the magnet.) Plot a graph: distance from one end of the magnet (x-axis) versus the number of nails lifted (y-axis). Draw a smooth curve through your data points. Is the magnet strongest at the very ends? Why is it important to shake the nails in a tin before reusing them?

2. Look up the geographic locations of the Earth's North Magnetic Pole and South Magnetic Pole. (See "Terrestrial magnetism" in the Encyclopaedia Britannica.)

3. Pages 394-398 of *Physical Science, a Basic Course* by J. C. Hogg, J. B. Cross and K. E. Vordenberg (Toronto: D. Van Nostrand Co. Inc., 1959), present a summary of most of the characteristics of magnets and magnetic fields that you have examined in these experiments.

II–11   MAGNETIC EFFECTS OF AN ELECTRIC CURRENT
(Demonstration and Student Activity)

Although Alessandro Volta had devised a means of maintaining an electric current in 1800, it was not until 1820 that Hans Oersted discovered that a magnetic compass needle deflected when placed beside a current-carrying wire. This discovery, which at first seemed to be a simple one, has made modern industry possible.

The following experiments will show you something about the relationship between electrical and magnetic phenomena. The name given to this field of study is electromagnetism.

NOTE: *Teachers may prefer to demonstrate Procedures 2 to 5 using a transparent compass and an overhead projector, and a heavy copper wire mounted in a transparent plastic base.*

APPARATUS REQUIRED (per station)
  Small magnetic compass
  75 cm of stiff copper wire
  2 wire leads with alligator clips
  (per class)
  2 dry cells or a power supply that provides 10 amperes at 6 volts
  cardboard square
  ring clamp
  fine iron filings
  2 support stands
  2 burette clamps
  3 meters of #22 stranded and insulated copper wire
  strong U-shaped magnet

Fig. II–11–1   The action of a magnetic compass in a region near an electric current

Procedure:

1. Repeat Oersted's discovery by placing a compass beside a copper wire and *very briefly* passing an electric current through the wire. (See Fig. II-11-1.)

NOTE: *When a good conductor directly connects the positive and negative*
terminal of a dry cell, the cell is said to be shorted. (How must the
gremlin perform in this situation?)

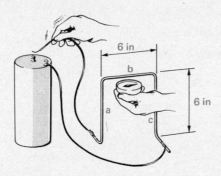

Fig. II–11–2   Determining the directions of magnetic lines of force near a current-
carrying wire

**What do you think caused the magnetic compass needle to deflect?
What term is used to describe the region in which the influence of a
magnet may be detected? (Review Experiment II-10.)**

2. Bend some stiff copper wire to form an upright square like that shown
in Fig. II-11-2. Clean the ends of this heavier wire so that good connections can be made between it and the wire leads. Place a dry cell in
the circuit, but leave the end of one wire disconnected except during
brief periods while making observations.

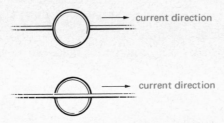

Fig. II–11–3   Compass above and below a current-conducting wire

       Hold a compass near the horizontal section of wire "b" as
shown in the diagram, first above and then below it. Each time, close
the circuit just long enough to determine the direction the compass
needle takes. Make two sketches such as those in Fig. II-11-3 showing
the wire conductor with the compass above it and then below it. Indicate the direction of the electric *current* and use an arrow head to
represent the N pole of the compass needle in the diagram.
**What does the direction of the compass needle indicate about the
direction of the magnetic lines of force around the conducting wire?
(Review Experiment II-10.) Are the lines of force in the direction of
the wire? at right angles to the wire? in some other direction?**

3. Repeat Procedure 2 after reversing the direction of the current by reversing the connections at the dry cell.
Are the results you obtained the same as those in Procedure 2? Explain.

4. Now hold the compass horizontally beside the vertical wire "a." Close the circuit briefly while observing the compass needle. Repeat this procedure several times, holding the·compass in a different position on a horizontal circle around the wire each time.

Sketch the vertical wire as in Fig. II-11-4 and show the compass in several positions around it. Indicate on your sketch whether the current travels up or down the wire and label the N pole of the compass needle in each position.

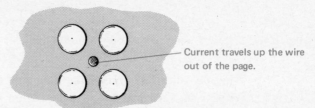

Fig. II–11–4   Compass in four horizontal positions around a current-carrying wire

Is the compass needle deflected in the same direction in every position around the vertical wire? Can you make a statement that describes the behavior of the compass under these circumstances?

5. Repeat Procedure 4 with the compass moving in a horizontal circle about vertical wire "c" in Fig. II-11-2. Sketch and label your observations as before.
How does the direction of the electric current through "c" compare with its direction through "a"? Does the current direction have any effect on the direction of the magnetic field around the wire?

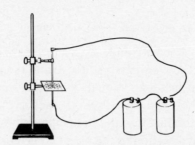

Fig. II–11–5   Mapping the lines of force around a current-carrying wire

†6. (Demonstration) Run a length of copper wire vertically through the center of a horizontal cardboard square which is supported by a ring clamp. (See Fig. II-11-5.) Sprinkle a light coating of fine iron filings

evenly on the cardboard around the wire. Use a battery of two dry
cells in series or a power supply that provides a direct current of 10
amperes at 6 volts , as shown in Fig. II-11-5.

Very briefly close the circuit while simultaneously tapping
the cardboard lightly with a pen so that the filings form a pattern.
Draw a diagram of this pattern. Include an end view of the vertical
wire in your diagram.

†7. (Demonstration) String a length of light, insulated, stranded copper
wire between two vertical support stands that have been placed about
2 meters apart as shown in Fig. II-11-6. The wire should sag slightly
so that it can swing freely. Connect a 3.0 volt battery (or a 6 volt, 10
ampere power supply) to one end of the wire. Hold a strong U magnet
so that it faces upward and so that the wire is centered between its
poles. Then momentarily close the circuit. With the magnet still
facing upwards, reverse the positions of its poles and again close the
circuit momentarily.

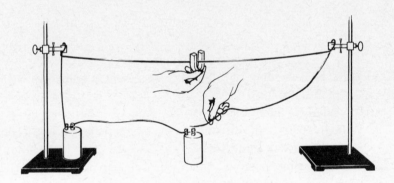

Fig. II–11–6   Interaction between a U-magnet and a current-carrying wire

NOTE: *RULES WHICH DESCRIBE THE PROPERTIES OF LINES OF*
FORCE:
  – Lines of force never cross.
  – Lines of force with the same direction tend to spread and separate
  from each other.
  – Lines of force tend to shorten if possible and thus behave like
  stretched elastic bands.
A "RULE OF THUMB" FOR PREDICTING THE DIRECTION
OF THE MAGNETIC FIELD OF A CURRENT-CARRYING
WIRE:
Imagine placing your right *hand* over the current-carrying wire with
thumb outstretched so that your thumb points in the direction of the

current. *Then imagine closing your fingers around the wire. Your fingers will then point in the direction of the lines of force.*

Questions:

*1. Two bar magnets with a compass between them are shown in the diagram. Ends X and Y of the bar magnets attract each other. The N pole of the compass faces X.

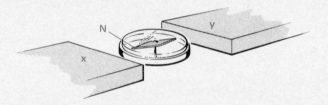

   (a) Sketch the lines of force between X and Y using arrows to show their direction.
   (b) What is the polarity of end X? of end Y?

*2. What happens to the direction of the magnetic field about a conductor when the current is reversed?

*3. The following diagram shows compasses in four positions around a vertical conductor. Sketch the diagram and draw in the lines of force which are causing each compass needle to behave as illustrated. Mark their direction.

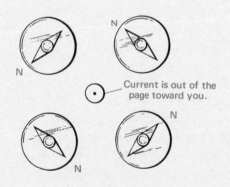

*4. A compass needle is shown under a current-carrying wire in the following diagram. Below the diagram, the same wire and compass are shown in cross-section as they would be seen when viewed from the left of the upper diagram. On the end view diagram, sketch the direction of the lines of force that cause the compass to assume this direction. Use your experimental results to indicate the direction of the current on both the top view and end view drawings.

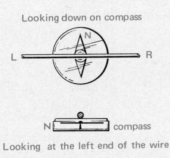

Looking down on compass

L ————————— R

N [========] compass

Looking at the left end of the wire

†5.(a) Sketch the three diagrams below in your notebook. Then use arrows to label the directions of the lines of force between the poles of the magnet in diagram (a).

(a) Lines of force about a U - magnet

(c) End view of wire conductor
     with current away from you

(b)

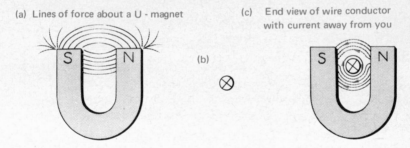

(b) The magnetic lines of force about a current-carrying wire form concentric circles. If you look at the end of such a wire when the current is *directed away from you*, the direction of these lines of force will be clockwise about the wire. Diagram (b) shows an end view of a conductor in which the current direction is away from you. Draw the lines of force about this conductor and label their direction.

(c) If a current-carrying wire and a permanent magnet are brought close to each other, their magnetic fields will interact. Such a situation has been illustrated in diagram (c) by combining diagrams (a) and (b). What feature of the lines of force shown will help you to predict that the wire will be forced upward?

(d) Name two changes you could make, each of which would cause the wire to move in the opposite direction.

(e) Sketch the shape and direction of the interacting magnetic fields when one of the changes you suggested has been made.

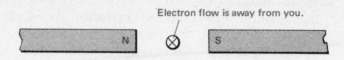

Electron flow is away from you.

††6. In which direction will the current-carrying wire in the above diagram be forced? To support your explanation, show the combined magnetic fields on the diagram.

†7. Test the "right hand" rule as stated following Procedure 7 by using it to predict the results which you obtained in Procedures 2, 3, 4 and 5 and those described in Questions 3, 4 and 5(b).

References and Suggestions for Further Investigation:

1. J. C. Hogg, J. B. Cross and K. E. Vordenberg discuss the magnetic effects of current-carrying wires on pages 399-400 of *Physical Science, a Basic Course* (Toronto: D. Van Nostrand Co. Inc., 1959).

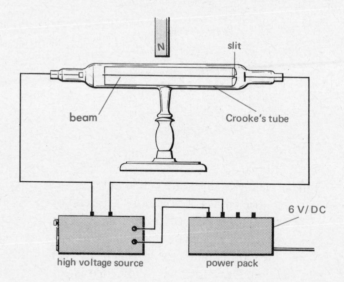

2. Cause an electric discharge across a laboratory Crookes's tube and observe the effect of electrons striking the fluorescent screen. (This effect is duplicated on your television set.) If necessary, reverse the leads to obtain a narrow beam. (See the diagram above.) OPEN THE CIRCUIT TO THE HIGH VOLTAGE SOURCE BEFORE CHANGING ANY CONNECTIONS. If a cathode ray tube is not available, a student model cathode ray tube may be substituted.

The light path which you see on the fluorescent screen is not the electrons themselves but the effect that these elctrons produce when they strike the fluorescent material. Nevertheless, the light path enables you to see the direction taken by the electrons.

Approach the electron beam with a magnet held perpendicular to the path of the electrons as in the previous circuit diagram. With the N pole leading, approach the tube first from above and then from the front. Repeat with the S pole facing the tube. Under what circumstances are the electrons deflected downward? upward? toward the screen? away from the screen? Do the free electrons move in the direction of the magnetic field or at right angles to the magnetic field? This experiment shows that it is the moving electrical charges in a current-carrying wire that produce the magnetic field around the wire. It also demonstrates why the Earth's magnetic field is capable of deflecting charged particles from space away from the Earth, thus protecting its inhabitants.

3. Some practical applications of cathode ray tubes are illustrated and discussed by H. L. Eubank, J. M. Ramsay and L. A. Rickard on pages 389-391 of their book *Basic Physics for Secondary Schools* (Toronto: Macmillan Co. of Canada Ltd., 1957).

II–12   MAGNETIC EFFECTS OF A CURRENT-CARRYING SOLENOID (Demonstration and Student Activity)

A straight current-conducting wire produces a circularly shaped magnetic field that is always at right angles to the direction of the wire. The direction of this magnetic field is reversed if the direction of the current is reversed.

A solenoid is a coil of many turns. What magnetic field will result if a length of current-carrying wire is wrapped in circles to form a coil or *solenoid*? Will the magnetic effect produced by each turn in the coil be recognizable or will the whole solenoid behave in a completely different manner? In this experiment you will have an opportunity to investigate these and other questions about solenoids.

APPARATUS AND MATERIALS REQUIRED (per station)
   7 meters of #22 stranded and insulated copper wire
   a 10 cm length of 5 cm diameter cardboard tubing as used in PSSC optics experiments (or a PSSC solenoid)
   magnetic compass
   2 dry cells
   copper bar
   soft iron bar

4½ in common iron nail
about 100 ½ in iron finishing nails
meter stick
2 wire leads fitted with alligator clips
empty tin can (such as a soup tin)
centigram balance (optional)
(per class)
cardboard and wooden blocks (or overhead projector and solenoid
*   mounted in a transparent plastic base)*
iron filings
6 volt/10 ampere power supply

Procedure:
PART A

1. Wind 20 turns of #22 stranded and insulated copper wire around a length of cardboard (non-magnetic) tubing as shown in Fig. II-12-1. (A pre-wound PSSC solenoid will also be satisfactory.)

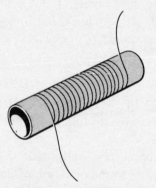

Fig. II–12–1   A solenoid – a coil of conducting wire

2. Using one dry cell, produce brief currents through the solenoid while testing the direction of the magnetic field in various positions around the solenoid with a magnetic compass. Reverse the direction of the current through the solenoid to determine whether or not the direction of the magnetic field is also reversed.

3. With the current in a given direction, sketch the solenoid and the directions of the compass needle at various positions around the solenoid. Then draw the lines of force around the solenoid as you did for the magnet in Procedure 1 of Experiment II-10. For simplicity, consider only the lines of force that lie in a horizontal plane cutting through the center of the solenoid. (It may be necessary to make allowances for the Earth's magnetic field.)
How does the pattern you obtain in this case compare with that obtained in Procedure 1 of Experiment II-10? Do the lines of force still

form a circle around each wire? What is the effect on the strength of the magnetic field of placing a number of wires side by side with the current through all of them in the same direction?

†4. Place your right hand on the solenoid (with fingers together and thumb at right angles to them) so that your thumb is pointing in the direction of the current in the wire. (See Fig. II-12-2.) With a compass needle determine whether your fingers point to the N end or the S end of the solenoid.

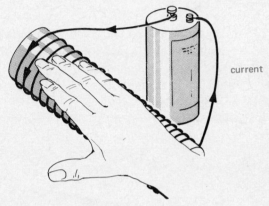

current

Fig. II–12–2   The right hand rule

Do your fingers point in the direction of the magnetic field, as they did for a straight wire?

The procedure you have carried out to predict the polarity of a solenoid is a variation of the right hand rule, which has been described. State the rule that applies in this case.

5. (Demonstration)

NOTE: Alternatively, this procedure may be carried out using the overhead projector and a solenoid of heavy copper wire that is mounted in a transparent plastic base.

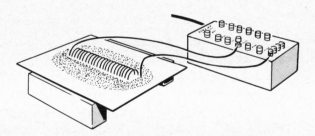

Fig. II–12–3   Observing the magnetic field about a current-carrying solenoid

Thread a length of copper wire into a sheet of stiff cardboard to form a solenoid as shown in Fig. II-12-3. Mount the cardboard on two wooden blocks and sprinkle iron filings evenly on the cardboard around the wire. Using a 6 volt 10 ampere direct current power supply, momentarily pass a current through the solenoid. Simultaneously tap the cardboard with a pencil.

What is the shape of a magnet which produces a magnetic field of the same shape as that of a current-carrying solenoid? (Use information from a previous experiment.)

PART B

6. Turn the air core solenoid you prepared in Procedure 1 until its axis points in an east-west direction. Place a compass about 15 cm from the solenoid as illustrated in Fig. II-12-4, and using a dry cell, pass a current through the solenoid briefly. If the compass needle deflects more or less than 15°, move the compass farther or closer until a deflection of approximately 15° is obtained.

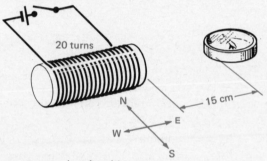

Fig. II–12–4   A compass near an air solenoid

How far away from the magnet must you hold the compass in order to obtain a deflection of about 15°? Why would placing the solenoid in a north-south direction not produce the desired deflection? (Hint: In what direction does a compass needle normally point?)

7. Insert a soft iron bar into the windings of the solenoid. Again close the circuit briefly and note the reaction of the compass needle. Repeat using a copper bar.

How far away from the magnet must you now hold the compass in each case to obtain a 15° deflection? Was the magnetic field strength of the solenoid increased in each case? What is the effect of placing a soft iron bar in a weak magnetic field?

8. Wrap 50 turns of insulated copper wire around a 4½ in common nail leaving sufficient wire at both ends to enable you to connect the coil to a dry cell.

9. Pile at least 100 finishing nails on the table. Using one dry cell, pass a current through the windings on the large nail and see how many small nails you can pick up with the *head* end of your *electro-*

magnet (See Fig. II-12-5.) Do not leave the cell connected any longer than it takes you to move the nails to your partner's hands. Count the nails and record the number. If you prefer not to count them, weigh them using a centigram balance.

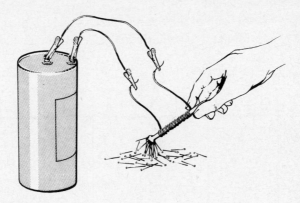

Fig. II–12–5　An electromagnet

What can you do to cause an electromagnet to lose most of its magnetism?

10. Place the nails you picked up with the electromagnet into an empty tin can and shake them vigorously to remove any residual magnetism before placing them back on the table. Then repeat Procedure 9 *at least* once.

11. Unwind 10 of the turns on the nail but do not shorten the wire. Repeat Procedure 10 and see how many nails you can now pick up. Make at least two trials. Count the nails and record the number.

12. Repeat Procedure 11 three times, but with 30, 20 and 10 turns respectively remaining on the nail. Do not shorten the wire. Each time see how many nails you can pick up, carrying out at least two trials for each case.

   Does the number of turns of wire in the electromagnet coil affect the strength of the resulting magnetic field? How?

13. Replace the single cell with a battery of 2 *equally strong* cells connected in series. Repeat the last observation of Procedure 12 with 10 turns still left on the nail.

   Compare the current produced by two dry cells connected in series with that produced by a single cell. How is the magnetic field strength of the electromagnet affected by this change in current?

†14. Using the data you collected for 1 dry cell, plot a graph: the number of windings (x-axis) versus the number of nails lifted (y-axis). (Alternatively, the number of windings versus the *mass* of nails lifted.) Comment on the shape of your graph.

Questions:

*1. How can the magnetic field strength of a solenoid be increased? List 3 ways.

*2. Why is soft iron rather than steel used as a core for most electro-magnets?

*3. In each of the figures shown below, indicate the direction of the current and the polarity of the electromagnet. Use the right hand rule.

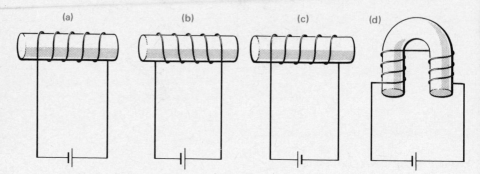

†4. With the aid of diagrams, explain how you can magnetize a long steel bar so that it will have north poles at each end and a south pole in the middle. Try it.

†5. The graphs below indicate the kind of relationship which exists between (a) the strength of an electromagnet and the number of turns of wire about it and (b) the strength of an electromagnet and the current through its windings. Use this information to answer the following questions.

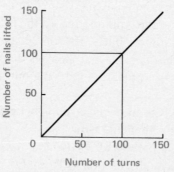 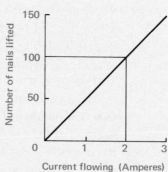

(a) The current through the windings of an electromagnet having 250 turns is 5 amperes. What current must there be in a similar electromagnet of 1,000 turns to produce an equally strong magnetic field?

(b) Two electromagnets have identical iron cores which are wound with 2,000 turns and 400 turns of wire respectively. What current in the 400 turns will produce a magnet as strong as that obtained by passing 0.20 amperes through the 2,000 turns?

References and Suggestions for Further Investigation:

1. With the aid of a diagram, describe the construction and operation of an electric bell. Your diagram should show the bell connected in an electrical circuit with a 3 volt battery and switch and should include the following: metal frame, gong, hammer, contact screw, return spring, armature, electromagnet and binding posts. Label the direction of the current and the polarity of the electromagnet.

2. Use a reference book such as an encyclopaedia to learn how electromagnets are used in telephones, radio speakers, television tubes, electric motors and automobile starters.

3. If you are interested in examining the properties and applications of current-carrying solenoids in greater detail, pages 305-307 of *Basic Physics for Secondary Schools* by H. L. Eubank, J. M. Ramsay and L. A. Rickard (Toronto: Macmillan Co. of Canada Ltd., 1957) discuss these topics.

II–13 APPLICATION OF PRINCIPLES: THE GALVANOMETER — INTERACTION BETWEEN A CURRENT-CARRYING COIL AND A PERMANENT MAGNET

You have clearly seen that

(a) a current-carrying wire has a magnetic field associated with it,

(b) the strength of this magnetic field increases when the current increases,

(c) solenoids are able to concentrate and thus strengthen the magnetic field of a current-carrying wire; the greater the number of turns, the greater the magnetic field produced,

(d) an iron core is capable of greatly increasing the magnetic field strength of a solenoid.

In previous experiments you have used devices called ammeters and voltmeters. These meters were made by applying the principles outlined above.

In this experiment you will build a simple device, a galvanometer, that can be used to detect an electrical current. No doubt your galvanometer will need to be improved before it can be used to measure currents accurately.

APPARATUS REQUIRED (per station)

About 75 cm of stiff (#10) copper wire
3 meters of #34 lacquered copper wire
4 strong permanent bar magnets
2 dry cells
support stand
burette clamp
meter stick

2 5 cm × 10 cm × 10 cm wooden blocks
2 cm × 2 cm square of emery cloth
masking tape
wire leads
(per class)
cutting pliers
two bunsen burners
a gas lighter

Procedure:

1. Take a length of stiff copper wire and bend it into a square which has sides that are about 15 cm long. The ends of the wire should extend parallel to each other from the middle of one side as shown in Fig. II-13-1. Bare the wire ends and bend each to form a small hook to which other wires can be connected.

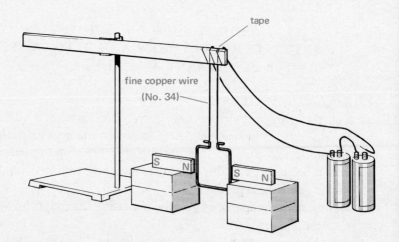

Fig. II–13–1   A galvanometer

NOTE: *Lacquered copper wire may appear bare but unless the lacquer, an insulating material, is removed from its ends, there will be no current. A bunsen burner flame can be used to burn the lacquer from the ends of such wire. Any remaining soot can be easily removed with emery cloth. (Two lighted burners at the front of the room will be ample for the whole class.)*

2. Connect a length of fine copper wire (#34) to the hook on each end of the loop. Be sure that all wire ends are bare so that good electrical contact can be made. Check to see that the two ends of the heavy wire loop are insulated from each other.

3. Suspend the square conductor from a meter stick by means of the two attached fine copper wires so that the bottom of the square is 1 or 2 cm above the table as shown in Fig. II-13-1. Using masking tape, secure the wires to the meter stick so that they are *no more than 2 cm* apart.

4. Use wooden blocks to support two permanent bar magnets in the same plane as the square conductor and on a horizontal line through its center. The N pole of one and the S pole of the other must face each other. (See Fig. II-13-1.)

5. Note the position and behavior of the coil when there is no current through it.
   Does the magnetic field produced by the bar magnets have any effect on the coil of copper wire when there is no current in it?

6. Connect the supporting wires to two dry cells in series as shown in Fig. II-13-1. Observe and record the behavior of the coil as the circuit is opened and closed a number of times.

NOTE: *The effect can be increased considerably by closing the circuit each time the wire square swings past the magnets in the direction in which it is pushed.*

7. Repeat Procedure 6 but change the direction of the current flow through the wire square by reversing the wire connections to the battery.
   Does the direction of the current affect the behavior of a current-carrying square in a magnetic field? Explain.

8. Repeat Procedure 7 using only one dry cell.
   How does this change affect the current in the wire square? Suggest how the wire square would behave if three dry cells were used. Try it.

9. Increase the magnetic field strength by using a pair of magnets on each block with their like poles together. You should now have two N poles on one side of the square and two S poles on the other side. Use two dry cells in series and momentarily close the circuit.
   How does the increased magnetic field strength affect the response of the coil?

10. Repeat Procedure 9 but turn one of the magnet pairs around so that the S poles of both magnet pairs face each other across the square. Close the switch and record the behavior of the square. Synchronize the opening and closing of the circuit to obtain a larger effect.
    How does the resulting effect differ from that in Procedure 9? Can you explain why? What would be the effect if the N poles faced each other? What would be the effect if you reversed the current while the N poles were facing each other? Try it.

11. Rearrange the magnets as shown in Fig. II-13-2 so that the N pole of one points toward one face of the square and the S pole of the other points toward the other face of the square. Momentarily close the switch and note the reaction of the square. Reverse the direction of the current and repeat.

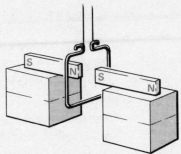

Fig. II–13–2   Does the position of the
                magnets affect the result?

Does the position of the magnets have any effect on the interaction of a current-carrying square and the permanent magnetic field? Explain.

12. Repeat Procedure 11 but reverse one of the magnets so that like poles face each other.
    Which side of the current-carrying square is the N pole end?

13. Remove the magnets and again close the circuit.
    What two requirements are there to cause the wire square to move?

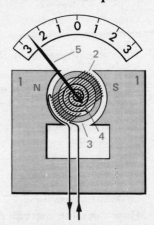

Fig. II–13–3   A galvanometer

NOTE: A sensitive galvanometer works in exactly the same way as the loop in the magnetic field that you have worked with in this experiment. However, as Fig. II-13-3 illustrates, numerous refinements have been made.

1. Two curved pole pieces produce a uniform magnetic field in the region of the movable coil.

2. The movable coil consists of very many turns of fine wire to increase the magnetic field of the coil. This coil pivots on very low friction bearings.

3. A soft iron core further increases the magnetic field strength of the movable coil.

4. A coiled spring produces a restoring force (in proportion to the displacement of the coil).

5. A needle is fixed to the coil to indicate the amount of deflection of the coil.

   In order to use a sensitive galvanometer for measuring larger currents, a conducting by-pass (shunt) is used so that there is only a small but constant fraction of the total current in the coil. Multirange milliammeters have a number of shunts, each with a different resistance, to allow for greater or lesser sensitivity.

   A galvanometer can be used as a voltmeter because the higher the voltage, the greater the current through the galvanometer. However, to increase the range of voltages it can measure, a galvanometer is usually connected in series with a high electrical resistance to limit the current.

Questions:

*1. What conditions are necessary to enable a coil to rotate? Draw a diagram of the arrangement of the equipment. Show the direction of the current in the coil and the direction of the magnetic field from the permanent magnets. If you can, use the right hand rule to determine the polarity of the coil.

*2. Under what conditions will a permanent magnetic field cause a current-carrying coil to *swing*? Use a diagram in your answer.

*3. Under what conditions will a permanent magnetic field have no effect on a current-carrying coil? Is it because no forces are acting? Explain.

*4. What features in the construction of a manufactured galvanometer enable it to detect small currents?

†5. Can a galvanometer be used to determine the direction of current? Explain.

†6. A galvanometer scale is sometimes marked in arbitrary divisions rather than in practical units such as milliamperes. Does this fact mean that a galvanometer is not capable of estimating the comparative sizes of small currents? Explain.

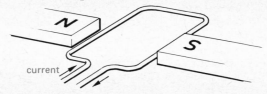

†7. Redraw the diagram above in cross-section. Draw in the shapes and directions of the magnetic fields and determine the direction of rotation of the coil.

References and Suggestions for Further Investigation:

1. If you are interested in reading about the interaction of current-carrying wires and permanent magnetic fields, pages 309-311 of *Basic Physics for Secondary Schools* by H. L. Eubank, J. M. Ramsay and L. A. Rickard (Toronto: Macmillan Co. of Canada Ltd., 1957) discuss and illustrate the principles involved.

2. The galvanometer which you built in Experiment II-13 can be quite easily modified to become an electric motor. Most of the modifications necessary are just what you would expect.

   (a) Use more windings in the moving coil to increase the magnetic field.

   (b) Insert a shaft through the center of the coil so that it can rotate with a minimum of friction.

   (c) Arrange for the coil to be supplied with electricity while it is turning.

   The following diagrams demonstrate one way of carrying out these modifications.

armature

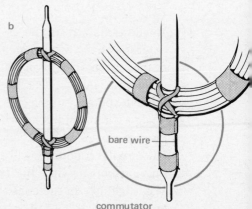

bare wire

commutator

Wind about 7 meters of #22 stranded and insulated copper wire onto a 12 cm diameter cylinder to form a compact coil. Remove the coil from the cylinder and use masking tape to hold the loops together. Both ends of the wire should protrude from the coil. Push a glass rod, whose ends have been drawn to a point in a bunsen flame, through the coil and secure it with masking tape.

Shorten the wires if necessary and remove their insulation in the region where they contact the glass rod. Then securely tape the bare wire ends on opposite sides of the rod leaving a bare section of each wire exposed on the glass. Tape a washer to the base of a support stand to serve as a guide for the lower end of the glass rod. Place a second washer in a burette clamp on the support stand to guide the upper end of the glass rod. The armature you have built should now rotate freely.

Bend two fairly stiff, bare, conducting wires and secure them to the base of the support stand with tape so that they brush against the bare coil ends (commutator) on opposite sides of the glass rod. These stiff wires are called brushes. Turn the armature so that the brushes make contact with the bare coil wire ends. Then place at least two magnets on wooden blocks in the same plane as the coil and in line with the center of the coil. The magnets should be on opposite sides of the coil with their unlike poles facing each other.

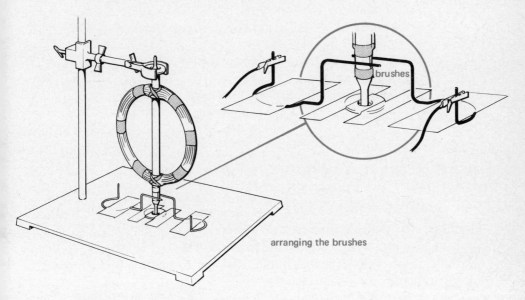

arranging the brushes

Use a 3 volt battery to pass a current through the coil armature via the brushes. A slight push should start the motor rotating. You may also find that a small change in the position of the magnets will improve the performance of the motor.

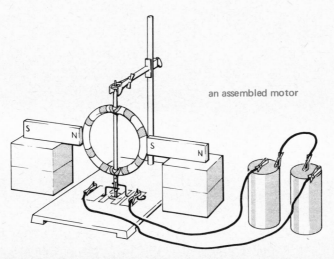

an assembled motor

Notice that the armature rotates continuously since the current is continually reversing its direction through the armature because of the rotating commutator.

Alternatively, purchase an inexpensive motor kit such as the Armaco 2 pole #TFT2 (or 3 pole #TFT3) and assemble it according to the printed directions provided.

3. If there is a St. Louis motor in your laboratory, compare its construction and operation with the motor you have constructed. A St. Louis motor is illustrated on page 397 of *Physical Science for Progress* by M. O. Pella and A. G. Wood (Englewood Cliffs, N.J.: Prentice-Hall Inc., 1964).

4. Pages 313-314 of *Basic Physics for Secondary Schools,* by H. L. Eubank, J. M. Ramsay and L. A. Rickard (Toronto: Macmillan Co. of Canada., 1957) describe the principles of operation of a simple electric motor.

II–14   INTERACTION OF A MOVING MAGNETIC FIELD AND SOLENOID

You have seen that when an electric current is passed through a solenoid a magnetic field is produced around the solenoid. This fact led Michael Faraday to wonder if the opposite was also true. By 1831 he had found the answer. In this experiment you will reproduce his results.

APPARATUS REQUIRED (per station)
A solenoid made by wrapping at least 30 turns of #22 stranded and insulated copper wire around a 5 cm diameter cardboard tube (or a PSSC-type solenoid)
galvanometer (or milliammeter)
2 bar magnets

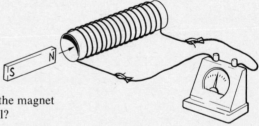

Fig. II–14–1   What happens when the magnet is pushed into the coil?

Procedure:

1. Connect the galvanometer and solenoid in an electrical circuit as shown in Fig. II-14-1. Then plunge the N pole of the bar magnet into the solenoid and note the response of the galvanometer needle.

What does the response of the galvanometer needle indicate? Does the galvanometer needle respond when the magnet is held stationary inside the solenoid?

2. Quickly withdraw the magnet from the coil and again note the response of the galvanometer needle.
   Is the needle deflected in the same direction when the N pole is withdrawn as when it is inserted?

3. Test the effect of speed by rapidly moving the magnet in and out of the solenoid. Then repeat the procedure, this time moving the magnet slowly in and out.
   Does the speed of the magnet have any effect on the reaction of the galvanometer?

4. Turn the magnet around so that the S pole moves into the solenoid. Repeat Procedures 2, 3 and 4.
   What difference is there in the galvanometer reaction from that obtained in Procedures 1, 2 and 3 respectively?

5. Place 2 magnets side by side with like poles together and plunge the combination into the solenoid as before.
   What is the effect on the magnetic field of substituting two magnets with like poles together? How does the addition of the second magnet affect the galvanometer deflection?

6. Reverse one of the magnets so that opposite poles face each other and repeat Procedure 5.
   What is the effect on the magnetic field of substituting two magnets with opposite poles together? How does the effect of this combination compare with that of a single magnet?

7. Hold a magnet stationary and move the solenoid over it so that the solenoid envelops the N pole of the magnet.
   How do the results compare with those in Procedure 1? Does it matter which moves—the magnet or the solenoid?

Questions:

*1. When a magnet is near a current-carrying coil, but not touching it, what enables the magnet to influence the coil? (What property of the magnet "makes contact with" the coil?)

*2. What causes the galvanometer deflection in Procedures 1, 2 and 3? What changes increase the deflection?

*3. If the galvanometer needle is first deflected in one direction and then in the opposite direction, what must have occurred?

*4. Summarize your results by answering the following questions.
   (a) What requirements must be satisfied in order to make an electric generator?

(b) How can the current produced be increased if a moving or changing magnetic field and a solenoid are used? (Give at least 2 ways.)

*5. The electric current produced in the conductor in this experiment was, like all other currents, the result of a potential difference between the "ends" of the conductor.

(a) Describe how the changing magnetic field affects the free electrons in the solenoid.

(b) What device can be used to measure the difference in the electrical condition between the two ends of the wire?

(c) Scientists are more inclined to speak of the voltage produced by an electric generator rather than the current so produced. Why?

*6. Why is current from a dry cell referred to as *direct current* or *D.C.*? Why is the current produced in this experiment by moving a magnet in and out of a solenoid (or vice versa) referred to as *alternating current* or *A.C.*?

*7. Is the electric current that you use in your home lighting produced by mechanical or chemical means? Is it A.C. or D.C.? If it is A.C., does it reverse at a regular frequency?

*8. There is a saying that "you cannot have something for nothing." How does it apply to the generation of electrical energy with a magnet and a solenoid?

†9. Draw two graph axes like those provided below, and, in turn, sketch graphs on each representing (a) the current produced in a closed circuit by a dry cell, and (b) the current induced in a closed circuit by moving a magnet in and out of a solenoid.

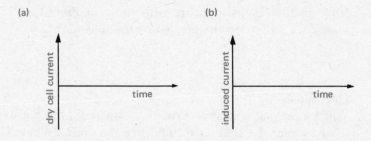

NOTE: *Many devices such as the ignition coil of an automobile engine, the transformer located on the "power" pole along your street, the transformer in your radio and the generators located in the power house at a dam site make use of the effect produced by changing the magnetic field in the region of the windings of a solenoid.*

References and Suggestions for Further Investigation:

1. If there is a small hand crank generator available in your laboratory, familiarize yourself with its operation. How do you make the light bulb glow dimly? brightly? What kind of energy do you use to operate the generator? What kinds of energy is it changed to? What kind of electrical current does your generator produce? Explain. Remove the light bulb and crank the handle. Is it easier to turn with the bulb in or out of the circuit? How then does the light bulb behave in the circuit?

2. Bring a strong permanent magnet close to the glass of a clear straight-filament (showcase) light bulb which is connected to an A.C. source. Observe the reaction of the filament. Explain why it behaves in this manner.

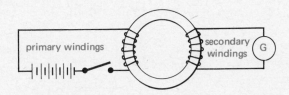

3. Construct a simple transformer by wrapping two coils of insulated copper wire around opposite sides of a soft iron ring. If an iron ring is not available, wind six or eight feet of #16 soft iron wire into a ring with a two inch inside diameter and tape it together so that none of the iron wire is visible. Connect one coil in series with about six dry cells and a switch. This coil makes up the primary windings. Connect the other coil or secondary windings of your transformer to a galvanometer as indicated in the diagram above. By closing the switch of the battery circuit for brief periods, determine how to induce a current in the secondary windings. Vary the number of turns in the primary and secondary windings as well as the number of dry cells in the primary circuit to determine some of the factors that influence the magnitude of the current induced in the secondary windings. Explain how this device works and list at least two types of transformers that are in everyday use. Refer to a book if necessary.

4. Pages 324-327 of *Physical Science for Progress* by M. O. Pella and A. G. Wood (Englewood Cliffs, N.J.: Prentice-Hall Inc., 1964), briefly discuss some theoretical and practical aspects of generators and transformers.

5. The phenomenon of physics called electromagnetic induction is discussed in considerable detail in almost every basic physics book. A brief summary of the principles involved is given on pages 317-320 of *Basic Physics for Secondary Schools* by H. L. Eubank, J. M.

Ramsay and L. A. Rickard (Toronto: Macmillan Co. of Canada Ltd., 1957) and on pages 433-439 of *Physical Science, A Basic Course* by J. C. Hogg, J. B. Cross and K. E. Vordenberg (Toronto: D. Van Nostrand Co. Inc., 1959).

6. If a cathode ray oscilloscope is available, ask your teacher to explain how it works. This device can be used to detect fluctuations in voltage. If the deflecting plates of the oscilloscope are connected to a dry cell, the pattern seen on the screen shows that the dry cell produces a very steady voltage. On the other hand, if the same deflecting plates are connected to the terminals of a 6.3 volt A.C. power supply, the pattern on the screen shows a regularly recurring change in the voltage, from positive to negative.

ATOMS, MOLECULES AND IONS

NOTE: *Before starting this unit it is essential that the first four experiments of Unit II have been completed. Students should proceed through this unit by first doing, in order, Experiments 1 to 5 of Section 1. After this, the experiments in succeeding sections may be done in any logical sequence.*

INTRODUCTION

To review some of your ideas about matter, imagine that you are observing a water solution through an extremely high-powered microscope which allows you to see the particles of matter. Without the aid of the microscope the solution appears to be homogeneous (the same throughout) and continuous. (See view 1 of Fig. III-0-1.) When a drop of this material is observed under your powerful microscope (view 2), it becomes apparent that the material is not continuous but is composed of minute particles (chemical units) that move in a random manner. With higher magnification (view 3) it can be seen that the particles of the solution are not all alike. A still greater magnification (view 4) enables you to classify these particles into three distinct types of chemical units, each of which, in this case, is a molecule. Each molecule is composed of different kinds and numbers of smaller particles (atoms) that are tightly bound together. In other cases we shall find that chemical units are not molecules.

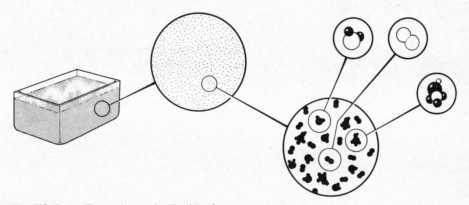

Fig. III–0–1   Four views of a liquid mixture

Each substance contains only one kind of chemical unit, which explains why each substance has only one particular set of properties. You can see (view 4) that there are three different kinds of molecules in the sample. The solution must therefore contain three distinct *substances*. Because our solution sample contains more than one kind of chemical unit, it is a *mixture*. Most common materials are composed of two or more substances and are therefore mixtures.

View 4 of the chemical units also shows that two of the substances are composed of more than one kind of atom and are therefore *compounds*. The third substance consists of only one kind of atom. It is therefore an *element*. All matter is composed of the atoms of one or more of the approximately 100 elements that exist. These ideas are summarized in Fig. III-0-2.

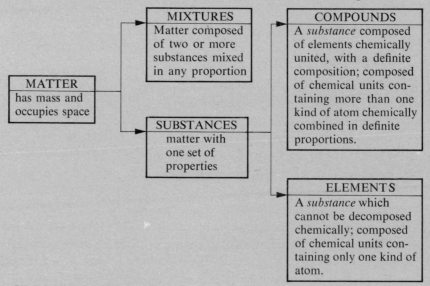

Fig. III-0-2 The classification of matter

In the discussion above we imagined that we had a microscope of sufficient power to observe chemical units and atoms. Since no such instrument is available in any classroom the existence of chemical units has had to be inferred from less direct observations. The following are observations that were important in the development of the foregoing ideas:

(a) Mass is never created or destroyed in a chemical reaction. (This suggests that atoms are never created or destroyed.)

(b) When a substance is decomposed, the masses of the resulting substances are always in the same ratio to each other. For example, when water is decomposed, it always yields eight times as much mass of oxygen as of hydrogen. Hence water must always be composed of 11.1% hydrogen and 88.9% oxygen by mass. Likewise, when different substances react chemically with each other, the mass of each substance that reacts and the mass of each substance that results are always in the same ratio to each other. For example, 23 mass units of sodium always combine with 35.5 mass units of chlorine to form 58.5 mass units of sodium chloride. Thus, chemical units of a substance that is composed of more than one kind of atom must always contain those atoms in the same proportion.

(c) Some substances cannot be decomposed by chemical means into other substances. (These substances are made up of one kind of atom.)

Such experimental evidence can be explained, as you have seen, by assuming that matter is composed of atoms and that a chemical reaction is simply a separation and/or rearrangement of these atoms to form new chemical units. The decomposition of water and the reaction between methanol and oxygen are illustrated below.

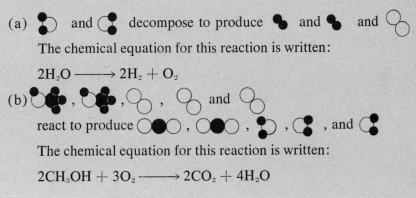

(a) ⬡ and ⬡ decompose to produce ● and ● and ◯◯

The chemical equation for this reaction is written:

$$2H_2O \longrightarrow 2H_2 + O_2$$

(b) ⬡, ⬡, ◯◯, ◯◯ and ◯◯

react to produce ◯●◯, ◯●◯, ◯, ◯, and ◯

The chemical equation for this reaction is written:

$$2CH_3OH + 3O_2 \longrightarrow 2CO_2 + 4H_2O$$

A substance that is composed of atoms of only one kind is an element. A substance that is composed of atoms of two or more elements combined in definite proportions is called a compound. Since the chemical units of compounds contain more than one kind of atom, they can be broken down into smaller chemical units, containing fewer atoms.

What you should know about matter can be summarized as follows:

1. Chemical elements are made up of extremely small particles called *atoms*.

2. All the atoms of an element are chemically identical to each other and chemically different from the atoms of every other element. Hence, each element has a constant set of properties that is different from the set of properties of every other element.

3. When two or more elements combine chemically to form a compound, a whole number of atoms of one element combine with a whole number of atoms of another element.

   (a) In a chemical unit of the resulting compound, the number of atoms of each element is fixed. (These numbers are always *whole* numbers and are usually small.) In any sample of the compound, therefore, the ratio of the number of atoms of one kind to the number of atoms of another is fixed. Since all the atoms of one element have the same mass, we can say that in any sample of the compound, the ratio of the *mass* of one element present to the *mass* of another element present is also fixed.

(b) Atoms do not merge or blend with one another but remain as bound particles occupying a position in the chemical unit.

(c) The mass of a compound formed in a chemical reaction is equal to the sum of the masses of the elements that combined.

(d) The properties of the compound formed are different from the properties of the elements that combined. This is well illustrated by comparing the properties of the elements sodium (poisonous) and chlorine (poisonous) with those of the compound sodium chloride (a food).

In Unit II you saw that friction between two objects can produce an electrostatic charge. The existence of these charges was explained by assuming that atoms are, themselves, composed of smaller particles, one of which is positively charged and another negatively charged. In this unit you will investigate the relationship between the electrical nature of matter and the chemical properties of matter.

Section I
A COMPARATIVE STUDY OF THE ELECTRICAL CONDUCTIVITY OF ELEMENTS, COMPOUNDS AND SOLUTIONS

III–1   ELECTRICAL CONDUCTIVITY OF THE CHEMICAL ELEMENTS

The term "element" applies to all substances which contain only atoms that are chemically identical. Since *all* other substances are compounds which result from combinations of the relatively few elements, the properties of elements are of great importance.

In this experiment you are provided with a number of samples of chemical elements. By making observations, try to find subsets of elements that have properties in common.

APPARATUS REQUIRED (per station)
> 2 dry cells
> 3 volt bulb in a porcelain receptacle
> wire leads
> milliammeter
> 2 test probes

MATERIALS REQUIRED (per station)
> Samples of* Fe, Cu, Pb, Al, S, Si, C(graphite rod), Ni, Sn, Ag, Mn, Cd, Zn, Co, Cr, Bi, Mg, Sb and other elements that are available and safe to work with, including those present in air
> (per class)
> samples of Hg, I_2, Na, K, Ca, P, As, Ge, Se (grey form)
> *These samples may be shared by a number of groups.

CAUTION: Some of the elements you will be examining are poisonous. Treat them accordingly. Take particular care not to touch the elements listed under "Materials Required" (per class).

Procedure:

1. Record whatever physical characteristics you observe in each sample, including the elements present in air. You should investigate such properties as color, general appearance (shiny or dull), hardness, ability to bend without breaking, phase at room temperature (gas, liquid or solid), etc.

2. Test the electrical conductivity of each sample provided by placing it in a circuit with a 3 volt battery, a lamp and a milliameter as shown in Fig. III-1-1. Use the brush technique (page *111*) when first closing the circuit. Beside the name of each element, record the current

reading which results when the probes are pressed firmly into its surface. Compare these readings with that obtained by pressing the test probes together.

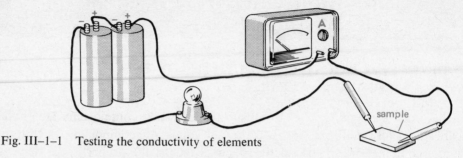

Fig. III–1–1   Testing the conductivity of elements

3. (Demonstration) If samples are available your teacher will help you extend your list by similarly testing the conductivity of Hg, I, Na, K, Ca, P (test under water), As, Ge, Se.

Questions:

*1. Make a copy of the Periodic Table on page *177*. Treat the squares containing the symbols of the elements which you tested as follows.
   (a) Color good conductors red. (Include all the elements you tested that allowed a current within 20 mA of that obtained when the probes were pressed together.)
   (b) Color non-conductors blue. (Include all the elements you tested that permitted no measurable current.)
   (c) Color poor conductors green. (Include all the other elements you tested.)

*2. The Periodic Table on page *177* shows two types of atoms – fastener atoms and ring atoms. What relationship is there between the type of atom and its electrical conductivity? How is the conductivity related to the element's luster (sheen)?

*3. Why are the elements copper and aluminum used for making electrical wires?

*4. What element would you choose to make a solid insulator?

*5. Why were such well known insulators as rubber, asbestos and porcelain not included in the list of elements to be checked?

†6. Try to draw a line on your Periodic Table that separates the good conductors from the poor conductors. The following additional information is provided to assist you. The number in brackets which follows the symbol is the atomic number. "Good," "poor" and "non" refer to conducting ability.

B (5) – poor, Ga (31) – good, In (49) – good, Tl (81) – good, Si (14) – poor, Ge (32) – poor, Sn (50) – good, P (15) – non, As (33) – poor, Sb (51) – good, Bi (83) – good, Se (34) – poor, Te (52) – poor, Po (84) – good.

PERIODIC TABLE OF ELEMENTS

COMMON RADICALS

Name	Formula	Type		Name	Formula	Type
Carbonate	CO_3			Bisulphate	HSO_4	
Chlorate	ClO_3			Sulphate	SO_4	
Hydrogen carbonate or bicarbonate	HCO_3			Permanganate	MnO_4	
Hydroxide	OH			Chromate	CrO_4	
Nitrate	NO_3			Dichromate	Cr_2O_7	
Phosphate	PO_4			Acetate	$C_2H_3O_2$	
				Ammonium	NH_4	

Fig. III–1–2   Periodic table of the elements

The electrical resistivity (opposite of conductivity), of other solid elements is given in reference books such as the *Handbook of Chemistry and Physics* or the *Handbook of Chemistry*.

  ††7. The electrical conductivities of silicon and germanium make them very useful in solid state electronic circuits. Use a reference book to find out how these elements are treated to form N-type and P-type semiconductors.

   References and Suggestions for Further Investigation:
   1. The common physical properties of the metals you observed occur because of a common feature in their atomic structures. Consult a reference book or the Periodic Table in your classroom to determine the difference between the outer electronic structure of metallic atoms and that of non-metallic atoms.
   2. Electrical conductivity changes with temperature. At extremely low temperatures interesting changes occur in the properties of some elements. For example, some metals become superconductors at temperatures approaching –273°C. Consult a book on Cryogenics to learn more about this fascinating topic.
   3. Properties of metals and non-metals are discussed on pages 348-352 of *Matter – Its Forms and Changes* by Brandwein et al (New York: Harcourt, Brace and World, 1968).
   4. A chemistry book you will find interesting is *Chemical Magic* by L. A. Ford (Greenwich, Conn.: Fawcett Publications Inc., 1964).

III–2   THE ELECTRICAL CONDUCTIVITY OF COMPOUNDS

You have seen that the property of electrical conduction is related to some of the other properties of elements. For example, metals, which can be distinguished by their luster, are good electrical conductors, while non-metals, whose surfaces are dull, are generally poor conductors.

  In the model that was used to represent atoms, metallic atoms were represented by fasteners and non-metallic atoms by rings. The Periodic Table on page *177* shows the type of atom possessed by each of the familiar elements. Below this chart are shown various groups of atoms called radicals. Since the atoms in each radical remain together during most chemical changes that you will carry out, radicals may be considered to behave as units (like atoms) during these changes. You will notice that all of the common radicals listed, except ammonium, behave like "ring" atoms.

  What would be the electrical conductivity of a compound in which a "faster" atom had combined with a "ring" atom or of a compound in which a "ring" atom had combined with another "ring" atom? (Compounds formed by combining fastener atoms with other fastener atoms are not common.)

PART A   TESTING THE ELECTRICAL CONDUCTIVITY OF TABLE SALT (A FASTENER-RING COMPOUND) AND SUGAR (A RING-RING COMPOUND)

APPARATUS REQUIRED (per station)
>   2 dry cells
>   3 volt bulb and receptacle
>   wire leads
>   test probes
>   100 ml breaker
>   multirange milliammeter
>   plastic teaspoon
>   stirring rod

MATERIALS REQUIRED
>   Sodium chloride
>   sugar

Procedure:

1. Connect two dry cells, a 3 volt bulb, a milliammeter and two probes in series, as you did in Experiment III-1. (See Fig. III-1-1.)
2. Close the circuit, first using the brush technique, by bringing the two probes together. Observe and record the resulting current.
3. Place a teaspoonful of sodium chloride (table salt) on a sheet of paper and test its conductivity as you did in Experiment III-1. If possible, place a single grain of the NaCl between the probes.
   Is solid sodium chloride a good conductor? (How does the current produced compare with that of Procedure 2?)
   Test your own conducting ability by holding a probe in each hand.
   Would your ability as a conductor interfere with the results of Procedure 3 if your hands touched both probes?
4. Place about 50 ml of water in a 100 ml beaker and test the conductivity of the water by immersing the two probes to a depth of about 2 cm. Hold the two probes parallel to each other and about 1 cm apart as shown in Fig. III-2-1.
   Is tap water a good conductor of electricity?
5. Now add the teaspoonful of the sodium chloride used in Procedure 3 to the water and stir. When the NaCl has dissolved, retest the conductivity of the solution as in Procedure 4.
   Is the NaCl solution a better conductor than water? than dry sodium chloride?
   During this test, observe the submerged portions of the two probes.
   What is forming at each electrode?

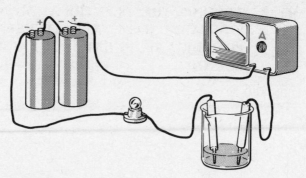

Fig. III–2–1   Does tap water conduct electricity?

6. Wash the beaker. Dip the probes into clean water and dry them with paper towelling. Then repeat Procedures 3, 4 and 5 using a tea-spoonful of table sugar (sucrose) instead of sodium chloride.
Is table sugar ($C_{12}H_{22}O_{11}$)a good conductor as a solid? when it is in solution?

NOTE: In sugar, hydrogen behaves like a ring atom.

Questions:
*1.(a) Did a chemical change occur at the probes when they were connected to the battery and immersed in a solution of (i) NaCl (ii) table sugar? Give reasons for your answers.
(b) In which case was there a current?
*2. Of what kind of chemical units is the element copper composed?
*3.(a) What is a substance?
(b) Copper and sodium chloride belong to the two major subsets of substances. What kind of substance is copper? sodium chloride?
*4. Is an aqueous (water) solution of sodium chloride, written NaCl(aq.), a substance? Explain your answer.
*5. You know that solids maintain their shapes whereas aqueous solutions do not. In view of this fact, do you think that the particles that compose a substance can move more freely in a water solution or in the solid phase? Explain.
*6. What evidence do you have that the sodium in solid sodium chloride is quite different from the element sodium? Consider luster, electrical conductivity and chemical behavior.
*7.(a) If sodium were liquefied, mixed with another melted metal and then cooled, would the resulting solid alloy (a solution of metals) conduct electricity? (Hint: Does brass, an alloy of copper and zinc, conduct electricity?)
(b) Sodium reacts with chlorine to produce sodium chloride. Does this latter substance conduct electricity?

PART B   A CLOSER EXAMINATION OF A METALLIC ELECTRICAL CONDUCTOR

In Part A you examined electrical conduction in a water solution of a compound. This type of conduction is called *electrolytic* (e-lek-troh-LI-tik) conduction. In this experiment you will try to determine the effect on a metal of passing an electric current through it. You can then make better comparisons between conduction in metals and conduction in water solutions.

APPARATUS REQUIRED

> *3 volt light bulb*
> *2 dry cells*
> *electric wire*
> *2 alligator clips*
> *a 30 cm length of stiff metallic wire (different groups should use wire made of different materials)*
> *centigram balance*

Procedure:

7. Determine the mass of a 30 cm length of metallic wire to the nearest centigram (0.01 gm).
8. Place the wire in a circuit as shown in Fig. III-2-2 and allow a current through it for about 2 minutes.

Fig. III–2–2   Does any mass change occur in a conducting wire?

Do you notice any change in the appearance of the wire when there is a current through it?

(Especially observe the points where the wire is connected to the rest of the circuit.)

9. Disconnect the wire and again determine its mass.

Has there been any significant change in its mass? Compare your results with those of other members of the class.

Questions:

*1. From your work in Unit II you know

  (a) that an uncharged metallic wire contains equal numbers of protons and electrons.

  (b) that only electrons move in the wire when it conducts electricity.

  (c) that in a circuit the number of electrons moving into and out of the conducting wire in any given time is equal.

From this information, what conclusion would you draw about the change in mass in a current-carrying wire? Does this prediction agree with your results?

*2. **The following is a model for a metallic conductor.** The members of the class can stand next to each other to form an open circle. (See Fig. III-2-3.) Each person in the line is given a marble or styrofoam ball which he can pass along. When he is holding a marble, a student represents a *neutral* atom containing a weakly bound electron. The line represents a length of metallic conductor. A box containing marbles is placed at one end of the line and a similar, empty box at the other end of the line. The teacher stands beside the full box in order to supply "electrons" to the "conductor."

  When – and only when – the teacher hands a marble to the nearest "atom" with the command "pass," everyone in the line passes his marble (electron) to the person standing on one side of him, at the same time receiving a marble (electron) from the person on his other side. The student at the other end of the line puts his extra marble into the "receiving" box. Note the time lag between the teacher passing a marble at one end and a marble falling into the receiving box at the other end.

Fig. III–2–3   Model for a metallic conductor

  (a) What particle is moving in the circuit?

  (b) Are all of the "atoms" neutral at all times?

  (c) Is the "electron" given to the wire the same one that is removed at the other end? Could this electron eventually travel through the wire?

  (d) Is the "conductor" changed as a result of the "current" it has conducted?

  (e) Non-conducting atoms also have electrons. What must be the difference between an atom which is a conductor and one that is not a conductor?

*3. The diameter of the nucleus of a copper atom is only 1/10,000 as large as the diameter of the complete atom. What occupies the remainder of the available space?

†4.(a) In a cubic centimeter of copper there are 8.4×10^{22} copper atoms, each of which has 29 electrons. How many electrons are there in a cubic centimeter of copper?

  (b) If you could take 8.4×10^{12} electrons away from a short length of copper wire 1 cm^3 in volume it would have a very large electrical charge. What fraction of the atoms would have lost an electron?

  (c) From (a) and (b) can you understand why a charged copper wire looks the same as an uncharged wire?

PART C TESTING A LARGE VARIETY OF SOLUTIONS FOR ELECTRICAL CONDUCTIVITY
(May be demonstrated)

APPARATUS REQUIRED (per station or per class)
> *As for Part A, plus 100 ml beakers to contain the solutions listed (about 20)*
> *paper towel*
> *a beaker of clean water*

MATERIALS REQUIRED
> *0.1 M solutions of potassium iodide, glycerine ($C_3H_8O_3$), lead nitrate, magnesium bromide, aluminum nitrate, barium chloride, sodium carbonate, glucose ($C_6H_{12}O_6$), iron (III) nitrate, copper (II) sulphate, tertiary butyl alcohol (C_4H_9OH), methyl alcohol (CH_3OH), potassium chromate, hydrogen chloride, hydrogen sulphate, hydrogen nitrate, hydrogen acetate, sodium hydroxide, ammonium hydroxide, barium hydroxide, potassium hydroxide**
>
> Teachers may wish to substitute comparable compounds.

Prelab Preparation:

1. Write the correct formulas for the compounds listed under "Materials Required." You may have to refer to the Periodic Chart on page *177* and you may find it helpful to imagine fitting fastener atom "spikes" into ring atom "holes." (Remember that all "spikes" and "holes" must be used when forming chemical units of compounds.)

2. After each compound formula write FsR if the compound combines fastener and ring atoms, and RR if the compound combines ring atoms with each other. Treat radicals as if they were atoms.

NOTE: *Hydrogen is able to behave like a ring atom in some situations and like a fastener atom in others. In the compounds whose formulas are provided in "Materials Required," hydrogen behaves like a ring atom.*

Procedure:

10. Add approximately 50 ml of each solution to a separate 100 ml beaker. Label each beaker according to its contents.
11. Using the same apparatus as in Procedure 4 of Part A, test the conductivity of each water solution, in turn, by lowering the probes into them to a depth of 2 cm. In each case, carefully observe and record any changes that may occur at the electrodes. Record the current for each solution. After each test, rinse the electrodes with water and dry them with a paper towel.

NOTE: *To make meaningful comparisons possible, the separation of the electrodes and the depths to which they are submerged should be kept uniform.*

Is there any relation between the conductivity of a solution and the occurrence of a chemical change (that is, the formation of new substances) at the electrodes?

Questions:

NOTE: *Substances whose water solutions conduct electricity readily are referred to as* strong electrolytes; *those whose water solutions conduct electricity only slightly are called* weak electrolytes; *those that do not conduct electricity at all are called* non-electrolytes.

*1. From your results, classify water and solutes used into the following three categories:
Non-electrolytes. A solution is a non-electrolyte if its conductivity is not significantly greater than that of water.
Weak Electrolytes. Include compounds whose solutions conducted between 1 and 10 milliamperes of current in this experiment.
Strong Electrolytes. Include all other compounds tested.
List the compounds tested under the proper headings in the following table.

NON-ELECTROLYTES	WEAK ELECTROLYTES	STRONG ELECTROLYTES

*2.(a) Using the rings and fasteners model, describe the compounds which are non-electrolytes (i.e. non-conductors). Use the list you prepared before you performed the experiment.
  (b) In terms of this model, generalize about the compounds that are electrolytes (that is, conductors in solution).

*3.(a) What relation did you notice between the conducting ability of the solution and the occurrence of a chemical change at the electrodes? Were there any exceptions?

   (b) Compare the conduction of a current in a copper wire with the conduction of a current in a solution. What evidence do you have that electrical conduction in a water solution of an electrolyte is quite different from conduction in a metal?

NOTE: *Electrical conduction in a metal is called* metallic conduction. *Electrical conduction accompanied by chemical change is called* electrolytic conduction.

References and Suggestions for Further Investigation:

1. Test the following materials to determine whether they are electrolytes: milk, coffee, tea, blood, saliva, gasoline, solvent, salad oil, cooking oil.

2. Determine how the conductivity of a water solution of sodium chloride varies as the concentration of the sodium chloride is increased.

3. Does a current in an electrolyte add heat energy to the solution? Can you relate your results to the amount of the current?

III–3 INVESTIGATING CHEMICAL CHANGE DURING ELECTROLYTIC CONDUCTION

You have observed that when a compound is composed of both metallic (fastener) and non-metallic (ring) atoms or radicals, its water solution will conduct an electric current. That is, compounds composed of metals and non-metals are generally electrolytes. You have also observed that the conduction of current by a water solution of an electrolyte is accompanied by chemical changes at both electrodes. A study of the nature of these chemical changes may reveal more about how a current is conducted in a solution and how electrolytic conduction differs from metallic conduction.

In this experiment you will study the conductivity of a solution in more detail.

PART A   ELECTROLYSIS OF COPPER (II) CHLORIDE

APPARATUS REQUIRED (per station)
    250 ml beaker
    2 1½ volt dry cells
    milliammeter
    wire leads

test probes
2 carbon electrodes

MATERIALS REQUIRED (per station)
   Blue litmus paper
   copper (II) chloride
   0.2 M CuCl₂ solution
   well diluted chlorine bleach

Procedure:
1. Look closely at a sample of dry copper (II) chloride.
   What color is it? Can you see any copper metal in the sample? Is it as flexible as copper?
2. Test the electrical conductivity of solid CuCl$_2$ with the apparatus you used in Experiment III-1. (See Fig. III-3-1.)

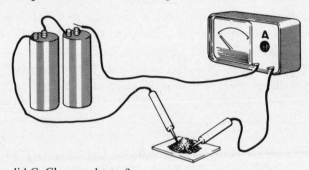

Fig. III–3–1   Is solid CuCl$_2$ a conductor?

Is dry, solid CuCl$_2$ a conductor of electricity? Does copper conduct electricity? Do your results therefore indicate that copper atoms undergo a change when they become part of a chemical unit of copper (II) chloride?

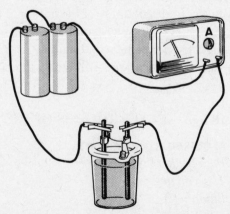

Fig. III–3–2   Observing the electrolysis of CuCl$_2$

3. Connect a 3 volt battery, a milliammeter and two clean carbon electrodes in series as shown in Fig. III-3-2. Add 150 ml of 0.2 M $CuCl_2$
   solution to a 250 ml beaker. Then place the carbon electrodes into
   this solution. Support them so that they do not touch each other.

4. Adjust the distance between the carbon electrodes to obtain a current
   of approximately 0.2 amperes (200 mA). Maintain this current for
   several minutes.
   **What do you observe happening at each of the electrodes after a short
   time? (You may have to raise the electrodes above the level of the
   solution to complete your observations.)**

5. Lower separate pieces of blue litmus paper into the solution near the
   positive and negative electrodes so that half of each paper is above
   and half below the level of the solution. After a few minutes, observe
   the color of the litmus papers.
   What change occurs in the color of the litmus paper at each terminal?

6. Dip a fresh piece of blue litmus paper into a small amount of diluted
   chlorine solution (bleach) so that it is half submerged.
   **Is the color change similar to the color change that occurred at one of
   the terminals in Procedure 5? If so, which terminal?**

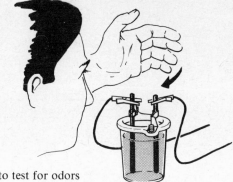

Fig. III–3–3   The correct way to test for odors

   Waft the air over the beaker toward your nose with your hand. (See
   Fig. III-3-3.) Do the same with the air over the container of chlorine
   bleach.
   What element do you think is forming at the positive electrode?

7. Open the circuit and remove the electrodes from the solution.
   What element do you think has formed on the negative electrode?

8. Reverse the connections to the electrodes so that the previously positive electrode is now a negative electrode. Place the electrode into the
   solution and close the circuit using the brush technique.

NOTE: *If the current is too great for the meter, use fewer cells for a time.*

   Observe and record the reaction at each electrode.

9. Maintain the current until gas again begins to form at the positive

electrode, then open the circuit and observe the electrodes.
What has happened to each electrode?

Questions:

*1. What evidence do you have that there was a current through the $CuCl_2$ solution?

*2.(a) Did the copper appear on the positive or negative electrode? (This electrode is said to be *plated* with copper.)

 (b) At which electrode was chlorine given off?

*3.(a) Did any change occur at the electrodes before the circuit was closed?

 (b) What, then, caused the chemical reaction to occur?

*4. In terms of the particles in an atom, explain why one electrode is negative and the other is positive.

*5. What is the function of the dry cell in the circuit?

*6. What is the function of the connecting wires in the circuit?

*7. Why is there no evidence of the elements copper and chlorine in the solid copper chloride and in the solution of $CuCl_2$?

PART B   IDENTIFYING THE COMPONENTS OF COM-POUNDS IN SOLUTIONS

In Part A you found that in neither copper (II) chloride nor its aqueous solution was there any indication of the presence of copper or chlorine. However, you found that when a positively and negatively charged electrode were placed in the solution so that the solution became part of an electrical circuit, copper and chlorine appeared. This behavior is rather unexpected.

APPARATUS REQUIRED (per station)
 Medicine dropper
 4 test tubes
 test tube rack

MATERIALS REQUIRED
 1 M $BaCl_2$ solution
 beakers or test tubes containing 0.1 M solutions of $K_2Cr_2O_7$, $CuSO_4$, K_2SO_4, KNO_3, and as many additional solutions as possible of compounds containing potassium, copper (II), sulphate, dichromate and nitrate. (Such solutions were used in Part C of Experiment III-2.)

Procedure:

10. Observe the colors of the various solutions of nitrate, sulphate, dichromate (dy-KROH-mayt), potassium and copper (II) compounds in water.

NOTE: *It is convenient to classify electrolytic compounds according to their*
          metallic and non-metallic components. For example, $CuCl_2$ may be
          classified as either a copper (II) compound or a chloride compound.

Suggest why $CuSO_4$ solutions are colored and K_2SO_4 solutions are colorless. From the colors of the various solutions, deduce the characteristic color that each of the following gives to its compounds in solution: potassium, copper (II), sulphate, dichromate and nitrate.

11. Use a medicine dropper to add a drop of 1 M $BaCl_2$ solution to each, in turn, of the test tubes containing solutions of KNO_3, $CuSO_4$, $CuCl_2$, KCl, K_2SO_4 and H_2SO_4.

In which solutions do obvious chemical changes occur? Which atom or radical was common to each of the solutions in which a reaction occurred?

Questions:

*1. What seems to be the color given to *compounds* by the following: potassium, copper (II), sulphate, dichromate, barium, chloride and nitrate?

*2. $LiNO_3$ forms a colorless solution. Predict the color of (a) a Li_2SO_4 solution (b) a $Li_2Cr_2O_7$ solution. Give reasons for your answer.

*3. Can you suggest a suitable test for the presence of sulphate in a compound? This test will be used to detect the sulphate component of $CuSO_4$ in Part C.

PART C   A MODEL FOR CONDUCTION IN SOLUTIONS
(Demonstration)

In Part B you observed that the presence of a common component in electrolyte compounds gave them a common color, e.g. $CuCl_2$, $CuSO_4$, and $Cu(NO_3)_2$ solutions are blue and $K_2Cr_2O_7$, $(NH_4)_2Cr_2O_7$, and $Na_2Cr_2O_7$ solutions are all orange. Does this mean that each of these compounds contains chemical units that are made up of two separable or separate parts?

The following experiment will further explore this possibility and try to relate this idea to electrolytic conduction in general.

APPARATUS REQUIRED (per class)
          2 250 ml breakers
          support stand
          2 utility clamps
          2 U-tubes with 4 2-hole rubber stoppers to fit the ends
          medicine dropper
          100 volt D.C. supply
          4 carbon rod electrodes
          wire leads with alligator clips
          stirring rod

MATERIALS REQUIRED

Clear gelatin
$CuSO_4$
$K_2Cr_2O_7$
1 M solution of $BaCl_2$
a saturated solution of KNO_3

Procedure:

11. In advance, your teacher will have prepared *separate* gels (semi-solid solutions) by dissolving about 1.5 gm each of $CuSO_4$ and $K_2Cr_2O_7$ in separate beakers containing 40 ml of hot water and then adding 1 teaspoon of gelatin to each beaker. While the water was still hot, each solution was stirred and poured into a separate U-tube until the tube was half full. It was then clamped to a support stand (Fig. III-3-4) and allowed to cool and gel.

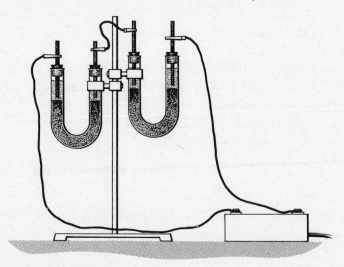

Fig. III–3–4   What happens to the colors?

To what components of the chemical units of $CuSO_4$ and $K_2Cr_2O_7$ can you attribute the blue and orange colors respectively?

12. Insert four carbon rods into four *two*-hole rubber stoppers which will fit into the ends of the U-tube. (The other hole in each stopper will allow any gases produced to escape.)

13. Add saturated KNO_3 solution to each arm of both U-tubes, using a medicine dropper to avoid disturbing the gel. Add this solution to within 1 cm of the top of each arm.

14. Adjust the carbon rods so that they do not penetrate the gel and carefully insert one of the stoppers from Procedure 12 into each of the U-tube arms. The carbon rods should enter only the upper portion of the KNO_3 solution in each tube.

CAUTION: 100 volts is extremely dangerous if the amperage is not limited.
Therefore, safety resistors must be included in the circuit described
below to limit the current to a maximum of 0.01 amperes. Fortu-
nately, these resistors are included in most power supplies manu-
factured for use in general science laboratories. Do not plug in the
power supply until all connections have been made.

15. Using electric leads with alligator clips, provide a single electric path from the $+100$ volt terminal of a D.C. power supply, through each U-tube solution in turn, and then back to the 0 volt (common) terminal of the power supply. (See Fig. III-3-4.) Then plug the power supply into an electrical outlet.

16. Maintain the current for at least 30 minutes. Make regular observations during this time.

17. After approximately 30 minutes, unplug the power supply and add one drop of $BaCl_2$ solution to the top of each arm of the $CuSO_4$ tube. Record your observations. (Take care to note which terminal is positive and which is negative in each of the U-tubes.) Recall the effect of $BaCl_2$ solution observed in Procedure 11.

**To which electrode did the orange color move in the $K_2Cr_2O_7$
solution? the blue color in the $CuSO_4$ solution? To which electrode
did the sulphate group migrate in the $CuSO_4$ solution? Can you suggest a reason why $K_2Cr_2O_7$ and $CuSO_4$ were used in gels?**

Questions:
*1. What noticeable changes occur when a $CuSO_4$ solution conducts electricity? How does this kind of conduction differ from conduction in a copper wire?

*2. What would happen if a negatively charged ebonite rod were brought near a positively charged pith ball?

*3. (a) What was the charge on the electrode which attracted
  (i) the blue color in the $CuSO_4$ solution (gel)?
  (ii) the orange color in the $K_2Cr_2O_7$ solution (gel)?
  (iii) the component of $CuSO_4$ that reacts with $BaCl_2$ solution?

  (b) What charge can you therefore associate with each of the particles that are colored?

  (c) What charge can you associate with the colorless component of $CuSO_4$?

*4. What do your observations suggest about the electrolytic compounds? Are they composed of neutral particles? Describe the particles moving about in an electrolytic solution.

*5. You found in Experiment III-2, Part C, that a chemical unit of an electrolyte is composed of a fastener-type atom and a ring-type atom. Using your answers to questions 2, 3 and 4, decide whether it is the fastener atom or the ring radical in $CuSO_4$ and $K_2Cr_2O_7$ which assumes a positive charge in a water solution of each electrolyte. Does the other atom or radical assume the opposite charge?

*6. Why does $CuSO_4$ conduct electricity only after it has been dissolved?

*7. Recall Part A of this experiment. The deposit which formed on the negative electrode in the $CuCl_2$ solution was copper, which is insoluble.

 (a) Where must the copper have come from?

 (b) To be attracted to the negative electrode, what must have been the charge on the particles in the solution which eventually formed the copper deposit?

 (c) What would happen when particles of this charge touched the negative terminal? (Could your answer explain why the particles became insoluble?)

*8. To answer the following questions, recall what you learned in Unit II.

 (a) Describe the atoms of an object that is neutral.

 (b) What happens to some of the atoms of an object that is positively charged? negatively charged?

 (c) What is the normal charge of a sample of $CuSO_4$? of a sample of water?

 (d) What, therefore, is the total charge of a water solution of $CuSO_4$?

 (e) If there are positively charged particles (which can be neutralized to form metallic copper) in a water solution of $CuSO_4$, what also must exist in the solution?

 (f) What will these other particles (mentioned last in "e") tend to do when positively and negatively charged electrodes are placed in the solution?

 (g) From experimental results, determine the sign of the charge on copper (II), sulphate, chromate and potassium in water solutions of electrolytic compounds.

*9. When the imaginary electrolytic compound MX is dissolved in water, it *dissociates* into positively charged M particles, written M^+, and negatively charged X particles, written X^-. When these particles are subjected to an applied voltage as shown in the diagram, toward which electrode (positive or negative) will the M^+ particles travel? the X^- particles?

*10. An atom of copper has 29 protons. This number is never changed by any chemical reaction. You have seen in several experiments that the charged copper particle found in water solutions of compounds containing copper always moves toward the negatively charged electrode. Will the number of electrons on a charged copper particle be greater than, equal to, or less than 29?

*11. Does the charged dichromate radical have more electrons than protons? Towards which electrode does the charged dichromate radical travel? Explain.

*12.(a) Which particles in a $CuSO_4$ solution react with $BaCl_2$ solution?
  (b) What is the charge of this kind of particle?

References and Suggestions for Further Investigation:

1. Does a current in a solution generate a magnetic field like a current in a wire? You may wish to refer to page 262 of *A Sourcebook of the Physical Sciences*, by Joseph et al (New York: Harcourt, Brace and World Inc., 1961).

III–4 OBSERVING THE ELECTRICAL PROPERTIES OF ZINC CHLORIDE–SOLID, DISSOLVED AND MOLTEN. (Demonstration)

The problem of explaining how an electrolyte conducts a current baffled chemists for many years. Many great scientists tackled the problem. Among those searching for an answer was a young Swedish scientist named Svante Arrhenius (ar-RAY-nee-us). For two years he experimented with electrolytic solutions by passing currents through each solution and recording the results. Finally, on May 17, 1883, all the pieces of data tumbled into place and the *Ionic Theory* (eye-ON-ik) was born. Arrhenius postulated that electrolytes in solution consist of electrically charged atoms or groups of atoms, which he called *ions* (EYE-onz). He further postulated that these ions move independently of each other, once the substance is dissolved. Since solutions have no net charge, he reasoned that the effect of all of the positively charged ions was neutralized by the effect of all of the negatively charged ions.

When a metallic and a non-metallic atom acquire a charge, as a result of combining with each other, there is a dramatic change in their properties. For example, there is no odor of chlorine from a solution of copper chloride and the copper (II) ions in the solution are blue instead of a copper color. Also, copper, normally insoluble in water, becomes soluble when it becomes part of the compound $CuCl_2$.

In this experiment you will use the ionic theory to determine the way the electrolyte zinc chloride conducts a current.

APPARATUS REQUIRED (per class)
>   *250 ml beaker*
>   *2 dry cells*
>   *carbon electrode*
>   *copper electrode*
>   *milliammeter*
>   *wire leads*
>   *test probes*
>   *#18 nichrome wire (or stainless steel)*
>   *large cork*
>   *2 electrodes*
>   *plastic spoon*
>   *evaporating dish*
>   *ring clamp*
>   *asbestos gauze*
>   *support stand*
>   *bunsen burner*
>   *3 volt bulb and receptacle*

MATERIALS REQUIRED
>   *0.2 M solution of $ZnCl_2$*
>   *solid $ZnCl_2$*

Procedure:

CAUTION: Zinc chloride is poisonous if taken internally. Be sure to wash your hands after doing the experiment.

1. Add a solution of $ZnCl_2$ to a 250 ml beaker and test its conductivity as you did in Procedure 4 of Experiment III-3. (See Fig. III-3-2.) Connect a copper electrode to the negative terminal of a battery and a carbon electrode to the positive terminal. Close the circuit by placing the electrodes into the solution and maintain a current for several minutes. Use the Ionic Theory to predict what substances are produced at the electrodes.

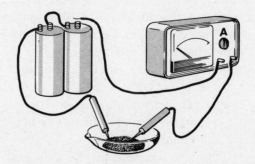

Fig. III–4–1   Testing the conductivity of $ZnCl_2$

2. Place about 1 teaspoonful of solid $ZnCl_2$ in an evaporating dish.
3. Check the conductivity of the solid $ZnCl_2$ as shown in Fig. III-4-1. **Does solid $ZnCl_2$ have the same conductivity as solid NaCl and solid $CuCl_2$?**
4. Place the dish on asbestos gauze supported by a ring clamp and a support stand and heat it with a bunsen burner flame until the $ZnCl_2$ just melts. After it has melted, maintain only sufficient heat to keep it molten.

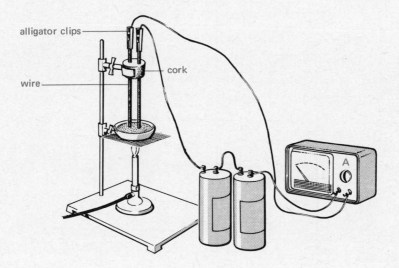

Fig. III–4–2   Does molten $ZnCl_2$ conduct electricity?

5. Prepare nichrome wire electrodes so that they can be easily handled by pushing two 15 cm lengths of the wire through a large cork. (See Fig. III-4-2.) Observe the initial condition of the electrode ends. Check the conductivity of the molten zinc chloride by inserting the ends of the nichrome wire electrodes into the liquid $ZnCl_2$. (See Fig. III-4-2.)

NOTE: Because their temperature is lower than that of the liquid $ZnCl_2$, the electrodes will initially become coated with solid $ZnCl_2$, which acts as an insulator.

Leave the electrodes in the molten liquid for several minutes after the solid $ZnCl_2$ coating has melted.
Can you observe any evidence of chemical changes while the electrodes are submerged in the molten $ZnCl_2$?
6. Remove the electrodes and wash off any adhering $ZnCl_2$.
Is there any noticeable change in the appearance of the electrodes? If so, what reaction(s) do you think has (have) occurred? Does liquid $ZnCl_2$ consist of charged ions?

PERIODIC TABLE OF ELEMENTS

1 H^+ Hydrogen																	2
3	4											5	6	7	8 O^{2-} Oxygen	9	10
11 Na^+ Sodium	12 Mg^{2+} Magnesium											13 Al^{3+} Aluminum	14	15	16 S^{2-} Sulphur	17 Cl^- Chlorine	18
19 K^+ Potassium	20 Ca^{2+} Calcium	21	22	23	24 Cr^{2+} Cr^{3+} Chromium	25	26 Fe^{2+} Fe^{3+} Iron	27 Co^{2+} Co^{3+} Cobalt	28 Ni^{2+} Ni^{3+} Nickel	29 Cu^+ Cu^{2+} Copper	30 Zn^{2+} Zinc	31	32	33	34	35 Br^- Bromine	36
37	38	39	40	41	42	43	44	45	46	47 Ag^+ Silver	48	49	50	51	52	53 I^- Iodine	54
55	56 Ba^{2+} Barium	57	72	73	74	75	76	77	78	79 Au^+ Au^{2+} Gold	80 Hg^+ Hg^{2+} Mercury	81	82	83	84	85	86
87	88	89															

COMMON POLYATOMIC IONS

Ammonium	NH_4^+	Nitrate	NO_3^-
Acetate	$C_2H_3O_2^-$	Carbonate	CO_3^{2-}
Chlorate	ClO_3^-	Chromate	CrO_4^{2-}
Hydrogen Carbonate or Bicarbonate	HCO_3^-	Dichromate	$Cr_2O_7^{2-}$
Bisulphate	HSO_4^-	Sulphate	SO_4^2
Hydroxide	OH^-	Phosphate	PO_4^{3-}

Fig. III–4–3 Periodic table of the common monatomic ions

NOTE: 1. *Elements are arranged in the Periodic Chart according to their atomic number, the number of protons possessed by each atom of the element. For example, since the atomic number of sodium is 11, each sodium atom (which is neutral) contains 11 protons and 11 electrons.*
2. *A copper (II) ion is represented by the symbol Cu^{2+}, which shows that the atom has lost 2 electrons.*
3. *A chloride ion is represented by the symbol Cl^-, indicating that it has gained 1 electron.*

Questions:

*1. Use the information in the Periodic Chart on page *196* to determine how many electrons and protons there are in
(a) a zinc atom.
(b) a zinc ion.
(c) a chlorine atom.
(d) a chlorine ion.

*2. Toward which electrode did the zinc ions (Zn^{2+}) move? the chloride ions (Cl^-) move? Why?

*3. When the zinc ions come in contact with an electrode that has an excess of electrons, what happens to the zinc ion to change it to a zinc atom?

*4. When the chloride ion comes into contact with an electrode that has a deficiency of electrons, what happens to the chloride ion to change it into a chlorine atom?

*5. As you learned in Unit II, two requirements must be met before the "gremlin" in the dry cell can do his job. First, electrons must be removed from the negative terminal: in this case they were removed by zinc ions. Second, electrons must be added to the positive terminal: in this case, by chloride ions. What effect does this process have on a milliammeter in the wire part of the circuit?

*6. Explain how it is possible for electrons to flow from a battery to one electrode in an electrolyte solution and from the other electrode back to the battery, without any conduction of free electrons through the solution. (Refer to questions 5 and 10.)

*7.(a) An electric current occurs during the movement of *any* charged particles. When electrons are flowing from the battery to one electrode and from the other electrode back to the battery, is there, in fact, a current through the electrolyte?
(b) What particles constitute the electric current through the solution?

*8. Refer to the Periodic Table of atoms and the Periodic Table of ions.
(a) What relationship is there between the type of atom (whether it

is a ring atom or a fastener atom) and the kind of charge (positive or negative) it gains when it becomes an ion?

NOTE: *It is helpful to think of the spikes of fastener atoms and radicals as electrons which can be captured and removed to "fill" the holes of ring atoms or radicals. The number of spikes on a fastener atom or radical is the number of electrons it loses when it combines chemically with a ring atom; and the number of holes on a ring atom or radical is the number of electrons it gains when it combines chemically with a fastener atom.*

(b) What can you say about the charges on the ions of elements all in the same vertical column of the Periodic Chart.

*9.(a) Use the information on page *196* to write the chemical formulas of the following compounds: zinc chloride, calcium nitrate, sodium sulphide, ammonium bromide and aluminum sulphate.

(b) Above the symbol of the metallic and the non-metallic component of each formula, write the size of the net charge on the ion. For example, write SrI_2 as $Sr^{2+}I^-_2$. (Each atom of strontium, element 38, loses two electrons to a non-metallic atom; each atom of iodine, element 53, captures one electron from a metallic atom.

(c) Write a chemical equation for each of the above compounds to show the dissociation of ions when it is dissolved in water. For example, when SrI_2 is in the solid phrase, its ions are not free of each other, shown by the fact that it is a very poor conductor of electricity. After it has dissolved, its ions move independently; they are said to have *dissociated* themselves from each other.)

e.g. $SrI_2 (s) \rightarrow Sr^{2+} (aq) + 2I^- (aq)$

NOTE: *The letters in brackets after the formulas in the above equation have the following meanings:*
(s) means the substance is a solid,
(aq) means the particle or chemical unit is in water solution.

The equation above states that one chemical unit of solid strontium iodide dissociates in water to form one strontium ion and two iodide ions.

A Model of Electrolytic Conduction:

*10. The model of a metallic conductor given in Question 2 on page *182* can easily be modified to describe electrolytic conduction. Create a gap in the center of the conductor or the line of students. (See Fig. III-4-4.) This gap is where the electrolytic conduction is to take place. The student on each side of this gap represents an electrode atom. The positive electrode is on the "empty box" side of the gap and the negative electrode, on the "full box" side. In the solution (gap) between the electrodes, equal numbers (for simplicity) of positive and negative ions (students) may move about. It is advisable that the students representing the electrodes and the ions be labelled. "Electrode" atoms and "conductor" atoms each have one marble, being neutral; "positive ions" have no marbles, since they lack one electron; and "negative ions" each have two marbles since they possess one extra electron.

Fig. III–4–4   Model of electrolytic conduction

When, as before, the teacher hands a marble to the student on the end of the conductor and gives the command "pass," everyone in the line passes his own electron and receives another in his other hand. This charge flow creates a negative charge (an excess of one electron) at the negative electrode and a positive charge (a deficiency of one electron) at the positive electrode. Immediately, a positive ion is attracted to the negative terminal, where it removes the extra electron, and a negative ion is attracted to the positive terminal, where it gives up an electron. As a result of losing their net charges, both ions have become atoms, and may sit near their electrodes.

The entire procedure which began with the word "pass" may be repeated until no more ions exist.

NOTE: *You should realize that this process is a model of the simplest electrolytic conduction possible.*

(a) What charged particles move to cause the electric current in an electrolyte?
(b) Why does a chemical change always accompany electrolytic conduction?

References and Suggestions for Further Investigation:

1. The development of the Ionic Theory by Svante Arrhenius illustrates well the way man's knowledge advances. You can read a very interesting account of Arrhenius' work on pages 140-154 of *Crucibles – The Story of Chemistry* by Bernard Jaffe (Greenwich, Conn.: Fawcett Publications Inc., 1961).
2. A discussion of the Ionic Theory is presented on pages 190-200 of *Modern Chemistry* by C. E. Dull et al (Toronto: Clarke, Irwin and Co. Ltd., 1953).
3. A model for electrode reactions is clearly presented on pages 127-129 of *Chemistry – Experimental Foundations* by R. W. Perry et al, (Englewood Cliffs, N.J.: Prentice-Hall Inc., 1970).

Section II
PROPERTIES OF IONIC AND COVALENT COMPOUNDS

III – 5   COMPARING IONIC AND COVALENT COMPOUNDS

In the previous experiment you observed that *molten* $ZnCl_2$ will conduct electricity. In the process, chlorine gas forms on the positive electrode and zinc forms on the negative electrode. This fact shows that zinc and chloride ions exist in pure zinc chloride just as they do in a water solution of zinc chloride. Compounds such as zinc chloride, whose chemical units consist of ions, are called *ionic compounds*. Ionic compounds generally contain both metallic and non-metallic components (fastener and ring units according to our model).

What can be said about the compounds which consist only of non-metals (including hydrogen, which often behaves like a non-metal)? The chemical units of these substances do not consist of ions; they are molecules made up of atoms bound together by a type of bonding called *covalent* bonding. Compounds consisting entirely of non-metals are called *covalent compounds* because of the nature of the bonds between the atoms in their molecules.

There are, then, two general classes of compounds: ionic compounds and covalent compounds. In Part A of this experiment you will compare some of the properties of an ionic compound (NaCl) with those of a covalent compound (paraffin).

NOTE: Paraffin consists of more than one covalent compound. It is very difficult to separate its constituents since they are very similar in their composition and properties. Paraffin is chosen for this experiment because it is inexpensive and readily available. The behavior of any of the covalent compounds in paraffin is, however, very similar to the behavior of paraffin.

PART A   COMPARING SODIUM CHLORIDE
AND PARAFFIN

APPARATUS REQUIRED (per class)
   Stereomicroscope or hand lens
   microscope slide
   bunsen burner
   support stand and ring
   crucible
   pipestem triangle
   single edge razor blade
   two 100 ml beakers
   4 test tubes
   test tube rack
   (per class)
   paraffin
   sodium chloride crystals prepared in advance by allowing a saturated
       solution to evaporate slowly in a large petri dish
   granular sodium chloride
   carbon tetrachloride (CCl_4)
   KNO_3 crystals

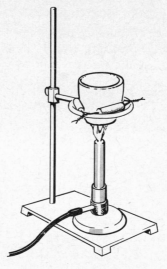

Fig. III–5–1   Comparing the melting point of paraffin and NaCl

Procedure:
1. Place several NaCl crystals and pieces of paraffin on a microscope
   slide and observe them with a stereomicroscope or a hand lens.
   Describe any differences between the appearances of the two
   materials, in a diagram if possible.
   Which substance appears to have greater regularity in its structure?

2. Attempt to crush a single piece of each material with your finger nail. **Which substance is harder? Which is more brittle?**

3. Determine whether NaCl or paraffin has the higher melting point by placing a small quantity of each in turn in a crucible supported on a pipestem triangle, ring and support stand as shown in Fig. III-5-1. (Do not use large NaCl crystals.) Heat the sample slowly at first; then gradually increase the heat until the sample melts or until the crucible reaches maximum temperature. Beware of spattering in the early stages of heating.
Which sample melts at a lower temperature? Which material, therefore, has the greater attraction between its chemical units?

4. Choose a fairly large crystal of NaCl and place the sharp edge of a single edged razor blade parallel to one of its flat surfaces. Give the top of the blade a sharp blow with a pen. Repeat the procedure with a second crystal, but this time place the blade diagonally across the crystal.
In what direction(s) does an NaCl crystal split?
Do the same with a piece of paraffin and describe any differences in the results.

CAUTION: The following procedure should be carried out in a well ventilated room. Do not inhale CCl$_4$ vapor.

5. (Demonstration) Place a pinch of sodium chloride into each of two test tubes and a similar amount of paraffin in each of two other test tubes. Add water to a depth of 2 cm to one of the tubes containing NaCl and one containing paraffin. Add the same amount of carbon tetrachloride to the other two tubes and immediately place stoppers on them.
Which of the two liquids is the best solvent of NaCl? From your observations, is this liquid effective in dissolving other electrolytes? Does this liquid effectively dissolve the non-electrolyte paraffin? Carbon tetrachloride is useful as a solvent. Which type of compound do you expect it to be effective in dissolving?

Questions:
*1. Describe the following properties of wax and sodium chloride: crystal structure, cleavage (ability to split along a plane), hardness, brittleness, melting point, solubility in water, solubility in CCl$_4$.

*2. Predict the physical properties of KNO$_3$ and then check your predictions. (If large crystals of KNO$_3$ are not available, grow them by allowing a saturated solution to evaporate slowly.

*3.(a) Imagine that you are provided with a large number of positively and negatively charged balls that will not lose their charge on contact with each other.

(i) How do a positively and a negatively charged ball affect each other?

(ii) How do two negatively charged balls and one positively charged ball arrange themselves if they are brought together?

(iii) How then, do a large number of these balls arrange themselves? (Think of adding positively and negatively charged balls to the group one at a time.) Give the arrangement first in two dimensions (on a flat surface) and then in three dimensions.

(iv) Do you expect the three-dimensional arrangement to have a regularity to its structure? Does it cleave to form smooth faces?

(v) Would a solid composed of ions in this way be hard? Would it have a high melting point?

(vi) Which type of solvent "molecule," one that has electrical charges at its ends or one that is entirely neutral, would be more effective in dissolving (pulling away the ions of) the material?

(b) What can you conclude about the composition of NaCl, an ionic compound?

*4. (a) Imagine that you are provided with a large number of balls with no net electrical charge.

(i) If these balls have a slight attraction for each other, how would a large number of them arrange themselves?

(ii) If you pushed down on the top surface of the assembly obtained in 4(i), how would the balls react?

(iii) What would the "melting point" of such a substance depend on?

(iv) If the balls were replaced with sausage shaped objects (like paraffin molecules), how would the assembly react when you pushed down on it?

(b) What can you conclude about the composition of paraffin, a covalent compound?

PART B   RECOGNIZING IONIC AND COVALENT COMPOUNDS

In this part of the experiment you will observe samples of a number of different compounds. On the basis of their physical properties you will classify them as covalent or ionic compounds.

MATERIALS REQUIRED (per class)

Samples of calcium nitrate, methyl alcohol, potassium iodide, glycerine, glucose (dextrose) that has been carefully *melted and then cooled, sodium acetate, magnesium bromide, carbon tetrachloride (in sealed container)*

Procedure:

1. By looking at each of the materials listed above, attempt to classify each as either an ionic or a covalent compound. Record your results under two headings: Ionic Compounds and Covalent Compounds.

Questions:

*1. What were some of the properties you used to distinguish between these two classes of compounds?

*2. To which group do you expect most of the living material in your body belong?

References and Suggestions for Further Investigation:

1. The natures of the covalent and the ionic bond are discussed on pages 337-342 in *The Physical Universe* by K. B. Krauskopf and A. Beiser (Toronto: McGraw-Hill Book Company, 1967).

2. Ionic bonding is concisely outlined on pages 12-16 of *Atoms, Crystals and Molecules* by A. H. Drummond, Jr. (Middletown, Conn.: American Education Publications, Inc., 1965).

Section III
ELECTROLYSIS

III–6 "MAGIC" WRITING BY MEANS OF ELECTROLYSIS

You have learned that solutions of electrolytes contain charged particles called ions. If it were not so, your eye muscles could not function to move your eyes across this page! The nervous system that signals muscles to move depends on the properties of ionic solutions. This example is only one of many that illustrate how greatly your life is affected by electrochemical processes. Numerous products that you use daily are produced electrochemically. The process of using electrical energy to produce chemical changes is called *electrolysis*.

In the first part of this experiment you will investigate a "magic" writing process which uses an electrolytic reaction. As you perform this experiment, apply what you have previously learned to explain what happens.

PART A

APPARATUS REQUIRED (per station)

2 dry cells

4 pieces of filter paper

> 3 wire leads with alligator clips
> a 6 in × 6 in sheet of aluminum foil (or other common metal)
> a 3½ in nail to serve as a pen
> steel wool
> test tube
> graduated cylinder
> stirring rod

MATERIALS REQUIRED

> *A freshly prepared water solutions of:*
>   *starch**
>   *0.5 M potassium iodide*
> *a solution of iodine in methyl alcohol*
> *The starch solution may be prepared by putting a small amount of
> starch into boiling water.

Procedure:

1. Mix about 15 ml of KI solution and a few drops of starch solution in a test tube.
2. Lay a piece of filter paper on a square of clean aluminum foil and moisten the paper with the prepared KI starch mixture.

Fig. III–6–1   Scientific magic

3. Using wire leads with alligator clips, connect the aluminum foil to the negative terminal and a nail "pen" to the positive terminal of a 3-volt battery as shown in Fig. II-6-1. Do not allow the nail to touch the aluminum foil, causing a short circuit.
   Slowly print your name with the tip of the nail on the moistened filter paper.
   What "magic" do you observe?
   Can you use your pen connected to your circuit to "write" on your neighbor's paper? Explain.
4. Remove the used filter paper and replace it with a new dry one. Try "writing" on the dry filter paper.
   Does the "magic" work?

Moisten the dry filter paper on which you have written with water and again try "writing" on it.

Does any writing appear?

5. Repeat Procedure 4 but this time moisten a piece of filter paper with KI solution only (without the starch).

6. Now add a little starch to the filter paper, using a stirring rod to spread it over a small area. Try writing across this area.

Can you see your writing now?

7. Repeat Procedure 5 using only starch solution to moisten a piece of filter paper. Try writing again. Record your results.

8. Add a drop of starch solution to a beaker of water. Then add a drop of iodine solution.

What is the function of the starch? Do you recall using iodine as a test for the presence of starch in a previous course? Can starch be used as a test for the presence of iodine?

PART B (Demonstration)

To help you to understand what has occurred, your teacher may arrange the following demonstration, which shows the reaction on a larger scale.

APPARATUS REQUIRED
> *2 dry cells*
> *eye dropper*
> *small test tube*
> *1 1½ volt bulb and receptacle (or milliammeter)*
> *2 carbon electrodes*
> *1 U-tube (15 mm)*

MATERIALS REQUIRED
> *50 ml of KI solution*
> *starch solution*

Procedure:

1. Set up the apparatus as shown in Fig. III-6-2. Use carbon rods for both electrodes. Pour KI solution into *one arm* of the tube until it is 2 cm from the top.

2. Place the electrodes in position and close the circuit using the brush technique. Check your circuit to determine which electrode is positive.

Describe what happens at the electrodes.

3. After 5 minutes, withdraw a sample from each arm of the U-tube with an eye dropper and add it to a separate test tube containing a small amount of starch solution.

Do both samples affect the starch solution in the same way? What do your observations indicate?

NOTE: *The reaction at the negative electrode is not a simple loss of charge by K^+ ions. Instead, water molecules are decomposed. The reaction is shown by the equation:*

$$2H_2O(l) + 2e^- \rightarrow H_2(g) + 2\,OH^-(aq)$$

$2e^- = 2$ electrons from the cathode

(g) means that H_2 is a gas

This decomposition reaction takes place more readily than the reaction $K^+(aq) + 1e^- \rightarrow K(s).$

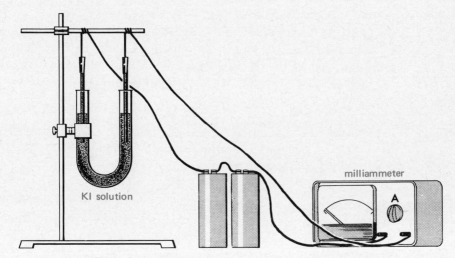

Fig. III–6–2   Electrolysis of Kl solution

Questions:

*1.(a) List the ions present in an aqueous solution of KI, showing their charges.

(b) Which of these ions will be attracted to the positive electrode? negative electrode?

*2. From the experimental evidence and your answer to Question 1(b), write the equation for the reaction at the positive electrode.

*3. How does the reaction at the positive electrode explain the "magic" writing observed in Part A?

*4. Molten sodium iodide conducts electricity and thus behaves like an electrolyte. What ions are present? Write the equation for the reactions that would take place at electrodes placed in this liquid substance.

†5. Chlorine is used very extensively as a bleaching agent in homes and in industry (particularly in the manufacture of high grade pulp). There are two methods of producing chlorine commercially. A less

important method is to electrolyze (use electricity to decompose) molten sodium chloride. The more important method is to electrolyze an aqueous (water) solution of sodium chloride. The reactions that occur are similar to those in the electrolysis of aqueous KI (Na^+ behaves like K^+ in this situation). Write the reactions which occur at both electrodes.

†6. How many grams of chlorine could be produced from the electrolysis of 117 gm of sodium chloride?

†7. In the reaction described by the following equation, what mass of Cl^- ions is formed from 32.5 gm $FeCl_3$? (The mass of an ion is practically the same as the mass of an atom, since the mass of a few electrons is so small compared to the mass of a nucleus.)

$$FeCl_3(s) \rightarrow Fe^{3+}(aq) + 3Cl^-(aq)$$

††8. What mass of $CuSO_4$ is required to produce 112 gm Fe^{2+} in solution if the equation for the reaction is:

$$Fe(s) + Cu^{2+}(aq) \rightarrow Fe^{2+}(aq) + Cu(s)$$

III-7 ELECTROPLATING

As you watch a river or stream it may not occur to you that it is a source of energy which can be used to produce chemical reactions. The province of British Columbia, for example, has an abundance of this energy source and relies on it heavily. Outstanding examples of the present use of electrical energy in that province are the aluminum industry at Kitimat and the lead-zinc smelter at Trail.

In the previous experiment you saw that electrical energy could be used to produce a chemical reaction. In this experiment you will carry out an electrolysis reaction in which copper metal is deposited. During the experiment, you will investigate the relation between the amount of electrical charge that is supplied by the battery and the amount of copper that is deposited as a result.

APPARATUS REQUIRED (per station)
  2 *12.5 cm ✕ 2 cm copper electrodes (see the note about their
      required surface area after Procedure 3)*
  electrode holders
  5 wire leads with alligator clips
  250 ml beaker
  2 dry cells
  milliammeter
  1 ft. of #28 nichrome wire or other resistance wire
  centigram balance

MATERIALS REQUIRED

6 M HCl solution for cleaning electrodes

250 ml CuSO₄ – acid solution made by adding 200 gm CuSO₄· 5H₂O and 150 ml of 6 M H₂SO₄,* (or 50 ml conc. H₂SO₄) to 1 liter of water. ADD ACID TO WATER, NOT WATER TO ACID.

methyl alcohol

steel wool

*The purpose of the H_2SO_4 is to improve the quality of the deposit.

Procedure:

1. Thoroughly clean the copper electrodes by first dipping them in 6 M HCl, washing off the acid with running water and then drying them with a paper towel. (Do not touch the electrodes with your fingers after you have cleaned them; handle them with paper towelling.) Lay each electrode on a piece of towelling and thoroughly polish it with fine steel wool. Again wash it and wipe it with a dry towel. Scratch a distinctive mark on one end of each electrode to distinguish one electrode from the other.

2. Determine the mass of each electrode to the nearest centigram (0.01 gm) and record it in your notebook.

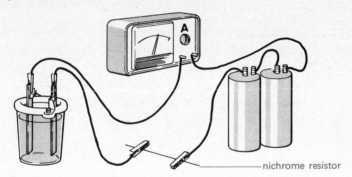

nichrome resistor

Fig. III–7–1   Electroplating with copper

3. Set up the apparatus as shown in Fig. III-7-1 *but do not close the circuit.* Connect one electrode to the negative terminal of a 3 volt battery and the other to a short length of nichrome wire. This wire will allow you to control the current by varying its conducting length and thus its resistance. Connect the other end of the nichrome wire to the positive terminal of the battery via a milliammeter between the resistor and the positive battery terminal.

NOTE: To obtain a hard deposit of copper, the solution should be no warmer than room temperature. Also, 200 milliamperes of current should be used for each 20 cm² of the negative electrode exposed in the solution. For example 200 milliamperes of current should be used if the elec-

trode is 2 cm wide and 5 cm deep in the solution. (Remember that the electrode has two sides!) The instructions which follow assume that 20 cm² of the negative electrode area is being plated.

4. Add sufficient $CuSO_4$- acid solution to the 250 ml beaker to immerse the electrodes to the depth appropriate to the current you are going to use. Adjust the electrodes if necessary but take care not to touch them directly with your hands.

CAUTION: Because of the acid present, this solution must not touch your skin or clothing. Dry up any drops with paper towelling. If some of the solution does touch you, wash it off with large quantities of water and inform your teacher.

5. Check to see that the electrodes are parallel and about 3 cm apart; set the milliammeter at its maximum scale and close the circuit briefly using the brush technique. If the meter responds correctly, close the circuit for *brief* periods while you adjust the length of nichrome wire in the circuit and, if necessary, the distance of separation between the electrodes, in order that the intensity of the current is 200 milliamperes.

6. When you have made the necessary adjustments, close the circuit and record the time.

7. Maintain 200 mA of current for at least 20 minutes. While you are waiting, you may answer some of the questions at the end of this experiment. Record the finishing time when you open the circuit. Your teacher may assign different times to different groups to test the effect of time on the amount of copper plated.

8. After the circuit has been opened, remove the copper electrodes, noting which was positive and which negative. Wash them well with water, dip them in alcohol and then allow the alcohol to evaporate.

9. When the electrodes are dry, again determine and record their masses.
   What is the change in the mass of each copper electrode?

10. If different times were taken to plate the copper by various groups in the class, record your results on a class data sheet.

Questions:

*1. Which electrode was electroplated with copper (or gained mass), the positive or the negative?

*2. Which electrode lost mass?

*3. How did the gain in mass of one electrode compare with the loss in mass of the other?

*4. What reaction occurred to cause the mass of one of the copper electrodes to increase during the experiment? Write the equation for this reaction.

*5. Suggest what reaction occurred to cause the mass of the other electrode to decrease during the experiment. Write the reverse of the equation you wrote in Question 4. Does this equation describe the reaction you suggested?

*6. You will recall from your work in Unit II that a milliammeter measures the rate of flow of charge in milliamperes just as a water meter measures the rate of flow of water in gallons per minute.

(a) If water flows from a pipe at the rate of 8 gallons/minute, what quantity of water has left the pipe in 20 minutes?

(b) What is measured, therefore, by the product of the electric current and the time during which it is maintained?

Answer Questions 7, 8 and 9 only if different student groups carried out the electroplating for different lengths of time.

*7. Using the class data, draw a graph with the change in mass of the negative electrode along the y-axis and the time along the x-axis. Draw the best possible fit line through the points. On the same set of axes, draw a second graph using a different color of ink to show the change in mass of the positive electrode versus time.

*8. What generalization can you make about the relation between the amount of copper deposited and the time during which there is a constant current?

*9. The chrome on the bumper of a car is electroplated on. If a certain thickness of chromium can be deposited in 40 minutes, how long will it take to deposit a layer twice as thick?

*10.(a) In view of your answer to 6(b), what is the relation between time and the amount of charge which flows, if the amount of current is constant?

(b) What, then, is the relation between the amount of copper deposited and the charge supplied by the battery?

††11. Given the following facts:

(a) When there is a current of 1 ampere (1000 milliamperes) approximately 6 billion billion (6×10^{18}) electrons pass a point in the circuit every second.

(b) To neutralize and thus deposit each copper atom, 2 electrons are required.

(c) About 6×10^{23} copper atoms have a mass of 63.5 gm.

how many grams of copper would be deposited if a current of 10 amperes were passed through Cu^{2+} solution for 1800 seconds?

References and Suggestions for Further Investigation:

1. Directions for making your own electroplating and electrolysis apparatus can be found on pages 193-203 of *Chemistry Experiments at Home for Boys and Girls* by H. L. Heys (London: George G. Harrop and Co. Ltd., 1959).

2. Faraday's discovery of the laws of electrolysis and pictures of his apparatus are given in *Michael Faraday* by H. G. Andrew, The Nuffield Foundation (Harmondsworth, Middlesex, England: Longmans/Penguin Books, 1966).

3. Instructions for making electrolytic rectifiers and capacitors are given on pages 234-252 of *Adventures in Electrochemistry* by Alfred Morgan (New York: Charles Scribner & Sons, 1959).

Section IV
ELECTRON TRANSFER DURING CHEMICAL CHANGES

III–8   THE FORMATION OF IONS – ELECTRON TRANSFER

You have established that ions exist in solution, but how are ions formed?

You have already learned that atoms are neutral particles since they possess equal numbers of electrons and protons. However, atoms can spontaneously capture more electrons. In fact, some atoms, particularly those of non-metals, are much more stable when they have one or more extra electrons. But in order for one atom to gain an electron, another atom must lose one. Thus, whenever an atom gains or loses an electron, there is an electron *receiver* and an electron *donor* (DOH-ner).

For example, when an Na atom (with one easily removable electron) and a Cl atom (with a strong tendency to gain one electron) collide, the Cl atom captures the removable electron of the Na atom. In the process, a Na^+ ion and a Cl^- ion are simultaneously formed. Energy is released, showing that an assembly of chloride ions and sodium ions is more stable than an assembly of chlorine atoms and sodium atoms. The oppositely charged ions, Na^+ and Cl^-, attract each other, so that in large numbers they form a crystal, but the Na^+ ions are not capable of recapturing their lost electron from Cl^- ions.

There are, however, other means by which a positive ion can regain its electron(s). For example, if a metallic ion X^+ collides with metallic atom Z, it may be capable of capturing some of its electrons. Consider, for example, the reaction between zinc metal and hydrochloric acid.

When zinc reacts with hydrochloric acid, hydrogen gas and zinc chloride result. Chemists write the equation as follows:

$$Zn(s) + 2HCl \text{ (aq)} \longrightarrow ZnCl_2 \text{ (aq)} + H_2 \text{ (g)}$$

Consider the kinds of particles that compose the reactants and products.

In the reactants: Zinc metal consists of neutral zinc atoms; hydrochloric acid solution contains the ions H^+(aq) and Cl^-(aq).

In the products: Zinc chloride solution contains the ions Zn^{2+} (aq) and Cl^- (aq); hydrogen gas consists of molecules, each of which contains two neutral hydrogen atoms.

Since ions in solution are dissociated from each other, we rewrite the chemical equation as follows:

$$Zn(s) + 2H^+(aq) + 2Cl^-(aq) \longrightarrow Zn^{2+}(aq) + Cl^-(aq) + H_2(g)$$

A study of this equation reveals that changes occur only in the zinc atoms and hydrogen ions. Chloride ions remain unchanged. The change that takes place in the hydrogen ions is described by the *reaction statement*:

$$2H^+ (aq) \longrightarrow H_2 (g)$$

This shows that the hydrogen ions gained electrons. To make this statement an equation, we include these electrons:

$$2H^+ (aq) + 2e^- \longrightarrow H_2 (g)$$

If hydrogen ions gained electrons something else must have lost them. Consider the change in the zinc atoms indicated by the following reaction statement:

$$Zn (s) \longrightarrow Zn^{2+} (aq)$$

This shows that zinc atoms lost electrons, or

$$Zn (s) \longrightarrow Zn^{2+} (aq) + 2e^-$$

Since no other changes occurred, electrons must have been transferred from the zinc atoms to the hydrogen ions. The equation describing the net overall reaction can be recovered by adding the two equations above.

$$2H^+ + 2e^- + Zn (s) \longrightarrow H_2 (g) + Zn^{2+} (aq) + 2e^-$$

In Part A of the following experiment, you will study similar reactions in which electrons are lost by atoms of various metals and gained by hydrogen ions, as in the reaction between zinc and hydrochloric acid. In Part B you will observe the process of electron transfer further.

APPARATUS REQUIRED (per station)
> *6 test tubes*
> *test tube rack*
> *10 ml graduated cylinder*
> *wood splint*

MATERIALS REQUIRED
> *Mossy zinc*
> *small pieces of aluminum, magnesium, lead and copper*
> *iron nail or paper clip*
> *steel wool for cleaning metals*
> *3 M hydrochloric acid*
> *liquid detergent soap*

PART A   REACTION BETWEEN VARIOUS METALS AND HYDROCHLORIC ACID

Procedure:

1. If necessary use steel wool to clean thoroughly a piece of each metal listed under Materials Required. Then place a sample of each in a separate test tube. Label each tube according to its contents. (See Fig. III-8-1.)

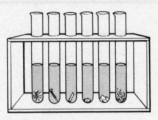

Fig. III–8–1   Which metals react with hydrogen ions?

2. Add approximately 5 ml of dilute HCl to each test tube. Test any gas produced by inserting a burning splint. It may be helpful to trap the gas in the test tube for a short time before inserting the splint.
Does bubbling occur in each test tube? What does it indicate? Do the pieces of metal appear to be decreasing in size?
Compare the rate of each reaction with the rate of the reaction between zinc and hydrochloric acid. (If you add several drops of liquid detergent to each tube you will be able to see any bubbling more clearly.)

Questions:

*1. Which of the above metals would not make suitable containers for storing hydrochloric acid? Explain.

*2. Describe two different ways of producing hydrogen gas.

*3. If you wished to etch your initials into a sheet of iron how could you do it, using a chemical reaction?

*4. Write the equation for the reaction between Zn and HCl in your notebook. Under this equation write the corresponding equations for the other metals which reacted with HCl. Write ionic compounds as separate ions. (Use the information in the Periodic Chart on page *196* to determine the charges on these ions.)

*5.(a) Write the equation that describes the loss or gain of electrons by the hydrogen ions in each reaction.

   (b) Write the reaction statement that describes the loss or gain of electrons by the metallic atom in each reaction. (Remember that not all metallic ions have the same charge.)

*6. From which metallic atom(s) were the hydrogen ions unable to take electrons?

*7. In each of the cases in which a reaction occurred there was an electron transfer from atoms to ions. What signs indicate that electron transfer may have taken place from the zinc atoms to the hydrogen ions?

*8. What is one way in which you can convert aluminum atoms to aluminum ions?

*9. Which metals have atoms with less ability than hydrogen atoms to keep their "removable" electrons? Which have more?

PART B   INVESTIGATING OTHER CASES OF ELECTRON TRANSFER

In this part of your experiment, you will again be observing chemical reactions in which electron transfers occur. In this case, however, you will use a solution containing copper (II) ions, $Cu^{2+}(aq)$, instead of hydrogen ions. As a result, no gas will form but you will observe a different reaction. By carefully observing the surfaces of the metal samples you should be able to determine what is occurring.

APPARATUS REQUIRED (per station)
     5 test tubes (18 × 150 mm)
     test tube rack

MATERIALS REQUIRED
     0.5 M $CuSO_4$ solution
     strip of copper
     lead
     iron (nail)
     zinc
     aluminum
     steel wool

Procedure:
1. Pour about 10 ml of $CuSO_4$ solution into each of five 18 × 150 mm test tubes.
2. Thoroughly clean pieces of copper, lead, iron (a nail will do), zinc and aluminum with a piece of steel wool and drop a piece of each sample into a separate test tube containing the $CuSO_4$ solution. Label each tube according to the metal it contains. Observe the samples for some time. Do not immediately terminate experiments that appear to show no results. If possible, allow the test tubes to stand overnight. **In which of the test tubes did you observe a chemical reaction? (In which tubes did the metals become plated with copper?) Did any change occur in the color of the solution in these tubes? What does such a change indicate?**

3. Dip a small piece of steel wool briefly into some $CuSO_4$ solution. What change do you observe in the steel wool when you remove it?

4. Do not pour the used $CuSO_4$ solution into the sink, but empty it into a waste container such as a large beaker.
   Can you suggest a reason for not pouring the $CuSO_4$ solution down the sink?

Questions:

*1. What substance formed on the surface of each of the metals which reacted?

*2. Which of the above metals could be used to make a container for storing a solution of copper sulphate?

*3. (a) How can you get rid of the blue color in a solution of copper sulphate? Explain why your method works.

   (b) In what form (atoms or ions) does copper exist in a solution of copper (II) sulphate? copper metal?

*4. From which metallic atoms can copper (II) ions, Cu^{2+}(aq), take away electrons?

*5. Write a reaction statement to show the loss or gain of electrons by copper (II) ions when they become atoms (in copper metal).

*6. Write reaction statements to show the loss or gain of electrons by atoms of the metallic reactants when they become ions.

*7. Which particles (ions or atoms) were the electron receivers? electron donors?

*8. Which metals have atoms with less ability than copper atoms to keep their "removable" electrons?

*9. The following equation describes how an atom of the imaginary element M is converted to a metallic ion with a charge n+ as a result of a chemical reaction with Cu^{2+} ions:

$$M \text{ (s)} \longrightarrow M^{n+} \text{ (aq)} + ne^-$$

NOTE: *The reactions for which you have written reaction statements in Questions 5 and 6 are called* half reactions. *Since in your experiment, the net charge of the resulting solution was unchanged, the number of electrons lost by the metal's atoms in forming ions must have been equal to the number of electrons gained by the copper ions when they became atoms of solid copper. For example, for the metal chromium you would write:*

$$Cr(s) \longrightarrow Cr^{3+}(aq) + 3e^-$$

for the half reaction of the metal forming its ions. For the copper half reaction you would write:

$$Cu^{2+}(aq) + 2e^- \longrightarrow Cu(s)$$

One atom of chromium gives up three electrons whereas one ion of copper captures only two electrons. In order to describe the experi-

mental fact that the solution does not become charged you must show in your equation that the number of electrons lost by one metal is equal to the number gained by the other metal. You must therefore show in your equation that you need two chromium atoms for every three copper ions, that is:

$$2 \ Cr(s) \longrightarrow 2 \ Cr^{3+}(aq) + 6e^-$$
$$3 \ Cu^{2+}(aq) + 6e^- \longrightarrow 3 \ Cu(s)$$

By adding these half reaction equations together you will obtain a total equation of:

$$2Cr(s) + 3Cu^{2+}(aq) \longrightarrow 2Cr^{3+}(aq) + 3Cu(s)$$

which shows that the net charge of the solution does not change.

Write total equations for the chemical reactions between Cu^{2+} ions and the atoms of each of the metals on which copper plating was observed.

References and Suggestions for Further Investigation:

1. Cut and bend a sheet of copper, zinc or aluminum foil to look like a Christmas tree and suspend it so that it is immersed in a beaker containing 0.1 M silver nitrate. (Be very careful not to allow the silver nitrate solution to touch your hands, your clothes or the lab bench because it stains badly.) How can you explain the snow covered tree you obtain? If you want white snow, keep the container in the dark while the reaction is taking place. (A zinc tree in a lead nitrate solution also gives an interesting result.)

2. A spectacular view of the reaction between copper metal and silver nitrate may be obtained by using a projecting microscope. Use a piece of copper wire and a solution of silver nitrate. What would happen if you replaced the copper wire with steel wool? The same apparatus may be used to observe crystallization of $CuSO_4$ from a saturated solution or the dissolving of a large crystal.

III–9   THE NATURE OF THE "GREMLIN" IN A DRY CELL
   (Demonstration)

In the previous experiment you learned that copper ions reacted with zinc atoms, forming copper atoms and zinc ions. During the process, copper ions seized electrons from the zinc atoms; that is, zinc atoms were donors of electrons and copper ions, receivers of electrons.

In Unit II you used a gremlin to help you understand and predict what happens when a dry cell is used in an electrical circuit. Now that you have observed electron transfer between atoms and ions, it is possible to explain the source of energy of a dry cell.

In this experiment you will study what happens when the two half reactions during an electron transfer reaction occur in separate locations. In this case, the transfer of electrons cannot be accomplished by direct contact between two particles involved, but can occur if a conducting wire is provided between the two locations.

APPARATUS REQUIRED (per class)
> *250 ml beaker*
> *1.5 volt flashlight bulb and receptacle or milliammeter*
> *wire leads with alligator clips*

MATERIALS REQUIRED
> *3 M HCl*
> *10 cm of clean copper wire*
> *10 cm of clean magnesium ribbon*

Procedure:
1. Add 200 ml of 3 M HCl to a 250 ml beaker. Feel the beaker to estimate its temperature.

CAUTION: To avoid letting acid touch your clothing, dry up all drops with paper towelling.

2. Wind approximately 10 cm of clean copper wire into a fairly narrow coil, 4 cm long. Connect the coil to a bulb and receptacle as shown in Fig. III-9-1. Do not place the coil in the acid solution yet.

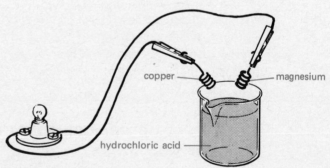

copper ——   —— magnesium

hydrochloric acid ——

Fig. III–9–1 What produces the electric current?

3. Attach a similarly coiled 10 cm length of clean, coiled magnesium ribbon to the other binding post of the lamp receptacle.
4. Holding the lamp, lower the *copper* coil only into the acid solution. **Do you notice any bubbles of gas? Does the lamp light?**
5. Remove the copper coil and then very briefly lower only the magnesium ribbon into the acid. Withdraw it quickly. **Do you observe any gas bubbles? Does the lamp light?**

6. Now lower both the magnesium and the copper coil into the acid solution.
   At which electrode(s) are bubbles formed? Does the lamp light? What happens to the magnesium ribbon?
   Feel the beaker to estimate its temperature now.
   Has any change in temperature occurred? What characteristics of a chemical change did you observe?

Questions:

*1. What is required in an electric circuit to make the light glow?

*2. In Unit II you learned that each circuit must have a *source* of electrons and a *receiver* of electrons as well as a continuous path for the flow of charge. What evidence is there that all of these requirements were met in the above chemical system? Name the source of electrons, the receiver of electrons and the means by which the electrons moved from the former to the latter.

*3. How was the difference in charge *maintained* to keep charge flowing? (Hint: What was it that made the electrons move? When did the light go out?)

*4. Consider the "gremlin" model of a cell in terms of your present knowledge of a cell. You should be able to see that there are really *two* "gremlins" in a cell—one is a chemical reaction which gives up electrons at one electrode (electron donor); the other is a chemical reaction which captures electrons at the other electrode (electron receiver). In the cell you have just made, the reaction at the magnesium electrode was

$$Mg(s) \longrightarrow Mg^{2+}(aq) + 2e^-$$

and the reaction at the copper electrode was

$$2H^+(aq) + 2e^- \longrightarrow H_2(g)$$

   (a) What atom, molecule or ion was the electron donor? the electron receiver?

   (b) At which terminal were electrons "left behind" as atoms became ions in solution?

   (c) At which terminal were electrons removed (captured) as ions in solution became atoms?

   (d) How were electrons transferred from one half reaction to the other?

   (e) What kinds of charge moved in the solution?

*5. Write the equation for the total chemical reaction between magnesium and hydrochloric acid.

*6. Why did the light not glow when you dipped only the copper electrode into the solution (Procedure 4)? when you dipped only the magnesium ribbon into the solution (Procedure 5)? What do your answers tell you about the requirements of a chemical cell?

*7. Give several reasons why this cell would not be useful in a flashlight.

†8. Use a book to find the kind of chemical change that takes place in a common dry cell.

    (a) Write equations for each of the half reactions and then give the total chemical equation.

    (b) What is the purpose of MnO_2 in a dry cell?

A Further Application of the People Model:

An exercise that may help clarify your thinking about the operation of an electrochemical cell is the "people" model, which uses each member of the class (with a marble) to represent an atom. (See page *198*.) You should be able to decide the various roles necessary and how they must interact with one another.

III – 10   THE ELECTROCHEMICAL CELL – A STUDY OF MINIMUM REQUIREMENTS

The way in which you produced an electric current in Experiment III-9 is much more elaborate than the way in which Luigi Galvani discovered the phenomenon on September 20, 1786.

    Galvani had performed a series of experiments showing that muscles underwent violent contractions if an electric discharge was passed from a Leyden Jar (or lightning), through the nerve controlling the muscle, to the ground.

    He was trying to determine whether a frog's leg would undergo the same muscular contractions in calm weather as it did when there was lightning. He had used brass hooks to penetrate the spinal cord of the dead frog and was about to hang it on an iron rail. But when the brass hooks touched the iron rail, he observed a noticeable contraction of the frog's leg muscles.

    He repeated his experiment using different kinds of metals found that the contractions were always present, more violent with some combinations of metals and less violent with others. Since he was using no source of electrical charge he concluded that the animal itself must contain a source of electricity. He called the electricity Animal Electricity.

    A fellow Italian, Alessandro Volta, became very interested in this strange phenomenon. He claimed that Galvani's hypothesis of Animal Electricity was wrong, and that the electricity was a result of the conditions of Galvani's experiment.

    In this experiment you will study something about Volta's argument.

APPARATUS REQUIRED (per station)
2 250 ml beakers
milliammeter
wire leads with alligator clips

MATERIALS REQUIRED
>   *Sodium chloride*
>   *sucrose (sugar)*
>   *2 copper electrodes*
>   *other electrodes (preferably with the same dimensions as those of the*
>   *copper) made of zinc, aluminum, lead, carbon, glass, plastic, wood*
>   *5 cm of bare copper wire*
>   *5 cm of magnesium ribbon*
>   *steel wool*

Procedure:

1. Add 200 ml of water to a 250 ml beaker and dissolve three teaspoon-fuls of sodium chloride in it.
    Is NaCl an electrolyte?

2. To each terminal of a milliammeter, connect a wire lead which has an alligator clip on the free end. Set the meter to its maximum scale. Bring the alligator clips into contact with each other.
    Is there any current? Record your reading.

3. Connect one of the alligator clips to a copper electrode and the other to a zinc electrode with the same dimensions. Hold the electrodes parallel to each other 2.5 cm apart. Watch the meter while you slowly lower the two electrodes into the beaker of sodium chloride solution. (See Fig. III-10-1.)

Fig. III–10–1   What makes an electrochemical cell?

NOTE: You should try to keep the exposed area of the electrodes and the distance between them constant during the entire experiment. Make sure that you clean the electrodes by polishing them with steel wool.

Is there any current? If so, record the maximum intensity which occurs immediately after the electrodes have been immersed. If there is a current, note which electrode is negative and which is positive.

4. Wash the electrodes thoroughly and repeat Procedure 3, but this time use a different beaker containing water instead of NaCl solution. After you have tested the water, add two teaspoons of sugar.
    Is there a current when there is no electrolyte?

5. Replace the zinc electrode with a copper one so that both electrodes are made of the same metal and repeat Procedure 3.
    Is there a current when both electrodes are made of the same metal?

6. Using various combinations of two electrodes from those listed under Materials Required, again repeat Procedure 3. Take care to maintain a 2.5 cm distance between the electrodes in each case. Note which electrode is negative and which is positive for each pair of metals.
    Which pair produced the greatest current? Which pairs, if any, produced no current?

7. Attach 5 cm lengths of copper wire and magnesium ribbon to the two terminals of a milliammeter using wire leads. Place the ends of the two pieces of metal in your mouth, but do not allow them to touch each other. Cover the ends of both pieces with saliva.
    What do you observe? What does this observation indicate about saliva?

8. If you are adventurous, touch a metallic filling in one of your teeth with the magnesium.
    What is your sensation?

9. A simple "lie detector" can be made with the apparatus in Procedure 7. (A very sensitive galvanometer is preferable.) Instead of putting the electrodes in your mouth, have someone hold an electrode tightly between the thumb and forefinger, one in each hand. Better results are achieved if the fingers have been moistened in a solution of NaCl. Startle the person holding the electrodes observing the current at the same time.

Questions:

*1. What are the requirements for the production of an electric current when two metal electrodes are placed in an electrolyte? (Compare the results of Procedures 3 and 4; 3 and 5; 3 and 6.)

*2. Given that body fluids contain electrolytes, explain the movement of the frog's leg in Galvani's experiment. Recall that he used one metal at one end of the nerve in the spinal column and a different metal at the other end and then brought the other ends of the two metals into electrical contact with each other through an iron rod.

*3. Explain why the contractions of the muscles in the frog's leg were more violent with some pairs of metals than with others.

*4. How could you produce an electric current using a penny, a dime and some sea water?

†5. The atoms on the negative electrode are the electron donors. Use this fact to list the elements tested in order of their ability to donate electrons, placing the best electron donor at the top of the list.

References and Suggestions for Further Investigation:

1. A very interesting account of the work of Galvani and Volta is given in a pamphlet called *The Discovery of the Electric Current* by G.

Van Praagh, The Nuffield Foundation (Harmondsworth, Middlesex, England: Longmans/Penguin Books, 1966).

2. Another book that outlines the discovery and investigation of the electrochemical cell as described by Galvani and Volta (as well as many experiments that you can perform) is *Frogs and Batteries* by Leo E. Klopfer (Chicago: Science Research Associates, Inc. 1964).

3. Make a voltaic pile by piling dimes and pennies alternately, separating them by newspaper that is wet with a salt solution.

4. Using a reference book, study some of the models chemists have devised to explain why some atoms are better donors of electrons than others.

III–11   CORROSION – UNWANTED ELECTRON TRANSFER

You have seen a car with large holes "eaten" in its fenders. The problem of corrosion becomes very noticeable in regions where salt is placed on the roads in winter to help melt the ice and snow. Another problem, closely linked to this one, is the leaking of aluminum roofs where they have been fastened with iron nails.

In this experiment you will study the problem of corrosion as an application of the principle of the electrochemical cell.

APPARATUS REQUIRED

      Bare copper wire
      2 large glass containers (e.g. widemouth jar)
      centigram balance
      2 elastic bands
      2 plastic bags

MATERIALS REQUIRED

      2 pieces of aluminum foil or sheet aluminum, 2 in $\times$ 4 in
      2 iron nails
      strips of other metals such as zinc, copper and lead (optional)
      NaCl
      KCNS solution
      and possibly strips of other metals such as zinc, copper and lead
      methyl alcohol

Procedure:

1. Clean a 2 in by 4 in piece of Al foil or sheet Al with a piece of steel wool and determine its mass to the nearest centigram.

2. Repeat Procedure 1 with an Fe nail.

3. Connect the Fe nail to the A1 foil with a piece of bare Cu wire.

4. Prepare a NaCl solution by dissolving 3 teaspoons of NaCl in a large jar containing about 200 ml of water.

5. Lower the two metals into the solution until only the Cu wire is out of the solution. (See Fig. III-11-1.) Do not allow the two metals to touch each other. (You might want to check the direction of electron flow, if any, by temporarily placing a milliammeter into the circuit.)

Fig. III–11–1   Studying corrosion

6. Cover the jar with a plastic bag and secure it with an elastic band to prevent evaporation and leave the apparatus for at least 1 week.

7. At the end of about a week, remove the pieces of metal from the jar and detach the copper wire.

8. Wash both pieces of metal thoroughly with water, wipe them with a paper towel, dip them in alcohol and allow them to dry.

9. When both pieces of metal are completely dry, determine their masses.

10. Different groups within the class may perform Procedures 1 - 9 with different pairs of metals, e.g. Zn – Cu, Al – Cu, Zn – Fe, Pb – Cu. Each group should also prepare a control – a second bottle containing exactly the same metals and solution, but with the metals unconnected by copper wire.

11. If you have used iron as one of the metals, test the solution for the presence of the Fe^{3+} (aq) ion with a few drops of KCNS solution. If Fe^{3+} (aq) ions are present, the solution will turn blood-red.

Questions:

*1. When an iron nail is used in aluminum roofing, does the roof leak because the nail becomes smaller, or the hole becomes bigger, or both?

*2. To prevent a steel tank or a steel boiler from rusting, magnesium bars are often placed inside it. These bars are connected to the tank and become negative with respect to it because magnesium gives up electrons more readily than the elements in steel. There is then a small electric current between the bars and the tank. The magnesium thus corrodes fairly rapidly as its atoms form ions but the steel or iron in the tank is protected because its atoms make up the positive electrode and do not form ions in this kind of reaction.

(a) Which of the metals in your experiment was the positive electrode?

(b) Which has the greater ability to give away electrons, aluminum or iron?

References and Suggestions for Further Investigation:

1. The corrosion of iron and some experiments you can perform are described on pages 269-275 of *Adventures in Electrochemistry* by Alfred Morgan (New York: Charles Scribner's Sons, 1959).

III-12   THE DANIELL CELL — ELECTRON TRANSFER AND ION MIGRATION (Demonstration)

In Experiment III-11 you learned that different pairs of metals yield different currents when they are used as electrodes (as a result of the different voltages produced). You have learned that metallic atoms differ in the strength of the attraction by which they hold outer electrons. Recall, for example, that zinc reacted readily with hydrochloric acid while copper would not react at all. (Experiment III-8.) In other words, zinc atoms will give electrons to hydrogen ions, but copper atoms, which hold their outer electrons more strongly than do hydrogen atoms, will not.

In this experiment, you will study one such reaction more closely.

APPARATUS REQUIRED (per class)
Insulated copper leads with alligator clips
cotton wool or glass wool
3 U-tubes
1 demonstration galvanometer (a milliammeter will do)
2 250 ml beakers

MATERIALS REQUIRED
1 piece each (approx. 1 cm × 10 cm) of Zn and Cu
200 ml of 0.5 M $CuSO_4 \cdot 5H_2O$ solution (29 gm/200 ml)
100 ml 0.5 M $Zn(NO_3)_2 \cdot 6H_2O$ solution (14.7 gm/100 ml)
0.5 KNO_3 solution
a sugar solution
methyl alcohol

Procedure:

1. Fill a U-tube with 0.5 M KNO_3 solution and insert a glass wool plug at each end of the tube.
2. Add 100 ml of 0.5 M $CuSO_4$ solution to one 250 ml beaker and 200 ml of 0.5 M $Zn(NO_3)_2$ solution to another.
3. Place a copper electrode in the $CuSO_4$ solution and a zinc electrode in the $Zn(NO_3)_2$ solution. Connect the electrodes to a demonstration galvanometer (or a milliammeter).
   Is there any current? Is the circuit complete?
4. Set the galvanometer (or milliammeter) to its greatest range. Then place the two beakers close to each other and, quickly inverting the U-tube, place it with one arm in each beaker, so that it forms a liquid bridge between the two solutions. You may have to reverse the connections to the meter. Make sure that no large air bubbles cause a gap in this bridge. (See Fig. III-12-1.) If possible, switch the meter to a more sensitive range.

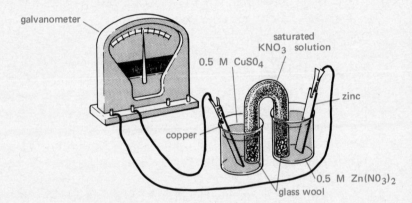

Fig. III–12–1   Is there evidence of movement of charges?

Is there any current? If so, in which direction are electrons flowing? Does the current begin immediately as you close the circuit? Does the current vary? Can you explain the role of the U-tube containing KNO_3 in the circuit? (Hint: What makes up a current in an electrolyte solution?)

5. Withdraw each of the electrodes in turn from its beaker.
   Is there still a current when one of the electrodes is not in its solution?
6. Substitute another copper electrode for the zinc electrode.
   Is there still a current?
7. Repeat Procedure 3 but replace the U-tube with one containing a solution of sugar.
   Is there any current? Is sugar an electrolyte?
8. Repeat Procedure 7, replacing the sugar solution with methyl alcohol.

9. Repeat Procedure 7, replacing the sugar solution with some of the $CuSO_4$ solution.
   Is there a current flow?

Questions:

*1.(a) In which direction do the electrons flow in the wire conductor?
   (b) Use this information to determine which electrode is the electron donor and which electrode is the electron receiver. Which atoms, zinc or copper, hold their electrons more tightly?

*2. What kind of solution must you have in the U-tube to allow a current?

*3. Why does the cell not produce current when both electrodes are copper? (Hint: Consider the ability of metals to hold electrons.)

*4. What would happen if, instead of placing the zinc electrode in $Zn(NO_3)_2$ solution and providing a liquid bridge from this solution to the $CuSO_4$ solution, you placed the zinc electrode directly into a solution of $CuSO_4$? (Hint: Review your data from Part B of Experiment III-8.)

*5. Using the answers to Questions 1 and 4, write the equations for the half-reaction which took place at each electrode.

References and Suggestions for Further Investigation:

1. The operation of a Daniel Cell and the reactions which occur in it are very clearly presented on pages 286-288 of *Chemistry* by M. J. Sienko and R. A. Plane (New York: McGraw-Hill Book Co. Inc., 1961).

III–13   **A CHEMICAL ANALYSIS OF ELECTRON TRANSFER IN AN ELECTROCHEMICAL CELL**

In Experiment III-3, you carried out the following chemical reaction:
$$Cu^{2+} (aq) + 2Cl^- (aq) \xrightarrow{\text{electrolysis}} Cu (s) + Cl_2 (g)$$
From this chemical equation you can see that both ions lose their charges in the reaction. Since the solution does not become charged, both ions must lose their charges at the same time. Because the products are *less* stable than the reactants, energy is required for this process to occur. This energy was provided in Experiment III-3 by a separate chemical change that took place in the dry cells used.

In a later experiment (III-8, Part A), you observed this reaction:
$$Zn(s) + 2H^+ (aq) + 2Cl^- (aq) \longrightarrow Zn^{2+} (aq) + 2Cl^- aq) + H_2 (g)$$
By again studying the equation, you can conclude that zinc atoms became ions while hydrogen ions lose their charges. In this case, no energy has to be provided since the products are more stable than the reactants. In fact, noticeable heat is produced during the reaction. The reason why the reaction occurs is

related to the fact that an H^+ ion has a greater attraction for an electron than does a zinc atom.

In this experiment you will study a different reaction, one in which you will be able to trace the formation of the ions more directly. As a result, you will be able to determine what has taken place.

APPARATUS REQUIRED (per station)
>   3 test tubes
>   labels
>   U-tube
>   platinum or stainless steel electrodes (from electrolysis of water apparatus)
>   milliammeter
>   2 wire connectors

MATERIALS REQUIRED
>   0.1 M $FeSO_4$ solution (freshly prepared)
>   0.1 M $Fe_2(SO_4)_3$ solution
>   0.1 KCNS solution
>   saturated bromine water ($Br_2(aq)$)
>   2 M H_2SO_4

Procedure:

PART A   IDENTIFICATION OF THE IONS THAT WILL BE USED OR FORMED IN PART B OF THIS EXPERIMENT

1. Label and number three test tubes for identification.

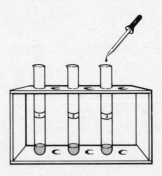

Fig. III–13–1   Which ion is identified by potassium thiocyanate solution?

2. Add freshly prepared iron (II) sulphate solution to the first two test tubes, and a solution of iron (III) sulphate to the third test tube, to a depth of 3 cm. (See Fig. II-13-1.) List the ions present in each test tube.

3. To test tube 1 add a few drops of 0.1 M potassium thiocyanate solution. This solution undergoes color changes which indicate the presence of certain ions.
   What color change do you notice?

4. Observe the color of the solution in test tube 2 and the color of bromine water, $Br_2(aq)$. Add, drop by drop, about 20 drops of bromine water to the solution in test tube 2.
   What is the color of the resulting solution? Is it the color you expect from a simple physical mixing of the two solutions? If not, what change do you think the bromine must have undergone? (Hint: A solution of sodium bromide is colorless.)

5. To test tubes 2 and 3 add a few drops of 0.1 M potassium thiocyanate solution.
   What change is evident? What ion is in test tube 3 that is not in test tube 1? What do you therefore conclude about the change that has taken place in test tube 2 involving the iron (II) ion?

   Questions:

*1. The iron (II) ion has the symbol Fe^{2+} to indicate that it has two fewer electrons than protons. Iron (III) has the symbol Fe^{3+}.
   (a) What is the difference between the number of electrons in Fe^{3+} ions and the number in Fe^{2+} ions?
   (b) What has therefore happened to the iron (II) ions in test tube 2?

*2. The change in the iron (II) ions of test tube 2 must have been caused by the presence of bromine atoms since the same change was not evident in test tube 1. What then do you suppose happened to the bromine atoms?

*3.(a) Using the symbol e^- to represent an electron, write a half reaction equation to describe the change that occurred in the iron ions.
   (b) Write a second half reaction equation to describe what happened to the bromine atoms.

NOTE: *You should not proceed beyond this point until you have clearly established in your mind what electron transfers have taken place.*

PART B   ANALYSING A CHEMICAL CHANGE IN AN ELECTROCHEMICAL CELL (Demonstration)

7. Fill a U-tube to within 5 cm of the top with 2 M sulphuric acid. (If the tube has side arms, fill the tube to within 2 cm of the side arms.)

8. Then, using a medicine dropper, carefully add a 2 cm layer of bromine water to one of the U-tube arms. Very carefully add a 2 cm layer of iron (II) sulphate solution to the other arm, using a medicine dropper so that it does not mix with the acid solution. (See Fig. III-13-2.)

9. Insert platinum electrodes into the bromine water and iron(II),solu-
phate layers.

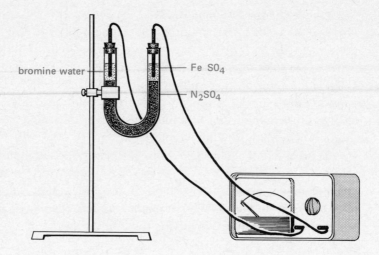

Fig. III–13–2   What chemical changes occur at the electrodes?

10. Connect the two electrodes to a milliammeter using the brush technique. If there is a current in the wrong direction, reverse the connections to the milliammeter. After about 5 minutes, remove the
electrodes.
**Is there any change in the color of the bromine layer? What does this
change indicate?**

11. Test the solution in the arm of the U-tube that contains Fe^{2+} (aq)
with a few drops of potassium thiocyanate.
**What color change do you notice? What does this change indicate?
Has any electron transfer occurred?**

Questions:

*1. Which particles (molecules, atoms or ions) were the electron donors?

*2. Which particles (molecules, atoms or ions) were the electron re-
ceivers?

*3. What is the difference between the ways in which the electrons were
transferred when the Fe^{2+}(aq) was mixed directly with Br_2(aq) in
Part A and when the acid separated the two solutions?

*4. Write the equation for the half reaction that occurred in the Br_2(aq)
arm and in the Fe^{2+}(aq) arm.

*5.(a) Does the reaction take place spontaneously, (i.e. without the aid
of an external energy supply)?

(b) Which are therefore more stable, the reactants or the products?

References and Suggestions for Further Investigation:

1. Look up the topic "fuel cells" in your library. Fuel cells supply much of the energy requirements of space capsules.
2. Chemical generation of electrical energy is discussed in Chapter 6 on pages 117-135, and fuel cells are described on pages 119-125 of *Chemistry in the Space Age* by Marjorie H. Gardner (New York: Holt, Rinehart and Winston, Inc., 1965).
3. Some interesting experiments on electron transfer are described on pages 172-177 of *Chemistry – Collected Experiments*, ed. by B. J. Stokes, The Nuffield Foundation (Harmondsworth, Middlesex, England: Longmans/Penguin Books, 1967).

III–14   THE LEAD-ACID STORAGE CELL: FURTHER APPLICATION OF ELECTRON TRANSFER
(May be Demonstrated)

One of the better known electrochemical cells is the 2 volt lead storage cell. It is commonly used in a car battery. Car batteries consist of either three or six cells of this type (depending on whether they are 6 volt or 12 volt batteries) connected in series. In the following investigation you will first study the method by which this cell is made and then use it to operate a small electrical device.

APPARATUS REQUIRED (per station)
   2 pieces of lead (approx. 6 in $\times$ 1 in)
   steel wool
   2 insulated wire connectors with alligator clips at both ends
   1 600 ml beaker
   6 volt D.C. power supply or 4 dry cells in series
   electric bell or a 3-volt light bulb

MATERIALS REQUIRED
   400 ml 6 M H_2SO_4
   steel wool

Procedure:
1. Clean the lead electrodes thoroughly with steel wool.

CAUTION: Take care not to let any H_2SO_4 solution touch your clothes or skin. If it does, wash the area it touches with large quantities of water.

2. Set up the apparatus as shown in Fig. III-14-1 with both lead electrodes partly immersed in the H_2SO_4 solution. Connect a small electric bell (or a 3 volt light bulb) to the lead electrodes as shown. **Does the bell ring?**

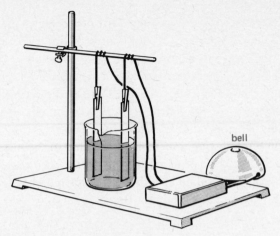

Fig. III–14–1   Bell connected to two lead electrodes

3. Remove the electric bell and in its place connect a 6 volt battery or power supply as shown in Fig. III-14-2. Mark each lead terminal according to its electric charge. Record your observations of the effect at each terminal when the circuit is closed.

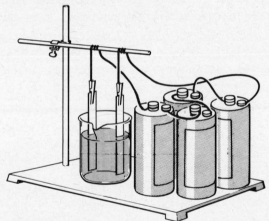

Fig. III–14–2   Charging a lead storage cell

4. Disconnect the 6 volt source after about 10 minutes. Examine the two electrodes and describe any change which has occurred.
5. With the electrodes in the acid, reconnect the bell or bulb to them in place of the power source.
   Does the bell ring? Is there any evidence of chemical change? What is the appearance of the electrodes when the cell is completely discharged? Have the electrodes returned to their original condition?

   Questions:
*1. What conditions for a chemical cell are not present before this cell is charged?

*2. What do the bubbling and the changed appearance of the electrodes during charging indicate? Do both electrodes look the same after charging?

*3.(a) Are the conditions of an electrochemical cell present after the charging?

(b) What must have occurred as a result of the electrical energy supplied during the charging?

*4. During the discharge of the cell, the half reaction at one electrode is

$$Pb(s) + HSO_4^-(aq) \longrightarrow PbSO_4(s) + H^+ + 2e^-.$$

(a) Does lead lose or gain electrons in this reaction?

(b) While the cell is discharging, does this electrode supply electrons to or take electrons from the external circuit (the part of the circuit outside the cell)?

(c) While the cell is discharging, what must happen to electrons in the half reaction at the other electrode?

*5. The density of sulphuric acid is greater than that of water. When a car battery is well charged, the density of the electrolyte is 1.3 gm/cm^3, indicating that the concentration of sulphuric acid is high, and when it is discharged the density is about 1.1 gm/cm^3, indicating that there is very little sulphuric acid in the cell. (The density of pure water is 1 gm/cm^3.) The overall, reversible reaction in the cell is:

$$Pb(s) + 2HSO_4^- + 2H^+ + PbO_2 \longrightarrow 2PbSO_4(s) + 2H_2O$$

(a) If the reaction were going from left to right would the cell be charging or discharging?

(b) What is the formula of the brown substance which appears on one of the electrodes when the cell has been charged?

†6.(a) Why does an automobile use a rechargeable cell instead of some of the other cells you have studied in this course?

(b) Why does a car battery not become discharged even when the car has been operating for some time?

References and Suggestions for Further Investigation:

1. Automobile manufacturers are experimenting with rechargeable cells that could replace the combustion engines of cars. Learn more about the kinds of cells they are using by locating articles on this topic in a scientific journal such as *Scientific American.*

2. You can make a simple hydrogen-oxygen fuel cell by electrolyzing a 1 M solution of NaOH with carbon electrodes. More details can be found on page 432 of *Chemistry: The Sample Scheme Stages I and II: The Basic Course* ed. by M. J. W. Rodgers, The Nuffield Foundation (Harmondsworth, Middlesex, England: Longmans/Penguin Books, 1967).

Section V
REACTIONS INVOLVING IONS

III–15   REACTIONS BETWEEN IONS IN SOLUTION

When a crystal of sodium chloride is placed in a beaker of water, water molecules attract the Na^+ and Cl^- ions and pull them away from the crystal. The dissociated ions with their accompanying water molecules then move more or less independently in the solution. The concentration of these ions in the solution increases as the crystal dissolves. As the ions move through the solution, they frequently collide with ions of the opposite charge and may temporarily remain attached because of electrostatic attraction. The random pattern of attachment and separation can be likened to that of a frantic dance in which partners are continually being exchanged. If a solution that is saturated with these ions is cooled, the "dance partners" collect in larger groups to form crystals that settle and continue to grow at the bottom of the container.

If two or more electrolytes are placed in the same sample of water, the dance becomes more involved since there are now four or more possible ways in which ions can combine with ions of the opposite charge. If the ions in one of these combinations attract each other more strongly than the water molecules which tend to separate them, the substance formed will no longer remain dissolved. An insoluble solid substance formed in this way is called a *precipitate*. Sometimes, oppositely charged ions form a substance that decomposes to release a gas. Once such gas molecules have escaped from the solution, the reaction cannot be reversed.

APPARATUS REQUIRED (per station)
6 test tubes
test tube rack
6 labels

MATERIALS REQUIRED
6 M H_2SO_4
0.1 M solutions of: $Pb(NO_3)_2$, NaI, Na_2SO_4, $NaC_2H_3O_2$ and Na_2CO_3

Procedure:
1. Add a 3 cm depth of each of the following 0.1 M solutions to a separate test tube: $Pb(NO_3)_2$, NaI, Na_2SO_4, $NaC_2H_3O_2$, and Na_2CO_3. Label each test tube with the name of the solution in it. Write down the ions that are present in each of the solutions. (See Fig. III-15-1.)
2. To each of the test tubes containing solutions of NaI, Na_2SO_4 and $NaC_2H_3O_2$ add a depth of 1 cm of $Pb(NO_3)_2$ solution.

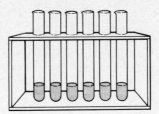

Fig. III–15–1   Five electrolytes

In which test tube(s) did a precipitate result?
For each of the tubes in which a precipitate resulted, write down the four combinations of positive and negative ions that could result when the solutions involved were mixed.
To arrive at the formulas of the substance(s) that were precipitated, consider the possible ion combinations in the solutions that did *not* form precipitates.

3. Slowly add a 1 cm depth of 6 M H_2SO_4 solution to the test tube containing Na_2CO_3.
What does the observed behavior indicate?
Write down the four combinations of positive and negative ions that are possible in this mixture of solutions.
Which of these combinations was most probably involved in the observed chemical change? (Hint: Which does not contain a metallic ion?)

Questions:
*1. Write the ionic equations (balanced equations showing how the ions reacted) for the reactions which took place
   (a) in the test tube containing $Pb(NO_3)_2$ and NaI.
   (b) in the test tube containing $Pb(NO_3)_2$ and Na_2SO_4.
*2. Do the results of this experiment indicate that ions of dissolved substances move independently and separately in a solution? (Is the negative ion of a soluble electrolyte tightly held by its positive ion in an aqueous solution?)
*3. In cases where precipitates formed, what caused the ions of the precipitating substances to move out of solution?
*4. If all of the water in a mixture of the solutions $Pb(NO_3)_2$ and $NaC_2H_3O_2$ were evaporated, what products would you expect to remain?
†5. The compound H_2CO_3 readily decomposes as follows:
$$H_2CO_3(aq) \longrightarrow CO_2(g) + H_2O(l)$$
Write the ionic equation for the reaction that took place in the solution when H_2SO_4 and Na_2CO_3 were mixed.

References and Suggestions for Further Investigation:

1. To test your understanding of the behavior of ions in solution, slowly add a 0.1 M solution of H_2SO_4 to a 0.1 M solution of $Ba(OH)_2$ while two electrodes (from the conductivity of solutions apparatus) are immersed in the $Ba(OH)_2$ solution. Why does the conductivity first decrease and then increase? Is a point reached when there is almost no current? Why?

III–16 A QUANTITATIVE STUDY OF THE IONIC REACTION BETWEEN BARIUM CHLORIDE AND POTASSIUM CHROMATE

In the last experiment you observed that when certain electrolytes are mixed, oppositely charged ions combine. When the binding force of such combinations is not sufficiently strong, the ions will again separate. However, when the binding force is greater than the force of attraction between water molecules and the ions, a pricipitate, a covalent liquid, or a gas results.

In this experiment you will use what you have learned about ionic reactions to study a reaction between two electrolytes. You will combine known quantities of $BaCl_2$ and K_2CrO_4 to determine whether or not they combine in definite proportions.

It may be helpful to explain your observations in terms of the following model. Imagine that you are holding a dance. If only girls (pure $BaCl_2$) are present or only boys (pure K_2CrO_4) are present, dance partnerships cannot occur. If more girls than boys are present (more $BaCl_2$ particles than K_2CrO_4 particles), the number of partnerships possible is limited by the number of boys. Likewise, if there are too many boys, the number of partnerships is limited by the number of girls. Only when there are equal numbers of girls and boys will everyone find a partner, so that no one is left out (there is no excess of one of the reactants).

APPARATUS REQUIRED (per station)
Centigram balance
100 ml graduated cylinder
10 ml graduated cylinder
2 250 ml beakers
stirring rod
medicine dropper
5 small test tubes
test tube rack
masking tape

MATERIALS REQUIRED
> *BaCl₂*
> *K₂CrO₄*
> *0.1 M solutions of KI and NaCl.*

Procedure:

1. Weigh, to the nearest centigram, 4.16 gm of $BaCl_2$ in a beaker. Dissolve it in 30 ml of water and add the solution to a graduated cylinder. Then bring the level of the solution up to exactly 40.0 ml with water. Use a clean medicine dropper to add the last few drops. Remember to have your eye level with the top of the solution and to read the level of the *bottom* of the meniscus. Pour the solution into a 250 ml beaker and mix it thoroughly with a stirring rod.
   What ions are present in this solution? What color is the solution?

2. Carefully rinse out the graduated cylinder and repeat Procedure 1, this time using 3.88 gm of K_2CrO_4.
   What ions are present in this solution? What color is the solution?

3. Using masking tape, a 10 ml graduated cylinder and water, calibrate a medicine dropper so you can tell when 1 ml of liquid has been drawn into the dropper.

4. Use the clean calibrated medicine dropper to add exactly 5 ml of the K_2CrO_4 solution to each of the five test tubes. Label these test tubes 1 to 5. (See Fig. III-16-1.)

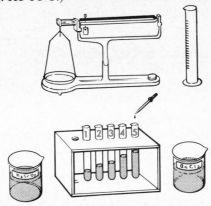

Fig. III–16–1   Which test tube contains little excess reactant?

5. Rinse the medicine dropper and use it to add the following carefully measured volumes of the $BaCl_2$ solution to the test tubes. To test tube No. 1 add 3 ml of $BaCl_2$ solution; to No. 2, add 4 ml; to No. 3, add 5 ml; to No. 4, add 6 ml; to No. 5, add 7 ml.
   What color is the precipitate that is formed in each test tube?

6. Stir the contents of each test tube with a clean stirring rod. Leave the tubes overnight to let the residues settle.

7. While you are waiting for the precipitate to settle, determine the effect of mixing equal volumes of 0.1 M KI and NaCl solutions in a separate test tube.
   Does a precipitate form? What, therefore, must be the precipitate in each of the test tubes 1 to 5?

8. After the residues have settled, note the color of the solution above the residue in each test tube (this solution is called the supernatant liquid) and carefully measure the height in centimeters of the precipitate in each tube.
   What does the color change of the super natant liquid indicate about the amount of reaction in each case? How do the amounts of precipitate depend on the amounts of solution used? Why does the amount of precipitate not increase when you use 6 and 7 ml of $BaCl_2$?

9. From test tube 1, withdraw about 1 ml of the supernatant liquid with an eye dropper and divide it equally between two small test tubes labelled 1A and 1B.

10. Add five drops of $BaCl_2$ solution to test tube 1A and stir. Let any precipitate that forms settle, before adding another drop.
    Does the last drop also cause precipitation?

11. Clean the medicine dropper and treat test tube 1B as you did test tube 1A, but add 5 drops of the K_2CrO_4 solution instead of the $BaCl_2$.
    Which ion was not completely removed from solution in test tube 1?

12. Repeat steps 9, 10 and 11 for each of the other test tubes (2 to 5). (Label the test tubes appropriately.)
    Which test tubes from 2 to 5 still contained an ion that reacted with $BaCl_2$ solution? K_2CrO_4 solution?

   Questions:
*1.(a) When the supernatant liquids from test tubes 1 to 5 were tested with $BaCl_2$ solution, which produced a reaction?
  (b) When the supernatant liquids from test tubes 1 to 5 were tested with K_2CrO_4, which produced a reaction?

*2. Would you obtain a precipitate in every case if you added either $BaCl_2$ or K_2CrO_4 to the original solutions in the 5 test tubes? Why or why not?

*3.(a) What does a reaction with $BaCl_2$ indicate about the supernatant liquid?
  (b) What does a reaction with K_2CrO_4 indicate about the supernatant liquid?

*4. If, in one of the A or B test tubes (Procedures 10, 11 and 12), you obtained a reaction with the first three drops of one of the reactants but not with the next drop, what would you conclude?

*5.(a) In which of test tubes 1 to 5 were both reactants used up most completely?

(b) In what way did the color change of the supernatant liquid indicate the completeness of the reaction?

*6.(a) Calculate the mass of each electrolyte you added to the test tube described in Question 5(a). (Hint: Recall how many grams of each of the reactants you dissolved in the original 40 ml of each solution.)

(b) For this test tube, what is the value of the ratio

$$\frac{\text{mass of } BaCl_2 \text{ (gm) added}}{\text{mass of } K_2CrO_4 \text{ (gm) added}}?$$

(c) Compare your ratio with those of other groups.

*7. Use the Periodic Chart on the back cover to calculate the masses of a chemical unit of $BaCl_2$ and a chemical unit of K_2CrO_4; use the same chart to calculate the ratio

$$\frac{\text{mass of a chemical unit of } BaCl_2}{\text{mass of a chemical unit of } K_2CrO_4}.$$

*8. How do the ratios calculated in Questions 6(b) and 7 compare?

*9. In this experiment, did the reactants obey the Law of Definite Proportions? ("A compound is found to have a definite composition no matter how it is prepared.") Explain.

*10.(a) Write an ionic equation for the reaction in this experiment. Indicate the phase (s, l, g, or aq) of each ion and chemical unit involved.

(b) Write the net ionic equation for this reaction by leaving out of the equation in (a) those ions which did not change. (Such ions are often referred to as *bystander* ions.)

†11.(a) How many grams of K_2CrO_4 would be required to react completely with 103 grams of $BaCl_2$?

(b) How many grams of $BaCrO_4$ would be produced by this reaction?

Section VI
CLASSIFICATION OF ELECTROLYTES

III-17 CLASSIFICATION OF ELECTROLYTES

You have learned that a soluble compound can be classified as a strong electrolyte, a weak electrolyte or a non-electrolyte. Since there are so many different electrolytes, it is necessary to subdivide them further in order to study them.

One of the properties used to classify an electrolyte is the effect of its water solution on a dye called litmus (LIT-mus). A chemical extracted from a lichen, litmus changes its color in the presence of certain kinds of electrolytes.

Such color-changing compounds are called *indicators*. There are many chemicals that can be used as indicators. Ordinary tea (watch it change color when you squeeze some lemon juice into it) and phenolphthalein (fee-nol-THA-lee-in), which you will use later in this experiment, are two other examples.

Another way of classifying electrolytes is to observe their behavior with an active metal such as magnesium.

Both means of distinguishing between electrolytes will be used in the following experiment. Once you have classified the compounds by indicators and magnesium you can look for similarities in the formulas of the compounds within a class or subset.

Since there are so many electrolytes to be tested it is recommended that the class work as a team. You will be assigned five samples to test, one of which is water.

Prelab Preparation:

Before going to the laboratory, make up a full page data table with the following headings:

ELECTROLYTE (name)	FORMULA	COLOR CHANGE OF LITMUS	COLOR CHANGE OF PHENOLPHTHALEIN	REACTION WITH MAGNESIUM

APPARATUS REQUIRED (per station)
   4 in $\times$ 4 in glass plate
   stirring rod for each solution
   5 test tubes
   test tube rack
   test tube brush

MATERIALS REQUIRED
   0.1 M solutions of the following:
      (a) NaOH, KOH, Ca(OH)$_2$, NH$_4$OH
      (b) KCl, HNO$_3$, H$_2$SO$_4$, HC$_2$H$_3$O$_2$
      (c) NaCl, KNO$_3$, Al$_2$(SO$_4$)$_3$, Na$_2$CO$_3$
      litmus paper (red and blue)
      phenolphthalein solution

Procedure:

1. Place 5 tiny squares each of red and blue litmus paper on a glass square. Add approximately 5 ml of each of the solutions in Group (a) under "Materials Required" to separate, clean, labelled test tubes. Add 5 ml of water to a fifth clean, labelled test tube. In turn, insert a clean stirring rod into each of the solutions and the water, and touch

the rod to a dry piece of red and a dry piece of blue litmus paper. (See Fig. III-17-1.) Note any change in color that occurs.

Fig. III–17–1   Testing solutions with litmus

2. Complete the first three columns of your table (see Preparation) for the four electrolytes which you tested. If no color change occurs, write "none."
   What difference is there between the effects of the electrolytes on litmus paper and the effects of water on litmus paper?
3. Add 1 or 2 drops of phenolphthalein to each of the five test tubes and record the result of each reaction in the fourth column of your table. (See Fig. III-17-2.)

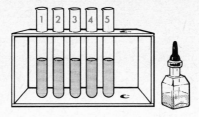

Fig. III–17–2   Testing solutions with phenolphthalein

   What difference is there between the effect of the electrolytes and that of water on phenolphthalein?
4. Carefully wash each of the test tubes using a test tube brush and add a fresh 5 ml sample of each of the same solutions and water to the same test tubes. Cut five 0.5 cm lengths of magnesium ribbon and add one of them to each of the test tubes. In the fifth column of your data table, record which electrolytes are reacting with magnesium quickly, which slowly, and which not at all.
   Is there any difference between the effect of each of the electrolytes and that of water on the magnesium?
5. Again wash each of the test tubes, label four of them according to the electrolytes dissolved in the solutions of group (b) under "Materials

Required." Test the effect of the four electrolytes of group (b) on red and blue litmus paper and phenolphthalein using the same procedure as in Procedures 1 and 3. Record these reactions in your table.

In what way(s) do the results for group (b) electrolytes differ from those for group (a) electrolytes? Include the reactions with water in the comparison.

6. Repeat Procedure 4 with this group of electrolytes.

In what way(s) do the results for group (b) electrolytes differ from those for the electrolytes in group (a) and that of water? What difference(s) do you observe in the rate of the reaction with magnesium between group (a) and group (b)?

7. Repeat Procedures 5 and 6 using the electrolytes in group (c) under "Materials Required."

Do the electrolytes in this group behave in a similar manner toward indicators (litmus and phenolphthalein) and magnesium?

Questions:

*1.(a) Study the set of electrolytes that caused blue litmus paper to turn red. Compare the formulas of these compounds. Can you find any subset containing electrolytes with similarities in their composition?

(b) Since each of the solutions tested is an electrolyte, each must have contributed positive and negative ions to the solution. Write equations showing what positive and negative ions are released in the solution. To help you, the following example is provided:

$$MgCl_2(s) \longrightarrow Mg^{2+}(aq) + 2Cl^-(aq)$$

NOTE: *Remember that radicals (with the exception of ammonium, (NH_4^+)) act as single atoms; they do not break up into smaller particles when they are dissolved in water.*

*2. Answer Question 1 for the electrolytes that caused red litmus to turn blue.

*3. Answer to Question 1 for the substances that caused no change in either red or blue litmus.

*4.(a) A solution always turns blue litmus red when a certain ion is present. What ion is this?

(b) A solution always turns red litmus blue when a certain ion is present. What ion is this?

NOTE: *Solutions that turn blue litmus red are said to be* acidic. *Solutions that turn red litmus blue are said to be* basic.

*5. Did the electrolytes that reacted with magnesium all have the same effect on litmus? Are they acidic or basic?

*6.(a) Consider the solutions that reacted most rapidly with magnesium. Are they weak or strong electrolytes? (Refer to your results in Part (c) of Experiment III-2.)

(b) Write the formula of each of the electrolytes that reacted *most* rapidly with magnesium. What element do they all have in their formulas?

†7. Among the electrolyte solutions of group (c) you will have observed one that was acidic but did not apparently contain the H^+ ion and one that was basic but did not apparently contain the OH^- ion. If these two ions were indeed present in each case, what substance provided them?

NOTE: *Many metallic (positive) ions react with water to produce H^+ ions and many non-metallic (negative) ions react with water to produce OH^- ions.*

†8. If you have been able to test the gas released when certain electrolytes reacted with Mg, you will have found it to be hydrogen (H_2). In each of these reactions, neutral Mg atoms were converted to Mg^{2+} ions. Write the equation for the reaction between H^+ ions and Mg atoms.

†9. If the rate of the reaction between H^+ ions and Mg atoms depends on the concentration of hydrogen ions (H^+) present, what is suggested about the degree to which hydrogen acetate forms ions?

NOTE: *Hydrogen acetate is also known as acetic acid. Although its chemical units are for the most part molecules, when these are in the presence of water molecules, a small fraction of them are caused to break up into positive H^+ ions and negative $C_2H_3O_2^-$ ions.*
This process is called ionization *and is shown in the following equation:*

$$HC_2H_3O_2 \xleftarrow{\quad\longrightarrow\quad} H^+ + C_2H_3O_2^-$$

The small forward pointing arrow shows that ionization is slight while the larger reverse pointing arrow shows that the recombination of H^+ and $C_2H_3O_2^-$ ions occurs much more easily. Thus, the concentration of H^+ ions in a solution of acetic acid never reaches a large value. This acid is therefore known as a weak acid.

References and Suggestions for Further Investigation:

1. Observe the color change in tea as you add hydrochloric acid or sodium hydroxide.
2. The measure of H^+ ion concentration in a solution is called pH. Indicator paper which shows different colors at different pH values is

used by aquarium hobbyists. Use this paper to test the pH of common materials (e.g. soil water from various locations).

III–18   REACTIONS BETWEEN ELECTROLYTES (ACIDS AND BASES)

In the previous experiment you learned that solutions of electrolytes can be grouped into three categories according to their reaction with litmus paper or phenolphthalein. Those that turn blue litmus red and leave phenolphthalein colorless are called *acidic solutions*. Those that turn red litmus blue and phenolphthalein pink are called *basic solutions*. Finally, those that have no effect on red or blue litmus and leave phenolphthalein colorless are called *neutral solutions*. The source of an acid's properties has been found to be the hydrogen ion (H^+). (Since hydrogen atoms have only one electron, a hydrogen ion is a hydrogen nucleus. This is a single proton or, in rare instances, a proton and a neutron.)

The source of a base's properties is often the hydroxide ion (OH^-). The two ions mentioned above (H^+ and OH^-) form water if combined.

$$H^+(aq) + OH^-(aq) \longrightarrow H_2O(l)$$

In the following experiment you will observe what happens when acids and bases are mixed. You will also discover the action of acids on compounds which contain the carbonate ion (CO_3^{2-}).

APPARATUS REQUIRED (per station)
   5 test tubes
   test tube rack
   medicine dropper

MATERIALS REQUIRED
   0.1 M HCl
   0.1 M H₂SO₄
   0.1 M NaOH
   cream of Tartar (KCH₄H₄O₆)
   baking soda (NaHCO₃)
   epsom salt
   alum
   limestone
   chalk
   litmus paper
   dropping bottle of phenolphthalein solution

Procedure:

1. With an eye dropper held vertical, add 10 drops of hydrochloric acid solution to a test tube. Then add 5 ml of water and 1 or 2 drops of phenolphthalein.

CAUTION: *To prevent damage to clothing, wipe dry any drops of spilled acid with paper towelling.*

2. Wash the eye dropper thoroughly and fill it with sodium hydroxide solution. Holding the dropper vertical, add the sodium hydroxide to the acid drop by drop until the phenolphthalein just turns pink. How many drops are required?
   What does the color change indicate? Is the test tube warmer than before? If you wish, you may add HCl and NaOH alternately to the neutral solution.

3. Repeat Procedures 1 and 2, replacing the HCl with a solution of sulphuric acid (H_2SO_4) of the same concentration (0.1 M) as the hydrochloric acid.
   What difference(s) did you find?

4. Place sufficient cream of tartar (a household acid) into a test tube to just fill the rounded part. Add 10 ml of water and shake well to mix. Use a stirring rod and test the solution with red and blue litmus paper to determine if the solution is acidic, basic or neutral.
   Does all of the cream of tartar dissolve? Is its solution acidic or basic?

5. Add one or two drops of phenolphthalein indicator to the test tube and then 5 ml of NaOH solution. Stir the contents with a stirring rod and place the test tube vertically in a test tube rack.
   What happens to the color of the solution in the region close to the undissolved cream of tartar?
   After a short time, stir the contents of the test tube and again allow the test tube to stand.
   Has more of the cream of tartar dissolved? Suggest what is happening. (Relate your observations to those in Procedure 2.) Is a solution of cream of tartar strongly acidic? Explain.

6. Cream of tartar is often used with baking soda ($NaHCO_3$) in baking. To see why, place enough baking soda in a large test tube to fill the rounded part. Add a depth of 5 cm of water and a pinch of cream of tartar.
   What do you observe? What effect would this behavior have on cake batter?

7. The action of an acid on a carbonate is used as a test for the presence of a carbonate. Use this information to determine which of the following materials contains carbonate: epsom salt, chalk, alum, limestone.

Summary and Additional Notes:

Compounds that result when metals combine with non-metals are commonly composed of positive, metallic ions and negative, non-metallic ions. It is because of the strong electrical attraction between the oppositely charged ions that these substances are solid, crystalline and generally hard. The general name *salt* is given to those ionic compounds which have a positive ion other than H^+ and a negative ion other than OH^-. (Many salts such as Na_2SO_4 do not contain any H^+ or OH^-; other salts, such as $NaHSO_4$ and $Cu(OH)Cl$, do.)

Many non-metals combine readily with other non-metals. The resulting substances, which are not ionic, are composed of neutral chemical units called molecules. Such substances are often gaseous or liquid when the molecular mass is low (e.g. CO_2, H_2O).

Hydrogen sometimes behaves like a metal and at other times like a non-metal. Because of this, some hydrogen compounds when dissolved in water are able to change from the covalent (molecular) type, typical of combinations of non-metals, to the ionic type, typical of compounds containing both metals and non-metals. For example, when hydrogen nitrate (nitric acid) molecules are added to water, the following reaction occurs:

$$HNO_3\ (l) \longrightarrow H^+\ (aq) + NO_3^-\ (aq)$$

In this reaction, which is typical of acids, hydrogen nitrate molecules contribute protons (hydrogen ions) to the water solution.

The difference between a strong acid and a weak acid lies in the degree to which such ionization occurs. For example, hydrogen acetate (acetic acid) is a weak acid because only a small fraction of its molecules become ionized. (See the note following Question 9 on page 243 .)

Hydrogen ions have the following properties in water solutions:

(a) H^+ ions react with some (but not all) metals to give hydrogen gas and a metallic ion in solution, e.g.

$$Mg\ (s) + 2H^+\ (aq) \longrightarrow Mg^{2+}\ (aq) + H_2\ (g)$$

(b) H^+ ions react with hydroxide ions to form water molecules, e.g.

$$H^+\ (aq) + OH^-\ (aq) \longrightarrow H_2O\ (l)$$

(c) H^+ ions react with carbonate ions in two stages. (Only the second stage, in which CO_2 molecules result, will have been obvious in your experiment.)

$$CO_3^{2-}\ (aq)\ or\ (s) + H^+\ (aq) \longrightarrow HCO_3^-\ (aq)$$
$$HCO_3^-\ (aq) + H^+\ (aq) \longrightarrow H_2O\ (l) + CO_2\ (g)$$

Questions:

*1. What ions are present in a water solution of HCl? NaOH? H_2SO_4?

*2. Write equations which show the ionization that results when the following are dissolved in water: hydrogen chloride, sodium chloride and hyrogen sulphate. (There are two stages of ionization when H_2SO_4 is dissolved in water. When an H_2SO_4 molecule has lost one H^+ ion, the resulting HSO_4^- ion may lose another H^+ ion.)

*3. Of all the ions that you listed in Question 1, which pair could combine and remain combined in the presence of water molecules? If this pair combined, which remaining pairs would form strong electrolytes?

*4. It is possible to cause NaOH solution to react with HCl solution so that a neutral solution results. (Here, "neutral" means "neither acidic nor basic" – it does not mean electrically neutral.) What will the products of this chemical change be?

*5.(a) Write the equations for the neutralization reaction
   (i)   between NaOH and HCl,
   (ii) between H_2SO_4 and NaOH.
  (b) What kind of electrolyte is formed by the reaction between an acid and a base?

*6. Why did it take more drops of NaOH to neutralize the H_2SO_4 in Procedure 3 than to neutralize the HCl in Procedures 1 and 2? (Refer to the equation you wrote in answering Question 5.)

†7. Suggest a similarity between the reactions that occurred in Procedures 2 and 3 and those that occurred in Procedures 5 and 6.

†8. Given that the formula of cream of tartar is $HKC_4H_4O_6$ (only the first hydrogen forms H^+ ions in water), write the equation for the reaction between cream of tartar and NaOH. (This reaction is a neutralization reaction.)

References and Suggestions for Further Investigation:

1. An interesting experiment that shows the relative mobilities of hydrogen and hydroxyl ions is described on page 45 of *Chemistry Takes Shape, Book 3*, an excellent book by A. H. Johnstone and T. I. Morrison (London: Heinemann Educational Books Ltd., 1967).

   The apparatus required is similar to that used in Part C of Experiment III-3. Make a solution of gelatin in water, add a tablespoonful of KNO_3 and sufficient universal indicator to turn the mixture a deep green. Pour this mixture into two U-tubes to within 3 cm of the top and allow it to set. Now pour 1 M HCl into the right-hand arm of each U-tube and 1 M NaOH into the left-hand arm. Allow one of the tubes to stand and slowly mix by itself. Insert two electrodes into the arms of the second tube and connect a battery to them so that the positive terminal is in the HCl solution. Color changes of the indicator will show how quickly the two ions (H^+ and OH^-) move.

UNIT **IV**   **W. H. Rasmussen**

SOUND AND WAVE MOTION

INTRODUCTION

Many of your experiences come from listening to sounds; indeed, aside from sight, hearing is the main means by which you obtain information from the world around you. You have learned to recognize the hum of a bee and the bark of a dog. More important, you have learned to use sound to communicate with other people.

The sounds that you experience are many and varied. This suggests that the nature of sound is complex. In this unit you will conduct experiments with sound and then with models that represent sound to show what sound is and how it is produced, transmitted and detected.

IV–1   REQUIREMENTS FOR SOUND

What conditions are required to produce, transmit and detect sound?

APPARATUS REQUIRED
> *Tuning fork*
> *rubber mallet (e.g. one-holed stopper on a pencil)*
> *pith ball on string*
> *large container for water*
> *ruler*
> *(per class)*
> *bell in vacuo apparatus*
> *vacuum pump*
> *vacuum wax*
> *rubber tubing*
> *glass tubing*
> *3 – 6 volt D.C. power supply*
> *fine copper wire (#34)*
> *wire leads*
> *audio oscillator with amplifier (or 16 mm movie projector)*
> *speaker (or Galton's whistle)*
> *helium gas supply*

Fig. IV–1–1   Holding the base of a vibrating tuning fork against your elbow

Procedure:
1. Strike one prong of a tuning fork with a rubber mallet. (Never strike a tuning fork with a hard object.) Now perform the following tests:
   (a) Touch the surface of water with the prongs of the fork.
   (b) Touch a suspended pith ball with the prongs of the fork.
   (c) Touch your elbow with the *base* and then with the prongs of the fork. (See Fig. IV-1-1.)

What effect did the tuning fork have on the water and the pith ball? What effect did it have on your elbow? What do these effects tell you about the motion of the fork?

2. Touch your throat while you hum.

   What is apparently happening as you hum?

3. Project ¾ of the length of a 30 cm ruler beyond the edge of a table. Hold it firmly in place by pressing the supported end to the table. Now pluck the free end with the thumb of your other hand to produce a sound.

   What causes the sound to stop eventually? From the above investigations, what is apparently necessary for the production of sound?

4. Hold an object in your hand and slowly move it back and forth.

   Does it produce an audible sound? Explain. What additional requirement is there for the recognition of sounds by your ear?

5. Suspend an electric bell by means of fine conducting wires from a sealed rubber stopper at the top of a sealed bell jar. (See Fig. IV-1-2.) Connect the bell to dry cells or a power supply so that it rings loudly. Use a vacuum pump to remove as much air as possible from the jar while the bell is ringing.

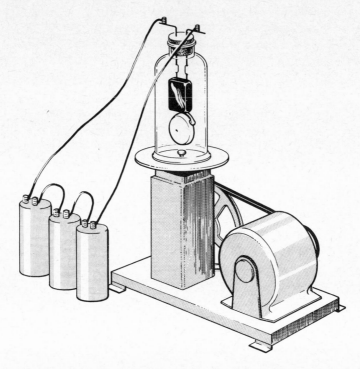

Fig. IV–1–2   What is necessary for the transmission of sound?

What happens to the sound as the air is withdrawn from the jar?
Allow air to re-enter the jar while the bell is still ringing.

What do you observe as air re-enters the bell jar? Therefore, what is required if sound is to be transmitted?

6. (Demonstration)

NOTE: *A Galton's whistle may be used if the equipment described is not available.*

To produce sounds caused by vibrations of different rates (different frequencies), connect an audio frequency generator to an amplifier and speaker as shown in Fig. IV-1-3. (If the frequency generator or oscillator has a sufficiently high wattage output, an amplifier may not be required. Alternatively, explore the possibility of using a microphone jack plugged into a 16 mm movie projector.) Vary the sound frequency by turning the control knob on the audio frequency generator.

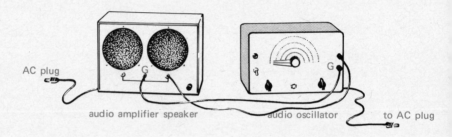

Fig. IV–1–3   Connecting an audio oscillator to an amplifier and speaker

What is the highest frequency that you can detect? What range of frequencies can you hear? Do you have any hearing gaps in this range? If the frequency of a sound is above your range of hearing, how could you tell that the sound exists? Therefore, for sound to be observed, what is required in addition to a source and a medium for its transmission?

7. (Demonstration) Take a breath of helium gas. With your lungs full of helium, speak to the class.

CAUTION: *Make certain that it is helium and not another gas.*

What effect does helium have on the sound of your voice?

Questions:

*1. What are the three general requirements for sound?

*2. When a tuning fork is struck with a mallet, it receives an amount of energy. What has happened to this energy when the fork ceases to vibrate?

*3. If a huge asteroid collided with the Moon, could someone on the Moon hear a sound? Through what medium?

*4. Vibrations are used to clean a chimney, but no sound can be heard by someone in the house. Explain.

*5. Horses rotate their ears forward when they observe an object in front of them. What does this response indicate about the path taken when sound travels from the source to the receiver? If sound travelled in a circular path, would you be able to locate the source?

*6. What evidence do you have that sound normally travels in all directions from its source?

†7. Suggest why increasing your distance from the source of sound decreases the volume of the sound you hear.

References and Suggestions for Further Investigation:

1. Reading pages 76-78 of *Physics is Fun, Book Two* by Jardine (London: Heinemann Educational Books Ltd., 1967) will give you an increased understanding of the transmission of sound through air.

2. For a diagram and brief description of the ear, consult pages 357-358 of *Modern Physics II* by Dull, Metcalfe and Brooks (New York: Holt, Rinehart & Winston Inc., 1962) or pages 235-236 of *A School Physics* by C. W. Kearsey (London: Longmans Green & Co. Ltd., 1962).

3. Pages 8-15 of *Science Experiments With Sound* by Harry Sootin (New York: W. W. Norton & Co. Inc., 1964) discuss and suggest further experiments with vibrating bodies.

4. Read about the many uses of ultrasonic sound such as sonar, detecting flaws in metals, homogenizing milk, cleaning tools, performing "bloodless" surgery, precipitating smoke, drilling teeth.

5. Recently, infrasonic sound experiments have revealed important facts about the effects of these low frequency vibrations on our bodies. Try to find information about these discoveries.

NOTE: *Experiment IV-3 requires a piece of apparatus called a Crova's disc. This note gives you advance notice so that you will have time to prepare the apparatus. For instructions on how to make it, turn to "NOTE", page 257*

IV–2 MEDIUMS WHICH TRANSMIT SOUNDS

From the previous experiment, it is apparent that sound requires a *vibrating source*. Although a vibrating body is the cause of audible sounds, not all sounds produced by vibrating bodies are audible. You could not hear the infrasonic sound produced by a slowly vibrating ruler, nor could you hear ultrasonic fre-

quencies above approximately 20,000 vibrations/second. It is apparent, therefore, that hearing a sound depends on your sensitivity to the frequency of the
sound. A person with good hearing can hear any sound with a frequency between 20 vib./sec. and 20,000 vib./sec. A third condition for sound to be
audible is the presence of a vibrating medium between the source and receiver.
This condition is absent when a bell vibrates in a vacuum. No sound is heard;
therefore, air is necessary to transmit sound from the bell to your ear. The air
serves as the highway or *medium* that carries the sound.

This experiment is designed to test the ability of liquids and solids to
serve as sound mediums.

APPARATUS REQUIRED (per station)
>   *Tuning fork*
>   *rubber mallet*
>   (per class)
>   *a large water container with a flat bottom in which a wooden block*
>   *can be floated*
>   *wooden block*
>   *tuning fork with resonance box*
>   *4 tin cans*
>   *cord*
>   *nail and hammer*

Procedure:
1. Touch the bone behind your ear with the base of a vibrating tuning
   fork. (See Fig. IV-2-1.)

Fig. IV–2–1   Does sound travel through bone?

**What difference in loudness do you notice between the sound heard
when the fork is in contact with the bone behind your ear and the
sound heard when it is not? Through what material or materials must
the vibrations have been transmitted to the inner ear when the fork
was held in contact with the bone?**
2. Touch your lips and your teeth with the base of the fork.
   Which is the better medium – flesh or bone?

3. Press your ear to a desk or table top. Now touch the table with the base of a vibrating tuning fork.
   Is the table a better or worse medium than air?
   Press your hand on the table top a short distance from a vibrating fork that has its base in contact with the table.
   What is happening to the table?

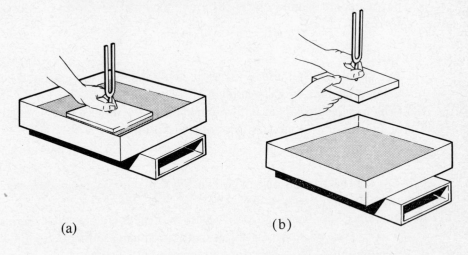

(a)   (b)

Fig. IV–2–2   The block and vibrating tuning fork are held first in and then out of the
               water

4. Assemble the apparatus illustrated in Fig. IV-2-2. Float a wooden block inside a large container of water which is resting on a resonance box from which the tuning fork has been removed.
   Press the base of a vibrating tuning fork firmly against the floating block and listen with your ear in front of the open end of the resonance box.
   Did the vibrations travel through the water?
   Repeat the procedure with the block suspended above the water. Press the fork against the block with the same amount of pressure used in the previous case.
   What difference do you notice? Is water a good medium for sound?
5. Punch small holes in the centers of the bottoms of two tin cans. Pass one end of a 6 ft cord through each of the holes and tie large knots in the cord so that it cannot be pulled through the holes. Use each can as a speaker and receiver to communicate with your partner. Alter the tension in the cord to determine what effect this change has on the ability of the cord to transmit sound. Try different sounds such as those produced by tapping the can or scratching the cord.
6. Cross your cord line with that of another group so that the taut cords touch each other at only one point. Stroke the cord near your can.

What paths along the cords are now available to the sound that originates at your can? What effects are produced? What takes place in the string while sound is being transmitted? (Are the vibrations that you initiate being transmitted?)

7. Test the relative abilities of materials such as wood or metal to transmit sound. Use the plumbing or the walls to communicate with your partner some distance away. You will have to use a form of Morse Code.

Questions:

*1. In general, which phase of matter (solid, liquid or gas) appears to be the best medium for transmission of sound?

*2. Why was the block placed in and then out of the water to test whether or not water is a medium for sound transmission? (Hint: Through what other medium did sound travel to your ear from the tuning fork?)

*3. The approach of a train can be detected earlier by listening at the steel rails. Explain.

*4. You must supply energy to an object to make it vibrate. Why then is it reasonable to expect an object that is producing sound to gradually stop vibrating? What happens to its energy?

References and Suggestions for Further Investigation:

1. Pages 78-79 of *Physics is Fun, Book Two* (London: Heinemann Educational Books Ltd., 1967) by Jardine discuss sound transmission in liquids and solids.

2. The speeds of sound in various mediums are discussed on pages 246-248 of *A School Physics* by C. W. Kearsey (London: Longmans, Green & Co. Ltd., 1962).

IV–3 SOUND WAVES (Part Demonstration)

You have seen that a vibrating object causes adjacent materials to vibrate; for example, the table vibrated when touched by the vibrating fork. The sound was heard more distinctly when you placed the fork in contact with your ear bone. It must, therefore, have caused the bone behind your ear to vibrate.

When sounds are received, energy has been transferred from the source to the receiver. It is reasonable to believe that air, like solids, also transmits sound by means of vibrational motion. In this experiment the transmission of sound through air will be described by the use of models which demonstrate this vibrational motion.

APPARATUS REQUIRED (per class)
> *Crova's disc and slotted disc**
> *rotator*
> (per class)
> *4 marbles*
> *grooved ruler*
> *flat wire coil ('slinky')*
> *1 in diameter spring about 6 ft long when unstretched*
> *a 12 ft length of 1½ in wood dowelling*

*NOTE   A spiral for a Crova's disc can be made quickly by drawing a line from the center to the circumference on a rapidly rotating disc that is 2 or 3 ft. in diameter. Your pencil must move with a constant speed to produce a uniform spiral. A stationary disc to be placed in front of the spiralled disc should have a slot of approximately the dimensions shown in Fig. IV-3-1.

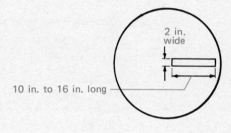
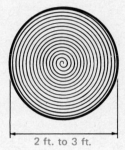

Fig. IV–3–1   Construction of a Crova's disc

Procedure:

1. Place 3 marbles equidistant from each other along the groove in a ruler so that they are close to, but not in contact with, each other. Strike one of the end marbles with a fourth rolling marble.
   What do you observe about the resulting motion of each of the marbles? How was the energy from the first marble transferred to the last marble?

Fig. IV–3–2   The loops at one end of the slinky are compressed and then released

2. Stretch a slinky a moderate amount along a table or on the floor. Have your partner hold one end of the slinky in a fixed position, and gather about 10 or 15 loops at the other end to form a compressed section. (See Fig. IV-3-2.) Now release several of the loops while still holding the end of the slinky.

How does the released compression travel along the slinky? In what directions do the loops of the slinky move? In what way do these motions resemble those of the balls in Procedure 1?

NOTE: *Care must be taken to avoid tangling the slinky or permanently distorting it by stretching it beyond its elastic limit.*

3. Create similar compressions by regularly vibrating one end of the slinky in the direction of its length. What do you observe about the separation of individual pulses? Does the separation between two consecutive pulses vary as they move down the slinky? If so, how? **What does this observation tell you about the speed of each pulse?**

NOTE: *The movement of the disturbance along the slinky is called a* wave. *When the passage of the disturbance causes the particles of the transmitting medium to move back and forth in the direction in which the wave travels, the wave motion is called* compressional. *A single displacement travelling through a medium is called a* pulse wave. *When regularly recurring vibrations cause a train of pulses to travel through a medium, the number of vibrations past a point in a second is called the* frequency of the wave train. *The distance between successive pulses of the wave train is called the* wavelength.

4. Create pulses of different *amplitude* (different amounts of compression).
   Is the speed of the pulse affected by the amplitude?

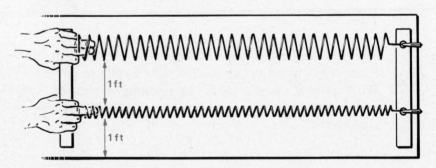

Fig. IV–3–3   Comparing sound velocities in different mediums

5. Lay a taut 1 in diameter coiled spring alongside the taut slinky of equal length so that the springs are parallel, 1 ft apart and situated with their ends opposite each other. (See Fig. IV-3-3.) Produce simultaneous pulses in the two springs. Do not overstretch either of the springs.
   How do the velocities of the pulses in the two springs compare? Each of the springs represents a different medium for the transmission of compressional waves. Does the medium affect the velocity of the

pulse? **What does this sound model suggest about the relative speeds of sound in mediums such as air, water and steel?**

When compressional waves were produced in the springs, especially in the 1 in diameter spring, the pulse did not disappear at the other end but returned to you.

What sound phenomenon does this reflection of the pulse represent?

6. Secure the center of the spiralled (Crova's) disc, previously prepared, to a motor rotator and cause it to rotate so that the spiral appears to expand.

    What point represents the source of the sound waves? What do the lines represent?

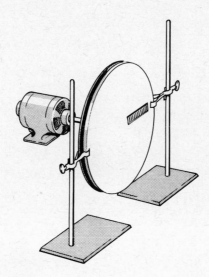

Fig. IV–3–4   Crova's disc assembled

7. Place the slotted disc in front of the spiral disc as shown in Fig IV-3-4. Rotate the spiralled disc and view the pattern through the slot of the stationary disc. Describe the apparent motion of the lines.

NOTE: *The motion of the slinky and the apparent motion of the lines of the Crova's disc closely resemble the motion of sound waves when air is transmitting sound. Fig. IV-3-5 represents the motion of air in response to a vibrating tuning fork. The sound radiates in all directions but, for simplicity, only a small section of the vibrating air has been shown.*

When the tuning fork prongs spread, as in Fig. IV-3-5(a), a region of compressed air appears on the outer edge of each prong. The molecules in this region move outward to reduce the pressure. In so doing, new regions of compressed air are formed that continue to move out at a constant speed. When the tuning fork prongs move close together as in Fig. IV-3-5(b) a rarefaction appears on the outer edge of each prong. The air outside this region rushes in to equalize the pressure, forming a rarefaction at a new region further removed from the fork. The rarefaction continues to move outward at the same velocity as the compression. The prongs move outward again as in Fig. IV-3-5(d) and a second compression is formed, Fig. IV-3-5(e). This cycle repeats itself as long as the prongs vibrate. It is important to realize that individual molecules move back and forth only short distances in the direction in which sound moves. The waves that result are therefore compressional waves. Only the compressions and rarefactions travel outward from the source. They travel at a constant speed. The distance between consecutive compressions or rarefactions is called the wavelength.

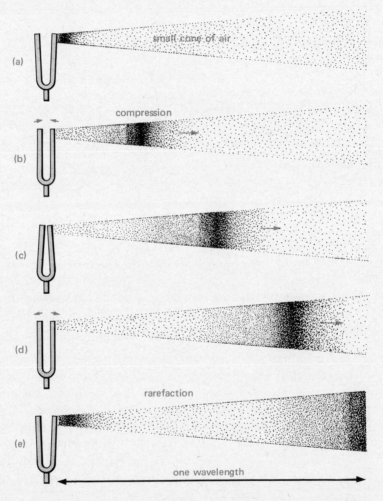

Fig. IV–3–5   Regions of compression and rarefaction move outward while the particles of air move only back and forth

8. Stretch 1 in diameter spring along the floor and create compressional waves in it.
   How does the speed of the reflected pulse compare with the speed of the initial pulse?

9. Reflection is more readily apparent if you use a suspended slinky. Suspend a slinky on cords that are at least 2 ft long and attached to the slinky at equal intervals (every 6 or 10 loops). Attach the other ends of the cords to a long board such as a 12 ft length of 1½ in diameter wood dowelling that is tied to the ceiling. (The use of dowelling allows the appartus to be rolled up and stored at ceiling level when not in use.) Adjust the lengths of the supporting cords so that, when the cords hang vertically, the center axis of the stationary slinky is a straight line. Tie the ends of the slinky to rigid supports. (See Fig. IV-3-6.) This slinky will also be used in later experiments to study more complex motion of air molecules.
   Use the suspended slinky to compare the speeds of the initial and reflected waves.

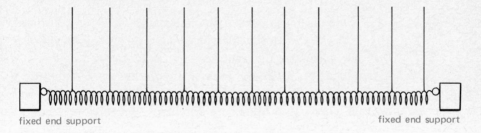

fixed end support   fixed end support

Fig. IV–3–6   Reflected waves in a suspended slinky

   If sound reflects from walls in a similar manner, how will the speed of the echo compare with the speed of the initial sound?

10. Stand at a measured distance of at least 100 ft from a large wall and face it. Clap your hands or two boards together and have your partner measure and record the time that elapses before the echo returns. Using the time taken and the total distance travelled (twice the distance to the wall), calculate the speed of sound in air.

11. Clap your hands in the classroom.
    Can you detect an echo? How could you demonstrate that an echo is produced even though it cannot be heard? What does your inability to detect an echo in a small classroom tell you about your sense of hearing?

Questions:

*1. What examples can you cite to support the argument that air can be compressed and rarefied?

*2. Suppose you are observing a very long but orderly convoy of military trucks on a highway and you make the following observations:
The spacing between adjacent trucks is constant and equal to 100 ft (measured between the centers of successive trucks).
Every minute 20 trucks pass.

(a) How many trucks heading toward you are within one minute of reaching you? The answer to this question is the number of trucks that will pass you each minute or the frequency in trucks per minute.

(b) How far away is the farthest of the trucks referred to in (a)?

(c) Therefore, how fast does this truck travel in feet per minute?

(d) Answer Questions (a), (b) and (c) when the truck spacings are 'l' ft and the number of trucks passing per minute is 'f.' Express the relationship between the speed 'v', the wavelength 'l' and the frequency 'f' of the trucks in the convoy.

(e) Suppose that the trucks accelerate to a new speed when they reach a certain point on the road (for example, when they reach new pavement).

  (i) Is the distance between them affected?

  (ii) Is the "frequency" with which they pass an observer on the new pavement different from that in Question 2(a)?

*3. A large number of cars move down a straight highway so that they remain 2 miles apart. An observer standing on the side of the road notices that a car passes him every 4 minutes (15 cars every hour). How fast must the cars be moving? Express your answer in mi/hr.

*4. A machine gun fires 10 bullets every second. If the bullets travel 2,000 ft/sec, how far apart are they as they fly through the air?

*5.(a) The compressions in a slinky are 4 ft apart and the frequency of vibration of the free end is 5 vib/sec. At what speed do the compressions travel in the slinky?

(b) The compressions created in air by a tuning fork of frequency 256 vib/sec are 4.3 ft apart. What is the speed of sound waves in air?

*6. If the end of a slinky is held loosely, a pulse arriving at that end will not be reflected. What happens to the energy of the pulse? What situation does this correspond to in sound?

*7. When sound waves arrive at a wall, what three things can happen to the sound energy?

References and Suggestions for Further Investigation:

1. If you have a Savart's wheel, perform the following experiment. Hold a strip of thin cardboard against the wheel teeth while rotating the wheel at various speeds. Compare the sounds produced. You have

probably noticed the same effect while holding a piece of cardboard against a spinning bicycle tire. Be very careful not to touch the rotating wheel because it can cut your finger.

2. Hold a tapered nozzle on the end of a rubber tube near the holes of a rotating Siren disc. Blow air at the holes through the nozzle at various distances from the center of the disc. Explain the resulting effect. See if you can make the disc play musical notes.

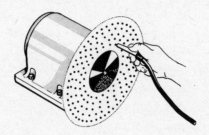

3. Pages 20-26 of *Science Experiments With Sound* by Harry Sootin (New York: W. W. Norton & Co. Inc., 1964) describe the use of the above two pieces of equipment. Experiments that illustrate reflection phenomena are listed on pages 32-35.

4. Pages 248-253 of *A School Physics* by C. W. Kearsey (London: Longmans, Green & Co. Ltd., 1962) discuss echoes and their use.

IV–4   REPRESENTATION OF A SOUND WAVE (Demonstration)

The simple graphical representation of a sound wave whose energy is diminishing is illustrated in Fig. IV-4-1. A diagram of actual air pressure conditions appears directly below the graph.

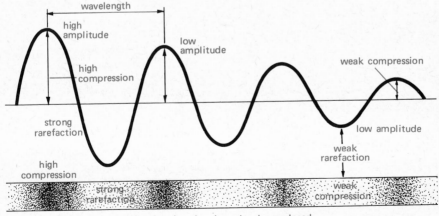

Fig. IV–4–1   Using a graph to represent sound waves

The pattern produced by sound waves on the screen of an oscilloscope is similar to the pattern above and can be used to analyse the wave. Both the wave length and amplitude (which is related to the energy) of a sound can be easily observed.

APPARATUS REQUIRED (per class)
Oscilloscope
microphone
fixed frequency sound sources such as tuning forks with frequencies of 256, 320, 384, 512 and 576 cps (or an audio oscillator and combination audio amplifier and speaker)
rubber mallet
16 mm movie projector

Procedure:
1. Turn on an oscilloscope and adjust it to obtain a horizontal trace across the center of the screen. (If you do not obtain a trace, try varying the intensity and adjusting the vertical and horizontal centering knobs in turn.) When you have established a trace, focus it to a sharp line. Center the trace using the centering knobs and adjust the horizontal gain so that the trace length is approximately ¾ of the screen.
2. Attach a microphone to the oscilloscope. If there is no microphone jack on the oscilloscope it will be necessary to run two leads from the vertical input and ground posts to the microphone, as shown in Fig. IV-4-2. (For greater amplification, insert the microphone jack into a 16 mm movie projector and connect the input and ground posts to the two wires of the speaker.)

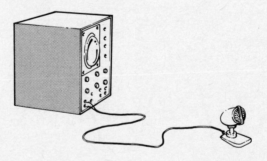

Fig. IV–4–2   Leads from the microphone can be used instead of a jack

3. Use your ear to compare the sounds produced by the various tuning forks when they are caused to vibrate.

4. Place the microphone close to a 256 cycle/second (middle C) tuning fork that is mounted on a resonance box. Adjust the vertical gain and, if necessary, the vertical input to obtain a pattern on the screen that has a fairly large amplitude. Now adjust the sweep time of the electron beam across the tube face until you establish a stationary pattern of 4 waves as in Fig. IV-4-3. If the oscilloscope screen is lined with a grid, adjust the horizontal gain so that the total trace is 8 grid spaces long and adjust the horizontal centering so that the trace begins on a grid line.

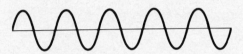

Fig. IV–4–3   A sound wave as it appears on an oscilloscope

On the screen, how long is the representation of one wave?
5. Now in turn place the microphone near other vibrating, mounted forks with the frequencies listed in "Materials Required." Do not adjust the oscilloscope except when necessary to make very slight sweep time adjustments to stabilize the pattern. Record the number of cycles or wavelengths that appear when each fork is vibrated. Compare the representations of the wavelengths of the various sound waves produced by the forks, i.e., calculate the ratio:

$$\frac{\text{total length of the pattern}}{\text{number of waves in the pattern}}$$

for each frequency. Comparisons are possible because the number of waves seen on the screen in each case occurs within very nearly the same time interval. (Although the wavelength shown on the oscilloscope is not the actual wavelength, it is a scaled model of it.)
How do the wavelengths compare? How do the ratios of the wavelengths compare with the ratios of the frequencies written on the forks? If the frequency is doubled, what happens to the wavelength? How is the pitch of a sound related to its frequency?
6. Ensure that the vertical input is set at its most sensitive range (you have probably had it on this setting) and adjust the vertical gain to near maximum. Place the microphone at a convenient distance from a vibrating fork so that the amplitude of the sound wave as shown on the oscilloscope is large and easily measurable. Measure the distance to the fork. Now double the distance to the fork and record the new amplitude of the wave. (This procedure must be carried out

quickly so that the amplitude of the vibration of the fork does not have time to be reduced considerably.) Check your results by repeating the procedure, this time starting at the farther position and then moving to the nearer position.

How was the amplitude affected by the distance of the fork from the microphone? Explain why.

Questions:

*1. Describe the change(s) you would hear in the characteristics of the sounds if the wave graphs changed as follows:

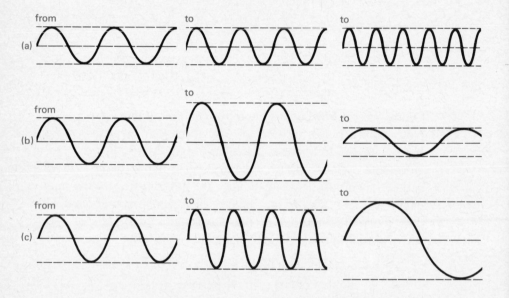

*2. Why is a child's voice higher pitched than an adult's voice?

*3. Suggest how you can prevent the amplitude of a sound wave (related to its loudness) from decreasing so rapidly as you move away from the source. (How do cheerleaders sometimes solve the problem?)

*4. In what ways is the oscilloscope a better instrument than your ear for recording sounds?

*5.(a) From the results you obtained in Procedure 5, what can you say about the speeds of waves of different frequencies in the same medium? (Hint: recall the relation you derived between frequency, wavelength and velocity.)

(b) If a soprano and a baritone sing a duet, will their synchronization be affected if the listener moves further away? What does this experience tell you about the relative speeds of sounds of different pitch?

†6. Explain how you would use an oscilloscope, a sound amplifier and a microphone to check the acoustics (sound properties) of a room.

References and Suggestions for Further Investigation:
1. A discussion of a cathode ray tube, the working part of an oscilloscope, is contained on pages 326-328 of *Matter and Energy – Foundations of Modern Physics* by J. H. MacLachlan, K. G. McNeill and J. M. Bell (Toronto: Clarke, Irwin & Co. Ltd., 1970).

IV–5   NATURAL FREQUENCY

Different objects vibrate with different natural frequencies. In this experiment you will observe the natural frequencies and physical characteristics of a variety of vibrating bodies. Then objects with similar natural frequencies will be arranged with some physical connection to each other. Finally, objects with dissimilar natural frequencies will be so arranged, so that the vibrational motion of one can affect the motion of another.

APPARATUS REQUIRED (per station)
  4 identical one-hole stoppers
  nylon string
  cord
  meter stick
  2 different masses (200 gm, 500 gm)
  2 C-clamps
  4 paper clips
  masking tape
  (per class)
  a clock with a sweep second hand

  1 different and 2 identical tuning forks mounted on resonance boxes
  resonating tube
  lycopodium powder (or cork dust)
  soft leather chamois (or rag)
  resin or alcohol
  a suspended slinky

Procedure:
1. Suspend a pendulum from a table as in Fig. IV-5-1. Start the pendulum swinging with a small amplitude and record the time taken for 10 complete swings (from A to B and back again to A). Repeat this procedure to obtain a second reading. Calculate the frequency of the

pendulum in each case, (i.e. the number of complete vibrations in 1 second). Since you know that there were 10 vibrations in the time you measured, this can be easily done.

How do the observed frequencies for the two trials compare with each other?

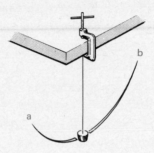

Fig. IV–5–1   Vibration of a pendulum

2. Repeat Procedure 1 using the same pendulum with a string of shorter length (about one half as long).

How can the frequency of a pendulum be increased? (Allow for experimental error.) What can be said of the frequencies of pendulums of the same length? What can be said about the frequencies of pendulums of different lengths?

3. Clamp a meter stick to a table as shown in Fig. IV-5-2, so that 90 cm of the meter stick extends beyond the table. Secure a 200 gm mass at the free end with masking tape.

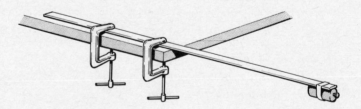

Fig. IV–5–2   Vibration of a meter stick

NOTE: *Do not overstrain the meter stick by using too great a mass or too large an amplitude of vibration.*

Determine and record the time taken for 20 vibrations of the meter stick and calculate the frequency. Repeat the procedure and compare the two frequencies.

4. Repeat, using a 500 gm mass on the end of the meter stick.
   How does the natural frequency of vibration of the meter stick depend upon the mass attached?

5. Attach a horizontal cord (or length of rubber tubing) to two rigid supports (two support stands or bench tops will do) and suspend four pendulums as in Fig. IV-5-3. The pendulums should be tied tightly to the horizontal cord. Pendulums A and C should have the same lengths; pendulum B should be longer than A, and pendulum D, shorter. Start pendulum A vibrating with a moderate amplitude. Watch all of the pendulums for some time.
   What happens to the other pendulums?

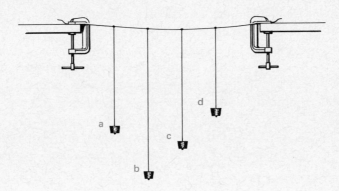

Fig. IV–5–3   The effect of one vibrating pendulum on another

6. Stop all motion. Then repeat Procedure 5 but this time start pendulum B vibrating.
   What now happens to the other pendulums?
   Stop the motion and repeat Procedure 5 for pendulum C and then D.
   How must their natural frequencies compare if one vibrating body is to transfer its vibrations to another?

7. Check your conclusions using identical tuning forks on resonance boxes. Strike one of two identical forks with a rubber mallet. Place one box adjacent to, but not in contact with, its twin as in Fig. IV-5-4. After a short period of time stop the vibration of the first fork.
   What has happened to the other fork?

8. Repeat Procedure 7 using two forks that differ in frequency.
   What happens to the fork that is not struck by the hammer?

NOTE: *When one vibrating object causes another object to vibrate, the vibration produced is said to be a sympathetic vibration. The object that so vibrates is said to* resonate.

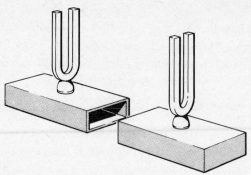

Fig. IV–5–4   Observing resonance

9. (Demonstration) The air in a tube such as an organ pipe also has a natural frequency of vibration. This can be demonstrated using a resonating tube. Set up the resonating tube as shown in Fig. IV-5-5. Make certain that the metal rod is clamped firmly, exactly at its midpoint. Spread a fine, even line of lycopodium powder or cork dust uniformly along the tube and slide the tube over the rod as shown in Fig. IV-5-5. Adjust the elevation of the rod so that the metal disc at the end of the rod is not in contact with the tube. Twist the tube on its axis so that the powder is on the verge of slipping down.

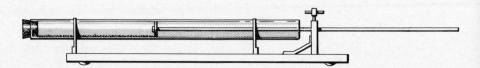

Fig. IV–5–5   A resonating tube

10. Put resin (or alcohol) on a rag or a piece of chamois leather and use it to stroke the outer end of the rod. You can tell whether or not the rod is vibrating by the high-frequency squeaking sound that results. Adjust the distance from the metal disc to the stopper, one cm at a time, by sliding the glass tube. Do this until a distinct pattern forms in the powder when the rod is stroked. If you have the correct adjustment the powder will respond vigorously.

If the vibrating rod causes the air in the tube to vibrate, how must the frequencies of vibration of the rod and the enclosed air column compare? Make a sketch of the pattern formed by the powder. What do you observe about the spacing of the dust piles? Where would you expect dust to collect – at points where the air is vibrating or where it is at rest?

11. Readjust the distance from the metal disc to the stopper by moving the tube.

    Does the air in the tube resonate for other lengths of the tube?

†12. If you have the time and patience, you can clamp the rod in a different position so that it vibrates at a frequency that is a multiple of its previous frequency. With the rod in this position, it is easy to demonstrate that the air inside the tube has more than one natural frequency.

13. The suspended slinky used in Experiment IV-3 can be used as a model to demonstrate the motion of the air in the resonating tube. Use a meter stick to create "standing" compressional waves in the coil, that is, a stationary pattern in the coil. (See Fig. IV-5-6.) The frequency you choose will determine the type of compressional wave that results. You may need to practice creating these waves to avoid producing lateral motion in the spring. A successful method is to develop the wave gradually by allowing the slinky vibration to guide the frequency you apply. With careful manipulation of the meter stick, you can make the slinky vibrate in 1, 2, 3, 4, 5 or more distinct sections. The fundamental frequency of the slinky is produced when it is made to vibrate in only one section (all of the waves moving to the left and then all to the right). Harmonics or overtones are produced when the slinky vibrates in 2 or more sections.

    Where do the compressions and rarefactions occur? If the air in the resonating tube vibrates in this manner, which point(s) on the spring represents where the dust would collect, (that is, where the spring moves the most or the least)?

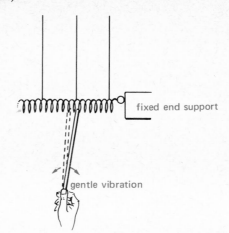

Fig. IV–5–6   Producing standing
              waves in a slinky

NOTE: *Points along the tube where the air does not move or points along the slinky where the coils do not move are called* nodes. *Points halfway between nodes, where the motion is at a maximum, are called* antinodes.

Questions:

*1. Why do pendulum clocks tick at a constant rate hour after hour?
*2. If a pendulum clock was gaining time, how would you adjust it?
*3. You can make a playground swing move through a larger and larger arc by pushing on it each time it reaches the end of its swing.

(a) How does the frequency of your pushes compare with the frequency of the swing?

(b) What would happen if you pushed on it briefly while it was moving rapidly towards you?

(c) What would happen if you pulled on the swing at a regular frequency that was out of step with the natural frequency of the swing?

*4. Why does the rod produce a sound when it is stroked?
*5. The waves produced in a resonating tube are called "standing waves." Why? (Hint: Remember the patterns produced in the slinky.)
*6. What other musical instruments use vibrating air to produce sounds? What general relation do you notice between the size of the instrument and the pitch of the sound it produces?
*7. Why do wind instruments have air vents?

References and Suggestions for Further Investigation:

1. Natural vibrations are discussed on pages 44-47 of *Science Experiments With Sound* by Harry Sootin (New York: W. W. Norton & Co. Inc., 1964).
2. For students who prefer a more detailed analysis of vibrating objects, the discussion on pages 170-175 of *Physics for the Inquiring Mind* by Eric M. Rogers (Princeton: Princeton University Press, 1960) is recommended.
3. Choose a long cardboard tube (one used for storing maps would be ideal). Light a bunsen burner and place the tube over the burner so that the flame is enclosed. For greater effects slip a slightly larger tube over the first tube to vary its effective length. Describe what happens.
4. Cheshire's disc gives an effective representation of the motion of air in a tube. For instructions on the construction of this apparatus refer to page 34 of *Model Making for Young Psyicists* by A. D. Bulman (London: John Murray, 1963).

IV–6   TRANSVERSE (S) WAVES (Demonstration)

The waves that you have studied in previous experiments have been compressional waves. Such waves are also called longitudinal or *P waves*. (See the introduction to Exercise V-6.) Sound travels through air as P waves. Many musical instruments, however, vibrate in a transverse manner. For example, although a violin string produces compressional waves in the air, it vibrates at right angles to its length.

A wave is called a P wave if the medium vibrates in the direction in which the wave is travelling. When you vibrated the slinky in previous experiments the wave travelled down the length of the coil and the coil loops vibrated in a direction parallel to the coil. A transverse wave will also travel down the slinky but small segments of the medium will vibrate in a direction perpendicular to its length. Surface water waves are another example of transverse wave motion.

There are many similarities between compressional and transverse wave motions. Examination of Figues IV-4-1 and IV-4-3 shows that the graphical method used to represent the compressional wave has the shape of a transverse wave. You should not, however, confuse these graphs with actual transverse waves.

In this experiment, you will be introduced to the basic properties of transverse waves.

APPARATUS REQUIRED (per class)
> *Slinky*
> *4 C-clamps*
> *meter stick*
> *2 long 1 in dameter coil springs*
> *rubber tube*
> *suspended slinky*
> *sonometer*

Fig. IV–6–1   Forming a transverse wave in a slinky

Procedure:
1. Create a pulse wave in a stretched slinky by moving the end through a complete sideways vibration as shown in Fig. IV-6-1.
   Describe the pulse wave in the slinky. In what direction do the coils of the slinky move? In what direction does the pulse wave move?
2. Clamp one end of each of three mediums (a slinky, a coil spring and a rubber tube) to a rigid support as shown in Fig. IV-6-2. Support these mediums on a smooth table or on the floor. Clamp the other end of the rubber tube to a meter stick and hold the other ends of the two coils firmly to the meter stick so that the coils are parallel to each

other and to the rubber tube. If necessary, adjust the lengths of the mediums so that all are subjected to a slight tension. (See Fig. IV-6-2.)

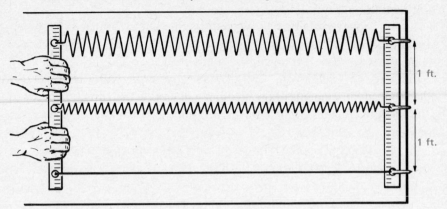

Fig. IV–6–2   Producing transverse waves

3. Give the meter stick a lateral (sideways) jerk.
   Describe the patterns produced in the mediums. Do the waves travel at the same velocity in all three mediums? If not, list the mediums from fastest to slowest. What happens to the amplitude (amount of lateral displacement) as the wave moves down the medium? Why?
   What happens to each wave when it reaches the rigid end? What do you observe about the velocity of the waves before and after they strike the rigid end?

4. Attach two identical 1 in diameter coils to a rigid support and place them on a table or on the floor so that they lie parallel to each other. Apply the same tension to the coils and produce a transverse wave as in Procedure 3. Compare the wave motions and the speeds of the wave in the two springs.
   Now alter the tension of one of the two coils and repeat the sideways jerk. Again compare the wave motion and the speed of the waves in the two coils.
   What effect does changing the tension have on the wave motion?

5. Again equalize the tensions in the two coils and in turn produce simultaneous waves of various amplitudes.
   How is the speed of the wave affected by its amplitude?

NOTE: *In Experiment IV-5 you observed that when air resonates in a tube, echoes are produced that interfere with the incident pulses. The places where compressions and rarefactions from the incident, and reflected waves pass each other and cancel each other out do not change with time. The result is a "standing" wave, a wave that has nodes or regions where no motion occurs. This effect also occurs with transverse waves when crests and troughs travelling in opposite directions meet and add to zero amplitude in the same places, called nodes.*

6. Create a small-amplitude, transverse, standing wave in the suspended slinky (Fig. IV-3-6) by displacing it laterally (at right angles to its length) at its central point and releasing it. Vibrate the slinky in its fundamental mode, as in part (a) of Fig. IV-6-3. Record the time taken for 10 vibrations.

7. Now select an appropriate frequency to create a small amplitude wave as in part (b) of Fig. IV-6-3. Move the slinky laterally at the position of an antinode, one quarter of the way along its length. Again record the time taken for 10 vibrations.

   How do the two times measured compare? How do the frequencies compare? Can you calculate the time for 10 vibrations when the slinky vibrates as in part (c)? Try it to test your answer.

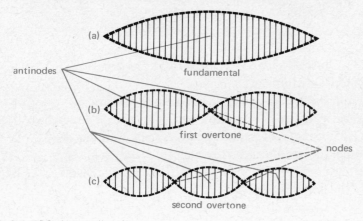

Fig. IV–6–3   Modes of vibrations of a spring; transverse standing waves

8. Pluck a sonometer string while it is being tightened.
   What happens to the pitch as the tension of the string is increased? What then happens to the resonant frequency of the string as you tighten it?

9. Shorten the length of a sonometer string by using a bridge as in Fig. IV-6-4.
   How are the pitch and frequency affected by changing the string length?

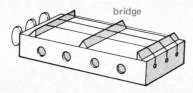

Fig. IV–6–4   A sonometer

10. Adjust two strings of different diameter so that they have the same length and tension.
    Which string produces the highest pitch and frequency?

Questions:

*1. Sketch the diagram below. Label a wavelength and a position of maximum amplitude. Three pulses have been started at the left end of the coil. In what direction are the coil loops moving? In what direction(s) is the wave moving?

Draw arrows from the labelled points to represent the directions and speeds of the coils at these points. (Use longer arrows to indicate greater speed.)

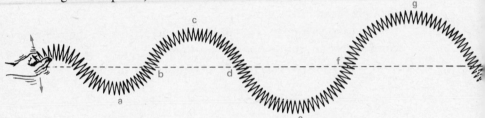

*2. What factors affect the velocity of a transverse wave in a coil (i.e. how can the medium be changed)?

*3. Explain why the coil *appears* to move forward.

*4. What evidence do you have that energy travels down the coil?

*5. Give examples of transverse waves that occur in nature.

*6. What factors affect the resonant frequency of a string?

*7. How are the overtone frequencies of a string related to the frequency of the fundamental?

*8. Why do power lines produce high pitched sounds in very cold weather?

*9. Why does an arctic wind over the ocean sound different from a tropical wind over the same surface?

†10. Why do you not usually see standing, transverse waves in water? Under what conditions might you see standing water waves?

†11. Why are violin strings mounted on hollow wooden frames?

†12. Why does a guitar produce a different sound from a violin even when it is producing the same note?

IV–7   MUSIC AND NOISE (Demonstration)

In past experiments you observed two major characteristics of sound waves that determine the kind of sound you hear. One factor was frequency (pitch); the other was amplitude (loudness). However, when the same note is played on two different instruments, the sounds produced differ even though their pitch and amplitude are the same. The reason for this difference is the subject of this experiment.

APPARATUS REQUIRED (per class)

> *Oscilloscope*
> *microphone*
> *mounted tuning forks as follows: 2 with frequency 256 cps and 1 with frequency 512 cps*
> *audio oscillator (2 audio oscillators if possible)*
> *audio amplifier with speaker*
> *plasticine*
> *musical instruments (e.g. a xylophone, clarinet, trumpet, oboe, french horn, tuba, flute, piccolo etc.)* (Instruments with a short vibrational duration such as a drum are not satisfactory.)

Procedure:

1. Adjust an oscilloscope and microphone as in Procedures 1 and 2 of Experiment IV-4.
2. Adjust the vertical gain and sweep time to obtain a stationary pattern with a convenient amplitude when the microphone is held close to a vibrating tuning fork. Then create an unpleasant noise, by scratching glass, for example.
   How do the wave patterns of the noise and the sound from the tuning fork and the noise compare? What feature distinguishes the wave patterns of noises?
*3. Hold the microphone to your mouth and whistle a note.
   Is the frequency uniform? Is the sound a noise or a note?
4. Play a note on a musical instrument such as a xylophone. Adjust the sweep frequency so that the pattern is stationary.
   What does the pattern look like? Sketch it.
5. Play the same note on several other instruments. You may have to adjust the sweep time slightly to hold the pattern stationary.
   Sketch each pattern. In what respects do the graphs of these similar sounds differ?
6. In turn, play two notes on a xylophone that are one octave apart. Sketch the pattern of each note as it appears on the oscilloscope. Then, simultaneously play the same two notes on the xylophone.
   What is the resulting pattern? Is it a composite of the single patterns? Therefore, is air able to transmit waves of two different frequencies at once? Give a reason for your answer.
7. Adjust the oscilloscope so that you obtain a standing pattern of four waves when the microphone is held near a tuning fork vibrating at 256 cycles/sec. (See Fig. IV-7-1.)
8. Now place the microphone between the open ends of two resonance boxes on which are mounted tuning forks that vibrate at 256 cps and 512 cps respectively. (See Fig. IV-7-2.)

Sketch the resulting pattern. Does it resemble the patterns produced by any of the instruments used in Procedure 5?

Fig. IV–7–1   Oscilloscope pattern

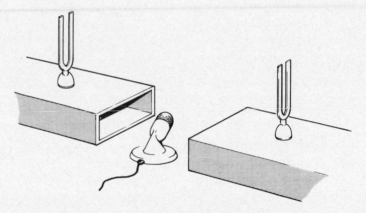

Fig. IV–7–2   Observing two waves simultaneously on an oscilloscope

9. Place a microphone between the resonance box of a 256 cps tuning fork and the speaker of an audio amplifier. (See Fig. IV-7-3). Vibrate the tuning fork and, if necessary, adjust the oscilloscope to again obtain a stationary pattern of four waves as in Fig. IV-7-1. Turn on the audio oscillator and set its dial at 768 cps. This is accomplished when 12 stationary waves appear on the screen. Adjust the amplifier so that the amplitudes of both waves are the same. Now produce both sounds simultaneously. Fine adjustments of the audio oscillator frequency may be necessary to achieve a standing pattern. A stationary pattern of four waves should occur. Repeat this procedure using the oscillator to generate frequencies of 1024 cps, 1280 cps or 1536 cps (i.e. multiples of 256 cps or overtones of the sound produced by a vibration of 256 cps).

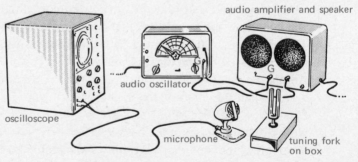

Fig. IV–7–3   Superimposing two notes

NOTE: *Alternatively, if two audio oscillators are available, both may be con-*
nected to the same amplifier and speaker. This would make the tuning
fork unnecessary.

Describe or sketch the patterns that result. Are any of these patterns
similar to those produced by the instruments you used in Procedure 5?

10. Repeat the above procedure using 256 cps and 512 cps vibrating
forks in addition to an oscillator-produced frequency of 768 cps,
1024 cps or 1280 cps. Locate the microphone so that all the sounds
have the same amplitude on the oscilloscope when they are produced
separately.

Describe or sketch the patterns that result.

11. Place two mounted 256 cps tuning forks so that they face each other
and stick small pieces of plasticine on the prongs of one fork. Start
the two forks vibrating.

Describe the sound produced. Observe the pattern on the oscillo-
scope. What happens to the amplitude?

(The above procedure can be accomplished with greater ease by using
the audio oscillator and one tuning fork or 2 audio oscillators. Slowly
adjust the frequency of the oscillation from about 230 to 280 cycles/
second.)

What happens to the amplitude as you approach a frequency of 256?
as you go from 256 to 280?

NOTE: *The pulse effects produced are called* beats.

Fig. IV–7–4   Observing "beats"

Questions:

*1. Why does the same note have a different sound on different instru-
ments?

*2. How does the frequency of middle C (256 cps) compare with the fre-
quencies of the first and second overtones? The first overtone is a C
note one octave above middle C; the second is the G note above that.

†3. Could a violin string play the notes C and A simultaneously? Why or why not?

†4. How is the frequency of *beats* that are produced by two similar tuning forks affected by making the frequencies of the two forks more alike?

References and Suggestions for Further Investigation:

1. Pages 375-379 of *Modern Physics* by Dull, Metcalfe and Brooks (New York: Holt, Rinehart & Winston, Inc., 1962) and pages 283-290 of *Physics For Our Times* by Marborger and Hoffman (New York: McGraw-Hill Book Company, 1967) give a good account of musical notes, chords and scales.

2. Experiments with music are discussed on pages 68-88 of *Science Experiments With Sound* by Harry Sootin (New York: W. W. Norton & Co. Ltd., 1964) and pages 84-85 of *Physics Is Fun* by Jardine (London: Heinemann Educational Books Ltd., 1967).

IV-8   WAVES IN TWO DIMENSIONS

The transmission of compressional and transverse wave motions demonstrated in previous experiments has been limited to one dimension. The demonstration of many of the properties exhibited by wave motion has been prevented because of this limitation. In this experiment, a ripple tank will be used to produce two-dimensional water waves. Although the waves are transverse in nature, you can use them to explain properties of sound waves (which are actually compressional waves) because of their similar properties.

APPARATUS REQUIRED

Ripple tank
150 watt, straight filament clear bulb light source
lamp support
wire screen strips
rubber hose
plane reflector
curved reflector
thick glass refracting plate
semi-circular glass lens
2 paraffin blocks
large beaker
vibrating source (meter stick, stiff wire, 2 small cork stoppers, C-clamp variable) phase wave generator, rheostat, 6 volt power source, leads
several sheets of white paper

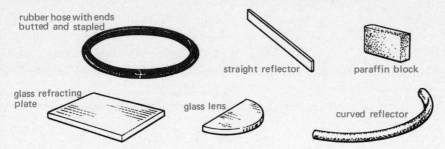

rubber hose with ends butted and stapled

straight reflector

paraffin block

glass refracting plate

glass lens

curved reflector

Fig. IV–8–1   Ripple tank apparatus

You may find equipment other than that illustrated in Fig. IV-8-1 equally useful.

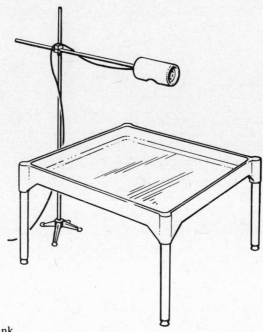

Fig. IV–8–2   Ripple tank

Procedure:

1. Assemble the ripple tank as shown in Fig. IV-8-2 and add water to a depth of 1 cm. Place the light source over the center of the tank and adjust the filament so that it is vertical. (If you look, from a point close to the lamp, at the lamp's reflection in the water, you should see a point image of the filament in the water. Alternatively, you could place the lamp under the ripple tank to produce patterns on the ceiling of the room. Place wire screen "beaches" around the tank border so that no reflection occurs when you create a wave in the center of the tank. Adjust the height of the light source so that the wave pattern

is focused sharply on a screen made from sheets of white paper. It may be necessary to add or remove water to focus the waves properly.

2. Switch off the room lighting. With the tank light source on, dip your finger in the water at the center of the tank. Observe on the screen the wave pattern that is produced by a point source.

   What does the resulting pattern reveal about the direction of the waves?

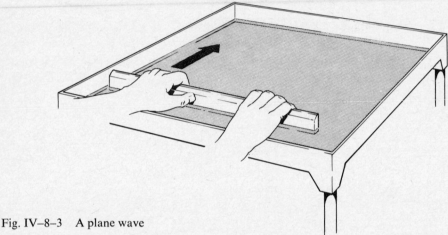

Fig. IV–8–3   A plane wave

3. Produce a straight pulse by giving a ruler or a rod in the water a short, brisk push, as in Fig. IV-8-3. Describe the wave.

4. Form a circle with a rubber hose and place it in the water. At its center, dip your finger in the water.

   Where do the reflected waves simultaneously cross each other? What do your observations suggest about the speed of the incident and reflected waves?

foci

Fig. IV–8–4   Ellipse

5. Partially flatten the circle to form an ellipse as in Fig. IV-8-4. Dip your finger as close as possible to one of the foci. If you succeed, all the reflected waves will collect at one point.

   Where do the reflected waves collect? Try to explain why.

6. Place a straight reflector in the water. Using the ruler as in Procedure 3, produce a straight wave parallel to the reflector. Describe the reflected wave.

7. Produce a straight wave that strikes the straight reflector at an angle of 45°.
   In what direction is the wave reflected?
8. Produce a circular wave with your finger. Describe how this wave reflects from the straight barrier. The position of the source of waves (your finger) is at the center of the growing circular wave.
   From similar observations, where does the source of the reflected waves appear to be?
9. Repeat Procedure 6 using the curved reflector, first with its convex side and then with its concave side toward the advancing straight wave front. Next use a point source and observe the reflected wave. (You may prefer to use a vibrating point source such as that described in Procedure 14.) Compare the shapes of the incident and reflected waves in each case. Describe how the reflected wave is affected by the position of the point source. Explain.

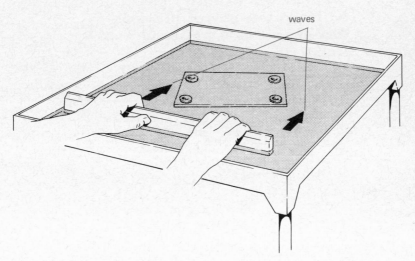

waves

Fig. IV–8–5   Passing waves over a refracting plate

10. Place a thick glass refracting plate in the water to alter the depth of the water significantly. If necessary raise the plate by placing it on metal washers so that the plate is just barely covered with water. With the ruler and refracting plate arranged as in Fig. IV-8-5, generate a straight wave. Describe the appearance of the refracted wave (the wave above the refracting plate).
    Does a change in the medium affect the direction of straight waves if these waves strike the boundary at an angle?
11. Repeat Procedure 10 using a glass semi-circular lens placed as shown in Fig. IV-8-6.
    Does the refraction effect cause the waves to be focused to a point?

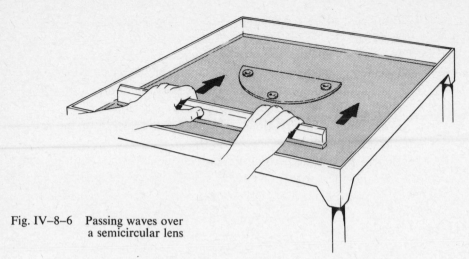

Fig. IV–8–6   Passing waves over
                    a semicircular lens

12. Place two paraffin blocks and a ruler as in Fig. IV-8-7. Generate waves with the ruler. Describe what happens to straight waves when they pass the edges of the paraffin blocks.
    What evidence do you have that sound can also travel around corners?

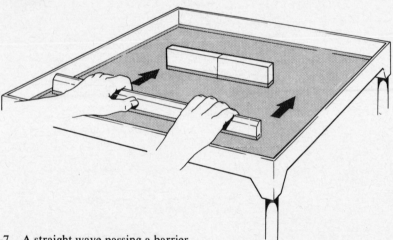

Fig. IV–8–7   A straight wave passing a barrier

13. Separate the paraffin blocks to form a narrow gate. Generate straight waves parallel to the blocks.
    What happens to the straight waves as they pass through the gate?

14. A simple vibrating source is shown in Fig. IV-8-8. A meter stick is attached to a solid support so that 60 cm extends beyond the supporting edge. A stiff wire is wrapped around the end of the meter stick with its ends extended downward and a cork stopper is pushed onto each wire end. Adjust the height of the stoppers so that they produce satisfactory waves when the meter stick is vibrated. Study the wave pattern produced.

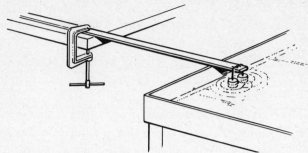

Fig. IV–8–8   A simple two source wave generator

NOTE: *A more sophisticated source like that shown in Fig. IV-8-9 may be available.*

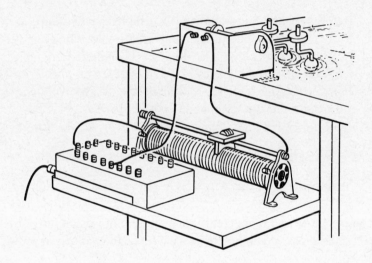

Fig. IV–8–9   A commercial two point source wave generator

15. Bend the wire so that the stoppers are now about 5 cm apart. Again produce a wave pattern by vibrating the meter stick. Study the resulting pattern and compare it with the pattern obtained in Procedure 14. **What is the effect of increasing the separation between the corks? Can you explain what is happening to produce the observed pattern? In what sound experiment did you observe "constructive" and "destructive" interference of waves?**

Questions:
*1.(a) If you stood at the center of a large circular building and shouted, would you hear a loud echo? Explain.

 (b) What echo effect would probably result if you made a sound at one of the foci of a large elliptical building (such as the Mormon Tabernacle in Salt Lake City)?

*2. From your observation of water waves passing through a narrow gate, describe the corresponding effect of sound waves passing through a doorway.

*3. Why is a large slightly concave screen often placed behind an orchestra when it plays in a large building or in a park?

†4. Water waves were focused (brought to a point) by a convex refracting plate because water waves travel slower in shallow water. Explain how you could focus sound by using a gas that reduces the speed of sound. (What shape of container would you put the gas in?)

†5. Why is it sometimes possible to hear an orchestra clearly in one part of a large building and hardly hear it at all in another part of the building, even if you are equally close and unhampered by barriers?

References and Suggestions for Further Investigation:

1. More complex sound phenomena are discussed on pages 263-267 of *A School Physics* by C. W. Kearsey (London: Longmans, Green & Co. Ltd., 1962) and pages 220-224 of *Matter and Energy – Foundations of Physics* by J. M. McLachlan, K. G. McNeill and J. M. Bell (Toronto: Clarke-Irwin and Co. Ltd., 1963).

2. Recommended PSSC films: *Simple Waves*; *Sound Waves in Air*.

IV-9   THE NEGATIVE EFFECTS OF NOISE

It is becoming more and more clear that excessive noise can have severe effects on people. Partial or even complete hearing loss can result from prolonged subjection to loud noises. A second effect is the reduction in safety caused by the difficulty of communication in noisy surroundings. A third, less measurable effect of noise, is its effect on human nature. One needs only to observe the irritability of people in noisy surroundings to realize that noise has a negative effect.

The trend towards a highly mechanized society is increasing the normal noise level considerably. It is therefore important that you become aware of the possible effects of noise to avoid living conditions that are detrimental to your health.

A unit used to measure the loudness of a noise is the *decibel*. The following table interprets decibel levels in terms of common noises.

DECIBEL LEVEL	NOISE
130	hydraulic press, rock drill at 3 ft
120	jet plane passenger ramp
110	loud motorcycle
100	pneumatic jackhammer

90	heavy truck at 20 ft
80	average factory
70	noisy office or classroom
60	conversation at 3 ft
50	quiet streets
40	quiet home
20	rustle of leaves
0	quietest noise audible to a child

As people grow older their hearing becomes less acute, even when they are not exposed to loud noises. However, if they are exposed to loud noises the rate of hearing loss is increased. Research indicates that noises below 85 decibels are, in general, not harmful. As the noise level increases beyond that level, hearing damage occurs.

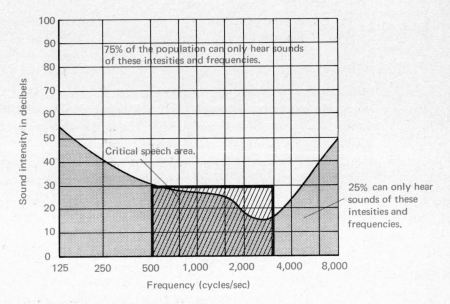

Fig. IV–9–1   Chart used to evaluate hearing loss

A chart commonly used to evaluate hearing loss is shown in Fig. IV-9-1. The threshold level (the level where sounds are just audible) is measured for various frequency ranges between 125 cycles/second and 8,000 cycles/second. The critical range of sound frequencies is between about 500 cycles/second and 3,000 cycles/second, the frequency range generally used in conversation. As can be seen from Fig. IV-9-1, a threshold level above 30 decibels in the speech range is considered to represent hearing impairment. Most research suggests that mild impairment exists at a threshold even lower than 30 decibels.

The table below describes the hearing capabilities of individuals with various threshold hearing levels.

THRESHOLD LEVEL	CHARACTERISTICS
less than 16 decibels	no difficulty with faint speech
16-30 decibels	has difficulty with faint speech
31-45 decibels	has difficulty with normal speech
46-60 decibels	has difficulty even with loud speech
61-90 decibels	can hear only amplified speech
more than 90 decibels	cannot understand amplified speech

APPARATUS REQUIRED

Tuning forks of various frequencies
audio-oscillator and combination amplifier and speaker

Procedure:

1. Connect the audio-oscillator to the combination amplifier and speaker. If the speaker is of reasonably good quality, the loudness will be constant, even when you vary the frequency of the audio-oscillator. Listen to the sound as the frequency of the oscillator is varied from 0 to 20,000 cycles/sec.
   Does your ear respond equally well to all frequencies, (that is, are sounds of all frequencies equally loud)? If not, for what range of frequencies (approximately) is your hearing most acute?

2. Compare the threshold levels of various members of the class by vibrating a tuning fork. As the sound level of the fork passes below the threshold level of each member, he can signal the fact that he can no longer hear the sound. Many trials will probably be necessary to distinguish between threshold levels. The people being tested should be at equal distances from the source. If there is any doubt that the loudness is the same at the positions of all the observers, they could change positions between trials. Compare the average threshold level of the class with that of any older person. If you can find people who have experienced long periods of high noise levels, you can determine their threshold levels and compare them with that of the class. If your oscillator, amplifier and speaker have very fine adjustments, it may be possible to test the threshold levels at many frequencies.
   In what range of frequency do adults show the greatest amount of hearing loss?

3. Attempt to conduct normal conversation while the amplifier is blaring. Vary the frequency of the noise to observe the effect of the frequency of a loud noise on normal conversation.

What frequency range causes the greatest amount of interference? Why?

4. Observe the irritability caused in yourself by high noise levels. It may already be apparent from the previous procedures.

References and Suggestions for Further Investigation:

1. The extent of hearing damage due to noise depends upon both the sound level and the length of time that an individual is subjected to it. Use research information and an estimate of the sound level and duration of electronically amplified music in order to determine what hearing loss, if any, you may receive by listening to it.

2. Describe various devices that can be used in industry to prevent hearing loss. (A source of information is the Workman's Compensation Board.)

3. Using available research data, prepare a reasonable safety code for the sound levels of working conditions.

4. What are the recognized hearing safety standards in your area?

5. What noise regulations are there in your residential district?

6. Describe the operation of a sound-level meter. What are the purposes of the A, B and C weighting scales?

7. Refer to "A Brief Study of a Rational Approach to Legislative Control of Noise," Division of Applied Physics, National Research Council of Canada, Ottawa, 1968, and *Handbook of Noise Measurement*, Sixth Edition, A. G. P. Peterson and I. E. Gross (West Concord, Mass.: General Radio Co. 1967).

Anand S. Atal

THE PLANET EARTH

NOTE: *It is desirable that wave motion (Unit IV) be studied before attempting this unit.*

INTRODUCTION

Man has always been curious about the Earth, and has wondered about and feared natural phenomena such as earthquakes, volcanoes, huge sea-waves and lightning. Hindus used to believe that a round earth was brought up from the ocean floor to rest upon the tusks of Varaha, one of their gods whose upper half resembled a boar. According to this belief, earthquakes occurred when God Varaha became tired and shifted to a more comfortable position. Romans believed that volcanoes erupted when Vulcan, their god of fire, stoked his furnace and that audible volcanic explosions resulted when he hammered his anvil. Before Columbus undertook his voyage to the new world, he was warned that his ships would perish in a giant waterfall at the edge of the flat Earth. In 1650 A.D., an Archbishop estimated Sunday, October 23, 4004 B.C. to be the day of creation. Many people accepted his conclusion.

These ideas may seem strange to you; however, without such attempts to explain natural phenomena, modern Earth Science would never have developed. It is through man's curiosity that questions such as the following have been answered: What is the shape and size of the Earth? How old is the Earth? What causes earthquakes and volcanic eruptions? Why are continents higher than the ocean floors? What is the Earth made of? Why do we sometimes find the remains of ancient fish and marine life in the rocks on mountain tops? What are the other planets in our solar system like? How does our Earth differ from other heavenly bodies?

An Earth scientist considers Earth in its entirety, including its atmosphere and magnetic field. To him it is a planet in a solar system within a vast universe. The Earth is unique when compared to the other planets and satellites in our solar system. For example, a piece of lunar rock picked up by an Apollo astronaut had been sitting in that same position for about 150 million years! Can you name a few natural features in your locality which have remained unchanged for the last million years or even the last ten thousand years?

        The Earth may be considered to consist of four major divisions. (See Fig. V-0-1.)

1. The *atmosphere* – a canopy of air that surrounds us
2. The *lithosphere* – a rocky crust that supports terrestial life and protects us from the hot interior
3. The *hydrosphere* – a collective name for all bodies of water including rivers, lakes and oceans

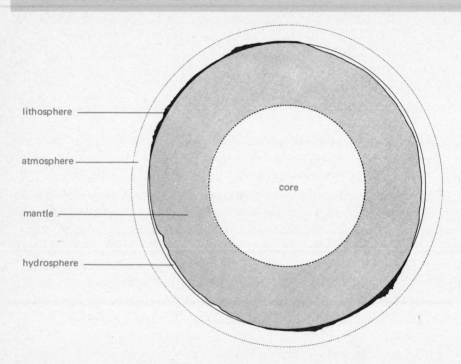

Fig. V–0–1   Major subdivisions of Earth (not to scale)

4. The *mantle and core* – the Earth's hot interior

        The presence of an extensive atmosphere and hydrosphere is necessary not only to plant and animal life (collectively referred to as the *biosphere*) but also to the processes which change the planet. In the first three exercises of this unit you will investigate the general characteristics of the three outer divisions of the Earth and the forces that constantly modify and reshape the lithosphere.

V-1   THE LITHOSPHERE

Man's continuing exploration of the Earth's surface has provided the following data.

FEATURE	DISTANCE
Thickness of the Earth's crust below the continents	7-30 miles
Thickness of the Earth's crust below the oceans	3-10 miles
Height above sea level of the highest point on Earth (top of Mount Everest)	29,028 ft (5.5 mi)
Height above sea level of the highest point in Canada (top of Mt. Logan, Yukon)	19,850 ft (3.8 mi)
Height of tallest building in the world (Empire State Building, New York)	1,250 ft (0.24 mi)
Average height of the continents above sea level	2,700 ft (0.51 mi)
Average depth of the oceans below sea level	12,400 ft (2.35 mi)
Depth below sea level of deepest part of the ocean (Mindanao Trench in the Pacific)	36,200 ft (6.85 mi)
Depth of deepest drill hole (for oil in Texas)	25,000 ft (4.7 mi)

APPARATUS REQUIRED (per station)
  2 sheets of graph paper
  metric ruler

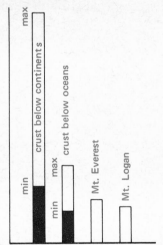

Fig. V–1–1   A bar graph (histogram)

Procedure:
1. Choose a suitable scale (such as 1 cm = 2 mi) and plot a bar graph as in Fig. V-1-1 that shows the distances given above. Use the vertical

axis (y-axis) to represent the various distances and equal spaces along the horizontal axis to represent each of the ten features listed. Label each bar of your graph.

2. Choose a larger scale (such as 1 cm = 500 mi) and draw a second bar graph to show how the thickness of the Earth's crust compares with the following approximate distances.

Diameter of the Earth (from pole to pole) 7,900 mi (12,600 Km)
Diameter of the Earth (at the equator)   7,926 mi (12,700 Km)
Thickness of the Earth's mantle   1,800 mi (2,900 Km)
Diameter of the Earth's core   4,340 mi (6,900 Km)
Diameter of the Moon   2,160 mi (3,460 Km)
Maximum thickness of the lithosphere   30 mi (48 Km)

How does the thickness of the Earth's crust (lithosphere) compare with the diameter of the Earth? How would you describe man's efforts to build onto and drill into the Earth's surface?

3. Drilling has shown that as one moves deeper into the Earth's crust, the temperature rises nearly $1C°$ for every 200 ft of depth or about $27C°$ for every mile ($16.8C°$ for every Km). If this rate of temperature increase is constant, calculate the temperature
   (a) in a mine whose depth is 10,000 ft (3,048 m);
   (b) at the bottom of an oil well 25,000 ft deep (7,600 m);
   (c) at a depth of 30 miles (48 Km);
   (d) at the center of the Earth.

Is your calculated temperature at the center of the Earth reasonable? (The temperature of the Sun's surface is estimated to be 6,000°C.) Estimate the depth beneath the surface of Earth at which iron would melt. (The melting point of iron is 1,200°C.)

4. The mass density of the rocks comprising the lithosphere ranges between 2.7 and 3.3 gm/cm^3. If we assume an average density of 3.0 gm/cm^3, the pressure at a depth of 1 meter is

$$3.0 \text{ gf/cm}^3 \text{ x } 100 \text{ cm} = 300 \text{ gf/cm}^2.$$

NOTE: The weight, on the Earth, of a mass of 3.0 gm is 3.0 gram force (3.0 gf).

Calculate the pressure at a depth of:
   (a)   3,000 meters (approximately 10,000 ft),
   (b)   8,000 meters (approximately 25,000 ft),
   (c) 48,000 meters (approximately 30 miles).

NOTE: For comparison, air pressure at sea level is approximately 1000 gf/cm².

†5. By using Newton's Laws of motion and gravitation and knowing the altitude and period of revolution of a satellite orbiting the Earth, the Earth's mass has been computed to be 6.0×10^{24} Kg (six followed

by twenty-four zeroes). The radius of the Earth $= 6.4 \times 10^6$ m (approx.) Calculate the average mass density of the Earth from this and the following data.

$$\text{Volume of a sphere} = \tfrac{4}{3}\,\pi\,r^3$$
$$\text{mass density} = \text{mass/volume}$$

How does your calculated average density of the Earth compare with the average density of the lithosphere (3 gm/cm³)? Try to account for the difference.

Questions:

*1. Study Fig. V-1-2. You will notice that relatively light granitic rocks overlie a denser basaltic layer to form the continents. The basaltic layer completely envelopes the Earth. The lower boundary of the lithosphere is a zone named the "Mohorovicic Discontinuity" (commonly called "Moho"). It is named after its discoverer, a Yugoslavian seismologist Andrija Mohorovicic (moh-hoh-ROH-vi-chich) In order to study the material in and beneath this discontinuity geologists one day hope to drill through the crust into the region beneath the Moho called the mantle. Project Mohole, as it is appropriately called, is a plan by United States scientists to drill a deep hole through the crust from a floating ocean platform. A test hole was drilled off the coast of California, but the project has been abandoned because of its high cost.

(a) Why would a drilling site located over the ocean be preferable to one located over a continent? (Examine Fig. V-1-3.)

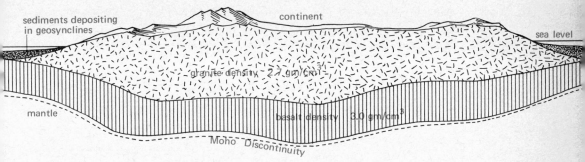

Fig. V–1–2 The two main layers of the lithosphere and the Moho Discontinuity

(b) Why do continents project above sea level? (Hint: Compare the densities of the various materials which make up the lithosphere.)

(c) Why is the basaltic layer lower under the continents than it is under the oceans?

(d) If geologists have never drilled into the mantle, how do they know of its existence? (If you are unable to answer this question now, you will be able to do so when further evidence for the mantle's existence is presented in a later exercise.)

(e) Continents are being worn down continually by erosion. The eroded material is carried down to the ocean basins by rivers. How will this large scale movement of material affect the balance of forces between the weight of the crust and the upward thrust of the mantle? (The upper part of the mantle has plastic properties that allow it to flow.)

*2.(a) What fraction of the Earth's radius is the depth of the lithosphere?

†(b) If the Earth with all its surface features were reduced in scale to the size of a soccer ball, would this ball be as rough as sand paper or as smooth as polished steel? Give reasons for your answer.

†(c) On the same scale, would the oceans be thicker than the film of water that would form on the ball if it were wet? Support your answer with approximate calculations.

*3. Would you expect the material in the core of the Earth to be solid, liquid or gaseous? (Hint: What is the probable effect of pressure on the hot material at the core?)

†4. Suggest several explanations for the fact that the temperature of the lithosphere increases with increasing depth. (Hint: Are there chemical or other processes that may be occurring to produce this heat energy?) Does one of these explanations provide a clue to the origin of the Earth?

References and Suggestions for Further Investigation:

1. Read about "Project Mohole." What problems were encountered that have so far prevented its successful completion?

2. The various layers of the Earth are described on pages 4-8 of *Earth Science: The World We Live In*, Fourth Edition, by Samuel N. Namowitz and Donald B. Stone (New York: American Book Co., 1969).

3. Various dimensions of the Earth are described on pages 70-76 of *Investigating the Earth*, Earth Science Curriculum Project (Boston: Houghton Mifflin Co., 1967).

V-2 THE ATMOSPHERE

You live and move about at the bottom of an ocean of air. Consequently you may take for granted the role that air plays in the maintenance of life on Earth. Imagine yourself trying to survive on the surface of the Moon. What problems would you encounter due to the lack of an atmosphere?

In the following exercises you will investigate the properties and composition of the Earth's atmosphere, and some of the important effects of air pressure.

PART A   LAYERS OF THE ATMOSPHERE

MATERIALS REQUIRED (per station)
>   2 sheets of graph paper
>   ruler
>   pens or pencils of several colors

Procedure:

The following data was obtained from rocket flights above White Sands, New Mexico, U.S.A. (Adapted from the *Handbook of Physics and Chemistry, 49th edition.*)

ALTITUDE ABOVE SEA LEVEL	AVERAGE TEMPERATURE OF THE ATMOSPHERE	AVERAGE PRESSURE OF THE ATMOSPHERE
0 Kilometers	17°C	760 mm of Hg
10 ”	−43°C	210 ” ” ”
20 ”	−63°C	42 ” ” ”
30 ”	−38°C	9.5 ” ” ”
40 ”	−13°C	2.4 ” ” ”
50 ”	− 3°C	0.75 ” ” ”
60 ”	−13°C	0.021 ” ” ”
70 ”	−63°C	0.054 ” ” ”
80 ”	−83°C	0.010 ” ” ”
90 ”	−63°C	0.0019 ” ” ”
100 ”	−33°C	0.00042 ” ” ”
’ ”	’	’
’ ”	’	’
160 ”	+297°C	1.5×10^{-6} ” ” ”

1. Plot a full page graph of altitude versus temperature of the atmosphere. Let altitude (0 to 100 Km) be represented by the vertical axis (y-axis) and temperature (between −100°C and +100°C) by the horizontal axis. Join the plotted points to form a smooth curve.

NOTE: *The Earth's atmosphere consists of the following layers.*

NAME OF LAYER	ALTITUDE ABOVE SEA LEVEL	TRANSITION ZONE
Troposphere	below 10 Km (approx.)	
		Tropopause
Stratosphere	10 to 50 Km (approx.)	
		Stratopause
Mesosphere	50 to 80 Km (approx.)	
		Mesopause
Thermosphere	above 80 Km (approx.)	

The layers are separated by transition *zones* rather than sharply defined boundaries. The altitude range of the various layers changes with latitude. Experts are not always in agreement about where boundaries occur.

2. Draw horizontal lines across your graph at the appropriate altitudes to indicate the position of the various layers that make up the atmosphere. Label the layers and the transition zones between them.
   Examine your graph and suggest at least one basis on which the atmosphere has been classified into various layers. Which of the layers has the lowest temperature? the highest temperature?

3. In addition to heat and visible light, the Sun also radiates ultraviolet rays, x-rays and cosmic rays which are harmful to many forms of life. Fortunately these forms of radiation are largely absorbed by the atmosphere. At altitudes above 60 Km, air molecules are transformed into charged ions by the absorption of this energy. Consequently, the region above 60 Km is also called the *ionosphere*. On your graph, shade and label the region referred to as the ionosphere. **Would you expect that electric currents occur in the ionosphere? Explain.**
   At altitudes between approximately 20 to 50 Km, ultraviolet rays are absorbed by oxygen (O_2) molecules, transforming them to less stable ozone (O_3) molecules. Show this zone on your graph and label it *the ozone layer*.

4. It is estimated that millions of meteors enter the Earth's atmosphere daily. Most of these meteors from outer space are "burned up" between the altitudes of 80 and 60 Km. Indicate and label this region on your graph.

5. Plot a second graph (or use a different color of ink and superimpose another graph on the first one) of altitude (y-axis) versus air pressure. Use the data in the table that precedes Procedure 1. (Some of the pressure values listed will be too small to plot.) Answer the following questions:
   (a) What evidence is there that air has weight?
   (b) Why is air pressure greatest at sea level?
   (c) Explain why air pressure decreases with increasing altitude.
   (d) Below what altitude would you expect to find about half of the total number of air molecules in the atmosphere? (At this altitude air pressure would be one-half of the pressure at sea level.) Label this altitude on your graph.
   (e) Estimate the air pressure at the top of Mount Everest (altitude 8.8 Km). Why would it be necessary to use special breathing equipment on Mount Everest?

Questions:

*1.(a) How does the rotation of the Earth affect the altitudes of the various atmospheric layers?

  (b) At what latitude would this effect be greatest? least?

*2. Why does the air temperature within the troposphere decrease with increasing altitude? (Hint: All atmospheric layers may not absorb the radiation from the sun equally well.)

*3. Suggest why air temperature within the stratosphere increases with increasing altitude. What causes this layer to behave differently from the troposphere?

*4. What is the importance of the ozone layer to life on the Earth? (Hint: What would happen if the Earth's upper atmosphere did not absorb harmful radiation?)

†5. With the help of a reference book, find out how the ionosphere aids communication by long and short radio waves.

PART B   COMPOSITION OF THE EARTH'S ATMOSPHERE

APPARATUS REQUIRED (per station)
  Drawing compass
  protractor
  metric ruler
  (per class)
  map of the world

NOTE: *Air at sea level that has had its water vapor removed has the following average composition:*

	Percentage Composition	Molecular Mass
Nitrogen (N_2)	78%	28
Oxygen (O_2)	21%	32
Argon (Ar)	0.93%	40
Carbon Dioxide (CO_2)	0.03%	44
All other gases	0.04%	

The percentage of water vapor (H_2O, molecular mass 18) in air fluctuates considerably, reaching a maximum of about 4%.

Procedure:

1. Draw a circle graph in which 360° represents the entire composition (100%) of dry air at sea level. Divide the 360° according to the percentage of each gas present. For example, on your graph, nitrogen would be represented by a sector whose bounding radii make an angle of $0.78 \times 360° = 281°$ with each other. Label each sector.

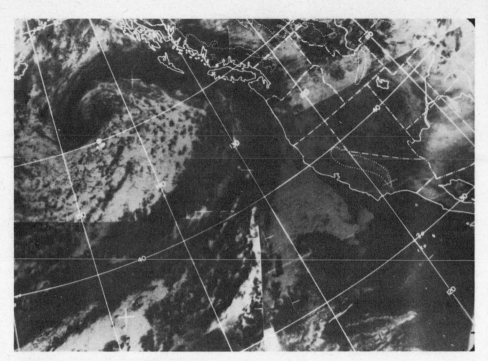

Fig. V–2–1   Satellite photograph of a weather system

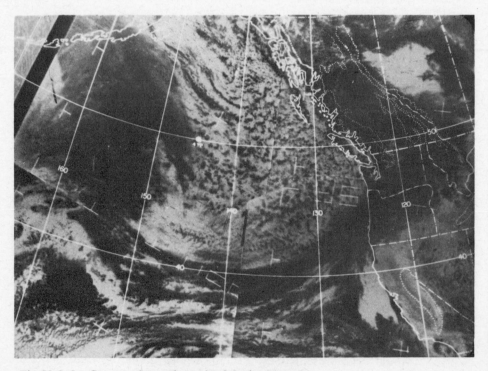

Fig. V–2–2   Can you detect the path of the jet stream?

2. Study the photograph in Fig. V-2-1. It was taken by an ESSA weather satellite from an altitude of about 900 miles. Answer the following questions that relate to the photograph:

   (a) What part of North America is shown in the photograph?

   (b) Estimate the area in square miles covered by the photograph. (Use an atlas to determine distances.)

   (c) The photograph has been compiled by joining smaller photographs taken at different times of the day. The various shades of gray are due to changes in light conditions. Ignoring these differences, what is represented by the dark areas in the photograph? the white areas?

   (d) The major feature shown in the photograph is a very large storm. Sketch in your note book the pattern of clouds associated with the storm.

   (e) Compare the shape of the storm with that of an eddy current in a rapidly draining sink. On your sketch, use arrows to indicate the directions of wind in various parts of the storm.

   (f) What is the general direction of movement of the storm, (clockwise or counter-clockwise)?

   (g) Storms serve to move moisture from the oceans to the relatively dry continents. What else do they move from one region of the Earth to another? Explain your answer.

   (h) Predict the general weather over British Columbia on this particular day. Give reasons for your prediction.

†3. Fig. V-2-2 is another composite photograph of a weather system. Clearly shown are bands of clouds that trace the paths of jet streams across the Pasific Ocean and over adjoining parts of the continent. Do jet streams follow a straight path?
   Over what parts of the continent's edge did the jet streams cross?

Questions:

*1. At a given temperature and pressure, a given number of molecules of any gas (regardless of its molecular mass) occupy the same volume. Which gas is therefore denser – air (O_2 and N_2) that contains a significant amount of water vapor (H_2O) or air that is dry?

*2. Keeping your answer to question 1 in mind, explain why a sudden drop in barometric pressure may indicate rain (or snow).

*3. List several reasons why most of our weather occurs in the troposphere.

*4. The total amount of water on the Earth is estimated to be approximately 1.29 billion billion tons (1.29×10^{18} tons). About 86.5% of this is in the oceans and only about 0.001% is in the atmosphere. Estimate the number of tons of water in the atmosphere.

*5.(a) In which latitudes do most storms originate? Explain why.
   (b) What is the source of energy for these storms?
   (c) What initiates the movement of large air masses within the atmosphere?
   (d) What would happen if air movement in all parts of the atmosphere ceased?

*6. Little change has occurred on the surface of the Moon for billions of years. Why has the Earth's surface changed so much during the same time period? List several reasons.

†7. What would be the effect on our lives if:
   (a) the percentage of O_2 in the atmosphere increased? decreased?
   (b) the percentage of CO_2 increased? (The percentage of CO_2 is increasing and some environmental scientists are becoming alarmed. Why?)

References and Suggestions for Further Investigation:

1. Read about jet streams, the huge rivers of air that occur in the upper levels of the troposphere at altitudes between 5 and 10 miles. Find answers to these questions:
   (a) How wide and deep are the air currents that make up the jet streams?
   (b) What is their speed?
   (c) Do they move in predictable directions or does their pattern of movement fluctuate rapidly and unpredictably?
   (d) What significance do jet streams have for commercial aircraft?
   †(e) What causes jet streams?

2. With the aid of reference books find the cause of the coriolis effect. How does this effect influence the weather in various parts of the world?

PART C   SOME EFFECTS OF AIR PRESSURE (Demonstration)

APPARATUS REQUIRED (per class)
   A vacuum pump and bell jar
   balloon
   100 ml beaker
   vacuum wax
   2 250 ml beakers
   small asbestos pad
   thermometer

an unopened bottle of pop
a thin 1 gallon metal can with an air-tight cap
tripod stand
bunsen burner
oven mits

Procedure:

1. Blow up a balloon until it has a diameter of about 10 cm. Place the balloon on a vacuum pump platform and cover it with a bell jar as shown in Fig. V-2-3. (To prevent the balloon from being drawn into the pump, cover the opening with a small beaker.) Seal the bell jar with vacuum wax and start the pump. Observe what happens to the balloon. Explain the observed effect.

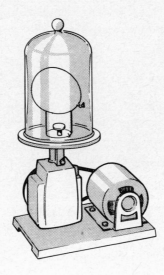

Fig. V–2–3   What effect does air pressure have on the size of the balloon?

2. Allow air to enter the bell jar and then remove the jar from its plat-form. Replace the balloon with a 250 ml beaker one-third full of water. Place the beaker on a small asbestos pad and insert a thermometer into the water. Position the thermometer so that tem-perature readings can be taken when the bell jar is replaced on the platform. Seal the bell jar in position and record the water tempera-ture. Start the pump and record the temperature at 1 minute intervals for about 20 minutes.
   How did the temperature of the water change as the air pressure above it was progressively decreased?

3. If the pump is a good one, in time you will notice some surprising effects in the water. (Do not run the pump for more than 20 minutes since water vapor condenses in the pump's oil.)

How does the observed phenomenon compare with the boiling of water? Were you able to freeze the water while it was still boiling?

4. Allow air to enter the bell jar, remove it and replace the beaker of water with another that is two-thirds full of a carbonated soft drink poured from a bottle that has just been opened. Replace the bell jar and start the pump. Observe the liquid in the beaker.

   What happens when the cap is removed from a carbonated beverage? Why? Does all of the gas in the liquid escape at normal air pressure? What happens when the air pressure above this liquid is progressively decreased? Did you notice small bubbles in the water during the early stages of Procedure 2 (before the water started to boil)? How is the solubility of a gas in a liquid related to the air pressure upon the liquid?

NOTE: For obvious reasons, the following procedure is a favourite with many teachers and it is quite possible that you have seen it before. Nevertheless, the experiment dramatically illustrates the tremendous force produced by atmospheric pressure.

5. Add water to a depth of about 1 cm to a one-gallon thin metal can. Place the can on a tripod stand *with its lid off* and heat the water to boiling. After the water has boiled for about 5 minutes, remove the source of heat and then *quickly* seal the can. USE OVEN MITS TO AVOID BURNED FINGERS. Allow the can to cool on the support stand.

   What happens to the can as it cools? Why was it necessary to boil the water for several minutes? What happens inside the can when the sealed can cools?

   Make a rough calculation of the surface area of the can. From this value calculate the force on the outside of the can due to the air pressure. (Atmospheric pressure at sea level is approximately 15 lb/in^2.)

Questions:

*1. How does a decrease in air pressure affect
   (a) the boiling point of water?
   (b) the solubility of a gas in water?
*2. If atmospheric pressure were to decrease considerably
   (a) which gas would escape from the water of the oceans and make it impossible for marine life to exist?
   (b) what effects other than escaping of gas from the oceans would occur? (Hint: Review Procedure 2, 3 and 4.)
*3. List several reasons why astronauts in space must wear special suits.
*4.(a) Calculate the force produced by air pressure of 15 lb/in^2 on one side of a book whose dimensions are 7 in by 10 in.

(b) Why does normal air pressure not cause you great discomfort?

†5.(a) Study the dial of an aneroid barometer. What pressure range indicates dry and sunny weather? stormy weather? Explain why.

(b) Suggest why a rapid drop in atmospheric pressure frequently foretells the approach of a storm.

(c) Suggest how an aneroid barometer could be adapted for use as an altimeter (an instrument for measuring altitude).

References and Suggestions for Further Investigation:

1. The aurora borealis or northern lights occur at altitudes ranging from 70 Km to 1000 Km. Find out how this phenomenon is related to the activity of sunspots and to the composition of the ionosphere.

2. The following references expand upon and provide additional information about the Earth's atmosphere: Chapter 7 of *Investigating the Earth* (Boston: Houghton Mifflin Co., 1967); Chapter 9 of *Focus on Earth Science*, M. S. Bishop, P. G. Lewis and R. L. Bronaugh (Ohio, U.S.A.: Charles Merrill Publishing Co., 1969); Chapter 33 of *Earth Science: The World We Live In*, Fourth Edition (New York: American Book Company, 1969).

V–3   THE HYDROSPHERE

The hydrosphere consists of all bodies of water on the lithosphere including lakes, river systems and the oceans. Oceans cover nearly 71% of the Earth's surface. In addition to serving as huge reservoirs of water, oceans also contain many other substances.

In the following experiment you will learn about the composition of sea water. Oceanographers and geologists are very interested in this composition since it provides many clues about the Earth's past environment.

APPARATUS REQUIRED (per station)
250 ml beaker
glass square (3 in × 3 in)
stirring rod
centigram balance
scoopula
bunsen burner
wire gauze with an asbestos center
support stand with ring
equipment used in Experiment III-2 to test the conductivity of electrolytic solutions

MATERIALS REQUIRED
    Red and blue litmus paper
    sea water (reconstituted sea water may be obtained by using marine
       mix sea salt available from aquarium suppliers)

Procedure:
1. Test a small sample of sea water with both red and blue litmus paper. Record your observations.
   Is sea water acidic, basic or neutral?
2. Determine and record the mass of a clean dry 250 ml beaker. Then add approximately 50 ml of sea water to the beaker.
3. Using the method of Experiment III-2, test sea water to determine if it conducts an electric current.
   Is sea water an electrolyte?
4. Determine and record the total mass of the beaker and the sea water it contains. Knowing the mass of the beaker, calculate the mass of the sea water.
5. Place the beaker on wire gauze on a ring support and evaporate the water by heating it gently. Do not cause the contents to spatter by overheating. Toward the end of the evaporation process, cover the beaker with a glass square. As soon as the evaporation is completed, remove the flame and allow the contents to cool.
6. Scrape any particles adhering to the glass square into the beaker using a scoopula. Again determine and record the mass of the beaker and its contents. Knowing the weight of the beaker, calculate the mass of the residue.
7. Calculate the ratio of the mass of the solid residue to the mass of your original sample of sea water.

$$\text{Percentage mass} = \frac{\text{mass of solids}}{\text{mass of sea water}} \times 100\%$$

Questions:
*1. Which hemisphere has more water – northern or southern?
*2. How does water eventually end up in the oceans?
*3. In what way(s) do large bodies of water affect the Earth's climate?
*4. If you were given samples of sea water from the Pacific, Atlantic, Indian and Arctic Oceans, would you expect them all to have similar characteristics (e.g. the same temperature, density, taste)? Explain your answer.
*5. An accepted value for the average percentage of solids in sea water is 3.5% If you obtained a significantly different result, give reasons for this difference.

†6. A chemical analysis of the dissolved salts contained in sea water yields these percentages by mass* i.e.,

$$\text{Percentage mass} = \frac{\text{mass of ion}}{\text{mass of solid}} \times 100\%$$

chloride ion – 55%, sodium ion – 30%, sulphate ion – 8%, magnesium ion – 4%, calcium ion – 1%, potassium ion – 1%, others – 1%. (Since solids make up 3.5% of sea water, it therefore follows that sodium ion makes up 1.05% and chloride ion 1.93% of the mass of sea water.)

*Adapted from "Salt and Things" in the Journal of Geological Education, Volume XV, No. 6, December 1967.

(a) The total mass of all sea water is estimated to be 1.1×10^{18} metric tons (1 metric ton = 2205 lbs). Calculate separately the mass of sodium ions and chloride ions dissolved in sea water.

(b) In what form (chemical compound) would you expect to recover most of the sodium and chloride ions when sea water is evaporated? Why?

(c) Where did the sodium and chloride ions in sea water originate? (Hint: Could quartz (SiO_2) or limestone ($CaCO_3$) be the source?)

(d) What rocks make up the bulk of the outer 15 miles of the Earth's crust? (If necessary, look back to Exercise V-1.)

†(e) Igneous rocks, on an average, contain about 2.8% sodium and only 0.14% chlorine (chloride) by mass. How would you therefore explain the fact that chlorine is the most prevalent constituent (by mass) of the salts dissolved in sea water? Name a geological process which may have contributed extra chlorine to sea water.

†(f) A comparison of the amounts of ions dissolved in sea water with the amounts dissolved in river water reveals an interesting difference. carbonate (CO_3^{2-}) ions, calcium (Ca^{2+}) ions and silicate (SiO_3^{2-}) ions make up nearly 67% of the salts dissolved in river water but only 1.5% of the salts in sea water. Account for the smaller proportion of these three ions in sea water. (Hint: Are there any physical or biological processes that constantly remove these ions from the sea water?) Explain your answers fully.

†(g) List reasons why the dissolved salts in sea water are of great interest to scientists all over the world.

†(h) It is estimated that a cubic mile of sea water contains more than 2 tons of gold. Can you suggest some practical and economical ways to recover this gold? Explain your answer.

†(i) Calculations of the amount of dissolved salts were once used in attempts to estimate the age of the Earth. Can you suggest why

these estimates fell far short of the present estimates? (Hint: Have oceans always existed in their present locations?)

†7. (a) Do biologists think that life on Earth originated on land or in water?

   (b) How does the mineral composition of sea water compare with that of your blood? (If necessary, find the answer in a reference book.)

References and Suggestions for Further Investigation:

1. Read about undersea features such as trenches, mid-oceanic ridges and continental shelves.

2. Sea water is now being commercially mined. Carry out library research to determine the means employed to extract various substances such as magnesium, bromine and iodine from sea water.

3. Chapters 10 and 13 of *Investigating the Earth* (Boston: Houghton Mifflin Co., 1967), Chapter 11 of *Focus on Earth Science* (Ohio: Charles Merrill Publishing Co., 1969) and Chapters 18-21 of *Earth Science: The World We Live In*, Fourth Edition (New York: American Book Company, 1969) provide interesting information about the hydrosphere.

V – 4   GEOLOGICAL TIME SCALE (may be done as a class project)

Man's life span is too short to enable him to observe directly either the dramatic and extensive changes which alter the surface of the Earth or the living organisms that inhabit it. Since the uplift of mountains and the movement of continental masses is only a fraction of an inch a year we are not aware of any change during our lifetimes.

It is estimated that at the present time, Canada (and North America) is moving westward at the rate of about an inch per year. At this rate, it will have moved a very significant distance of 16 miles in one million years. This is a very short time when compared with the estimated age of the Earth.

The following exercise will help you to appreciate the occurrence and duration of some significant events that have taken place since the birth of our planet.

APPARATUS REQUIRED (per station or per class)
   Roll of ticker tape
   meter stick

Procedure:

1. Using a scale of 1 cm equals 1 million years, mark the following distances from one end of the ticker tape. The end from which all dis-

tances will be measured represents the twentieth century. Label each mark according to the event that occurred at that time. (Alternatively, you may represent the age of each of the events by means of a bar graph as you did in Experiment V-1.)

EVENT	ESTIMATED TIME (MILLIONS OF YEARS AGO)
Most recent retreat of ice covering Canada	0.011 (11,000 years)
Beginning of Ice Age	1
Emergence of man	2.5
Estimated age of the Grand Canyon	6
Formation of Rocky Mountains	70
Age of dinosaurs	160
First mammals	225
First reptiles	300
First amphibians	400
First land animals	440
First vertebrates (fish)	500
First known animal (soft bodied)	1200
First known plants (algae)	3200
Oldest known rocks	3300
Formation of the Earth	4500 (?)

Questions:

*1. At certain times in the past, various parts of the Earth were subjected to intense upheaval by mountain-building forces. These upheavals resulted in significant changes in the environment and may have caused the extinction or modification of existing life forms followed by the evolution of new ones. These times of revolutionary change have been used by geologists to divide Earth's history into *eras*. Study the following chart which briefly describes these eras and then answer the questions which follow.

ERA	DURATION (MILLIONS OF YEARS)	BEGINNING (MILLIONS OF YEARS)	IMPORTANT CHARACTERISTICS
Cenozoic Era (Age of Mammals)	70	70	Cave man, ice ages, extinction of mammoths, man uses fire, whales, primitive horse, primitive mammals, Alps and Himalayas forming
Mesozoic Era (Age of Reptiles)	150	220	Uplift of Rockies begins, dinosaurs become extinct

Paleozoic Era (Age of Fishes and Amphibians)	380	600	Giant dinosaurs, birds with teeth, flying reptiles, egg laying mammals Tribolites extinct, evolution of insects, spiders and primitive reptiles Fish and invertebrates dominant, primitive amphibians, first land plants, primitive sharks, air breathing animals, corals, clams, starfish, seaweeds
Pre-Cambrian (Age of Invertebrates and Dawn of Life)	Late 2400	3000 (?)	Marine invertebrates develop, single celled primitive animals and plants, no fossil record
	Early Unknown	4550 (?)	Some early marine invertebrates, single celled primitive life, waterless earth, no fossil record

It is estimated that the Earth's crust formed over 4 billion years ago. No rocks or fossils corresponding to this period have been discovered.

(a) What differences would be noted in fossils contained in sedimentary rocks of various ages?

(b) The massive extinction of dinosaurs occurred at the end of which era?

(c) The large scale extinction of marine invertebrates (e.g. trilobites) occurred at the end of which era?

(d) Why is a major change in life forms generally associated with worldwide mountain-building movements?

(e) Why is it not possible to obtain a rock sample corresponding to the time when the Earth's crust was formed?

*2. Fig. V-4-1 shows a cross-section of rocks that have been exposed because of erosion by the Colorado River. Study it and answer these questions:

(a) Why is the Grand Canyon often referred to as a diary of the last billion years of the Earth's history?

(b) Study the chart which shows the Earth's eras and use this information to estimate the age (in millions of years) of the exposed rock layers in the Grand Canyon that are labelled A, B and C in Fig. V-4-1.

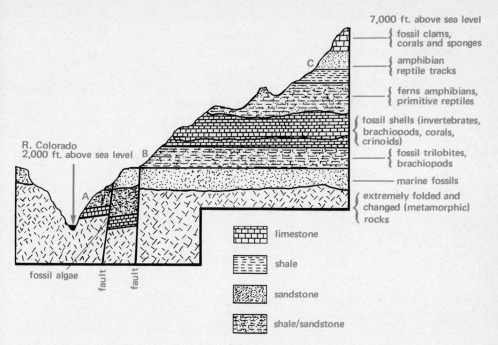

7,000 ft. above sea level
{ fossil clams,
{ corals and sponges

{ amphibian
{ reptile tracks

{ ferns amphibians,
{ primitive reptiles

{ fossil shells (invertebrates,
{ brachiopods, corals,
{ crinoids)

{ fossil trilobites,
{ brachiopods

— marine fossils

{ extremely folded and
{ changed (metamorphic)
{ rocks

R. Colorado
2,000 ft. above sea level

limestone

shale

sandstone

shale/sandstone

fossil algae

fault   fault

(Reprinted by permission of Scholastic Magazines, Inc., from *Science World*, © 1970 by Scholastic Magazines, Inc.)

Fig. V–4–1   A diagram of the cross section of rocks through Grand Canyon

References and Suggestions for Further Investigation:

1. Read Chapter 20, "The Geologic Scale" (pp 391-414) of *Focus on Earth Science* by Bishop and Lewis (Ohio: Charles Merrill Publishing Co., 1969).

2. If you could visit the North American continent as it was (a) 500 million years ago, (b) 80 million years ago, what present land features would you see? What features would you not see? Comment on the plants and animals of these periods.

DIASTROPHISM AND VOLCANISM

You have probably studied the geological processes of weathering, erosion and deposition in a previous course. How do these processes affect the surface of the lithosphere? Look at the natural features around your school. What did these surroundings look like a million years ago? Was there a school then? Were there mountains or valleys? What will these surroundings look like after another million years? What therefore is the general and cumulative effect of weathering and erosion upon the land surface? Would these effects occur if there were no atmosphere or hydrosphere? For how long has the Earth's surface been affected by erosion? It has taken an estimated 15 million years or more for the Columbia River system in British Columbia to reach its present state of erosion, Niagara Falls by comparison is a very recent feature, having formed as a result of the last ice age only 11,000 years ago.

The processes which tend to level the lithosphere are very slow; as a result, you may fail to appreciate their role in shaping the landforms around you. Given enough time, however, entire mountain ranges will be worn down and the resulting material will be deposited in the form of sediments. Gravity also plays an important role in these processes. Rivers can be regarded as huge conveyor belts that work ceaselessly to carry away weathered material and deposit it in low-lying areas. Where will all sediment eventually be deposited? Why have the oceans not been filled up with sediment?

It has been estimated that if weathering and erosion were to continue at the present rate, the surface relief (unevenness of the land surface) would entirely disappear within the next 50 million years. Since these processes have been going on for billions of years, why is the Earth's surface not flat?

Two processes which tend to undo the levelling effects of weathering and erosion are *diastrophism* and *volcanism*. Diastrophism is the process that moves and deforms the Earth's crust. Such movements occur when rocks respond to strains that develop within the crust. Often the result is an earthquake. Volcanism is the process that causes the movement of *magma* (molten rock material) both within the lithosphere and on the surface. Magma is called *lava* when it is expelled onto the surface. At such times, of course, volcanic activity is most evident. Without these two processes the Earth would be monotonously flat. British Columbia would resemble the Prairies and there would be no Rockies or Fraser Canyon.

V–5 VOLCANISM

Volcanic eruptions are the most dramatic evidence of the heat beneath the cooler lithosphere of the Earth. No one has yet observed the interior of the Earth directly and it is not likely that man ever will. However, man has long realized that he lives on a planet with a very hot and active interior. In this investigation you will study various types of volcanic cones and the type of material of which they are composed.

APPARATUS REQUIRED (per class)
Bunsen burner or hot plate
double boiler (or a beaker within a beaker)
oven mits (or beaker tongs)
thermometer

slide projector
(per station)
beaker
support stand with 3 in diameter ring
2 sheets of light cardboard (14 in × 9 in)
masking tape
protractor
pair of scissors

MATERIALS REQUIRED (per class)
Slides E1, E2A, E2B, E4, E7, E8, E11, E25 of the set of Earth
Science slides by the B.C. Science Teachers' Association*
block of paraffin wax
coloring material for the wax
(per station)
fine sand (0.5 mm)
coarse sand (2 mm) and gravel (3–4 mm)

*This set of slides may be ordered from the B.C. Teachers' Federa-
tion, 2235 Burrard St., Vancouver 9, B.C., Lesson Aids #M1.

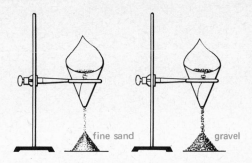

Fig. V–5–1   Studying the shape of a sandpile

Procedure:
1. Set up a support stand and ring as shown in Fig. V-5-1. Make a cone
   with a small opening (about 3 mm diameter) using a sheet of light
   cardboard (14 in × 9 in) and masking tape. Insert the cone into
   the ring as shown in Fig. V-5-1.
2. Fill the cone with fine sand and then allow it to empty so that the sand
   falls slowly but steadily through the hole onto a level sheet of cardboard placed about 10 cm below the base of the cone.
   What is the shape of the resulting sand pile?

Without disturbing the pile, use a protractor to help you estimate the "angle of repose." (See Fig. V-5-2.)

3. Add more sand to the pile as before.
   Does the angle of repose change with the size of the heap?

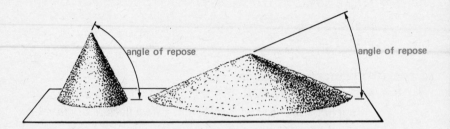

Fig. V–5–2   Does the size of sand grains affect the angle of repose?

4. Make a scale diagram of the resulting sand pile and label it. Indicate the approximate size of the sand grains used and the angle of repose.
5. Repeat Procedures 1-4 using coarse sand and then gravel. The hole at the bottom of the cardboard cone will have to be enlarged to allow gravel to flow through it. (See Fig. V-5-1.)
   Which grain size produces a cone with the largest angle of repose? with the smallest angle of repose?

NOTE: *The materials coming from a volcano can be both solid (cinders) and liquid (lava). The particles of the solid material may vary greatly in size.*

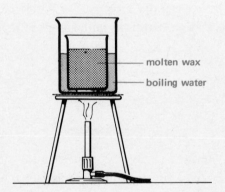

Fig. V–5–3   Melting wax in a double boiler

†6. (Demonstration) Carefully melt a block of paraffin wax either in a double boiler or in a beaker inside a larger beaker that contains water.(See Fig. V-5-3).You may add some coloring material to the

molten wax to make it more visible. (A small piece of wax marking pencil works well.) Allow the completely melted wax to cool to 60°C and pour the liquid wax slowly and carefully in stages over the top of the heap of coarse sand. Try to cover the entire cone.(See Fig. V-5-4). USE OVEN MITS OR A BEAKER CLAMP WHILE HANDLING THE CONTAINER OF MELTED WAX. Observe the way the molten wax covers the cone and how it becomes more sluggish as it cools while flowing down and around the cone.

Where does the wax solidify first? last? What forms at the base of the "volcano"?

Fig. V–5–4   What is the effect when molten material flows over colder granular material?

7. Make a diagram of the shape of the cone that is formed from the combination of sand and molten wax.
   In what way(s) does this cone differ from cones formed by sand or gravel? (Hint: How is its initial angle of repose affected?)

   Questions:
   *1.(a) What is the general relationship between the size of the particles used in the formation of a cone and the angle of repose of the resulting cone?
   (b) Under what conditions will the angle of repose of a volcanic cone be smaller – when the cone is made of solid cinders and ash or when it is made of rapidly cooling lava?

NOTE: *Volcanoes differ widely, according to the type of material ejected. Hawaiian volcanoes are non-explosive and expel large quantities of fluid lava while others may be more explosive, throwing up clouds of dust and ash, parts of the cone and huge blobs of lava which solidify before hitting the ground. The size of cinders in and around the volcanic cones is a testimony to the explosive violence of many volcanic eruptions.*

*2. Examine slides E7 and E8 which show two different types of volcanic activity.
   (a) What type of material (solid or liquid) is ejected by the type of eruption seen in slide E7? in slide E8?
   (b) Explain what cone shape will result from the material ejected by the eruption in E7? in E8?

†3. Use the library to answer the following questions.
   (a) What internal conditions might cause a volcano to eject a large quantity of cinders?
   (b) What internal conditions might cause a volcano to expel large quantities of lava relatively quietly?
   (c) What internal conditions might cause a volcano to expel both lava and cinders?
   (d) Why do many volcanoes have a quiet period between two eruptions?

*4. Examine slides E1, E2A and E2B which show three volcanic cones in widely separated parts of the world.
   (a) Estimate the angle of repose of the volcanic cones in each case.
   (b) What type of material (lava, cinders or both) may have gone into the making of each of these cones? Give reasons for your answers.

*5. Examine slide E4 which shows the inside view of a volcanic crater in Hawaii. Explain the significance of the layers visible on the crater walls.

*6. Examine slide E11 which shows an advancing stream of lava during a 1959 eruption of an Hawaiian volcano.
   (a) Explain the processes responsible for a gradual build-up of the volcanic islands of Hawaii from the sea floor during the last one million years.
   (b) Are these islands still growing in size?

*7. Examine slide E25 which shows a lava tunnel in Idaho (view looking outside from within the tunnel). Lava tunnels are not uncommon in many volcanic areas of the world. Explain how a lava tunnel may form. (Hint: A sluggish lava flow cools and hardens on the outside first.)

*8. Where is the source of the material coming out of a volcano (lithosphere, mantle or core)? Explain your answer with the help of a diagram. Refer to a text book.

*9. Explain why certain rocks resulting from the cooling of lava are characterized by air holes. (These rocks are called vesicular rocks.) (See Fig. V-5-5.)

*10. Why are many volcanic eruptions often preceded for a period of weeks by minor local tremors?

Fig. V–5–5   Vesicular lava and volcanic bombs

*11. Many major earthquakes are accompanied by one or more of the following effects.
  (a) Old volcanoes may suddenly become active.
  (b) Active volcanoes may cease their activity.
  (c) New "geysers" and hot springs may result.
  (d) Old geysers and hot springs may be reactivated.
  (e) Lava from active volcanoes may undergo minor changes in physical and chemical characteristics.
  Suggest reasons for each of the above effects. Use diagrams to illustrate your points.
†12. Are volcanoes activated by earthquakes or are earthquakes activated by volcanoes? Give reasons for your answer.
†13. Newly formed volcanoes look almost like a perfect cone. In the absence of a continuous volcanic activity, the cone may become progressively obscured by a ceaseless attack of water, wind and ice. The photographs in Fig. V-5-6 show three stages in the life of a volcano. Many geologists identify them as *active, dormant* and *extinct*. The time taken by a volcano to go through these stages will, of course, depend upon the general climate of the area.
  (a) What criterion is used in this classification of volcanic cones?
  (b) What part of a cone is generally most resistant to erosion? Explain.
  (c) From your study of the photographs, make a generalization that will help you in identifying each of these three types of cones.
  (d) Classify the volcanic cones referred to in Question 4 according to their condition.

active

dormant   extinct

Fig. V–5–6   Three stages in the life of a volcano

References and Suggestions for Further Investigation:
Use the library to carry out the following investigations.
1. Name the solid, liquid and gaseous kinds of volcanic debris (de-BREE) that are ejected from a volcano.
2. Make a chart of the physical characteristics that explain the difference between volcanic ash, dust, bombs (See Fig. V-5-5.), blocks, cinders and pumice. Why are they collectively referred to as "pyroclastic debris"?
3. Find out the names of volcanoes which are known to have ejected
   (a) predominantly solid materials (cinders and ash),
   (b) predominantly lava,
   (c) both solid materials and lava.
4. Determine the origin of the word "volcano."
5. (a) Prepare a report about one or more of the following famous eruptions:
      (i) Mt. Vesuvius
     (ii) Krakatoa
    (iii) Paricutin
     (iv) Mt. Pelee
      (v) Mt. Mozama (Crater Lake)
     (vi) Mauna Loa

(b) Where and when did these eruptions occur?

(c) What is the history of each volcano?

(d) What was the extent of the damage the eruption caused?

6. On a globe or world map, locate the following famous volcanoes: Mt. Fuji, Mt. Baker, Mt. McKinley, Mt. Ranier, Mt. Shasta, Mt. Mazama, Katmai (Alaska), Mayan (Philippines), Krakatoa, El Misti (South America). Locate them on an outline map of the world and keep this map for later comparison with a map of the earthquake zones of the world.

7. As shown in Fig. V-11-7 on page 353, fissure eruptions are caused when lava, pouring out of a network of cracks rather than a single vent, spreads over thousands of square miles. Two such famous series of eruptions took place in central British Columbia and in parts of western U.S.A. On the outline map of North America, trace the boundaries of these lava flows. Why are these areas called plateaus?

V-6 DETECTING AN EARTHQUAKE – THE SEISMOGRAPH
(May be demonstrated)

One of the most frightening natural events is a severe earthquake. This startling evidence of diastrophism occurs when the Earth's crust attempts to relieve itself of the strains that develop from enormous imbalances of internal pressure. These imbalances often result from the removal by erosion of tremendous amounts of surface material at one location and the deposition of this material at another location. The resulting stresses may result in cracking and buckling of large segments of the Earth's crust. Faults are deep fractures in the rock masses that comprise the lithosphere; earthquakes result when the crust moves along these faults.

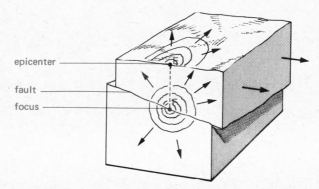

Fig. V–6-1   The epicenter is directly above the focus

Even a moderate earthquake can release an enormous amount of energy. Most of this energy is consumed in deforming the rocks in the immediate area of the disturbance. This source area, or *focus* of an earthquake, may be anywhere from a few miles to more than two hundred miles below the Earth's surface (on Canada's west coast, the focus of most earthquakes lies generally within 30 mi of the surface). The point on the Earth's surface directly above the focus of an earthquake is called the *epicenter*. (See Fig. V-6-1.) Where would you expect the maximum surface damage from an earthquake?

In Unit IV you learned that energy can travel from one location to another by means of waves. You also learned that there are two types of wave motion: compressional or P waves and transverse or S waves. It is by means of both of these wave types that part of the energy released during an earthquake is distributed over the entire Earth.

A seismograph is a device designed to detect and record such vibrations in the Earth's crust. (See Fig. V-6-2.) A seismograph consists of the following essential components:

(a) a large mass freely suspended from a rigid frame. (Because of its inertia, this mass will tend to remain stationary when the frame moves.)

(b) a device to record relative movement between this mass and the frame that is anchored to bedrock. This device can be constructed by attaching a pen (or stylus) to the mass and having it write on paper attached to the frame. If the paper is pulled beneath the pen at a steady rate, a continuous record of these movements can be obtained. Instead of a pen and paper, an arrangement of a beam of light and photographic paper may be used.

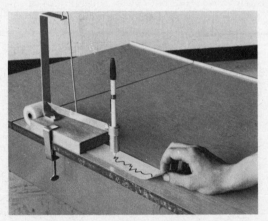

(Courtesy of Maple Leaf Distributors, Vancouver, British Columbia.)

Fig. V–6–2   A model seismograph

APPARATUS REQUIRED (per station or per class)
    Seismograph model with paper tape. (See Fig. V-6-2.)

NOTE: *As a separate project, students may design and assemble their own seismograph models.*

Procedure:
1. Set up a seismograph model as shown in Fig. V-6-2. Note the two essential components that were mentioned above.
   In which direction do the mass and the attached stylus move freely?
2. Without wasting too much paper tape, practice pulling it at a slow but steady speed and then a faster but steady speed under the stylus.
   Can your model detect very slight vibrations such as those produced by people moving around? What type of trace is obtained from a seismograph if there is no ground movement?
3. While you are pulling the tape *slowly* and steadily, have your partner represent an earthquake by quickly jerking the table in the direction of free movement of the stylus. Try varying both the speed and amplitude (related to the energy) of the jerks. (Review your work in Unit IV if you do not understand the meaning of these two terms.) Tear off the tape and label it "slow pull."
   How can you interpret the seismograph record (seismogram) to determine when quick, slow, strong and weak jerks occurred?
4. Repeat Procedure 3 but this time pull the tape more quickly. Again tear off the tape and this time label it "faster pull."
   What are the advantages of having the tape beneath the stylus move more rapidly? the disadvantages? Why would it be desirable for the recording paper in an actual seismograph to move at a constant speed?
5. Repeat Procedure 3 again but this time jerk the table first in a direction at right angles to the earlier one and then in an up and down direction.
   What are the limitations of your model seismograph? Can you rely on this model to record all the vibrations during an earthquake? Explain your answer. Suggest how these limitations in the model could be overcome.

Questions:
*1.(a) What is a wave?
  (b) Review Exercises IV-3 and IV-6. With the help of a diagram, show the two types of space waves that can be produced in a slinky?
      Describe both wave types in terms of the direction of the movement of the particles in the medium and the direction of propagation of the wave.
*2.(a) Suggest an arrangement that would allow a single seismograph to record Earth vibrations in both east-west and north-south directions simultaneously. (Use diagrams to illustrate your answer.)

(b) Suggest a modification that might be made in the seismograph model you used to enable it to record vertical Earth vibrations. (Use a diagram.)

(c) Why would at least three seismographs be required by an earthquake recording station to record both vertical and horizontal vibrations in all possible directions?

*3.(a) Below are the traces made during an earthquake by two different seismographs, A and B, at the same location. Which of the seismographs is more sensitive? Give a reason for your answer.

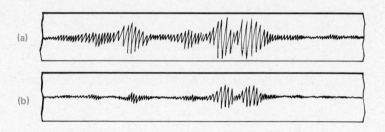

(b) List the factors that you feel limit the sensitivity of your seismograph model.

†(c) Suggest how you might use an arrangement consisting of a narrow light beam, a mirror and photographic film to modify your seismograph so that it can record very weak vibrations.

*4. How does the pattern of tracings on a seismogram depend upon the rate at which the recording tape is pulled? Explain your answer with the help of a diagram.

*5. How could you prevent a sensitive seismograph from recording local, unwanted vibrations like those produced by a heavy truck?

*6. What is the main source of the energy that is released during an earthquake?

†7. Aside from deforming rock and producing earthquake waves, what are some other ways in which the energy released during an earthquake may be "used up"?

References and Suggestions for Further Investigation:

1. If there is a seismograph station in your vicinity, arrange to visit the station and observe a seismograph in operation.

2. Read pages 347-354 of *Focus on Earth Science* (Ohio: Charles E. Merrill Publishing Co., 1969) and 224-234 in *Earth Science: The World We Live In*, Fourth Edition (New York: American Book Company, 1969).

V-7 LOCATING THE EPICENTER OF AN EARTHQUAKE

Modern seismic observatories are equipped with a number of sensitive, automatic recording seismographs. Each is tuned to record not only vibrations in a particular direction (e.g. east-west or vertical), but also vibrations within a particular frequency range (like a radio receiver). They are sufficiently sensitive to record tremors originating anywhere on the Earth. Sensitive seismographs use optical or electrical devices to amplify the movement of a stylus that is attached to a large, freely suspended mass. Their recording tapes are attached to a clock mechanism in order to indicate the time at which each vibration is received. (See Fig. V-7-2.)

Scores of such observatories are located all over the world, particularly in areas which experience frequent tremors. For example, in British Columbia, seismograph stations are located at Victoria, Port Hardy, Penticton, Fort St. James, Vancouver, Port Alberni and Mica Creek. Can you name some areas on the Pacific Coast of North America that experience frequent earthquakes?

An earthquake sets off several types of waves which are collectively called seismic waves. Before they reach a seismic station, some of these waves travel through the interior of the Earth and are thus called *body waves*; others travel along the Earth's surface and are accordingly called surface waves or *L Waves*. (See Fig. V-7-1.)

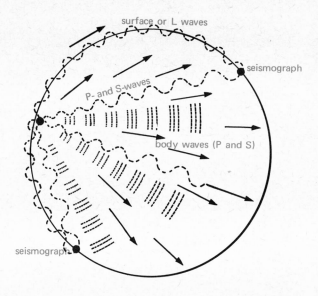

Fig. V–7–1   Path of earthquake waves from the focus to the recording station

There are two distinct types of body waves called P waves (for primus, because they arrive first) and S waves (for secondus, because they arrive second). As you have already learned in Unit IV, P waves cause the particles of the transmitting medium to vibrate in the direction of movement of the wave while S waves cause the particles of the medium to vibrate perpendicular to the direction of movement of the wave. (See Fig. V-7-1.) Both types of waves originate simultaneously in the focal zone of the earthquake. However, due to a difference in their speeds, recording stations do not receive these vibrations at the same time. In fact, the farther away the station is from the focus of the earthquake, the greater the difference in their times of arrival will be. Fig. V-7-2 shows a typical but simplified *seismogram* (record of an earthquake) that shows P waves arriving first, followed by S waves and finally L waves.

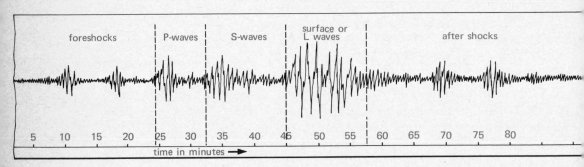

Fig. V–7–2   Seismogram

To see how these facts can be used by scientists to calculate the distance to the epicenter of an earthquake from their recording station, imagine the following situation.

Mike and Joanne are participating in a walk along a straight highway. Both start together and each maintains a constant speed but Mike walks 500 ft per minute and Joanne 400 ft per minute. Fig. V-7-3 shows graphically Mike's and Joanne's positions at regular time intervals as the walk progresses.

PART A   ANALYSING MIKE'S AND JOANNE'S WALKS

Procedure:

1. Study Fig. V-7-3 carefully and answer these questions.
   (a) What is the approximate distance between Mike and Joanne after they have walked for
      (i) 1 minute?
      (ii) 3 minutes?
      (iii) 10 minutes?

(b) If the walk started at 3:00 p.m., at what time will each have walked a distance of 2,000 ft?

(c) Joanne arrives 1 minute after Mike at a given location. How far has each walked to reach this location? (i.e. What is the distance of this position from the starting point?)

(d) What distance from the starting point will Mike reach 2 minutes ahead of Joanne?

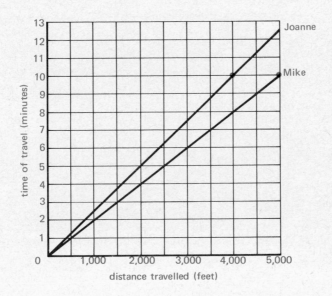

Fig. V–7–3   Graphs showing the travel times for Mike and Joanne

PART B   LOCATING THE EPICENTER

The techniques you have used in solving the problems above can also be applied to the problem of locating the epicenter of an earthquake.

APPARATUS REQUIRED (per station)
> 2 sheets of graph paper (8 in × 11 in)
> 2 outline (equal-area projection) maps of North America whose scale is known (may be traced on a stencil and mimeographed)
> a drawing compass
> a metric ruler
> set of colored pencils
> (per class)
> a globe or detailed map of the world
> a detailed map of Canada

Procedure:

The following data was recorded by seismograph stations in different parts of the world after a supposed earthquake that occurred at exactly 10:00:00 GMT (Greenwich Mean Time). The difference between arrival times of P and S waves was used at each recording station to calculate the distance of each station from the epicenter of the earthquake.

ARRIVAL TIMES OF THE EARTHQUAKE WAVES*
(All times in GMT)

LOCATION OF RECORDING STATION	DISTANCE FROM EPICENTER (Km)	TIME OF ARRIVAL OF P-WAVES (GMT) hr min sec	TIME OF ARRIVAL OF S-WAVES (GMT) hr min sec
Buenos Aires, Argentina	11,150	10: 13: 55	10: 25: 32
Halifax, Nova Scotia	4,400	10: 07: 38	10: 13: 45
Reykjavik, Iceland	5,660	10: 09: 10	10: 16: 29
Marseille, France	8,510	10: 11: 58	10: 21: 49
Edmonton, Alberta	820	10: 01: 59	10: 03: 18
Los Angeles, California	1,740	10: 03: 45	10: 06: 40
Ottawa, Ontario	3,520	10: 06: 30	10: 11: 42
Azores, Atlantic Ocean	7,360	10: 10: 56	10: 19: 48
Athens, Greece	9,710	10: 12: 55	10: 23: 39
Anchorage, Alaska	2,060	10: 03: 45	10: 07: 38

*Most of the data for this investigation was provided by Dr. Robert M. Ellis, Department of Geophysics, University of British Columbia, Vancouver, B.C.

1. Select a suitable scale and plot a graph with the distance from epicenter along the horizontal (x) axis and arrival times of P waves along the vertical (y) axis. Label the axes. Join the points with as smooth a curve as possible. Each partner should draw his own graph. **Can the origin be included as a point on your graph?**
2. Repeat Procedure 1 using the same set of axes but this time let the vertical axis represent the arrival time of S waves.
3. Label each plotted point on the graph by neatly printing the name of the recording station which contributed the information used. Also, label each curve to show whether it represents P waves or S waves. Provide a suitable title for the graphs.
4. On an outline map of North America (an equal-area projection map) mark with small x's the location of the various North American recording stations. Label these locations.

NOTE: *Maps which are not equal area projections will distort the distances.*

5. Reduce 2,060 Km (the distance from Anchorage to the epicenter) to the scale of your outline map, by dividing it by some convenient number. Using this scaled distance as the radius and Anchorage as the center, draw a circle on the map.
Is the earthquake epicenter located somewhere on this circle? Explain.

6. Repeat this procedure by drawing similar circles with appropriate radii around Edmonton and Los Angeles. The radii can be calculated by dividing the actual distance from the station to the epicenter by the number you used in Procedure 5.
Where is the epicenter of the earthquake located on your map?

NOTE: *If your arcs do not intersect at one point, locate the center of the "triangle" which is formed. (Point E in Fig. V-7-4(b).)*

Suggest why such a triangle is called the "triangle of error."

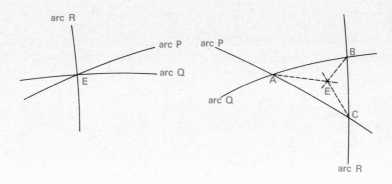

Fig. V–7–4   Locating the epicenter

Questions:
Answer the following questions with the help of your epicenter-location map and the travel-time graphs you have just drawn.

*1. Where in Canada (province and approximate locality) does the epicenter of the earthquake lie?

*2. (a) At what international time (GMT) did the earthquake occur?

    (b) What was the local time (Pacific Standard Time) in the epicenter region when the earthquake occurred? (You may consult a suitable reference book to answer this question.)

*3. Explain how the time and location of an earthquake are related to the damage to property and injury to people resulting from the earthquake.

*4. Use your plotted graph to determine the distance of a certain seismograph station from the epicenter if the first P waves arrived there

   (a)   8 minutes after the earthquake.

   (b) 13 minutes after the earthquake.

   (c) 20 minutes after the earthquake.

*5. Determine the distance of the recording station from the epicenter if the first S waves arrived there:

   (a)   8 minutes after the earthquake.

   (b) 12 minutes after the earthquake.

   (c) 20 minutes after the earthquake.

*6.(a) Do the speeds of P and S waves change as they travel through the interior of the Earth? Give reasons for your answer.

   (b) It took about 2 minutes for the P waves to travel a distance of 820 Kms to Edmonton. Compute the average speed of these waves in Km/sec and mi/sec (1 Km = ⅝ mi) between the epicenter and Edmonton.

   (c) Similarly, calculate the average speed of the P waves between the epicenter and Marseille (time: 12 minute; distance: 8510 Km).

 †(d) Recall your work with waves in Unit IV.

     (i) How do rigidity and density of a medium affect the speed of waves passing through it?

     (ii) P waves are found to travel faster when they travel a large distance inside the Earth. What does this indicate about the nature of the material in the Earth's interior?

*7. Review the situation in which Mike and Joanne walked along a highway at constant speeds.

   (a) What are the main differences between the graphs of their walk and the graph that you plotted for P and S waves?

   (b) Why are the two sets of graphs different?

 †(c) How does the difference in the arrival times of P and S waves change as the distance of the recording station from the epicenter increases?

 †(d) How is a recording station able to calculate its distance from the epicenter? Explain your answer.

*8.(a) A recording station is located 2,000 Km away from the epicenter of an earthquake. Calculate the difference between the times of arrival of the P and S waves at that station.

   (b) A recording station started receiving S waves ten minutes after it received the first P waves. What is the distance of the station from the epicenter?

   *9. Study Fig. V-7-2 and answer the following questions.
      (a) Which type of wave (P, S, or L) produces the strongest ground vibrations?
      (b) Which waves, therefore, are likely to cause most damage to property and life?
      (c) Why is it wise, except in special circumstances, to run out of a building immediately after the initial tremors?
  †10. Explain why seismograph stations rely upon the difference in the arrival times of P and S waves to compute their distance from the epicenter, rather than the time taken by only one of the waves to reach the station.

References and Suggestions for Further Investigation:
  1. The Apollo 12 astronauts left a sensitive seismograph on the Moon to record vibrations on the lunar surface. Later, after they had transferred safely to their command module, the lunar module was deliberately crash landed on the Moon. The impact caused strong vibrations which were faithfully recorded and transmitted back to Earth. What was the purpose behind this exercise? What surprising information about the interior of the Moon was obtained from the experiment?
  2. Why do L waves normally cause more damage to life and property than any other earthquake wave?
  3. Prepare a report recommending procedures to be followed by everybody in your school in the event of an earthquake. Give reasons for your recommendations. An excellent reference is *Safety and Survival in an Earthquake,* U.S. Department of the Interior/Geological Survey.

V–8 HOW EARTHQUAKES TELL US ABOUT THE EARTH'S INTERIOR

You have already learned that both types of seismic body waves travel through the Earth's interior, each with its own characteristic velocity. As they encounter changes in the medium (that is, rock layers with different physical properties) their velocities change. If they strike a boundary between different layers obliquely, they are refracted in the same way that light rays are refracted when moving from air into glass. (You observed refraction of water waves on crossing a boundary in a ripple tank in Experiment IV-9.) Waves may also be reflected at such boundaries, particularly if they strike them at a sufficiently large angle of incidence.

P waves travel almost twice as fast as S waves. In general, the velocity of P waves increases with depth since the rocks become heavier and are more rigid. Unlike P waves, S waves cannot pass through a fluid medium and this property has been used to determine the nature of rocks in the core of the Earth.

A knowledge of the velocity characteristics of these waves has been used to interpret seismograph data to develop a fairly comprehensive model of the Earth's interior. In this exercise you will learn how this is accomplished.

APPARATUS REQUIRED (per class)
  A large globe of the Earth or an unmarked globe

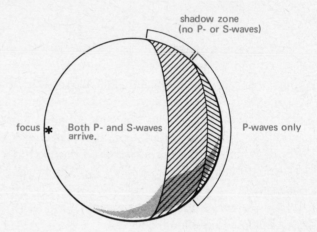

Fig. V–8–1   Seismograph stations at different locations on the Earth receive different data

Procedure:
1. Examine Fig. V-8-1. It shows that following an earthquake, seismograph stations at certain locations on the Earth may receive no S waves and only very faint P waves. These locations are in a belt called the "shadow zone" which extends around the Earth. Only P waves are received at seismograph stations located on the opposite side of the Earth from the focus of the earthquake.

   What condition(s) inside the Earth could be responsible for absorbing S waves while allowing P waves to travel through? (Hint: If necessary, reread the introduction.)

   In the light of these observations, which of the following Earth models is most reasonable? Give reasons for your choice.
   (a) The Earth has a hollow core.
   (b) The Earth has a hollow belt around a solid core like an inflated tube on a solid automobile wheel.
   (c) The Earth has a very dense and very hard central core.
   (d) The Earth has a molten (liquid) core.

2. Examine the Earth model shown in Fig. V-8-2 and answer the following questions.

   (a) How does this model account for the shadow zone observed after an earthquake?

   (b) How does this model account for the fact that only P waves arrive in the shadow zone?

  †(c) Suggest why body waves travel in a curved rather than a straight path.

  †(d) From an examination of Fig. V-8-2 what evidence is there that the inner core of the Earth is solid?

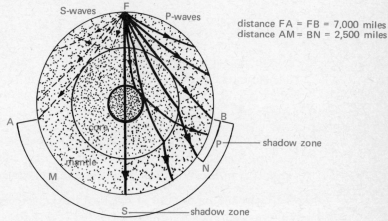

distance FA = FB = 7,000 miles
distance AM = BN = 2,500 miles

(From Hugh Grayson-Smith, *The Changing Concepts of Science*, © 1967. By permission of Prentice-Hall, Inc., Englewood Cliffs, New Jersey, U.S.A.)

Fig. V–8–2   The paths taken by S-waves travelling through the Earth are shown on the left and those of P-waves on the right. (P and S waves originate at the focus and travel in all directions)

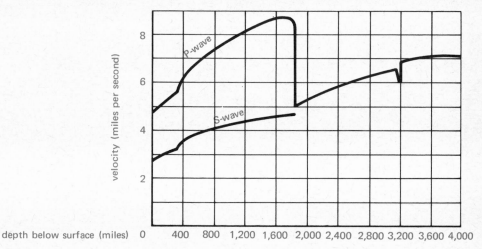

(By permission of Dr. Francis Birch, Hoffman Laboratory, Harvard University.)

Fig. V–8–3   Graph showing the change in velocity of P-and S-waves at various depths

3. By interpreting the difference in arrival times of those P and S waves that have been transmitted directly through the Earth, and those that have been reflected, it has been possible to calculate the velocity of these waves at various depths below the Earth's surface. Study the graph shown in Fig. V-8-3 and answer the following questions.

   (a) At what depth does the boundary between the Earth's mantle and its liquid core occur?

   (b) At what depth does the boundary between the Earth's liquid core and its solid inner core occur?

Questions:

*1. Use the information obtained from this and earlier exercises to draw a scale model of the Earth like that shown in Fig. V-1-1. Label the thickness of each zone. Include the Earth's atmosphere (altitude about 500 miles).

†2. Andrija Mohorovicic, a Yugoslavian seismologist, observed that a sudden change in the velocity of P waves occurred at a depth of about 25 miles. What important boundary occurs at this depth?

†3. Tell why the inner core of the Earth is believed to be solid and the outer core to be liquid.

References and Suggestions for Further Investigation:

1. Read pages 456-470 of *The Changing Concepts of Science* by Hugh Grayson-Smith (Englewood Cliffs, N.J.: Prentice-Hall Inc., 1967).

2. Read pages 321-335 of Chapter 21 entitled "Magnetism and Continental Drift" in *Physical Geology*, 3rd edition, by Leet and Judson (Englewood Cliffs, N.J.: Prentice-Hall Inc., 1965).

V–9   EARTHQUAKE DAMAGE

The frequency of earthquakes that are sufficiently large to cause damage may run as high as 100 a month. Most of them occur within the upper 30 miles of the Earth's crust in western Canada. Earthquake damage depends upon several factors such as distance from the epicenter, the nature of the ground over which buildings have been constructed, the design and materials used in the construction of buildings and the amount of energy released during the shock. Many deaths have occurred even during minor earthquakes in areas that are densely populated and where buildings are made of bricks or mud without proper bracing. During earthquakes, it is common for people to rush out of large buildings and into the streets where greater danger sometimes exists from falling objects. As a result of panic, many unnecessary deaths sometimes occur.

When the focus of an earthquake lies under the ocean, seismic sea waves called *tsunamis* (tsoo-NAH-mee) are produced. These can cause great damage to coastal cities at large distances from the epicenter.

In the following exercise you will locate regions of the world where most earthquakes occur and view pictures of damage that resulted from the 1964 Alaskan earthquake.

MATERIALS REQUIRED (per class)
> *A map of the world mounted on pinboard*
> *thumbtacks*
> *the most recent "World Almanac"*
> *slides D11 to D19 of the set of Earth Science slides available from the*
>   *B.C. Teachers' Federation Lesson Aid M-1*
> *slide projector*

Procedure:

1. Collect information about the locations of *major* earthquakes since 1900 and the locations of reported earthquakes during the past year with the help of a World Almanac. (See "Chronology of Year's Events".)

2. (Class project) Use thumbtacks to mark the locations of all earthquakes that occur on the Earth for the duration of the school year. These are reported in your daily newspaper.
   Do you see any pattern in the locations of these earthquakes? Describe the pattern.

3. Examine slides D11 to D19 and the accompanying notes of the slide set mentioned above. These pictures show the widespread damage and destruction resulting from an earthquake in Alaska in March, 1964. With the help of library research and these slides, answer the following questions.
   (a) What is meant by the Richter (RIK-ter) scale of earthquake magnitude?
   (b) How strong was this earthquake on the Richter scale?
   (c) List the various types of damage caused to land and man-made structures by the earthquake.
   (d) Prepare a report on the effects of the Alaskan Earthquake that were experienced in distant regions of the world. (Water in a swimming pool in Atlantic City, N.J., nearly 4,000 miles away,

was reported to have splashed due to the resulting vibrations.)

(e) What is a "tsunami"? What is its relationship to an earthquake? (Slide D12 shows the destruction caused by the tsunami that resulted from the Alaskan earthquake and which swept across almost the entire Pacific Ocean.)

(f) What damage did the tsunami cause on the coast of British Columbia?

(g) Prepare a brief description of two or more of the following major earthquakes of this century.
   (i) San Francisco Earthquake, 1906
   (ii) Tokyo, Japan Earthquake, 1923
   (iii) Chilean Earthquake, 1939
   (iv) Peruvian Earthquake, 1970

How do these earthquakes compare with the Alaskan Earthquake in magnitude and damage?

Questions:

*1. Earthquakes are generally confined to areas that are called earthquake belts. In a reference book find where these belts occur. Are you living in or near one?

*2. Why is the Pacific belt of earthquake zones also called the "Pacific Ring of Fire"?

†3. Write a well researched report on how buildings can be designed to resist earthquakes.

MINERALS AND ROCKS

Do you know the difference between a rock and a mineral?

A *mineral* is a naturally occurring solid which may be an inorganic compound or an element. (*Inorganic* means that the substance was not derived from living material.) Each mineral has a distinctive crystal structure and shows characteristic physical and chemical properties that may be used to identify it. Scientists who study minerals are called *mineralogists*.

A *rock* is a solid that forms a part of the Earth's crust and contains one or more minerals. Many rocks, such as granite, basalt and conglomerate, are mixtures of minerals whose proportions vary within a certain range. Others, like limestone and quartzite, have only one mineral in them.

Although more than 2,000 minerals have been identified, not more than a dozen of them make up most of the Earth's crust. You can learn to recognize them in the same way you recognize your classmates – by their physical characteristics. (Mineral identification through an analysis of chemical properties generally requires skills and equipment beyond the scope of this investigation.)

V-10   IDENTIFYING COMMON MINERALS

In the following exercise, you will observe several physical properties of minerals that can be used for their identification; because you will undertake a study of various rocks in succeeding exercises, you should remember the names and properties of the more common minerals.

MATERIALS REQUIRED
The following mineral samples:

NOTE: *With the exception of cinnabar, halite, sulphur and bornite, these minerals are available in a set provided by the Geological Survey of Canada.*

1. molybdenite (MoS_2)
2. graphite (C)
3. galena (PbS)
4. chalcopyrite ($CuFeS_2$)
5. pyrite (FeS_2)
6. hematite (Fe_2O_3)
7. magnetite (Fe_3O_4)
8. talc (hydrous magnesium silicate)
9. gypsum ($CaSO_4 \cdot 2H_2O$)
10. muscovite mica (complex hydrous potassium and aluminum silicate)
11. calcite ($CaCO_3$)
12. plagioclase feldspar (e.g. albite) (a mixture of calcium, sodium and aluminum silicates)
13. quartz (SiO_2)
14. siderite ($FeCO_3$)
15. potash feldspar e.g. microline (potassium and aluminum silicate)
16. garnet (a complex iron, magnesium, aluminum and calcium silicate)
17. asbestos (hydrous calcium, magnesium and iron silicate)
18. fluorite (CaF_2)
19. apatite [$(Ca_8(Cl,F)(PO_4)_3$]
20. pyroxene (calcium, magnesium and iron silicates)
21. biotite mica (complex hydrous potassium, aluminum, magnesium and iron silicate)
22. sphalerite (ZnS)
23. amphibole, e.g. hornblende, (complex magnesium, iron and calcium silicate)
24. cinnabar (HgS)
25. halite (NaCl)
26. sulphur (S)
27. bornite, called peacock ore (Cu_5FeS_3)

PART A   EXAMINING COLOR

Color is the most obvious property of a mineral; however, you should not rely on this property alone for identification since many widely different minerals have the same color. Also, certain minerals like quartz occur in a variety of colors (e.g. purple, smoky, milky, green, blue). Such differences occur because the color of a mineral is frequently determined by the kind and amount of impurities it contains. Moreover, the true color of a mineral may be masked by stains and weathering on its surface. In the field, it is often advisable to break a chip off a sample, allowing you to examine the fresh surface of a mineral.

Procedure:

1. Examine and record the color of each of the minerals in your set of samples. Do not confuse color with the sheen of the mineral. Describe the color by using one or a combination of two of the following colors: steel grey, lead grey, silver white, light grey, brass, white, grey (or greyish white), red, yellow, pink, brown, black (or brownish black), blue, green, colorless, etc.

NOTE: *In some samples, the mineral you are to examine may form only a part of the sample (e.g. molybdenite and asbestos). Other samples may contain more than one mineral. You must therefore examine each sample carefully to ensure that you are observing the correct mineral. When in doubt ask your teacher.*

Prepare a chart with the following headings and record *only* the minerals, their chemical composition and their color. Information about chemical composition is provided in the list of minerals found under "Materials Required." The properties of quartz have been entered for your reference. (Entries will be made in the other columns in later exercises.)

NAME OF MINERAL	CHEMICAL COMPOSITION	COLOR	LUSTER	HARDNESS	STREAK
quartz	SiO_2	variable; commonly colorless or milky	vitreous	7	none

CLEAVAGE PLANES	DENSITY COMPARED TO QUARTZ	CRYSTAL HABIT IF ANY	ANY SPECIAL CHARACTERISTICS
none	same	hexagonal if crystalline	striations on crystal faces, breaks unevenly, found in many colors.

2. Arrange the minerals in groups of common chemical composition, for example, oxides, sulphides, silicates.
Which group of minerals is most like common rocks? Which group contains minerals that resemble metals? Do the minerals in each of these groups have any other common characteristic?
3. Use a reference book to define what is meant by an *ore* mineral. **Which minerals in your samples are ore minerals? Which of the groups that you arranged in Procedure 2 contains ore minerals?**
4. Arrange the silicate minerals into two groups, according to their colors, under the headings DARK COLORED SILICATES and LIGHT COLORED SILICATES. Study the chemical composition of each silicate mineral.
Which element is common to the dark colored silicates?

NOTE: *Dark colored minerals frequently contain a significant amount of iron while light colored minerals contain mostly silicon, aluminum and oxygen.*

Questions:
*1. What familiar natural material has the same color as hematite?
†2. Many varieties of quartz and corundum are semi-precious stones. Their colors are variable because of the impurities present in them. Complete the following chart with the help of library research.

NAME OF STONE	COLOR	IMPURITIES PRESENT, IF ANY

(a) Varieties of Quartz (SiO_2)
  (i) rose quartz
  (ii) smoky quartz
  (iii) amethyst
  (iv) opal
  (v) jasper
  (vi) onyx
  (vii) chalcedony
  (viii) agate
  (ix) blood stone
  (x) carnelian
  (xi) chert (flint)

(b) Varieties of Corundum (Al_2O_3)
  (i) rubies
  (ii) sapphires
  (iii) emery

PART B   EXAMINING LUSTER

Luster refers to the quality of the light reflected by a mineral's surface.

MATERIALS REQUIRED (per station)
The mineral samples used in Part A

Procedure:
1. Record the luster of each mineral in your set in the fourth column of your chart. Use the following terms (or a combination of two) to describe the luster of the minerals.

TERM	DESCRIPTION
Metallic	shines like a metal
Non-metallic	
vitreous	glassy, like a broken piece of glass
resinous	like resin (pitch)
pearly	like a pearl
silky	like silk or rayon
greasy	like grease
dull	like dried mud or clay
adamantine	brilliant, like a diamond

2. Arrange the minerals into two groups, that is, minerals with *metallic* luster and minerals with *non-metallic* luster. Compare the groups with those in Procedures 2 and 3 of Part A.
   What other characteristics are common to the minerals with a metallic luster? (Hint: How do they compare in density and chemical composition?)

Questions:
*1. Describe how you would tell the difference between pieces of gold, glass, plastic, diamond and paper, all of the same size and shape, without touching them.
†2. How can you differentiate between a cut diamond and a colorless crystal of quartz? (Hint: Study the types of luster in Procedure 1.)

PART C   INVESTIGATING HARDNESS

Hardness is the resistance of a mineral to scratching. Minerals vary greatly in their hardness. In very hard minerals like corundum, atoms are held together by such strong chemical bonds that it is very hard to force them apart. It is therefore very difficult to scratch the surface of the mineral. The atoms of carbon in a diamond are bonded so strongly that diamond is the hardest of all naturally occurring substances. Hardness is a very important characteristic of a mineral.

The effect of chemical bonding is seen very clearly in diamond and graphite. Although both are chemically composed of only carbon atoms, their hardnesses differ greatly because their atoms are combined differently. (See Fig. V-10-1.) The 3-dimensional arrangement of carbon atoms in diamond produces a very hard substance while the 2-dimensional sheet-like arrangement of carbon atoms to form planes in graphite produces a very soft and slippery substance.

diamond

graphite

(From L. Don Leet and Sheldon Judson, *Physical Geology, Third Edition*, © 1965. By permission of Prentice-Hall, Inc., Englewood Cliffs, New Jersey, U.S.A.)

Fig. V-10-1   The way in which carbon atoms combine greatly affects the hardness of the resulting minerals

Friedrick Mohs (MOHZ), a German mineralogist, arranged certain common minerals in order of increasing hardness. His scale of mineral hardness has been widely used by mineralogists and prospectors for decades. You will find his scale useful for identifying many unknown minerals.

MOHS SCALE OF HARDNESS OF MINERALS

NAME	HARDNESS
talc	1 – very soft, soapy feel
gypsum	2 – fingernail scratches it
calcite	3 – copper penny scratches it
fluorite	4 – steel knife *easily* scratches it
apatite	5 – steel knife scratches it
feldspar	6 – steel file scratches it
quartz	7 – scratches steel and hard glass easily
topaz	8 – scratches quartz
corundum	9 –
diamond	10 –

A SIMPLIFIED HARDNESS SCALE WHICH YOU MAY USE
WITH THE SCALE ABOVE

NAME	HARDNESS
fingernail	2.5
penny	3.0
knife blade	5.5
scratches window glass	5.5
steel file	6.5

An examination of Mohs' scale might lead you to the conclusion that diamond is 10 times harder than talc but this is not so. Mohs simply arranged the minerals in order of their hardness. Each mineral listed can scratch but cannot be scratched by any mineral with a lower hardness. Talc, for example, can be scratched by all the minerals in the list while none of them can scratch diamond. It is estimated that diamond is nearly 1,000 times harder than talc and nearly 40 times harder than corundum.

APPARATUS REQUIRED (per station)
   A penny
   steel knife
   glass square
   steel file

MATERIALS REQUIRED (per station)
   Samples of talc, calcite, quartz, fluorite, apatite, feldspar, gypsum, molybdenite, garnet, pyrite, pyroxene, halite and sphalerite

Procedure:
1. Estimate the hardness of molybdenite, garnet, pyrite, pyroxene, halite and sphalerite. Use your fingernail, a penny, a pocket knife, a piece of glass (scratch *it* with the mineral), a steel file and the minerals listed in Mohs' scale. Surprisingly, almost all common minerals can be classified for hardness with these simple items.

NOTE: Fractions may be used to describe the hardness of a mineral that lies between the hardnesses of two minerals in Mohs' scale, e.g. pyrite has a hardness that lies between that of feldspar and quartz and is therefore rated 6.5.

Record the hardness of the mineral samples tested in the fifth column of your chart.
2. Compare the hardness of each mineral you tested with that given for the same mineral on the information sheet which accompanies the mineral set or in a suitable reference book.

Questions:

*1. Why are diamond drills used for drilling through rock formations in the Earth's crust?

*2. Why is talc used extensively as a base material in face-powders?

†3. Why does the value of a precious stone used for ornamental purposes depend not only upon its looks but also upon its hardness?

†4. Explain why there are no beaches of diamond, talc or calcite in the world while beaches of sand are almost universal. (Sand grains consist mainly of quartz.)

PART D   USING A STREAK PLATE TO DETERMINE THE STREAK OF A MINERAL

The color of a finely powdered mineral is often different from that of the mineral sample from which it is obtained. For example, brassy colored chalcopyrite produces a black powder. If you rub a mineral across a plate of unglazed porcelain it may leave a powder mark on the plate. The color of this mark is referred to as the *streak* of the mineral and the unglazed porcelain plate is called a *streak plate*. What is the streak of chalcopyrite?

Since the hardness (Part C) of a streak plate is about 6, minerals with a hardness of more than 6 will not have a streak. The lack of a streak for a mineral therefore tells you something about its hardness.

APPARATUS REQUIRED (per station)
Streak plate (or porcelain tile)

MATERIALS REQUIRED (per station)
Samples of galena, chalcopyrite, pyrite, molybdenite, feldspar, fluorite, calcite, apatite, garnet, gypsum, magnetite, sulphur, amphibole and sphalerite

Procedure:

1. Select several metallic and non-metallic minerals and rub them in turn on a streak plate. (Recommended minerals for this test are listed in Materials Required.) Since some of the minerals have a streak that has the same color as the streak plate and others have no streak, you will sometimes have to look carefully.
   Is the streak of minerals with a metallic luster lighter or darker than the color of the minerals? of the minerals with a non-metallic luster?

2. Record the streak of the minerals tested in the sixth column of the chart you prepared in Part A.

Questions:

*1. Hematite, which is often black, has a reddish-brown streak. What is the *true* color of the mineral?

*2. What is the streak of corundum? (Hint: Corundum has a hardness of 9.)

†3. Certain minerals do not have streak on the streak plate. Would they have streak if the streak plate were made of diamond? of talc? Explain your answer.

PART E   TESTING FOR CLEAVAGE

It is very easy to recognize mica because of the way it splits into sheets or flakes. Even a diamond crystal will break more easily along certain planes. (To recognize these planes of weakness in a large diamond crystal is a great challenge to a diamond cutter.) The tendency of a mineral to split or cleave more easily along certain planes is described as *cleavage*. Cleavage planes are governed by the arrangement of atoms or ions within a crystal and they occur in the planes across which the atomic bonds are relatively weak. Substances with no crystalline structure (such as agate and jasper) show no cleavage and are said to be amorphous.

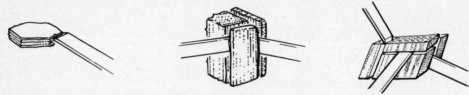

Fig. V–10–2   Cleavage may occur in one, two, three or more directions

Minerals that cleave may do so in one or more planes, e.g. mica cleaves in one, feldspar in two and calcite in three planes. (See Fig. V-10-2.) Usually, cleavage is better along certain planes than others. The planes of weakness show up as traces (straight lines) on some of the sides of a crystal so you do not have to break a mineral sample to discover its cleavage planes. (See Fig. V-10-3.)

(mica)
basal cleavage

cubic cleavage
(galena)

cleavage trace
rhombohedral cleavage
(calcite)

Fig. V–10–3   Traces of the planes of cleavage often show as lines on various faces of a crystal

If enough mineral samples are available, the following exercise may be carried out in small groups. Otherwise, it will be demonstrated.

APPARATUS REQUIRED (per station)
>   *Protractor*
>   (per class)
>   *hammer*
>   *sharp knife or chisel*
>   *hand lens*

MATERIALS REQUIRED (per station or per class)
>   *good samples of galena, calcite, feldspar, mica, halite, quartz*

Procedure:
1. Obtain a small piece of each mineral listed above and study each carefully with the aid of a hand lens. Try to identify definite cleavage planes by examining various crystal faces and determine the planes along which each mineral is likely to break.
    How many planes of weakness does galena have (parallel planes count as one plane)? What is the shape of a galena crystal? What is the difference between the cleavage planes of galena and calcite? (Both have the same number of cleavage planes.) Why does mica readily split into flakes?
2. As accurately as possible, trace outlines of the crystals of galena and calcite on a sheet of paper and measure the angles between their planes of cleavage.
3. (Demonstration) Break up the mineral samples carefully, by striking a sharp knife held along a cleavage plane with a hammer. Study the shape of the resulting pieces.
    Did the minerals break along the predicted planes of weakness?
    Record the cleavage of the minerals tested in the seventh column of your chart.

Questions:
*1. Common sand grains consist mostly of quartz and some feldspar. Explain why most quartz grains are rounded while most feldspar grains have rectangular sides. (This observation will be very helpful when examining crystals of these minerals in rock samples such as granite.)

PART F   COMPARING MASS DENSITIES

Minerals vary widely in their mass densities. The mass density of a mineral depends on the manner in which its atoms or ions are packed together within its crystals, as well as the masses of these particles. This property is therefore the most characteristic physical property of any mineral. However, since a precise determination of the mass density of a mineral is rather inconvenient for a geologist in the field, geologists learn to estimate relative mass densities.

In this exercise you will determine the relative mass densities of galena, calcite and quartz.

MATERIALS REQUIRED (per station)

> *Large samples of galena, calcite, quartz and other minerals that have approximately the same volume.*

Procedure:

1. Hold a sample of galena in one hand and a sample of quartz of the same volume in the other hand. Compare their weights.
Why will their weights tell you how their mass densities compare?
Complete the eighth column of your table for galena with one of the following terms: same, less, more, very much more, very much less.
2. Repeat Procedure 1 using samples of calcite and quartz which have approximately equal volumes.
3. Repeat Procedure 1 for as many other minerals as you have time for.

Questions:

*1. List the minerals you tested in order of decreasing mass density.
*2.(a) Use the chemical formula of each of these minerals and the Periodic Chart on the back cover of this book to find the mass of a chemical unit of each.
  (b) List each of these minerals in order of decreasing formula mass.
  (c) Does this list agree with that in Question 1?
  †(d) What factors affect the mass density of a substance in addition to its formula mass?
†3. The method you used to compare the mass density of a sample with the mass density of quartz is more successful for heavier minerals if you use large samples. Explain why.

PART G   EXAMINING CRYSTAL HABITS AND FORMS

The study of crystals is a highly specialized branch of mineralogy called crystallography. It is very rare to encounter minerals in nature that have perfectly developed crystals. As a means of mineral identification, therefore, crystal form may be of limited use to you. However, if you are familiar with the characteristic shapes of the crystals of common minerals these can be very useful clues to the identities of minerals.

Every mineral has a characteristic crystal form which, like hardness and cleavage, reflects its internal atomic or ionic structure. A crystal is a regular, geometric arrangement of these particles and therefore has a definite symmetry in its appearance. Based on these symmetries, all crystals can be grouped into six crystal systems. You can read about these crystal sytems in any good book about minerals.

Minerals are found either in *crystalline* or *amorphous* (non-crystalline) form. You should be able to distinguish between these two forms easily with some practice. Certain minerals like quartz occur in both crystalline (hexagonal) and amorphous (agate, jasper, etc.) forms.

Crystal habit refers to the typical shape of a crystal. A mineral may have more than one habit depending upon the temperature at which it crystallized in the parent rock. Some common crystal habits are cubic, columnar, tabular, hexagonal, rhombic, flaky (mica), bladed (like a knife-blade) and fibrous (asbestos). (See Fig. V-10-4.)

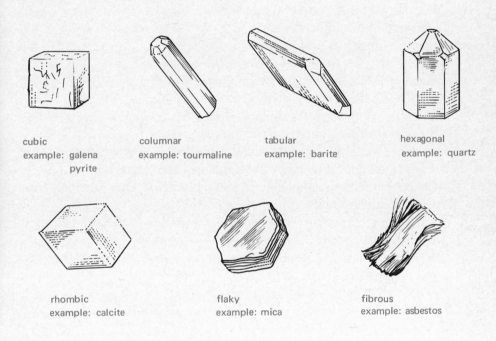

cubic
example: galena
pyrite

columnar
example: tourmaline

tabular
example: barite

hexagonal
example: quartz

rhombic
example: calcite

flaky
example: mica

fibrous
example: asbestos

Fig. V–10–4   Various crystal habits

APPARATUS REQUIRED (per station)
Hand lens or stereomicroscope

MATERIALS REQUIRED (per station)
Broken samples from Part E

Procedure:
1. Examine freshly broken pieces of calcite, quartz, galena (from Part E) and feldspar with a hand lens (or under a stereomicroscope if one is available).
Describe the shape of each of these crystals.
Record the habits of the minerals examined in the ninth column of your chart and use sketches to illustrate your observations.

Questions:

*1. Suppose you have a mineral with good cleavage along two perpendicular planes. What particular habit will be shown by the resulting pieces after cleavage has occurred? Explain. (Hint: Examine Fig. V-10-4.)

*2. Describe the habit of crystals of a mineral that has good cleavage in three planes that are perpendicular to each other.

PART H   IDENTIFYING OTHER CHARACTERISTICS

A few minerals have rather unusual properties that offer excellent clues to their identity. Some of these properties are:

1. Magnetism: Magnetite is attracted by a magnet.
2. Characteristic taste: Halite has a salty taste.
3. Striations (parallel threadlike lines on the faces of its crystals): Quartz and pyrite show striations on their crystal faces.
4. Variation in colors when the mineral is seen from different angles: Labradorite feldspar varies from irridescent blue to green.
5. Fluorescence in "black light" (mineral emits visible light when exposed to ultraviolet radiation): Fluorite, calcite and opal are fluorescent
6. Effervescence (fizzes when in contact with dilute acid): Carbonate minerals, particularly calcite and siderite, effervesce.
7. Fracturing in a particular way when struck with a hammer: Minerals with no definite planes of weakness tend to break in an irregular way; quartz breaks to form sharp edges and a surface like a clam shell. This type of fracture is called conchoidal fracture.

APPARATUS REQUIRED (per station)
        Magnet
        (per class)
        ultraviolet light source (see CAUTION)

MATERIALS REQUIRED (per station)
        3M HCl in dropper bottle

Procedure:

1. Test various minerals in your set with a magnet.
2. Use a medicine dropper to add a drop of 3M HCl to several minerals including calcite and siderite, to determine which are carbonates.
3. If a dark room and an ultraviolet light source are available, examine your minerals under ultraviolet "black" light.

CAUTION: To avoid damage to your eyes do not look directly at any ultraviolet light source.

4. Record any observed special characteristics in the last column of your chart.

Questions:

*1. Use the information sheet that accompanies the Geological Survey of Canada set of minerals and/or a good book on minerals to complete the chart on which you have recorded your observations. At the same time check your own observations to see if they agree with those in the reference material.

References and Suggestions for Further Investigation:

1. Read a biography of the Greek philosopher Archimedes and find out how he delighted his king by determining the purity of gold used in the king's crown without melting the crown.

V–11   ROCKS

The study of rocks provides geologists and prospectors with a great deal of information about the Earth. Rocks make up the lithosphere and contain minerals that are vital to our technology. To a geologist, rocks are like the pages in a history book of the Earth—a book that not only provides clues about the origin of the Earth but also records the changes that the Earth has undergone since its origin. A geologist who specializes in the study of rocks is called a *petrologist*.

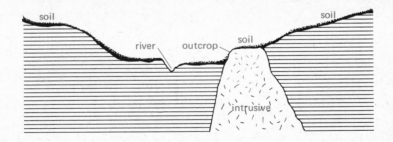

Fig. V–11–1   Outcrops reveal much about the rocks below the surface

Direct observation of the interior of the Earth is not possible; however, rocks reveal the conditions in the interior regions of the Earth beyond our reach. Fig. V-11-1 illustrates how a small exposure on the surface may be an extension (*outcrop*) of the massive rocks lying underneath and beyond our range of direct observation.

Rocks fall into three major categories depending on how they were formed:

1. *Igneous* rocks, formed by the crystallization of molten material called *magma* which is found beneath the Earth's surface at various depths. Magma that reaches the surface through an opening in the crust is called *lava*. (See Fig. V-11-7.)

2. *Sedimentary* rocks, formed by the consolidation of sediments derived from all types of rocks.

3. *Metamorphic* rocks, formed by the action of heat and pressure on pre-existing rocks beneath the crust.

The combined geological processes of weathering, erosion, deposition, volcanism and diastrophism keep the material of these rocks constantly in circulation, as indicated in Fig. V-11-2. However, the lithosphere obviously consisted mainly of igneous and metamorphic rocks during the beginning stages of the Earth's formation. Can you explain why?

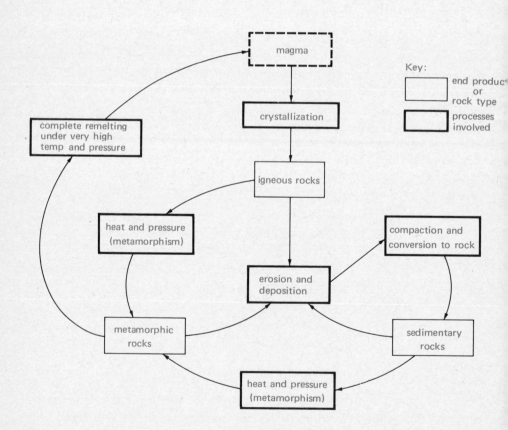

Fig. V–11–2   The rock cycle

PART A   IGNEOUS ROCKS

It is not possible to re-create in the laboratory the type of environment that exists in nature when igneous rocks are being formed. However, the first part of the following exercise will help you to appreciate how differences in the cooling rates of large bodies of magma produce differences in the sizes of crystals in the resulting igneous rocks.

APPARATUS REQUIRED (per station)
> *Hand lens*
> (per class)
> *1 liter beaker*
> *3 400 ml beakers*
> *beaker tongs*
> *stirring rod*
> *tripod stand*
> *asbestos gauze*
> *bunsen burner*
> *nylon thread*
> *glass plate to cover the 400 ml beaker*

MATERIALS REQUIRED (per station)
> *Samples of granite, syenite, gabbro, peridotite, feldspar porphyry,*
> *rhyolite, basalt, pink granite*, vesicular lava* (with air holes),*
> *obsidian**
> *saturated CuSO$_4$ solution*
> *slides E17 and E18 of the set of Earth Science slides provided by*
> *the B.C. Teachers' Federation (Lesson Aid No. M-I)*

NOTE: With the exception of those starred*, the rocks listed are available in an inexpensive set of rock chips provided by the Geological Survey of Canada. Rocks marked * may be obtained from a local rock and mineral dealer. Many people find rock collecting fascinating. While visiting such a collector take advantage of the opportunity to ask him about his hobby.

Procedure:

NOTE: Procedures 1, 2 and 3 may be demonstrated.

1. Pour 200 ml of a saturated CuSO$_4$ solution into each of three 400 ml beakers.
2. Treat each of the three beakers as follows.
   (a) Place beaker A in a location where it will be undisturbed and where temperature fluctuations are minimal.

(b) Using a glass stirring rod and a nylon thread to suspend a large "seed" crystal of $CuSO_4$ in the solution of beaker B. Place this beaker in the same location as beaker A. (See Fig. V-11-3.)

(c) Heat beaker C on an asbestos gauze placed on a tripod stand and allow its contents to evaporate to about ⅓ of the original volume. (See Fig. I-11-3.) Then cool the beaker and contents using beaker tongs to transfer the beaker to a cold water bath. Note the size of the crystals that form.

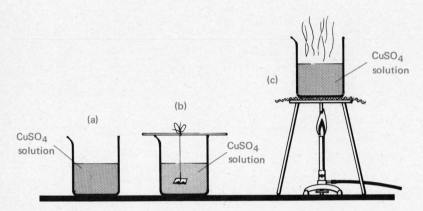

Fig. V–11–3   Observing the formation of crystals under different cooling conditions

3. After about 3 days carefully examine the crystals formed in each of the three beakers. Describe the shape, size and number of crystals in each beaker with the help of diagrams.
   In which beaker did the largest crystal(s) grow?
   Make a list of factors which determine the size and shape of crystals that grow in an evaporating saturated solution.
   In a cooling mass of liquid magma inside the Earth, where would you expect conditions to be similar to those in beaker A? beaker B? beaker C? (In a slowly cooling magma, heavier crystals formed at the top may drop sluggishly through the hot magma.)

4. Examine the following rocks with the help of a hand lens: granite, pink granite, syenite, gabbro, peridotite, feldspar porphyry, basalt, rhyolite, vesicular lava and obsidian. Divide these rocks into the following three categories.

   (a) *Plutonic* (intrusive) rocks – These rocks cooled slowly and at great depths. Such rocks contain fairly large crystals. (See Fig. V-11-4.)

   (b) Volcanic (extrusive) rocks – These rocks formed in cooling lava expelled to the surface from within the interior of the Earth. Such rocks contain either very tiny crystals or material which is apparently uncrystallized (volcanic glass). (See Fig. V–11–5.)

(c) *Intermediate* rocks – These rocks do not fall into either of the above categories. They contain material that may in part resemble lava and in part resemble well crystallized plutonic rocks. (See Fig. V-11-6.)

(From L. Don Leet and Sheldon Judson, *Physical Geology, Third Edition,* © 1965. By permission of Prentice-Hall, Inc., Englewood Cliffs, New Jersey, U.S.A.)

Fig. V–11–4   Plutonic rock (granite)

5. Examine the set of rocks that you have classified as plutonic rocks. **What are the characteristics, other than their crystal size, that are common to this group of rocks? Do you expect all plutonic rocks to have a similar composition? Give reasons for your answer.** Try to identify the various mineral grains in granite, pink granite and syenite. **Why is it possible for experts to distinguish the individual minerals which make up plutonic rocks?**

352

Fig. V–11–5   Volcanic rock (basalt)

Fig. V–11–6   Intermediate rock (porphyry)

6. Examine the set of rocks which you have classified as volcanic rocks. **Can you identify individual minerals in the volcanic rocks? Why is it difficult?**

7. Fig. V-11-7 shows how a large mass of magma may be injected into overlying rocks and sometimes allowed to reach the surface as lava. Suppose samples of igneous rock were taken from the locations numbered from 1 to 5. Use the headings in the following table and classify each of these samples as plutonic, volcanic or intermediate (as in Procedure 4). Also indicate the size of the crystals (large, small, both large and small or uncrystallized) in each sample. Give reasons for your decisions.

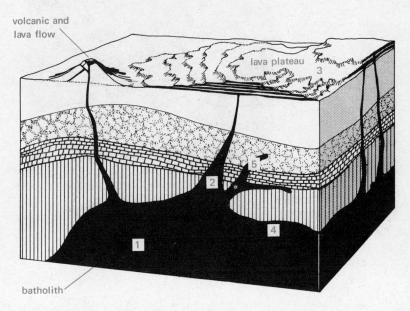

Fig. V–11–7   Magma injection into overlying rocks

SAMPLE NUMBER	CLASSIFICATION	SIZE OF CRYSTALS
1		
2		
3		
4		
5		

Why do rocks in a sill or a dike tend to be of a finer grain than those in a batholith (a large mass of intrusive igneous rock up to 15 miles deep within the lithosphere)?

8. A slowly crystallizing mass of magma deep below the Earth's surface that contains many fair sized crystals was squeezed out to the surface because of sudden crustal movements. This resulted in a type of rock containing fair-sized crystals in a very fine grained or glassy matrix. (See Fig. V-11-8.)

Which of the three groups of rocks in Procedure 4 best fits the above description?

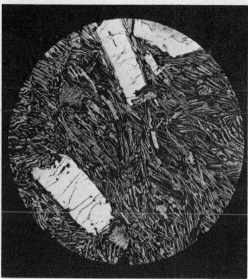

Fig. V–11–8   Magnified thin section of igneous rock containing larger crystals in a fine grained matrix

Questions:

*1. Why are igneous rocks regarded as the ancestors of all other types of rock?

*2. An estimated 5% of the lithosphere, by volume, consists of sedimentary rocks and 95%, of igneous and metamorphic rocks. On the other hand, sedimentary rocks cover about 75% of the land surface.

    (a) In which part of the crust (upper or lower) would you expect to find a larger percentage of igneous and metamorphic rocks? Justify your answer.

    (b) What important general conclusion(s) can you reach regarding the distribution of igneous, sedimentary and metamorphic rocks within the lithosphere? Justify your answer.

*3. Why are volcanic and plutonic rocks also referred to as "extrusive" and "intrusive" rocks respectively?

*4. Why would you not expect to find fossils in igneous rocks?

*5. In Exercise V-1, you learned that the lithosphere consists of rock layers of various compositions.

    (a) Name the two layers that make up the lithosphere.

    (b) What is the average mass density of the material in each of these layers? (See Fig. V-1-2.)

(c) Localized rock masses are believed to have been formed by the gradual cooling of a still-fluid magma. Which type of magma, the more dense or the less dense, would you expect to travel to the top before cooling to become surface igneous rocks?

(d) Explain why granite is the most common igneous rock on the Earth's surface.

*6. Are igneous rocks being formed now? Explain.

*7. With the help of Fig. V-11-7 and slides E17 and E18, explain the difference between a sill (E17) and a dike (E18) in terms of their relationship to overlying rocks.

†8. List some reasons why it is not possible to create in the laboratory the conditions under which igneous rocks are formed inside the Earth.

PART B   NAMING IGNEOUS ROCKS

Igneous rocks may be classified according to two characteristics:
1. the chemical composition of the parent magma,
2. the depth of cooling of the parent magma as determined by crystal size or rock texture.

To accurately name and classify igneous rocks requires the knowledge and experience of a petrologist. A microscopic examination of a thin section of a rock may also be necessary. However, with some practice, you may learn to sort rocks into the broad categories described below. This classification is based upon the proportion of quartz, potash feldspars (orthoclase), plagioclase feldspar (albite) and dark minerals present in the rock. Before you proceed with the following exercise, review Exercise V-4 and make sure that you can identify these important rock-forming minerals.

APPARATUS REQUIRED (per station)
Hand lens

MATERIALS REQUIRED (per station)
The rock samples that were used in Part A

Procedure:
1. Answer the following questions.
   (a) What element makes a mineral look darker? (Review your results of Experiment V-9.)
   (b) What is the color of potash feldspar? plagioclase feldspar?
   (c) Write three characteristics which you will use to distinguish between quartz and feldspar.
2. Fig. V-11-9 shows the percentage by mass of common metallic oxides contained by various types of igneous rocks. (The parent magmas of rocks A and E have been identified to assist you.)

ROCKS (A TO F) AND THEIR PARENT MAGMA CHEMICAL COMPOSITION %	A GRANITIC	B	C	D	E BASALTIC	F
1. SiO_2	70	48	60	73	49	45
2. Al_2O_3	14.5	18	16	13.5	14	6
3. $Fe_2O_3 + FeO$	3.5	9	6	2.5	13.5	13
4. MgO	1	7.5	2.5	.5	7	23
5. CaO	2	11	4.5	1	9	7.5
6. $Na_2O + K_2O$	8	3.5	8.5	8	3	2
Rest	1	3	2.5	1.5	4.5	3.5
Total Percentage by mass of $1 + 2 + 6$	92.5	69.5	84.5	94.5	66	53

Fig. V–11–9   The chemical composition of various types of igneous rock. (The data for this table was provided by Daly as reported in *Physical Geochemistry* by Smith.)

Study the composition of each rock type in Fig. V-11-9 and answer the following questions. (You need not know the actual names of the samples.)

(a) The composition of the parent magmas of all igneous rocks are one of two types – granitic or basaltic. Complete the following table in your notebook.

ROCK TYPE	PARENT MAGMA (GRANITIC OR BASALTIC)	REASON WHY YOU THINK SO
A	Granitic	
B	?	?
C	?	
D	?	?
E	Basaltic	
F	?	?

(b) Which of the two main magma types has the greater mass density? Justify your answer.

(c) Which of the six rocks listed above is darkest in color? Give a reason.

(d) Why is rock type F rarely seen on Earth? (Hint: What is unusual about its composition?)

3. In your notebook, complete the following table which lists some of the most common rock-forming minerals in the Earth's crust. (Refer to Exercise V-9 for their chemical compositions.)

MINERAL	APPROXIMATE CHEMICAL COMPOSITION

(a) Light colored
   quartz
   potash (or pink) feldspar
   plagioclase feldspar
   muscovite (white mica)

(b) Dark colored
   hornblend (a common variety
      of amphibole)
   augite (a common variety
      of pyroxene)
   olivine
   magnetite
   biotite (dark mica)

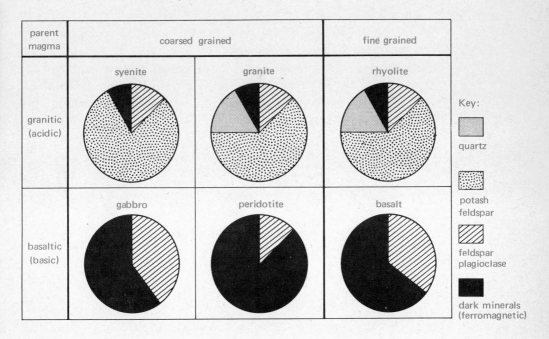

Fig. V–11–10 Relative abundance of various minerals in common igneous rocks

4. Fig. V-11-10 shows the relative abundance of quartz, potash feldspar, plagioclase feldspar and dark minerals present in several common igneous rocks. Use the information gained in Procedure 3 and carefully study Figures V-11-9 and V-11-10 to complete the following table in your notebook.

ROCK	POSSIBLE NAME FOR THE ROCK	INFERRED MINERAL COMPOSITION IN ORDER OF ABUNDANCE
A	Granite	potash feldspar, quartz, plagioclase feldspar, dark minerals
B	?	?
C	?	?
D	?	?
E	Basalt	
F	?	?

Questions:

*1. Extensive areas in many parts of the world (for example, southern India, western U.S.A. and central B.C.) are covered by basaltic lava flows. There are no similar and extensive granitic lava flows. Can you explain this phenomenon? (Hint: What type of liquid spreads more easily?)

*2. (a) Why is the granitic layer in the Earth's crust also called *Sial* [silica (SiO_2)-alumina (Al_2O_3)]?

   (b) Why is the lower basaltic layer called *Sima* [silica (SiO_2)-magnesia (M_gO)]? (Hint: Refer back to Procedure 3 and Fig. V-11-9 to examine the chemical composition of common rock-forming minerals.)

*3. Given below are proportions by mass of the seven most abundant elements within the first ten miles of the Earth's crust.

Oxygen	46.7%	Calcium	3.7%
Silicon	27.7%	Sodium	2.8%
Aluminum	8.1%	Potassium	2.6%
Iron	5.1%		

   (a) Suggest why silicon and oxygen make up nearly ¾ of the Earth's crust by mass. (Hint: Compare mass densities of various elements.)

   (b) What changes would you expect in the above figures if the average composition of the entire Earth were considered instead?

   (c) What is the effect of a larger concentration of iron on the density of a rock?

   †(d) How does the presence of iron in a rock affect its rate of weathering?

*4. Why are some countries rich in certain types of minerals while others are not?

†5. Canada is a country with enormous mineral wealth. Using reference material from the library, write an essay on the mineral resources in your province.

V–12 SEDIMENTARY ROCKS

Sedimentary rocks form more than three-quarters of the exposed rocks on the surface of the Earth. As their name indicates, these rocks have been derived from sediments like those you may commonly see around you, in deserts, river beds, beaches and on ocean floors.

Sediments are formed when various natural processes act upon rocks, such as alternate freezing and heating or weathering by solution. The parent rock cracks, then breaks into smaller sizes. In due course it is reduced in size from large boulders to pebbles and finally to fine particles of clay. The resulting sediments are carried by running water, ice, and/or wind, aided by gravity. They are deposited in lakes and ocean beds in the form of sedimentary layers of various thicknesses. When these sediments become compressed and compacted, they are cemented together and ultimately they change to rock.

Along with the sediments, plant and animal remains may be deposited. Fossils and deposits of coal and petroleum, common in sedimentary rocks, are unmistakable evidence of ancient forms of life that existed during the period of deposition of these sediments. The processes involved in the formation of sedimentary rocks are very slow but they have continued without interruption for billions of years. (See Fig. V-11-2.)

APPARATUS REQUIRED (per station)
> *Hand lens*
> *medicine dropper*
> *paper towelling*
> *hammer*
> *support stand base*

MATERIALS REQUIRED (per station)
> *rock samples of conglomerate, breccia, sandstone, shale, limestone, limestone (crystalline), rhyolite, basalt, granite, peridotite, gabbro*
> *3 M HCl in dropper bottle*

Procedure:
1. Examine samples of conglomerate, breccia (BRE-chee-a), sandstone, shale and both types of limestone with the help of a hand lens. On the basis of whether or not the rocks contain noticeable grains, separate the rocks into two groups as follows:

SEDIMENTARY ROCKS

CLASTIC ROCKS	NON-CLASTIC ROCKS
Rocks consisting of noticeable grains and fragments cemented together	Rocks formed when dissolved material was deposited out of water in solid form by chemical or organic means

2. Test all of these rocks for the presence of the carbonate radical with a drop of dilute HCl. Do they effervesce? Wash the rocks and use a paper towel to dry them after completing the test.
Which of the rocks contains the carbonate radical?

3. Try to identify individual grains in shale (sedimentary) and in rhyolite and basalt (volcanic).
Why is it almost impossible to identify mineral grains in these rocks?
List ways in which these three rocks resemble each other and ways in which they differ from each other.
Which of your conclusions will help you to distinguish between a sedimentary rock and a volcanic rock?

4. Examine the sedimentary rocks for the presence of fossils.
Which group of rocks (igneous, sedimentary, or metamorphic) is most likely to have fossils? Why?

†5. List at least five ways in which granite, gabbro and peridotite (igneous) differ from or are similar to sandstone, conglomerate and breccia (sedimentary).

6. Compare the shapes of individual grains in sandstone and conglomerate. Use a diagram.
Does the appearance of these rocks give any clue about how they originated?

7. (Demonstration) Use a hammer to crush a small piece of sandstone and another of granite on a support stand base.
Which of the rocks is easier to crush?
Examine the resulting single grains. Describe and sketch the shapes and relative sizes of the individual grains that you obtained.
Can you recognize any of the minerals that make up the rocks?

†8. Examine the samples of the two types of limestone (clastic and nonclastic). Suggest how they may have formed. Give reasons for your answers.

Questions:

*1. Answer the following questions after studying Fig. V-12-1 and the table that follows.

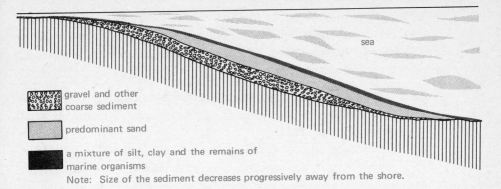

gravel and other
coarse sediment

predominant sand

a mixture of silt, clay and the remains of
marine organisms

Note: Size of the sediment decreases progressively away from the shore.

*Adapted from "Salt and Things" in the *Journal of Geological Education*, Volume XV, No. 6, December 1967.

Fig. V–12–1   Size of the sediment decreases progressively with the distance from the shore. Deep ocean sediments consist mainly of clay, mud and ooze*

SEDIMENT SIZE SCALE

NAME	SEDIMENT SIZE	ROCK FORMED BY COMPACTION	SPECIAL CHARACTERISTICS
boulder cobble pebble gravel	over 2 mm	conglomerate	If grains are angular, it is called breccia. (See Fig. V-12-2.)
sand	2 mm – $\frac{1}{16}$ mm	sandstone	grains visible to naked eye
silt	$\frac{1}{16}$ mm – $\frac{1}{256}$ mm	siltstone	grains visible with a hand lens only
clay	$\frac{1}{256}$ mm or less	shale	grains not visible, even with hand lens

(From L. Don Leet and Sheldon Judson, *Physical Geology, Third Edition,* © 1965. By permission of Prentice-Hall, Inc., Englewood Cliffs, New Jersey, U.S.A.)

Fig. V–12–2   Limestone

NOTE: *Limestone may be either clastic or non-clastic. It may form either by precipitation of calcium carbonate dissolved in ocean water or by the compaction of the shells of organisms that extract calcium carbonate from sea water.*

(a) If sandstone is formed from clear grains of quartz, why do we find sandstones with various colors? (Hint: What else is sandstone composed of?)

(b) Fossils are most common in limestone and shale. Why? (Hint: Remains of organisms are best preserved when as little oxygen as possible circulates through the sediment.)

(c) Examine the photograph in Fig. V-12-2 and explain how this limestone may have been formed.

(d) Describe the difference between sedimentary rocks that are formed from deposits close to shore and those formed from deposits farther from shore.

conglomerate   breccia

Fig. V–12–3   Conglomerate and breccia

*2. Examine Fig. V-12-3 and indicate the difference between the geological environments in which a breccia and a conglomerate are formed. (Hint: What is the effect of transport by running water upon the shape of the transported sediments?)

*3. A large sedimentary rock unit may show a gradation in the size of its sediments as shown in Fig. V-12-4.

(a) What geological conditions may have caused the sediment to be deposited in this way?

(b) Is the rock clastic or non-clastic?

(c) Suggest a suitable name for this type of rock.

†4. Interbanded layers of shale and sandstone are very common in nature. Suggest the circumstances in which such interbanded layers may have been deposited.

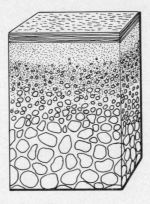

Fig. V–12–4 The size of sediment may vary with depth in a large sedimentary rock unit

†5. (a) Two layers of shale and sandstone (A and C in Fig. V-12-5) were deposited in approximately the same geological period. If the rate of supply of each kind of sediment was constant during deposition, why is the thickness of the sandstone greater than that of the shale?

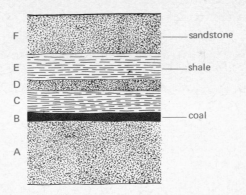

Fig. V–12–5 Interbanded shale and sandstone with a band of coal

(b) Arrange the sedimentary layers A to F according to their ages, listing the oldest first. Explain your answer.

*6. An "aquifer" is a rock unit that allows the free circulation of underground water through it. Which makes the better aquifer, shale or sandstone? Give reasons for your answer.

*7. Explain why geologists carefully examine sediments and soluble impurities carried in a stream during their search for ore bodies.

V–13   METAMORPHIC ROCKS

You have already learned that both pressure and temperature increase with depth inside the Earth's crust. Crustal movements, particularly those that result from large scale slippage along deep faults and folds within the lithosphere, may shift the surface rocks of today to deeper zones within the crust. The original characteristics of the rocks are then changed by the action of heat, pressure and/or chemically active solutions within and from beneath the lithosphere. While examining metamorphic rocks, you should consider the following questions.

1. What was the nature and composition of the original rock from which this metamorphic rock was formed?
2. To what *new* geological condition was the rock subjected? (Was it pressure, temperature, chemical solutions or a combination of these?)
3. What changes in the structure and composition of the original rock have been produced?

The processes of metamorphism of rocks may be divided into two main types:

1. *Thermal metamorphism.* This is primarily produced by the effect of heat on rock and the changes produced in the parent rock are often local.
2. *Regional metamorphism.* This is produced by an increase in pressure and temperature over a broad area. This process is normally accompanied by folding movements in the rock masses.

A detailed reconstruction of the geological history of metamorphic rocks requires a considerable knowledge of chemistry and mineralogy as well as a microscopic examination of the rocks.

In this exercise you will investigate some of the physical characteristics of a number of common metamorphic rocks.

APPARATUS REQUIRED (per station)
   Hand lens

MATERIALS REQUIRED (per station)
   Samples of quartzite, slate, talc schist, mica schist, garnet gneiss, garnet schist*, phyllite*, marble*, amphibolite, shale, limestone, sandstone
   (per class)
   Slides D-4, D-5, and D-10 from the set of Earth Science slides provided by the B.C. Teachers' Federation, Lesson Aid #M-I

NOTE: *With the exception of the rocks starred*, the rocks listed are available in an inexpensive set of rock chips provided by the Geological Survey of Canada.*

Procedure:

1. Use the hand lens to carefully examine the rocks listed above.
   Can you identify various minerals in granite, slate, talc schist and mica schist?
2. Divide the rocks into the following two categories:
   (a) *Foliated* – those which look directional or crusted with distinct banding and tend to cleave in parallel planes (e.g. talc schist). Examine slide D-10 to see what a foliated rock looks like.
   (b) *Non-foliated* – those which are rather homogeneous and dense with little or no indication of banding (or foliation).
3. Look at slides D-4 and D-5 of the set of geological slides and answer the following questions.
   (a) **What is the rock type shown in each case (igneous, sedimentary or metamorphic)? Give reasons for your answers.**
   (b) **What was the parent rock (igneous or sedimentary)? Explain your answer.**
   (c) **Indicate the agent(s) of metamorphism (e.g. heat, pressure and/or chemical action)? Explain your answer for each slide.**
   (d) **What is the degree of metamorphism (high, medium or low)? Explain your answer for each slide.**
   (e) **Briefly describe the geological environments to which the parent rock may have been subjected. Give a reason for your answer.**

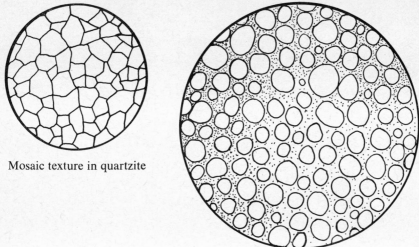

Mosaic texture in quartzite

Fig. V–13–1

Sandstone under microscope

Questions:

*1. Figure V-13-1 shows how thin sections of sandstone and quartzite might look through a microscope.
   (a) Briefly explain what might have happened to sedimentary sandstone during metamorphism.

(b) What evidence is there that the parent rock did not melt completely during metamorphism?

†(c) Compare the change of sandstone to quartzite with the change of snow flakes into a snowball when you press them with your palms.

(d) Which is more dense, sandstone or quartzite? Explain your answer.

(e) Explain why you would expect the chemical composition of sandstone and quartzite to be similar.

*2. Marble is metamorphosed limestone.

(a) Explain why marble is found in a wide variety of colors.

(b) Why is marble preferable to limestone as a building stone?

†(c) Why does marble contain larger crystals of calcite packed against each other?

*3. From your observations of various metamorphic rocks, complete the following table.

PARENT ROCK	METAMORPHOSED ROCK	PHYSICAL CHARACTERISTICS (color, mineral composition, texture, foliation)
limestone	marble	
sandstone	quartzite	
basalt	chlorite schist (low degree of metamorphism) amphibolite or amphibolite schist (high degree of metamorphism)	
granite	granite gneiss	
shale	gneiss slate	

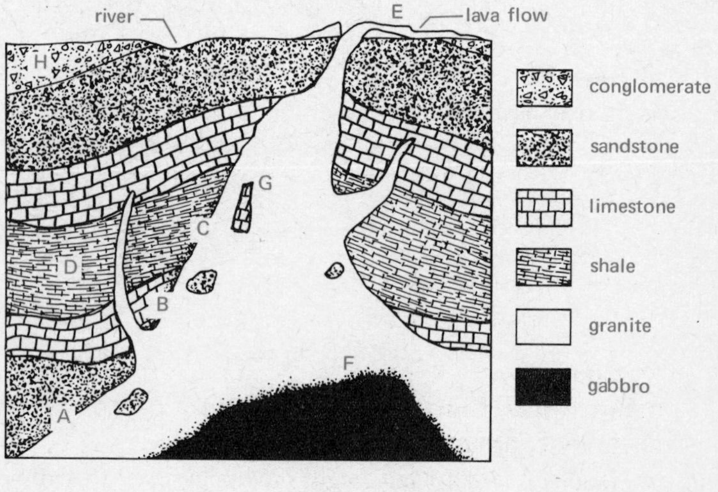

Fig. V–13–2   Molten magma intruding into layers of sedimentary rock

†4. Study Fig. V-13-2 which shows the results of the intrusion of molten magma into layers of sedimentary rock. The hot magma melts or bakes the rocks but does not change them to a free flowing fluid.

 (a) In which regions would heat be a major factor in producing metamorphism?

 (b) Prepare a table like the one below in your notebook and complete it with the help of the diagram and the table completed in Question 3. (The two types of metamorphism are described in the introduction to this exercise.)

LOCATION	PARENT ROCK	NAME OF METAMORPHIC ROCK PRODUCED	TYPE OF METAMORPHISM
A	Sandstone	Quartzite	Thermal
B			
C			
D			
E (Think!)			
F			
G	Also called Xenolith		
H (Think!)			

 (e) Which of the two intrusions (gabbro or granite) is younger? Explain your answer.

M. C. Schmid & J. A. Petrak

RADIOACTIVITY

INTRODUCTION

When Henri Bequerel discovered radioactivity in 1896, he found an energy source far greater than man had ever imagined. It is so great that the disintegration of one single radioactive atom can easily be detected.

The electrical effects and the chemical effects which you have observed in Units II and III are the results of changes in the electron structure of atoms. The nucleus is never affected during these changes. On the other hand, the source of the energy of radioactivity lies in the nucleus of the atom. The nuclear forces that bind protons and neutrons together in the nucleus are enormous, compared to the electrical and magnetic forces that bind the rest of the atom together. Therefore, any change in the condition of the nucleus of an atom involves great amounts of energy.

The nuclei of most of the Earth's atoms have remained unchanged throughout the billions of years of their existence and will probably remain in their present condition for billions of years to come. However, a small number of naturally occurring atoms, such as uranium, thorium, radium and polonium, have nuclei which are not stable. In order to become stable, these nuclei may shoot out particles at great speeds. When stability has been achieved by this means, the nucleus may have changed to become the nucleus of an atom of a different element. In addition to the naturally occurring unstable radioactive atoms, artificially produced unstable radioactive atoms of all the elements have been produced by scientists (nuclear physicists) using very high energy equipment.

The stability of a nucleus is governed by the relative numbers of neutrons and protons it possesses. For example, a nucleus that has 8 protons and 8 neutrons (oxygen) is stable. However, one that has 8 protons and 9 neutrons (also oxygen) is very unstable. We call atoms of the same element whose nuclei have different numbers of neutrons (but, of course, the same number of protons), *isotopes* of that element. For example, three isotopes of hydrogen exist. Although each has one proton, they are distinct from each other because one of them has no neutrons, the second has one neutron and the third has two neutrons. The third isotope is radioactive.

VI–1   OBSERVING RADIOACTIVITY (Demonstration)

The following experiment will demonstrate a method by which the presence of radioactivity can be detected.

APPARATUS REQUIRED (per class)
Cloud chamber (dry ice type) with a safe radioactive source
a block of dry ice about 1 in thick and the diameter of the cloud chamber
methyl alcohol
black dye (if the construction of the cloud chamber requires it)
a very strong source of directed light (e.g. spotlight)
a wool square

NOTE: *There are many commercial versions of the original cloud chamber invented by C. T. R. Wilson in 1911. All are based on the fact that when air that is saturated with methyl alcohol (or a similar substance) is cooled without being disturbed, it will become supersaturated. When a rapidly moving particle travels through the cool supersaturated air, it leaves a "vapor trail" of condensed alcohol behind it, showing the path that the particle has taken. The same thing often happens on a larger scale when a jet airplane flies through air supersaturated with water vapor: it leaves a trail of condensed water vapor.*

Procedure:

1. Rest the dry ice on suitable insulation such as a thick newspaper. Then place the metal base of a cloud chamber directly onto the dry ice.
2. Cloud chambers which require dry ice to cool the methyl alcohol usually have their sides partly covered with dark absorbent material to serve as a wick from which methyl alcohol can evaporate. Thoroughly moisten this material with methyl alcohol. Then carefully clean the top (observation window) of the cloud chamber, and place the upper part of the chamber onto the cold metal base. (Your apparatus may allow you to moisten the wick material by simply placing a thin layer of alcohol on the metal base.) The base should provide a black background.
3. Direct a horizontal beam of light from a powerful source so that it shines across the chamber as shown in Fig. VI-1-1.
4. Insert a radioactive source into the chamber as shown in Fig. VI-1-1. (Commercial suppliers usually mount these in the eye of a needle.)

The temperature inside the chamber ranges from –78°C at the base to about 20°C (room temperature) at the top. The region where the supersaturated condition of the air occurs is just above the base; it is here that the radioactive source should be located.

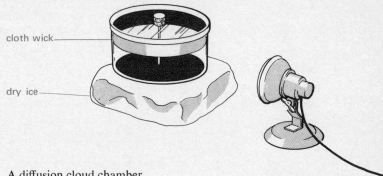

cloth wick

dry ice

Fig. VI–1–1   A diffusion cloud chamber

5. Look for evidence that fast particles are moving away from the source. If you are *too* successful and obtain too many tracks, you will have to remove old tracks or they will make it difficult to see new ones. You can remove them by gently rubbing the top window with wool to produce an electrical charge on it. Your equipment may be provided with a 45 volt battery to achieve the same result.

   Questions:
*1. What additional equipment would you require to tell whether or not the particles emitted by the radioactive source were electrically charged? How could you tell the sign of their charge?
*2. Examine some cloud chamber photographs. (They can be found in almost all physics text books.) What evidence is there
   (a) that the emitted particles are influenced by electrical and magnetic fields?
   (b) that collisions with other nuclei sometimes occur?

VI–2   DETECTING RADIOACTIVITY WITH A GEIGER COUNTER

When a particle is "shot off" from the nucleus of a radioactive atom, it is traveling at a great speed. As a result, when it collides with air molecules it removes electrons from them and converts them to electricically charged particles called *ions*. Since some air molecules may capture the electrons knocked from other air molecules, both positive and negative ions may be produced. The particle emitted from the nucleus thus creates ions along its path until its speed becomes too low to cause ionization. In Exercise VI-1 it was these ions which served as centers of condensation, thus allowing the path of the particle to be seen.

The Geiger counter is another device that detects the formation of these ions. Normally, a gas is an excellent insulator. However, when emissions from a radioactive source have passed through the gas inside a Geiger tube, the resulting free electrons and ions cause an electric current when a voltage is applied across the tube. Since the ions rapidly become neutral again, the current exists for only a very short time. This current can be used to create sound, to flash a light or to operate a counter.

APPARATUS REQUIRED (per class)
     Geiger counter
     safe radioactive source (e.g. wristwatch with luminous dial)
     clamp to hold Geiger tube
     various materials (including lead) for shielding tests

Procedure:

1. Read the operating instructions for your Geiger counter. Then turn it on and gradually increase the Geiger tube voltage just until distinct clicks occur without a radioactive source being present. (A click is caused by a short discharge of current through the Geiger tube and therefore represents the passage of a particle through the tube.)

NOTE: *Our environment includes a small amount of radioactive material. Some of the radioactive isotopes present are the result of the explosion of atomic bombs, but most are natural. The concentration of these isotopes varies from place to place. In addition, fast moving particles (cosmic rays) from outer space strike the Earth's atmosphere and cause showers of secondary particles that have the same effects on Geiger counters as those from radioactive isotopes.*

2. Count the number of clicks that occur in ten seconds. Repeat this count several times. Remember that each click signifies the decay of a *single* atom.
   Do these clicks occur with a constant frequency? Therefore, is it possible to predict when a radioactive nucleus will "decay"?

NOTE: *There is no way of telling when a particular nucleus will decay. The decay of each radioactive nucleus is therefore known as a random event. However, the rate of decay of a large number of nuclei is absolutely predictable. This fact is used to determine the age of a sample of material containing radioactive nuclei.*

3. Locate a weak radioactive source at a sufficient distance from the Geiger tube so that separate clicks occur, on the average, about one per second. (See Fig. VI-2-1.) Turn the "window" of the Geiger tube toward the source. Count the number of clicks that occur in ten seconds. Repeat this counting about twenty times. Calculate the average

number of clicks per ten-second interval. Then repeat the counting another twenty times and again calculate the average number of clicks per ten-second interval. Compare these two averages.

Is the number of clicks in a ten-second interval predictable? Is the average number of clicks in a ten-second interval predictable?

Fig. VI–2–1   Observing the radioactivity of a luminous watch dial

4. Move the radioactive source closer to the Geiger tube and observe the effect.

Does moving the source closer actually increase the rate of nuclear decay? Suggest an explanation for the effect you observed in Procedure 4. (Hint: Why is the illumination from a light bulb greater when you are closer to the bulb?)

5. Try shielding the Geiger tube from the radioactive source by using various materials of various thicknesses. Avoid having too high a count before you insert the shielding. Remember that background radiation comes from *all* directions so that your shielding will probably have little effect on this radiation (unless the shielding completely encloses the tube).

NOTE: *It has been discovered that natural radioactivity produces three distinct effects. There are two kinds of particles which can be shot from such nuclei. One consists of two protons and two neutrons bound together as they would be to form a helium nucleus. These fairly massive, positively charged particles are called* alpha particles, *commonly represented by either $\propto$ or $_2He^4$. The latter symbol shows that the particle has 2 protons and a total of 4 nuclear particles (2 protons and 2 neutrons).*

The second particle that may be emitted from a nucleus is an electron. When it is emitted from a nucleus, the electron is called a beta particle, *represented by β or $_{-1}e^\circ$. The latter symbol indicates a charge of -1 unit and an effective mass of zero (since its mass is only $\frac{1}{1840}$ of the mass of a proton or a neutron).*

The third effect often accompanies the first two. It is radiation, not a particle. Therefore, it has no charge or mass. Just as x-rays are more powerful and pentrating than visible light, the gamma rays *produced in nuclear reactions are more powerful and penetrating than x-rays. Like alpha and beta particles, gamma rays can also cause molecules to ionize. The symbol for a gamma ray is γ.*

When molecules in our bodies are ionized, damage to cell tissues can result. Fortunately, our bodies can repair such damage if it is not excessive. Exposure to radioctivity is especially harmful when it affects the genes in reproductive cells.

Alpha and beta particles can be easily stopped by normal clothing. Most of the danger of radioactivity is from gamma radiation. Although $\propto$, β and γ radiation are the general result of natural radioactivity, man-made radioactive isotopes may emit many other types of particles, including neutrons ($_0n^1$) and protons ($_1H^1$). Many current research projects rely on the special properties of such isotopes.

Questions:

*1. What, in general, is the source of all radioactivity?

*2. What types of emission can occur from radioactive nuclei?

*3. Are all levels of radioactivity great threats to your health? Explain.

*4. How can scientists protect themselves from excessive gamma radiation while they are working with radioactive materials?

†5. Try to predict which would travel further in air, alpha particles or beta particles. Check your prediction in a reference book.

†6. Suggest why it would be important to find a sample of radium stolen from a hospital.

†7. Various isotopes are used extensively in research. Suggest the purpose of

   (a) feeding a radioactive iodine compound to a patient undergoing medical research,

   (b) providing carbon dioxide that contains radioactive carbon to plans during research on the activities within a leaf.

References and Suggestions for Further Investigation:

1. When particles of certain solid materials are struck by fast moving alpha or beta particles, light is produced. For example, a TV screen lights when it is struck by electrons. A luminous watch dial makes use of the same effect. The manufacturer mixes a radioactive material with a material that will fluoresce when it is struck by fast particles. The fluorescence is caused by the disturbance of the positions of the electrons in the atoms of the fluorescent material.
   Try this experiment at home. Stay in a completely dark room for at least ten minutes. When your eyes have become accustomed to the dark, hold the dial of a luminous watch or clock about 3 cm from your eye. If you look carefully, you can see tiny bright flashes occurring in the same irregular manner as the electric discharges in the Geiger counter.

2. The intensity of cosmic radiation reaching a point on the Earth is related to its geomagnetic latitude. The radiation is greatest near the

magnetic poles. One of its effects is the aurora borealis. What is another name for the aurora borealis? Why does it occur? Draw a diagram to help explain this phenomenon.

3. Pages 376-384 of *Matter and Energy, the Foundations of Modern Physics* by J. H. McLachlan, K. G. McNeill and J. M. Bell (Toronto: Clarke, Irwin & Co. Ltd., 1963) discuss and illustrate several ways in which nuclear energy can be detected and used. Some radiation hazards are also mentioned.

4. W. L. Ramsay and R. A. Burckley discuss auroras on pages 25-26 and pages 30-31 of their book, *Modern Earth Science* (Holt, Rinehart and Winston Inc., New York, 1965).

5. Pages 182-199 of *Physical Science for Progress* by M. O. Pella and A. G. Wood (Englewood Cliffs, N.J.: Prentice-Hall, Inc., 1964) discuss such aspects of radioactivity as its production, detection, uses and dangers.

VI–3   RADIOACTIVITY AND TIME

All radioactivity can be explained as the changing of unstable nuclear arrangements into more stable nuclear arrangements. Interestingly, this process is completely unaffected by heating, cooling, pressurizing, chemical treatment and so on, because these conditions do not affect the tightly bound nucleus.

Usually the atoms of a radioactive material achieve greater stability by always emitting the *same* kinds of particles and gamma radiation. In a few cases involving several stages of decay, alternative methods exist; on careful examination, however, these methods are found to produce the same end result.

Since the resulting stable nuclei no longer emit particles or radiation, the number of nuclei available for decay decreases as time passes. Thus, as time progresses, the radioactivity observed decreases. This reduction in the activity is most noticeable in radioactive substances that are least stable.

The history of a nucleus plays no part in deciding whether or not that nucleus will decay at a certain time. The decay pattern of a large number of radioactive nuclei, therefore, can probably be best understood by using a large number of dice. The element of chance in the decay of a nucleus is considered in the following model. First shake a large number of dice (representing radioactive nuclei) in a box and then empty them onto a table. Every die which has six spots facing up will be considered to represent a nucleus that has decayed to form a stable non-radioactive nucleus. It must, therefore, be removed from play, since it cannot decay further.

APPARATUS REQUIRED (per class)

A large number of dice or marked sugar cubes (at least 60) and a container to shake them in

Procedure:

1. Count and record the total number of dice being used.
2. Shake the dice well and empty them onto the table. Remove the number of dice showing 6 dots on the top surface, count them and record the number.
3. Place all the dice which are "still in play" back into the container and repeat Procedure 2.
   Will these dice "remember" that they have been shaken before? Will the number which appears on the upper surface of each die the second time be influenced by the previous throw?
4. Repeat the procedure until no more than two dice remain in play.
5. Plot a graph showing the number of "nuclei" remaining after a "throw" (y-axis) against the number of the throw (x-axis – one, two, three, etc.). Include the number of "nuclei" you started with (at 0 throws).

Questions:

*1. Describe the decrease in the observed "radioactivity" of your dice as time passed.
*2. Refer to the graph drawn in Procedure 5 to answer these questions.
   (a) After how many throws of the dice did only half of the "radioactive nuclei" remain?
   (b) After how many *more* throws did only ¼ of the dice remain? That is, how many throws did it take to go from half the original number of dice to ¼ of the original dice?
   (c) How do your answers to (a) and (b) compare?

NOTE: *It has been found that when there is a large number of radioactive nuclei in a sample the time taken for one-half of the nuclei in the sample to decay is constant, regardless of the history and the mass of the sample. This time is called the* half-life *of the radioactive element. It is a convenient characteristic to use when comparing radioactive samples.*

For example, the half-life of the uranium isotope $_{92}U^{238}$ that contains 238 nuclear particles (92 protons + 146 neutrons) is 4.5 billion years. The half-life of $_6C^{14}$, carbon 14 (6 protons and 8 neutrons) is 5760 years. The half life of $_2He^5$, helium 5, is 2×10^{-21} seconds!

*3. Suggest how scientists can use the value for the known half-life of an element such as uranium 238 to calculate the age of rocks containing samples of uranium 238. (Hint: They also know the isotope of the element that results after each kind of decay.)

References and Suggestions for Further Investigation:
1. It is hoped that you will find out more about nuclear reactions. Do you know, for example,
    (a) that in every nuclear decay, the source of the enormous energy which is released is the result of the complete disappearance of a small quantity of mass? What does Einstein's equation $E = mc^2$ have to do with this effect?
    (b) that when two small nuclei, such as hydrogen nuclei, collide with each other with sufficient force, they may remain attached and, as a result, lose a little mass which is converted to a relatively large quantity of energy? Read about the principle of the hydrogen bomb and about the source of the Sun's energy.
    (c) that under certain conditions some large nuclei can be bombarded by neutrons and made to split into two? Read about the use of uranium and plutonium to produce atomic power.

BIBLIOGRAPHY

GENERAL

Morholt, Brandwein and Joseph, *A Sourcebook for the Biological Sciences*. New York: Harcourt, Brace & World, Inc., 1966.

THE CELL

Butler, J. A. V., *Inside the Living Cell*. New York: Basic Books, Inc., 1959.

Hurry, S. W., *The Microstructure of Cells*. Boston, Mass.: Houghton Mifflin Co., 1964.

Jensen, W. and R. Park, *Cell Ultrastructure*. Belmont, Calif.: Wadsworth Publishing Company, Inc., 1967.

MacKean, D. C., *Introduction to Genetics*. London: John Murray & Co., 1968.

Pfeiffer, John, *The Cell*. Englewood Cliffs, N.J.: Prentice-Hall, Inc., 1964.

Swanson, Carl P., *The Cell*. Englewood Cliffs, N.J.: Prentice-Hall, Inc., 1964.

IDENTIFICATION OF MICRO-ORGANISMS

Haas, Hans, *Pond Life*. London: Young Specialist Series, Burke Publishing Co., 1969.

Jahn, T. L., *How to Know the Protozoa*. Dubuque, Iowa: William C. Brown Company, 1949.

Needham, J. G. and P. R., *A Guide to the Study of Fresh-Water Biology*. San Francisco, Calif.: Holden-Day Inc., 1966.

Palmer, C. M., *Algae in Water Supplies*. Public Health Service Publication No. 657. Cincinnati: U.S. Department of Health, Education and Welfare, 1959.

REGENERATION

Buchsbaum, R., *Animals Without Backbones*. Baltimore, Md.: Penguin Books, Inc., 1964.

FLOWER IDENTIFICATION

Cuthbert, M. J., *How to Know the Fall Flowers*. Dubuque, Iowa: William C. Brown Company, 1948.

Cuthbert, M. J., *How to Know the Spring Flowers*. Dubuque, Iowa: William C. Brown Company, 1949.

Lyons, C. P., *Trees, Shrubs and Flowers to Know in British Columbia*. Vancouver: J. M. Dent and Sons, 1952.

FLOWER STRUCTURE

Hill, Overholts, Popp and Grove, *Botany*. Toronto: McGraw-Hill Book Company, 1967.

GENERAL GENETICS

Biological Science: Patterns and Processes, Science Council. Toronto: Holt, Rinehart and Winston, Inc., 1966.

Bonner, D. and S. E. Mills, *Heredity*. Englewood Cliffs, N.J.: Prentice-Hall, Inc., 1964.

George, Wilma, *Elementary Genetics*. Second Edition. New York: Macmillan Company, 1965.

Mather, K., *Genetics for Schools*. London: John Murray Co., 1959.

McElroy, W. and C. Swanson, *Modern Cell Biology*. Englewood Cliffs, N.J.: Prentice-Hall, Inc., 1968.

DROSOPHILA GENETICS

Demerec and Kaufmann, *Drosophila Guide*. Washington, D.C.: The Carnegie Institute of Washington, 1961.

Glass, Bentley, *Genetic Continuity – a Laboratory Block*. Toronto: D. C. Heath & Company, 1965.

Stickberger, M. W., *Experiments in Genetics with Drosophila*. New York: John Wiley & Sons, Inc., 1962.

CHROMOSOME STRUCTURE

(Although this topic is not covered in this course many students may find this recent development interesting.)

Asimov, Isaac, *The Genetic Code*. New York: New American Library, Inc., 1963.

Beadle, G. and M. Beadle, *The Language of Life*. Garden City, N.Y.: Doubleday & Company, Inc., 1966.

Hutchins, C. M., *Life's Key – D.N.A.* New York: Coward-McCann, Inc., 1961.

HUMAN HEREDITY

Penrose, L. S., *Outline of Human Genetics*. New York: James H. Heinemann, Inc., Publishers, 1963.

Scheinfeld, A., *The Human Heredity Handbook*. Philadelphia: J. B. Lippincott Company, 1956.

Srb, M. A., Owen and Edgar, *General Genetics*. Second Edition. San Francisco, Calif.: W. H. Freeman & Company, 1965.

Stern, Curt, *Principles of Human Genetics*. Second Edition. San Francisco, Calif.: W. H. Freeman & Company, 1960.

Electricity and Magnetism

Eubank, H. L., J. M. Ramsay, and L. A. Rickard, *Basic Physics for Secondary Schools*. Toronto, Ont.: Macmillan Co. of Canada Ltd., 1957.

Hogg, J. C., J. B. Cross, and K. E. Vordenberg, *Physical Science, A Basic Course*. Toronto, Ont.: Van Nostrand Co. Inc., 1959.

Pella, M. O., and A. G. Wood, *Physical Science for Progress*. Englewood Cliffs, N.J.: Prentice-Hall, Inc., 1964.

Verwiebe, F. L., G. E. Van Hooft, and R. R. Suchy, *Physics, A Basic Science*. Toronto, Ont.: Van Nostrand Co. Inc., 1962.

Chemistry

Andrew, H. G., *Michael Faraday*. The Nuffield Foundation. Harmondsworth, Middlesex, England: Longmans/Penguin Books, 1966.

Brandwein et al., *Matter: Its Forms and Changes*. New York: Harcourt, Brace & World, Inc., 1968.

Drummond, A. H. Jr., *Atoms, Crystals and Molecules*. Middletown, Conn.: American Education Publications, Inc., 1965.

Dull, C. E. et al., *Modern Chemistry*. Toronto, Ont.: Clarke, Irwin and Co. Ltd., 1953.

Ford, L. A., *Chemical Magic*. Greenwich, Conn.: Fawcett Publications, Inc., 1964.

Gardner, Marjorie H., *Chemistry in the Space Age*. New York: Holt, Rinehart and Winston, Inc., 1965.

Heys, H. L., *Chemistry Experiments at Home for Boys and Girls*. London: George G. Harrop and Co. Ltd., 1959.

Jaffe, Bernard, *Crucibles – The Story of Chemistry*. Greenwich, Conn.: Fawcett Publications, Inc., 1961.

Johnstone, A. H. and T. I. Morrison, *Chemistry Takes Shape*, Book 3. London: Heinemann Educational Books Ltd., 1967.

Joseph et al., *A Sourcebook of the Physical Sciences*. New York: Harcourt, Brace & World, Inc., 1961.

Klopfer, Leo E., *Frogs and Batteries*. Chicago, Ill.: Science Research Associates, 1964.

Kranskopf, K. B. and A. Beiser, *The Physical Universe*. Toronto, Ont.: McGraw-Hill Book Company, 1967.

Lange, N. A., *Handbook of Chemistry,* Tenth Edition. New York: McGraw-Hill Book Co., 1967.

Morgan, Alfred, *Adventures in Electrochemistry*. New York: Charles Scribner's Sons, 1959.

Perry, R. W. et al., *Chemistry – Experimental Foundations*. Englewood Cliffs, N.J.: Prentice-Hall, Inc., 1970.

Rogers, M. J. W., ed., *Chemistry: The Sample Scheme Stages I and II: The Basic Course,* The Nuffield Foundation. Harmondsworth, Middlesex, England: Longmans/Penguin Books, 1966.

Sienko, M. J., and R. A. Plane, *Chemistry*. New York: McGraw-Hill Book Company, 1961.

Stokes, B. J., ed., *Chemistry – Collected Experiments,* The Nuffield Foundation. Harmondsworth, Middlesex, England: Longmans/Penguin Books, 1967.

Van Praag, G., *The Discovery of the Electric Current,* The Nuffield Foundation. Harmondsworth, Middlesex, England: Longmans/Penguin Books, 1966.

Weast, Robert C., ed., *Handbook of Chemistry and Physics*. Cleveland, Ohio: The Chemical Rubber Company, 1969.

Sound

Bulman, A. D., *Model Making for Young Physicists*. London: John Murray & Co., 1963.

Dull, Charles E., Metcalfe and Brooks, *Modern Physics II*. New York: Holt, Rinehart & Winston, Inc., 1962.

Jardine, J., *Physics Is Fun, Book II*. London: Heinemann Educational Books Ltd., 1967.

Kearsey, C. W., *A School Physics*. London: Longmans, Green & Co. Ltd., 1962.

MacLachlan, J. H., K. G. McNeill, and J. M. Bell, *Matter and Energy – Foundations of Modern Physics*. Toronto, Ont.: Clarke-Irwin Co., 1963.

Marborger, W. J. and C. W. Hoffman, *Physics For Our Times*. New York: McGraw-Hill Book Company, 1955.

Peterson, Arnold Cer Gustaf, and Erzin E. Gross Jr., *Handbook of Noise Measurement,* Sixth Edition. West Concord, Mass.: General Radio Co., 1967.

"A Brief Study of a Rational Approach to Legistlative Control of Noise," Report by the National Research Council. Ottawa: Division of Applied Physics, 1968.

Rogers, Eric M., *Physics For the Inquiring Mind*. Princeton, N.J.: Princeton University Press, 1960.

Sootin, Harry, *Science Experiments With Sound, II*. New York: W. W. Norton & Company, Inc., 1964.

Geology

Ager, D. V., *Introducing Geology*. London: Faber and Faber, 1961.

Baird, D. M., *A Guide to Geology for Visitors in Canada's National Parks*. Vancouver, B.C.: Geological Survey of Canada, 1966.

Baird, D. M., *Banff National Park – How Nature Carved its Splendour*. Vancouver, B.C.: Geological Survey of Canada, 1967.

Baird, D. M., *Yoho National Park – the Mountains, the Rocks, the Scenery*. Ottawa, Ont.: Canada Dept. of Energy, Mines & Resources, 1968.

Croneis, Carey and William C. Krumbein, *Down to Earth – An Introduction to Geology*. Chicago, Ill.: The University of Chicago Press, 1969.

Dempsey, Michael, *The Round World – Foundations of Geology & Geomorphology*. London: Sampson Low, Martson & Co., 1966.

Dictionary of Geological Terms. Washington, D.C.: American Geological Institute, 1960.

Ekman, Leonard C., *Scenic Geology of the Pacific Northwest*. Portland, Oregon: Binfords & Mort, Publishers, 1962.

Foster, Robert J., *Geology*. Merrill Physical Science Series. Columbus, Ohio: Charles E. Merrill Publishing Company, 1966.

Heimler, Charles H. and Charles D. Neal, *Principles of Science*. Book Two. Columbus, Ohio: Charles E. Merrill Publishing Company, 1966.

Hubbell, Lawrence, *The Earth – Investigating Science with Children*. Darien, Conn.: Teachers Publishing Corporation, 1964.

Investigating the Earth, Earth Science Curriculum Project. Boston, Mass.: Houghton Mifflin Co., 1967.

Leet, L. D. and Sheldon Judson, *Physical Geology*. Third Edition. Englewood Cliffs, N.J.: Prentice-Hall, Inc., 1965.

Marean, John H., Dudley G. Cate and Edward C. Coppin, *Earth Science – A Laboratory Approach*. Don Mills, Ont.: Addison-Wesley Publishing Company, 1970.

Mather, Kirtley F., *The Earth Beneath Us*. New York: Random House, Inc., 1964.

Namowitz, Samuel N., *Earth Science – The World We Live In*. Fourth Edition. New York: American Book Company, 1969.

Putnam, William C., *Geology*. New York: Oxford University Press, Inc., 1964.

Ramsay, William L., and Raymond A. Burckley, *Modern Earth Science*. New York: Holt, Rinehart & Winston, Inc., 1965.

Read, H. H., and J. Watson, *Beginning Geology*. Toronto, Ont.: The Macmillan Company of Canada Ltd., 1966.

Suchman, J. Richard and Lawrence McCombs, *Readings For Geological Enquiry – Resource Book*. Chicago, Ill.: Science Research Associates, 1968.

The World We Live In, Life special edition for young readers. New York: Golden Press, Inc., 1966.

Viorst, Judith, *The Changing Earth*. New York: Bantam Books, Inc., 1967. (Good Teacher Reference)

White, J. F., *Study of Earth – Readings in Geological Science*. Englewood Cliffs, N.J.: Prentice-Hall, Inc., 1962.

Wolfe et al., *Earth and Space Science*. Boston, Mass.: D. C. Heath & Company, 1966.

Historical Geology

Ames, Gerald, and Rose Wyler, *The Earth's Story*. Mankato, Minn.: Creative Educational Society Inc., 1967.

Hurley, Patrick M., *How Old Is The Earth?* Garden City, New York: Anchor Books, Doubleday & Company, Inc., 1959.

Shourd, Melvin L. and L. R. Wegenek, *Fossils; A Student Reference Book*. Toronto, Ont.: Webster Division, McGraw-Hill Book Company, 1969.

Simpson, George Gaylord, *Life of the Past – An Introduction to Paleontology*. New Haven, Conn.: Yale University Press, 1953.

Stokes, William Lee, *Essentials of Earth History*. Englewood Cliffs, N.J.: Prentice-Hall, Inc., 1966.

Atmospheric Science and Oceanography

Bridze, Ruth, *The Gulf Stream*. New York: The Vanguard Press, Inc., 1945.

Caidin, Martin, *Hydrospace*. New York: E. P. Dutton & Company, Inc., 1964.

Chapman, Sydney, "The Story of the International Geophysical Year". *IGY: Year of Discovery*. Ann Arbor, Mich.: The University of Michigan Press, 1968.

Flanigan, Dennis, ed., *Scientific American*. Vol. 221, No. 3. New York: Scientific American Inc., September, 1969.

Frosee, Aylesa, *Beneath The Land and Sea*. Philadelphia, Pa.: Macrae Smith Co., 1962.

Irving, Robert, *Hurricanes and Twisters*. New York: Alfred A. Knopf, Inc., 1955.

Lehr, Paul E., R. Will Burnett, and Herbert S. Zim, *Weather*. New York: Golden Press, Inc., 1965.

Ross, M. Grant, *Oceanography*. Columbus, Ohio: Charles E. Merrill Publishing Company, 1967.

Spilhause, Athelstan, *The Ocean Laboratory*. Mankato, Minn.: Creative Educational Society, Inc., 1967.

Stevens, William M., *Science Beneath the Sea, The Story of Oceanography*. New York: G. P. Putnam's Sons, 1966.

Wyckoff, Jerome, *The Story of Geology*. New York: Golden Press, Inc., 1960.

Volcanism

Bullard, Fred M., *Volcanoes, In History, In Theory, In Eruption*. Austin, Texas: University of Texas Press, 1962.

Simpich, Frederick Jr., *Fountains of Fire in Hawaii*, Vol. 117, No. 3. Washington, D.C.: National Geographic Society, March, 1960.

Vaughan-Jackson, Genevieve, *Mountains of Fire*. New York: Hastings House Publishers, Inc., 1962.

Volcanoes of the United States, Pamphlet of the U.S. Geological Survey. Washington: U.S. Dept. of the Interior, 1965.

Wilcoxson, Kent H., *Chains of Fire – The Story of Volcanoes*. First Edition. Philadelphia, Pa.: Chilton Book Company, 1966.

Earthquakes

Belyea, Helen R., *The Story of the Mountains in Banff National Park*. Vancouver: Geological Survey of Canada, 1960.

Earthquakes, Science Service – Science Program. Garden City, N.Y.: Doubleday & Company, Inc., 1968.

Hodgson, John H., *Earthquakes & Earth Structures*. Englewood Cliffs, N.J.: Prentice-Hall, Inc., 1964.

Lacopi, Robert, *Earthquake Country*. Menlo Park, Calif.: Lane Magazine & Book Co., 1964.

Leet, L. D. and F., *Earthquake Discoveries in Seismology*. New York: Dell Publishing Company, 1964.

Safety and Survival in an Earthquake, U.S. Geological Survey.

Volcanoes and Earthquakes

Coleman, Satis N., *Volcanoes – New and Old*. New York: The John Day Company, 1946.

Roberts, Elliott, *Volcanoes and Earthquakes*. New York: Pyramid Publications, Inc., 1967.

Thomas, Lowell, *Lowell Thomas's Book of the High Mountains*. New York: Julian Messner, Inc., 1964.

Vaughan-Jackson, Genevieve, *Mountains of Fire*. New York: Hastings House Publishers, Inc., 1962.

Wykcoff, Jerome, *Rock, Time and Landforms*. New York: Harper & Row, Publishers, Inc., 1966.

Rocks and Minerals

Jones, W. R., *Minerals In Industry*. Baltimore, Md.: Penguin Books, Inc., 1963.

Morrissey, C. J., *Mineral Specimens*. London: Iliffe Books Ltd., 1968.

Pearl, Richard M., *Gems, Minerals, Crystals and Ores*. New York: Golden Press, Inc., 1967.

Pearl, Richard M., *Popular Gemology*. New York: John Wiley & Sons, Inc., 1965.

Pearl, Richard M., *Rocks and Minerals*. New York: Barnes & Noble, Inc., 1967.

Richards, Horace G., *The Story of Earth Science – Rocks, Fossils and Minerals*. New York: J. B. Lippincott Company, 1959.

Specimens and Samples – Their Treatment and Use, Bulletin 18, Dept. of Mines and Petroleum Resources. Victoria, B.C.: Queen's Printer, 1967.

The Identification of Common Rocks, B.C. Department of Mines and Petroleum Resources. Victoria, B.C.: Queen's Printer, 1968.

Walker, John F., *Elementary Geology – Applied to Prospecting*, Dept. of Mines. Vancouver, B.C.: Best Printer Co., Ltd., 1965.

Zim, Herbert S., and Paul R. Shaffer, *Rocks and Minerals*. New York: Golden Press, Inc., 1964.

Radioactivity

Ramsay, W. L. and R. A. Burckley, *Modern Earth Science*. New York: Holt, Rinehart & Winston, Inc., 1965.